DIGITAL AUTHORITARIANISM IN THE MIDDLE EAST

MARC OWEN JONES

Digital Authoritarianism in the Middle East

Deception, Disinformation and Social Media

OXFORD

UNIVERSITY PRESS

Oxford University Press is a department of the
University of Oxford. It furthers the University's objective
of excellence in research, scholarship, and education
by publishing worldwide.

Oxford New York

Auckland   Cape Town   Dar es Salaam   Hong Kong   Karachi
Kuala Lumpur   Madrid   Melbourne   Mexico City   Nairobi
New Delhi   Shanghai   Taipei   Toronto

With offices in

Argentina   Austria   Brazil   Chile   Czech Republic   France   Greece
Guatemala   Hungary   Italy   Japan   Poland   Portugal   Singapore
South Korea   Switzerland   Thailand   Turkey   Ukraine   Vietnam

Oxford is a registered trade mark of Oxford University Press
in the UK and certain other countries.

Published in the United States of America by
Oxford University Press
198 Madison Avenue, New York, NY 10016

Library of Congress Cataloging-in-Publication Data is available

ISBN: 9780197636633

Printed in the United Kingdom
by Bell and Bain Ltd, Glasgow

CONTENTS

List of Figures vii

Acknowledgements ix

Preface xiii

Introduction: The Gulf's Post-Truth Moment 1

PART I
Digital Deception and the Pseudo-Reality Industries

1 Digital Authoritarianism, Deception
and Information Controls 29

2 The Deception Order and Pseudo-Reality Industries 47

Part II
Controlling Domestic Politics

3 Making Arabia Great Again: The Evolution of Digital
Media Power and Digital Populism in the Gulf 73

4 Automating Deceit: Authoritarian AI and Journoganda 101

CONTENTS

Part III
Trump and the War on Reality in the Gulf

5   The US Right-Wing–Saudi Anti-Iran Nexus   123

6   The Gulf Crisis Never Happened: Pseudo-Events
and Pseudo-Publics   141

PART IV
Projecting Influence Abroad

7   Foreign Interference in Elections, Revolutions and
Protests: From Iraq to Algeria   165

8   You Are Being Lied to by People that Do Not   181
Even Exist: The Pseudo-Journalist

9   Football Crazy: Sportswashing and the Pseudo-Fan   199

10   Covid19's Disinformation Superspreaders   213

Part V
Attacking Journalists and Silencing Dissent

11   Silencing Journalists: The Killing of Khashoggi   225

12   Attacking Women: Malinformation and Digital   247
Misogyny

13   Stigmatising Muslims: The Sisterhood of the
Muslim Brothers   261

Part VI
Adventures in Troll-land

14   Talking Pro-MBS Zombies   279

15   The Rise and Fall of Magnus Callaghan   287

     Conclusion: The Future of Deception and
Digital Tyranny   299

Notes   319

Index   373

LIST OF FIGURES

1   Overview of key terminology assessed
    according to veracity and intent   31

2   Number of accounts by country suspended by
    Twitter due to state-backed influence operations   91

3   Tweets by Donald Trump that were retweeted by a
    pro-Saudi network   97

4   Followers of news-related Twitter accounts in the
    MENA region, by country   106

5   Tweets from propaganda accounts and their content   111

6   Saudi regional news-related Twitter accounts showing
    changes in number of followers   115

7   A topical analysis of the articles published
    by the fake journalists   189

8   The number of times the name Khashoggi
    appeared in a Twitter trend in MENA countries
    during October 2018   233

ACKNOWLEDGEMENTS

This book has been the product of more than ten years of work, but it is the last five which have been the most crucial, and there have been so many who have helped me along the way. Of course, the usual caveats apply: I know I cannot possibly include everyone who has offered support or inspiration – and that pains me – so please forgive me in advance.

In general, my family, friends and colleagues have been a source of encouragement and resilience, especially as much of the writing of this book took place during Covid19.

Thank you to Michael, Alice and Farhaana at Hurst for all your help and support during the publication process. And thank you, too, to Mary for your wonderful copyediting.

Thank you dearly to the Scandinavian quarter. I am fortunate that some of my favourite Gulf scholars are also my best friends. Charlotte, Mari, Hind, I will never forget hanging out in Copenhagen and Helsinki. I count those days as among the happiest in recent memory. I approach every new conference hoping we can relive those heady times. You guys are among the warmest, smartest, and most inspirational people I know.

Alexei, I hope one day we will live in the same city. I always look forward to hanging out and listening to tasty Knopfler licks. Thanks always for your wisdom, insights and assistance, in both work and life.

Courtney, thanks for your chats on 90s rock, steakhouses and occasionally Gulf politics. I miss you Exeter Gulf Studies crowd – Claire B, Marc V, and Ross P, and my other Gulf studies friends and academics. Thank you to Andrew L, Khalid Al J, Kristian Ulrichsen, Marwan, Banu, Marc L, James, Gerd, Andreas, Mehran and Suzi – academics and in many cases friends. You've always got time for a discussion or some impromptu feedback.

Thanks to all those disinformation scholars who are fighting hard to preserve information integrity and truth: Claire W, Mahsa, Khadeja, Shelby, Akin, Peter and Adam R, you are all wonderful and brilliant human beings. To the team at the EEAS, thanks for all your work in tackling disinformation, and bringing like-minded people together to make a difference.

Abdullah, thanks for being a great friend; I always relish our long conversations where we set the world to rights. Dr Abdullah, thank you for your kindness, hospitality and wisdom.

Noha, thanks so much for all our hangouts, for your wisdom and moral support. Karine, Zahra, Andrew and Julien, thanks for all the wonderful food, fun chats and political venting.

My colleagues at HBKU have been an amazing source of support, especially during Covid19. Thank you to Hassan, Steven, Sophie, George, Wajdi, Hendrik and Amal.

Many thanks to all the assiduous journalists and producers I have spoken to over the years who have taken a passionate interest in disinformation and my research. Sarah L, Abdu, David, Jack, Katy, Omayma, to name but a few. Thanks too to all those on Twitter who follow my work.

To my friends Ghada, Jeremy, Reina, Julien: I always laugh so hard when we are together; it rejuvenates me and gives me inspiration to write.

Jonathan, thanks for being a great friend, and for all the memes. It's been great getting to know you. That's the real big story.

Raouf, I always enjoy our chats. Same with you Mohammad ElCalm Street. Heba, thanks for being so empathetic, kind and above all, a good human being. Fatima, thanks, too, for being such a good, non-judgemental friend and for being so supportive of me and my work.

My dearest friends from Durham: Siobhan, Pep, Jesper, Lara, Mike, Michael, Kirstyn, Victoria, Nadine, Dima. Michael, I owe you a beer and/or burger in Seattle

To all the students from Digital Humanities and Women's Studies who I have had the pleasure knowing, you are an inspiration and source of strength. I know you will go on to do wonderful things.

Big thank you to the staff at Calm Street, you were a lifeline during the pandemic and for the writing of this book.

To my wonderful nieces Elsie and Heidi, hopefully I will have seen you by the time this book comes out. To my mum, dad, Kate and my brothers Gareth and Owen, thank you for being such a great family.

To my growing collection of cats, thanks for destroying my sofa. I never liked it much anyway.

Thank you to Bob and Apex Legends for help keeping me sane during lockdown.

To Covid19, you're obviously the worst.

PREFACE

Liliane Khalil had everything. She was young, intelligent, and her career as a journalist was blossoming. It was 2011 and Khalil was writing about the Arab Uprisings. Wearing a pair of her favourite Jimmy Choos, Liliane stepped out with members of the British consulate in Atlanta, Georgia. It was a warm spring night and a huge moment for her: a gala celebration at the Hilton Hotel to celebrate the launch of the Atlanta bureau of the Bahrain Independent, a blossoming news organisation. Khalil, an up-and-coming journalist, would be heading the bureau. Quite an achievement at such a young age. She already had thousands of followers on Twitter, including many well-known journalists, politicians and academics.

Despite her short career, Khalil had already interviewed some very prominent names in the Arab world, such as Hanan Ashrawi and the king of Bahrain. She had been a guest speaker at New York University, Oglethorpe University, and had written for a number of international news outlets. Sometimes she'd work late at her various gigs, pausing only to fulfil the new obligation of our digital age, stopping to take a photo to post on social media, in this case, a photo of the CNN logo and posting it on Twitter. Her fame had come in large part off the back of the Arab Uprisings, but she was doing an important job keeping people informed of what was going on.

Khalil was also riding the wave of techno-utopianism. With people touting Facebook and Twitter as liberating platforms, it was great to see a young woman from the region able to make a name for herself through brave and outspoken journalism. Khalil was modest and humble too, writing for the big outlets such as TRT, but also emerging and little-known platforms such as BikyaMasr, a new Egyptian blog. Her job was dangerous too. After writing about an event in Libya, her Twitter account briefly disappeared – it had been hacked. Khalil re-emerged online again a few days later. She was OK, much to the relief of her followers, who included other well-known journalists, pundits and commentators.

Despite all this, one question lingered. Why would such an up-and-coming journalist take a relatively humble job at a small, new Bahraini outlet? But in the Gulf, with heavyweights like Al Jazeera and Al Arabiya emerging from Qatar and Saudi, maybe it was Bahrain's turn to contribute to the Gulf media renaissance. Yet just as Khalil's career was reaching new heights, things began to fall apart. I started asking questions. Sure Liliane Khalil was a rising star, still early in her career, but why was there so little evidence of her interviews with many of these famous figures? I could not find her interview with the king of Bahrain, or Ashrawi, or others. Other things did not add up. Why had Liliane Khalil, a journalist who appeared to be supporting the Arab Uprisings, backed the Bahraini regime? Why had she written a piece that promoted the propaganda issued by the Bahraini state, namely that the uprising wasn't a democratic revolution, but a religious movement inspired by Iran? Why had a Dutch academic, Katje Niethammer, taken issue with Liliane Khalil's misrepresentation of her work? Was Liliane being paid by the Bahrain government? Had she sold out, and taken a lucrative salary in exchange for journalistic integrity?

Perhaps contacting those who knew Liliane would be useful, maybe her colleagues at the Bahrain Independent. They did not respond to my emails, and appeared mostly to be preoccupied with smearing activists criticising the Bahraini response to the uprising. I contacted the Hilton Hotel in Atlanta to ask about the gala night, where she had photographed herself side by side with women from the British consulate. They said there was no such event. I contacted the British consulate in Atlanta to ask if the staff photographed in Liliane's photo were available for comment or interview. They denied that the women in the photo even worked at the consulate. Oglethorpe and NYU had no records of Liliane Khalil ever having given a talk. Other things began to unravel. A quick scan of some of the articles Khalil had posted showed they had been plagiarised. One article she had written for the Turkish site Sabah was actually copy-pasted from Reuters.[1]

The story got weirder. One of the images used by Liliane Khalil directed to the LinkedIn profile of a woman called Gisele Cohen. There were more too, other accounts using her photo and biography led to profiles called Lily Khalil, Victoria Nasr, Gisele Mizrahi, Gisele Azari and Gisele Khadouri – a veritable rabbit hole of slightly altered identities featuring the same photos. I compiled all these bizarre findings into a document and posted it online. Soon it went viral. Al Jazeera did an interview with me,[2] as did France24. The *Washington Post* wrote an article on it.[3] Soon media outlets were clambering to get an interview with the elusive Liliane Khalil. The only condition they placed was that she appear on camera. After all, one of the central questions was, is Liliane Khalil who she says she is, the attractive young woman in the photos? Liliane agreed to be interviewed onscreen on a number of occasions but always pulled out at the last minute.

After lashing out numerous times, and getting a publicist who also worked for a company doing PR for the Bahraini regime, Liliane agreed to a phone interview with me. The woman on the phone sounded older than the woman in the photo, and began her interview with a sob story, no doubt designed to elicit sympathy. She often attributed things to poor memory. In one instance I asked her about the time she had copied and pasted a Reuters article and claimed it as her own, but she said she was drunk and didn't remember. It became clear that Khalil was a fraud, but a fraud who had duped a few thousand people into following her. What's more, a fraud who had made grandiose claims, seemingly without anyone bothering to verify them.

Liliane Khalil was neither the first nor last fraudster to remind people, especially journalists, to be vigilant; but she was a new breed, exploiting digital media and regional conflict to spread pro-government propaganda. Many people put too much trust in social media, and do little to verify the veracity of what they consume. At the same time as Liliane Khalil, the world had been transfixed by a similar scandal. A gay Syrian-American who had been blogging from Damascus called Amina Amaraf suddenly disappeared, prompting fears that the Syrian regime had arrested her. This provoked a real-life manhunt, and journalists and activists raised alarm bells about her fate. However, it turned out Amina was a man called Tom McMaster, an American postgraduate student at the University of Edinburgh in Scotland.[4]

Techno-utopianism bought with it the notion of techno-naivety. The euphoria and hope engendered by the Arab Uprisings had often made people forget that technology was not just the tool of the protester or the revolutionary. It was also the tool of the propagandist, the fraudster and the state. It could be used for good or ill. Social media, a highly unregulated and easy to manipulate space, was ripe for such impostors. This book is not an epitaph for the demise of techno-utopianism, or liberation technology, but rather a reminder that hope requires vigilance and not complacency, and that power accumulates as nodes within networks. It is also a critique of the liberation paradigm, which served as political cover for neoliberal capital, which has sought to emphasise the internet and its spread as a means of creating new untapped frontiers for investment.[5]

With the rise of any new technology, unbounded optimism can serve to leave us off guard, blind to the insidious encroachment of malicious actors seeking to reaffirm or maintain control over a digital space that could, in a theoretically possible but likely unattainable context, offer us so much good. However, as the book shows, since the demise of Liliane Khalil, the rise of post-truth politics and deception have shown no sign of abating. It is unclear if we are becoming better at exposing manipulation, or if manipulation is getting worse, but the confluence of a breed of new populists, along with a disinformation industry facilitated by loosely regulated social media companies, is sustaining digital authoritarianism and illiberal practices in both the Middle East and North Africa (MENA) and across the globe. It is the hope of this book to shed light on the causes, nature and impact of this weaponised deception.

INTRODUCTION

THE GULF'S POST-TRUTH MOMENT

Over the past ten years, and in the wake of the Arab Spring, while writing about various aspects of Gulf politics and media, I have received death threats, threats of rape, and online pile-ons. I have had caricatures drawn of me as an Iranian puppet, and websites set up for the sole purposes of defaming me and other academics and activists.[1] I have had impersonators set up social media accounts and write to local newspapers with political opinions contrary to those that I hold. I have been the subject of multiple, often contradictory, smear campaigns. If my attackers are to be believed, I am both gay and homophobic, both an Iranian and Qatari stooge, both Shiʿa and an atheist, and at times a Western secret agent. My colleagues and friends have been sent malicious spyware that steals their passwords, monitors phone calls, and even records videos from their webcams. I have been banned from entering Bahrain for criticising government repression online, and even had my Twitter account temporarily suspended after numerous smear campaigns. I have drunk coffee with people who were later incarcerated for merely writing a tweet deemed too critical by their government. Over time, I have witnessed the psychological change and damage, within me, and others, who have been subjected to continuous online violence.

1

Welcome to the world of digital authoritarianism, where digital harassment, surveillance and disinformation are used in an attempt to control human behaviour. Digital authoritarianism is the 'use of digital information technology by authoritarian regimes to surveil, repress, and manipulate domestic and foreign populations'.[2] It includes a wide gamut of repressive techniques, including 'surveillance, censorship, social manipulation and harassment, cyber-attacks, internet shutdowns, and targeted persecution against online users'.[3] An increasingly worrying component of social media manipulation is disinformation and misinformation; terms often used interchangeably to describe attempts to manipulate public opinion or give the illusion of public support for specific issues. Although this book deals with multiple aspects of digital authoritarianism, its primary focus is on disinformation and deception through social media. Fundamentally, it asks how governments and other non-state actors use social media and digital technology to deceive and control citizens living in the MENA region, and more specifically, the Gulf region.

Disinformation and Fake News

From Washington, DC in the United States to Riyadh in Saudi Arabia, disinformation and what is sometimes termed 'fake news' is a global problem. It is part of what Claire Wardle describes as a growing 'information disorder'.[4] Since 2008, academic attention across disciplines, but especially psychology and communications, has been directed at understanding the purpose of disinformation.[5] However, while disinformation is not new, the digital technologies that are being exploited by those spreading disinformation are relatively recent. No longer are the more centralised mediums of television, print news and radio the sole – or indeed, the primary – means of distributing disinformation. The new reach afforded by digital media and social media platforms, abetted by the growing ubiquity of internet-enabled smartphones, is shifting the scale of the information disorder, and disinformation is fundamentally altering people's perceptions of established truths and facts.

This is no different in the Middle East and North Africa. As a profoundly unequal region, the impact and takeup of digital technology are varied and differentiated according to governmental, business and consumer adoption. The United Arab Emirates, Bahrain and Qatar are among the top countries in the world with regard to digital consumer adoption, 'with more than 100 per cent smartphone penetration and more than 70 per cent social media adoption' in 2016. This is higher than in many parts of the United States and Northern Europe. Yemen, on the other hand, is one of the poorest countries in the world, and this is reflected in the fact it has the lowest internet penetration in the MENA region.[6] Yet while internet penetration rates are increasing or have plateaued, social media is more subject to fluctuation. For example, use of Twitter and Facebook is declining in the MENA region in general, although Saudi is still the world's fifth-largest Twitter market, with 38% (10 million) of its population considered active users.[7] Although the use of Twitter, WhatsApp, Facebook and, to an extent, Instagram is generally falling across the Middle East, in countries such as Egypt, Facebook use is increasing.[8] Despite changing trends, the numbers of those using social media remain high. New platforms may rise and fall, but the reality of how we communicate has been irreparably changed by digital technology. As a result, the extant challenges such technologies pose for the spread of disinformation are not going to disappear any time soon.

The Growing Dangers of Deception

These dangers of the information disorder are becoming increasingly apparent. From the rise of those who reject vaccinations to those who believe the world is flat, fringe conspiracies are arguably becoming more mainstream thanks to a proliferation of alternative information sources abetted by an apparent rise in distrust in traditional authority, whether that be government communications offices or the mainstream media.[9] In his book on propaganda, Peter Pomerantsev argues that we are experiencing a 'war against reality'.[10] Here disinformation and deception seek to alter people's views on reality through the discrediting of 'experts', the sowing of alternative explanations, and playing on people's visceral emotions to make them feel more vulnerable and therefore receptive to falsehoods.

And it is serious. Disinformation can lead to indoctrination, which can lead to incitement. Depending on the nature of the indoctrination, incitement can lead to violence and even genocide. The Arab world has witnessed the tragedy of this. The rise of Daesh has widely been attributed to the ability of disinformation, propaganda and indoctrination to transcend global borders via digital technology.[11] Even Facebook has acknowledged that its platform was used to incite what has been described as 'genocidal' violence against Myanmar's Rohingya Muslim population.[12] The same was true in the 'closed' environment of WhatsApp, where one video, for example, claimed to show Rohingya cannibalising Hindus. Of course, it was found to be false, but the damage was done.[13] Hundreds, and possibly thousands, of people may have died during the Covid19 pandemic as a result of disinformation about the virus.[14]

The war against reality risks undermining many of the advancements in critical thinking, science and knowledge creation that have been made over the past few centuries. It is no surprise then that disinformation and the attendant term 'fake news' have become ubiquitous in the past decade. The terms, along with the expression 'war against reality', are bound up in the vocabulary of the 'post-truth' age, wherein 'objective facts are less influential in shaping public opinion than appeals to emotion and personal belief'.[15] The motivations for such falsehoods are myriad, and several explanations have been touted; false information makes companies more money, truth is boring, or disinformation for profit is itself a business model.[16] However, while financial gains in the realm of commerce are often the objectives of the service provider, the clients of such disinformation cannot be overlooked. After all, without demand, there is no supply, and the post-truth age has played out in specific ways in the Gulf region.

Another way to view fake news is not a fight about truth, but about power.[17] As Mike Ananny notes, 'Fake news "is evidence of a social phenomenon at play – a struggle between [how] different people envision what kind of world that they want."'[18] In the realm of politics, the terms post-truth and war against reality sometimes even seem like a quaint euphemism. Michael Peters is more forceful, and highlights the phenomenon of 'government by lying', whereby demagogues and those on the fringes of political life use online media to disseminate controversial and often fallacious content in order to obtain power as a means of promoting their view of reality through policy or legislation.[19] The phenomenon is not confined to authoritarian regimes, but is also being driven by well-established democracies traditionally thought to have a relatively robust media that allowed for some plurality of opinion. Democratic regimes have, with various levels of sophistication, deceived their people. Some of these lies, such as the claims that Iraq had weapons of mass destruction (WMD), were used to justify an immensely tragic war, the consequences of which are still being felt and will continue to be felt for generations. We should not delude ourselves into thinking that deception is the purview of regimes classified as authoritarian. It is an illiberal practice common to every regime type.

Having said that, a key distinction between illiberal and authoritarian regimes is the presence of the press. A functioning and critical media, free from state control, has always been considered a mechanism by which to expose such lies and hold governments to account, even if this happens after the purpose of the lie has been achieved.[20] However, despite the efforts of populists like Trump and Orbán, a free press, however precarious, still exists in most European countries and North America. That these institutions offer a key line of defence against the unfettered and unchallenged deception by autocratic leaders places them squarely in the realm of the enemy. For this reason, a cornerstone of the new age of deception has been the trope of demonising the media. Trump's exhortations of fake news media are not new. The German term *Lügenpresse*, or 'lying media', was used extensively in the nineteenth and twentieth centuries to discredit those media that contradicted the statements of particular political parties.[21] The term has even been used by the likes of Richard Spencer, an American neo-Nazi and president of the National Policy Institute. In addition to discrediting those news channels that criticise him or his allies, Trump has promoted a steady stream of news outlets that he believes are supportive of him, such as One America News Network (OANN). For Trump and other populists, the idea has been to discourage the exposure of potential supporters to criticism of Trumpism. While lying is not a partisan notion, in the current post-truth age the rise of right-wing populism has brought with it a tide of deceptive influence campaigns. The *Washington Post* revealed that President Donald Trump had made approximately 22,000 false or misleading claims by the middle of 2020.[22] Discrediting the press results from the existence of a pluralistic media system, and thus is indicative of a desire to undo that pluralism in favour of a more authoritarian approach.

Although figures such as Donald Trump might have pathological characteristics that encourage their tendency to govern through deception, the emergence of what has been described as 'truth decay'[23] has been partly spurred on by a loosely regulated digital environment. Without established safeguards and gatekeepers setting the agenda through vertically organised media platforms[24] as well as the deterioration of sovereign boundaries that separate national news from the international information ecosystem, disinformation has become detached from its parochial context. A tweet sent by someone in Hong Kong can be read instantly by someone in Argentina. Regardless of whether you agree with a message or not, the swift and immediate transmission of messages, however erroneous or truthful, has become accessible to the multitudes.

This is not to advocate for vertically owned media structures that maximise the control of certain gatekeepers. Naturally, the benefits of challenging traditional media monopolies should be clear by this point. Globalisation, satellite TV and now the internet have challenged the ability of dictators and democracies to control their own domestic ecosystems. Whether we like it or not, technological change has resulted, to some extent, in a regional and global pluralism. Digital citizen journalism, activism and open-source investigations have all contributed to creating new streams of accountability that promote transparency and openness. But this book is not about the positive aspects of our digital information ecosystem; it is about the manipulation of truths and facts designed to serve the agenda of powerful actors that primarily seek to censor and mislead their populations. It is about the 'deception order' that works together to enact a war on truth that threatens the shared reality in which we live, whether that's about medical science or harmful lies about a particular ethnic group. Fundamentally, it is about documenting weaponised deception that results in widespread suffering and misery, or the perpetuation of political systems that promote corruption and inequality.

It is important to note that disinformation transcends borders, and malign actors are using disinformation to influence the foreign policy of other countries to further their own interests. Digital globalisation does not necessarily respect the sovereignty of states or the increasingly porous digital boundaries embodied in the term 'world wide web'. The information ecosystems in liberal democratic states have, to varying extents, created a space in which institutions act transparently in order that their facts and 'truths' may be contested and validated. This creates a reciprocal level of trust that affirms and establishes the authority of institutions through their accountability to those whom they serve. And while partisanship over moral and ethical choices may thrive, the trust imbued by this reciprocal relationship, to no small extent, encourages a shared set of specific ideological values. This shared reality, while allowing for disagreement and conjecture, is still mostly bounded by a mutual set of assumptions about science, civility and the nature of truth – aspects socialised through state education and other hegemonic endeavours. However, the rise of post-truth politics has highlighted the fragility of this relationship, and the vulnerability of sovereign media ecosystems to the transnational nature of digital media. It is the functionality of software created as far afield as Silicon Valley, combined with the malicious intentions of specific bad actors, that are undermining this shared reality inside and outside their specific polity boundaries (assuming they are a state). Populists and bad actors, wherever they may be, are able to subvert these norms for their own ends.

Situating the Middle East

Despite this urgency, up until now the study of disinformation has tended to privilege a Cold War paradigm, which frames Russia and

China as forces undermining US and European security. The focus is rarely on the Middle East and Western-allied Gulf states. In a similar vein, there has been a tendency to focus on actors who produce their own capabilities, such as China and Russia. This is not to diminish such research, but simply to argue that there is a normative tendency to focus on these states as the main actors in the disinformation ecosystem. It is a field dominated by transatlantic security concerns. From a communications and political science perspective, much of the existing non-MENA literature is also focused on the disinformation propagated by the rise of the far right,[25] both in the United States and across Europe. This has been especially true within liberal democracies, which have often framed the rise of disinformation as being integral to the decline of democracy and to a renewed interest in libertarian or authoritarian principles. It also makes sense, as disinformation has arguably been both the product and symptom of the resurgence of populism. Parallels drawn with the rise of European fascism in the 1930s have also created an understandable sense of urgency in trying to understand the role of propaganda, deception and populism.

However, for those living in the Middle East, disinformation is all too familiar. But, like other regions beyond Europe and the English-speaking world, it is neglected by social media companies too. BuzzFeed's Craig Silverman notes how Facebook tended to be US-focused when dealing with disinformation.[26] Sophie Zhang, a former Facebook employee, highlighted how Facebook tended to ignore or delay dealing with platform manipulation in places that would not cause an overt PR backlash.[27] Conversely, it is this seeming indifference from tech firms in the so-called Global North that facilitates illiberal practices across vast swathes of the globe. It has become abundantly clear that the research agenda needs to focus on disinformation in the Middle East and Africa.[28]

Extant disinformation studies on MENA have tended to conform to Western foreign policy concerns, for example, Daesh and Iran as bad actors. The rise of Daesh has thrown into sharp relief the power of non-state actors to spread gruesome and morbid propaganda. It has also reflected the fact that disinformation or propaganda has tended to elicit interest from Western policymakers only when it poses threats to Western civilians or interests. Yet the rise of Daesh itself, both on- and offline, can partly be attributed to a tendency to ignore the initial indicators of a looming crisis before it breaks into the mainstream. Without wishing to undermine the importance of studying the likes of Daesh, or indeed, their disinformation, it tends to divert limited attention from the sheer scourge of disinformation generated by MENA state actors that are well integrated and legitimised within the international community.

Of course, this does not mean there is not a burgeoning network of scholars, activists, policymakers and journalists working to document and highlight the prevalence of disinformation in the Middle East. Fact-checking sites such as the Jordanian-based *fatbyanno* (meaning 'just check' in Arabic) and Misbar[29] have been pioneering Arabic-language fact checking. But they have their work cut out; with over 400 million Arabic speakers worldwide, and a media ecosystem plagued by disinformation, efforts are limited.[30] Much research has been issue-focused, with published articles seeking to elaborate on specific events, such as the murder of Jamal Khashoggi, or the Gulf Crisis,[31] or religiously framed Covid19 disinformation.[32] There are also emerging studies based on country cases and demography.[33] Sub-types of disinformation connected to cybersecurity, such as studies on 'hack and leak operations', shed important light on the minutiae of tactics and how they resonate in a regional context.[34] However, due to the need to highlight disinformation campaigns rapidly, the snail-paced aspect of academic publishing creates a lag around what is a rapidly changing and urgent problem.

The new methods required to do open source and forensic analysis are also creating a chasm in the literature between those working in the realm of computer science and the social sciences. Empirical studies are increasingly documented by reputable news outlets working with researchers, and research organisations focused on technology and digital forensics. The Citizen Lab, based at the University of Toronto, has published numerous forensic investigations on digital authoritarianism across the region, and for some time ran a periodical update entitled The Middle East and North Africa CyberWatch.[35] The Stanford Internet Observatory has also established relationships with companies like Facebook and

Twitter, and frequently publishes analyses of state-backed information operations emanating from the Middle East based on data provided on those countries.[36] Similarly, the Global Inventory of Organized Social Media Manipulation published annually by the Oxford Internet Institute interviews subject area experts to document the nature of disinformation in a worldwide context. The European Union is also beginning to resource tackling disinformation, and, as Mariatje Shaake has noted, 'Europe' is one of the only serious regulators of big tech.[37] Given the wide range of methods required to study and identify disinformation, it does not sit comfortably within a single academic discipline.

It can seem somewhat arbitrary to focus on countries equally when studying a whole region. The acronym MENA is a problematic term used to describe diverse populations, languages, historical experiences and political traditions, not to mention increasingly divergent foreign policies and domestic priorities. Nonetheless, without wishing to appear reductive, many of the states are still bound by common strands, especially with regard to religion, language and legacies of imperial or colonial domination. At the very least, it is a useful, albeit flawed, heuristic. In the context of this book, the MENA is also a nexus, where multiple actors compete for interest. Part of de-essentialising any region is to acknowledge that the 'deception order' is not confined to authoritarian states hermetically sealed into neatly packaged geopolitical regions.

While the role of the internet and digital media has spanned multiple disciplinary spheres, there is still a tendency within research on the region, and more broadly on the global context, to focus on the state as a key unit of analysis – whether in terms of state policies or state activities.[38] This is particularly true of relevant studies of authoritarian resilience in the region, which focus on regime survival.[39] Much of the capability of MENA-based actors comes from the utilisation of technologies and human resources from China, Europe and North America, which often permit such expertise to be shared on the basis that many of these countries share overlapping foreign policy goals

This is not to discount the role of the state, but rather to acknowledge it as one actor among many in the creation of digital authoritarianism, and that states, just as they interact with other entities, are also able to more easily project their power beyond borders when it comes to digital authoritarianism. An argument of this book is that digital authoritarianism involves a decoupling and despatialisation of authoritarian practices, beyond traditional state boundaries. Digital authoritarianism is a transnational endeavour, and new digital powers, nodes or hubs that project their influence electronically are emerging. An underlying element of this is neoliberation technology, discussed in the following chapter. So while these agglomerations of disinformation actors span continents, MENA here generally refers to the locations and populations targeted and exploited in the context of these operations, and that emanate from the deception order outlined in Chapter 2. At the same time, while the book deals with numerous case studies, the focus tends to be on events and actors in the Persian Gulf. Indeed, as this book argues, the politics of the Gulf region have resulted in numerous global deception operations since 2011.

With the majority of Gulf states rated by most indices as authoritarian, the need to understand digital illiberal practices is as pertinent as ever. The fact that the study of digital disinformation is relatively new, and that the Middle East is often overlooked, means that many pertinent questions remain unanswered. These questions span multiple disciplines, but especially International Relations, Political Science and Communications. In the area of Communications, Ferrara et al. note the urgent task of identifying the 'puppet masters'. Indeed, by exploring whom bots target, what they talk about, and when they take action, we might be able to determine who is behind them. Such inquiries overlap with the demands of IR theorists, who seek to understand 'why states and non-state actors use disinformation, and why disinformation appears to be ever more present in modern-day international politics than ever before'.[40] To do this we must first document and uncover deception operations, and then determine who is responsible, how they work, and on what scale they operate. We can do this by examining the discursive, tactical and strategic qualities of deceptive content. By answering these questions we can begin to understand who the largest deception players in the region are, and what it is they are seeking to achieve.

The Gulf's Post-Truth 'Moment'

With the above in mind, this book makes the case for a Gulf post-truth 'moment', a period of time characterised by the strengthening of digital authoritarianism and led primarily by the Gulf Cooperation Council (GCC) states of Saudi Arabia and the United Arab Emirates. The book seeks to explain both why this moment has emerged and its various modalities – i.e. what are the tactics and methods of deception? One of the overarching arguments is that the techno-optimism characterised by the Arab Uprisings that began in 2010 has given way to the rise of digital authoritarianism, a central tenet of which is deception. Social media and digital technology, which helped fuel the Arab Uprisings, is now being used as a tool of counter-revolutionary repression, particularly by certain Gulf states, to protect the authoritarian status quo across the MENA region, especially from perceived 'Islamist' threats and Iranian expansionism.

Although this book explores the chains of information operations across multiple states and actors, it focuses on the biggest players – in line with the normative tendency to focus on dominant actors. In particular, it argues that Saudi Arabia, and to some extent the United Arab Emirates, are the main projectors of digital media power in the Arabic-speaking Middle East. It is worth noting that it is somewhat facile to assume that all countries or entities are engaging in such behaviours equally. Certainly, almost all countries will engage in information operations, but it is more fruitful to base such analyses about bad actors and their use of disinformation on the known sources of disinformation rather than seeking to generate false parity by overstating cases. To do so would just be to reify the concept of equality of disinformation based on an arbitrary state-centric parity between vastly different actors, whether in the MENA or otherwise. Indeed, there is a reason why disinformation scholars often focus on the large powers such as Russia, China and Iran. Not all countries are equally powerful, populous, authoritarian and, as we shall see, deceptive. Indeed, a useful question that derives from this is: who are the deception superpowers in the MENA region?

By empirically documenting known disinformation campaigns, and the different and evolving forms of deception, this book lays out the case that Saudi Arabia in particular should be seen as a new digital superpower, at least in the realms of deception via social media, specifically Twitter. Here being a digital superpower involves using human resources and digital technology to launch influence operations on three fronts – domestically, regionally and internationally – in a sustained and evolving manner. The impetus for this moment can be seen as the unsurprising evolution and 'upgrading' of authoritarianism.[41] That is, the tendency for authoritarian regimes to upgrade their capacity to resist dissent and adapt to new challenges (such as social media).

The Gulf's post-truth moment can be characterised by the advent of a new era of Gulf politics, largely forged as an alliance between the Trump administration and the states of the UAE and Saudi Arabia. The Trump administration's policy of maximum pressure on Iran and its drive to encourage normalisation between the Gulf and Israel have bred a fertile ground for disinformation and deception synergies. This has overlapped with a new vision for the Middle East led chiefly by the rulers of Saudi Arabia and Abu Dhabi, Mohammed bin Salman (MBS) and Mohammed bin Zayed (MBZ). These two emerging autocrats have sought to place their respective nations at the helm of a new Gulf moment, one that seeks normalisation with Israel and increasing hostility towards Iran and political Islam. The Gulf's post-truth moment can also be defined by disinformation synergies, complementary disinformation narratives in which right-wing American policy and the foreign policy goals of the Saudi and UAE feed off each other in mutually reinforcing tropes.

A striking aspect of the Gulf's post-truth moment is the emergence of tyrannical and totalitarian tendencies. In order to create a 'permanent state of mobilisation' where citizens advocate and defend their new 'messianic' leader, totalitarian leaders often invoke external enemies in order to deflect from internal domestic criticism.[42] In the Gulf, Saudi Arabia and the UAE in particular have created an 'axis of evil' consisting of the Muslim Brotherhood,

Qatar, Turkey and Iran. Expressions of sympathy for these entities, as well as criticism of the Saudi and UAE governments, are firmly suppressed. As part of attempting to legitimise the re-orientation of Gulf politics, disinformation and propaganda efforts have focused around attempting to construct this axis of evil as a regional bogeyman threatening the GCC.

Crucially, this book highlights how the digital space in the Arab world is not a level or horizontal playing field in which individuals or states are competing equally: just as with more conventional military might, certain states pour more resources into their digital deception apparatus, which feed their varying strategic objectives. Similarly, as with any autocratic or totalitarian regime, personality of leaders matters when it comes to how those informational control strategies play out.

The Death of Techno-Utopianism: 'Neo-Liberation Technology and Post-Truth Industries'

A curious aspect of digital authoritarianism is how it fits in with the notion of techno-utopianism. After all, the arguments presented here raise an important issue: how has digital authoritarianism emerged so soon after a period dominated by effusive narratives about how technology would bring democracy to the Middle East? Despite the name, digital authoritarianism should not be seen as a concept that applies only to specific states that forgo democratic legitimacy in favour of absolutist-style rule. Nor should it be seen simply as the authoritarian appropriation of liberating technology.

On the contrary, digital authoritarianism and deception should be seen as a concatenation of illiberal practices undertaken by multiple actors, whether public or private, and whether situated in autocratic or democratic regimes.[43] It is a phenomenon in which multiple state and non-state actors are complicit in the creation of authoritarian assembly lines and disinformation supply chains. Here, actors with various interests and incentives provide and utilise methods in the service of a particular goal. The motivations for the end user might be political, such as power maintenance in the case of a political regime. For the service provider, whether that is a PR company in

London or a troll factory in Poland, the primary incentive might be financial. It is these relationships and transactions that underpin the facilitation, creation and perpetuation of authoritarian and illiberal behaviours across technology and across borders.

These constant transactions that occur around the globe result in what can be termed 'cyberwars' – that is, mediated contestations or battles between different parties and players in the digital world.[44] In this regard, cyberwars are the everyday contestations between regimes and their domestic or international opponents, 'but also geopolitical contestations between different regimes'.[45] Although cyberwars are a global phenomenon, the Middle East sometimes feels like the Wild West of the disinformation world – a place where anything goes. The reasons for this are rooted in the relations of a political ecosystem characterised by several factors. Cyberwars thrive in a space dominated by despotic regimes, seemingly with little oversight or concern from many of those institutions that create the tools being used, such as Twitter or Facebook. However, such regimes are often the perfect customers for a global disinformation and deception industry that seeks to exploit conflict in order to sell services or technologies that can aid and abet digital authoritarianism. When political relationships are favourable between these despotic states and the producers of technology, there are fewer barriers to the adoption of that technology (for whatever purposes). In this case, a positive relationship between most GCC states and the USA and Europe facilitates the transfer of goods, including technology, and thus illiberal practices.

This neoliberal logic, Paul Starr argues, has shaped the internet itself.[46] A fundamental aim of the neoliberal project 'has been to open up new fields of capital accumulation in domains hitherto regarded off-limits to the calculus of profitability'.[47] This includes private data, now harvested on a massive scale thanks to digital technology. The commodification of our private data through mass personal information disclosure to large tech companies can be termed what Shoshana Zuboff calls 'surveillance capitalism'.[48] Here an increasingly small number of monopolistic entities (tech corporations) extract our data with our limited consent and sell it to advertisers. The commodification of identity has been an advertising boon, incentivising for companies the disclosure of personal attributes and data to the extent that we have entered the most pervasive era of global surveillance ever.

Social media platforms in particular, premised on this extraction of self-disclosed data, are not just advantageous for advertisers, but for authoritarian regimes who seek to maintain control of their populations in different ways. Data profiles of subjects can be used to better understand, monitor and control human behaviour. It is in this context that the interests of authoritarian regimes and tech corporations align in the datafication of the subject. For authoritarian regimes the protection of individual privacy is problematic, as they endeavour to surveil their subjects and monitor any potential dissent. For tech firms, who consistently lobby against privacy laws, the protection of privacy is costly as it risks diminished advertising revenues.[49]

For this reason, it is important to get away from the paradigm of thought that frames technology as fundamentally liberating. Here 'liberation technology' is a term used to describe how optimists view the internet and digital technology as a means 'to empower individuals, facilitate independent communication and mobilization, and strengthen an emergent civil society'.[50] It is inextricable from the paradigm of 'techno-utopianism', a notion conceived in Francis Bacon's *New Atlantis* published in 1627, and which has come to be associated with a world in which technology ensures 'humans affluence, order, justice, and freedom'.[51] The converse of techno-utopianism is, of course, techno-dystopianism, popularised by the likes of Aldous Huxley's *Brave New World* and George Orwell's *1984*, which famously documented how technology will be instrumentalised as a tool that facilitates authoritarian rule, eugenics, and the growing inequality or heirarchisation of society. However, the utopian versus dystopian dichotomy is not necessarily useful.[52] Assuming a temporally bound and universal teleology for technology, in which there is only one evident outcome (utopian or dystopian) is deterministic, and negates power, culture and context.

However, the current 'moment' has been shaped by neoliberalism. Technology is both conceived of within specific social and political contexts and deployed in different ways. That many social media platforms have been created in Silicon Valley implies a certain logic of creation, a design ontology indicative of specific forces that produce those products, from the personal philosophy of a tech firm's CEO and the vision of programmers to the demands of funders and the regulations and processes that determine profit and growth. The idea of liberation technology is deterministic, carrying an implicit 'technology as reform/freedom' ontology that implies an inherent benevolence in its outcomes designed to promote political and social freedom in an American-centric sense.

There is a somewhat symbiotic relationship between the ontology of techno-utopianism and neoliberal thought. If neoliberalist thought positions as inevitable the beneficial nature of untrammelled corporate enterprise, the idea that tech companies in liberal democracies should be producing liberation technology is not an intellectual stretch, or a difficult notion to justify. This ontology of liberation has helped sell and justify the often-uncritical spread of technology. Perhaps unsurprisingly then, the neoliberal logic also has overtones of imperialism and colonialism. As Couldry argues, 'a political rationality operates to position society as the natural beneficiary of corporations' extractive efforts, just as humanity was supposed to benefit from historical colonialism as a "civilizational" project'.[53] Just as proponents of colonialism framed it as a civilising mission, techno-utopianism frames technology deterministically as a liberalising mission.

This cover of liberation belies a logic of extraction and commodification, itself a fundamental aspect of techno-colonialism, defined by Randy Bush as 'exploitation of poorer cultures by richer ones through technology'.[54] The incentive to find new markets and the desire of Gulf authoritarian leaders to exploit the surveillance-like logic of social media platforms, as well as to use the investment potential of their markets as leverage in defining the functionalities of platform, create an inevitable feedback loop. Extractive capitalism, which views data as a commodity with humans as a natural resource, is itself pivotal to digital imperial or colonial projects. Deregulated markets facilitate the monetisation of extraction, while authoritarian leaders crave data extraction from their populace.

So if liberation technology is to tech what the 'civilising mission' was to colonialism, then neoliberation technology is a more apt conceptualisation of the realities of the global spread of tech from their areas of conception. Indeed, if, as Paul Starr argues, neoliberalism has shaped the internet to create the problems of 'monopoly, surveillance, and disinformation', neoliberation technologies are the outputs that emerge and thrive in this system.[55] Just as 'Neoliberalism and authoritarianism are ... not inherently opposed to one another'[56], neoliberalism and thus neoliberation technology are a logical attendant to digital authoritarianism. So while liberation technology focuses on the positive impact on political structures and civil society, neoliberation technology indicates how the economic logic of neoliberalism has facilitated the proliferation of technologies in markets governed by autocratic actors, often on the flawed logic that such technology will bring freedom, or 'civility'. The critical side of the debate around how technology is used is often framed as the abuse, or 'misuse', of such technologies, which itself is based on a flawed assumption that negates social constructivism – that is, how technology is utilised depends on the socio-cultural environment in which it is consumed. Misuse is simply another form of use, and a euphemism for those forms of use that do not fit the idealised use of technology as a tool of liberation.

Thus, the term liberation technology is simply an ideal type at best, a propaganda tool at worst, eminently elusive, while neoliberation technology reflects how technology is so often developed and spread for the purpose of profit seeking (often using private data) to markets vastly different from those in which the technology was conceived. The notion of liberation technology is, at the very least, deceptive.

How to Study Deception

There is also another issue with studying disinformation; we can only analyse known campaigns. Theoretically, sophisticated disinformation operations are being conducted all the time but are not discovered. Inevitably, the focus has fallen on those countries or actors perceived to be generating a lot of disinformation – or, indeed, caught producing disinformation. So how does one study disinformation and deception? Disinformation research is rapidly evolving. Uncovering disinformation operations can require a complex suite of tools and skills that might not easily fall under conventional social science or humanities methodological umbrellas. Descriptive and data-driven approaches to social media analysis are less well suited to answering 'how, why and with what consequences [people] use social media'.[57]

On the other hand, quantitative methods are also imperative in understanding the scale of abuse or deception, and the scope of the potential influence of bad actors. They also can help us identify patterns of behaviour across large datasets that provide evidence for the presence of manipulation. As such, the research for this book has utilised a number of methods, including digital[58] ethnography, open-source research,[59] as well as computer-assisted analysis of datasets, including anomaly detection, corpus analysis, network analysis and, well, good old-fashioned investigative work. Indeed, traditional qualitative methods, underpinned by the development of computer-aided research,[60] combine to detail a richer and more comprehensive analysis of deception operations. Together, these techniques enable us to answer the questions of how, why and with what effects deception and digital authoritarianism are realised across the Arab-speaking world.

The primary research for this book has involved analysis of Arabic and English content, as those are the languages with which I am most comfortable. Much of this content has been extracted from Twitter. Over the past five years I have analysed millions of tweets and hundreds of hashtags. Twitter is more forgiving in terms of data gathering, which can be accessed via the Application Programming Interface (API). There are also other reasons to study Twitter. Studies have shown that, while engagement with fake news may be declining on Facebook, it is continuing to rise on Twitter.[61] Depending on the nature of the deception campaign, Facebook pages, YouTube videos and websites and news sites have all functioned as objects of study, whether as disinformation themselves or secondary sources. As always, there is also the judicious use of secondary sources, especially with regard to providing background on some of the geopolitical contexts in the region. Although much of the focus – and, indeed, deception – appears to take place on Twitter, this research refers to activity on other platforms where possible, and the synergies between legacy media, social media and other forms of deception.

Interviews have also been instructive, especially when trying to evaluate the impacts of some aspects of digital authoritarianism, such as cyber harassment, trolling or bullying. In general, more technical methodological notes and detail will be footnoted so as to avoid interrupting the flow of the narrative. Having said that, sometimes a description of bot detection is provided to give readers an insight into the process, as well as the scale of these operations. In addition to social media analysis, the book is also premised on exploring holistically the interplay of deception operations with more traditional media.

With social media companies and governments accused of being lax in tackling digital deception, the urgency of 'monitoring and active debunking of information is falling uncomfortably across different sectors',[62] from journalism to academia. Often the nature of deception research raises considerable ethical dilemmas. How does one deal with large-scale analysis of metadata of social media accounts? Can the need to tackle illiberal practices by deceptive actors justify certain processes of exposure and publication for the public good? Do suspected trolls and bots require the same level of sensitivity as human subjects, especially when they are attempting to deceive the researcher and others for the purpose of information operations?

In many regards, disinformation researchers are having to make their own judgements on this, largely due to the prevalence of the neoliberation paradigm which resists regulation – even against deception. Often, authoritarian regimes will selectively use arguments of privacy to protect their own techniques of repression, and attempt to instrumentalise attention to ethics as a way to legitimise a lack of transparency. The following passage offers some guidance on treating new forms of public data: 'Blogs, twitter feeds, public websites, chat rooms, and other comparable data sources are "public" in the sense that they are freely available to all web users, and "published" in the sense that the data is published on the web. In most cases uses of these sources should be classified as non-human subjects research, even when they include identifiers via videos, photos, and text. This is by virtue of the fact that they do not include private identifiable data because the data is publicly available'.[63]

Just as mixed methods can improve empirical research, collaborations with other researchers can bring technical expertise and area studies knowledge that is important to contextualising disinformation research. Much of the research here has been the work of personal investigations and social media analysis by myself over a period of ten years. However, it is important to recognise that the digital space and its affordances and functionalities promote forms of interaction that might differ from so-called meatspace ('real' life). The relationships accrued, and the speed by which one is accessible and can interact with others is a functionality particular to social media. Uncoupled from geographical restrictions, conversations, tips, investigations, and relationships can be instigated globally. Many of the investigations and revelations have been made possible by the ability to make connections with journalists, academics and activists across the world, especially those with an interest in disinformation and the Middle East. Frequently case studies have arisen because someone in a particular place, whether Algeria or Yemen, has alerted me to something suspicious. This, of course, is a strong advertisement for the role of digital media. Ultimately, this book is the end-product of duly acknowledged collaborative efforts and collective action, made possible by the public-service-oriented approach I have cultivated through writing on disinformation on blogs, articles or Twitter threads.

Structure and Style

For those who are familiar with, or have a general knowledge of, Middle East politics, many of these chapters can be read on their own. Although some chapters are more akin to conventional current affairs and academic writing within the area of media studies, digital humanities or area studies, others are more narrative focused (such as Chapters 14 and 15), intended specifically to be both entertaining and informative. The term 'entertainment' is not designed to trivialise the severity of disinformation, but rather capture the spirit of the often-bizarre nature of disinformation investigations. Certainly, while it is hoped that the book in its entirety is compelling in its own way, the decision to include narrative-focused elements is designed to more vividly capture the nature and experiences of the (dis)information space – which is a fundamentally serious issue.

There are good reasons for this. A well-known criticism of some academic writing is that it can be needlessly complex and inaccessible, and thus distract from the urgency of communicating important and topical research to broader audiences.[64] The style of this book is motivated by 'public impact scholarship', which is 'characterized by intentional efforts to create social change through the translation and dissemination of research to nonacademic audiences'.[65] An explicit aspect of this is not just more accessible writing, but more engaging writing and styles.[66] Narratives can (among other things) be used to maintain attention, provoke curiosity, and ultimately improve reader engagement with the text.[67] The same is true of vignettes, anecdotal narratives, auto-ethnographic reflections and variations in pace. Even the lengths of chapters, which have been kept relatively short, are designed to improve readability. The urgency of the disinformation problem only emphasises the need for accessible and engaging research on the topic.

The book's chapters are organised broadly into six parts. Part I, which includes Chapters 1 and 2, lays out the definitions of disinformation, propaganda and deception. It makes the case that 'deception' is perhaps a better term to accurately describe the nature of how false content is produced and disseminated. Chapter 2 defines the deception order – that is the disinformation supply chains, actors and authoritarian assembly lines that are responsible for the information disorder.

Part II charts the rise of the new deception superpowers in the Gulf region. Chapter 3 explores the rise of Saudi Arabia (and to a lesser extent the UAE) as a key player in the deception order. It notes how the vision of MBS has been key in forging Saudi as one of the world's largest digital deception actors. It also makes the argument that, based on known empirical measures of Saudi information operations, it is likely one of the most active social media manipulators in the world. Chapter 4 documents innovations in the digitisation of deception, most notably how automation is being used on Twitter to control Saudi Arabia's domestic social media news cycle, with a specific case study examining the use of Twitter bots to dominate domestic news across Saudi's 13 regions.

Part III begins to look at the relationship between international politics, and particularly US policy, in shaping the MENA's disinformation space and the Gulf's post-truth moment. Chapter 5 highlights in particular how the Trump administration's maximum pressure policy on Iran, with support from Saudi and the UAE, has created a maelstrom of disinformation in the Middle East pertaining to Iran, Qatar, Turkey and the Muslim Brotherhood. Chapter 6 emphasises how the Gulf Crisis was a quantum shift in the disinformation landscape that cemented the KUBE (Kingdom of Saudi Arabia, United Arab Emirates, Bahrain and Egypt) countries as dominant actors and, to an extent, innovators in the deception space.

Part IV examines the strategic projection of deception operations outwards from the Arabian Peninsula towards the international community. Chapter 7 explores potential Gulf deception operations in the wider Middle East, with particular reference to Iran, Lebanon and Algeria. Chapter 8 documents one of the most audacious deception operations ever discovered, in which a group of fake journalists likely connected to the UAE fooled dozens of legitimate news outlets into publishing state propaganda. Chapter 9 shifts towards Europe, and is a case study focusing on the attempted manipulation of Newcastle United fans following the failed bid for ownership by Saudi's Public Investment Fund (PIF). All chapters highlight the growing use of deception operations as an adjunct to Saudi's economic and political goals.

Part V emphasises the silencing of critics, a crucial aspect of the new digital authoritarianism. Chapters 10, 11 and 12 all look at the modalities of how critics of KUBE policies are attacked through the uses of deception operations. Chapter 11 focuses on the murder of Jamal Khashoggi, and particularly the attempted marginalisation of his death through smear campaigns and content manipulation. Chapter 12 discusses malinformation, hack-and-leak operations and the use of misogynistic attacks on women critical of Saudi and

Emirati policies. Chapter 14 discusses how Covid19 disinformation played out in the region, and how it even reflected tropes of the new regional vision advocated by the UAE and Saudi Arabia.

Part VI is more narrative focused, detailing the various alarming ways that unknown actors appropriate social media accounts to phish for human intelligence and spread pro-MBS propaganda.

Conclusion

This chapter began with a personal account of harassment, manipulation, abuse and deception, as well as their attendant psychological pain. Such treatment is ubiquitous for those journalists, academics, activists and citizens who have used digital media to criticise their governments, anywhere in the world, and especially during and after the Arab Uprisings. Some people are aggrieved by what I tell them, while others are dismissive, saying things like 'Why just not use social media?' Although this is a solution for some, all it does is allow the aggressors, the disinformation agents and the cyberbullies to win. In an age where our life chances and inclusion into an increasingly technology-dependent world are so often defined by digital privilege – that is, our competence, willingness and ability to adopt new and increasingly ubiquitous technologies – we cannot and should not be expected to just abandon the promise of technology-facilitated opportunities by letting malicious actors scare us away. Just as we should not retreat from any public space on account of malevolent forces seeking to shut down debate or intimidate those that challenge illiberal authoritarianism, we should not retreat from the digital space. To retreat is to simply ignore the suffering, not to make it cease to exist.

As it stands, the outcomes of neoliberation technology are increasingly clear. Digital espionage, cyberbullying, industrial-level hate speech, content manipulation and social engineering all plague the global digital space, and this is particularly the case in the Middle East. Despite the prevalence of such toxic practices, MENA lingers on the periphery of the more mainstream attention of disinformation analysts, such as Russia and Iran, partly because most GCC states are strategic allies of the states in which many of those tech companies reside. This book attempts to address this lack of focus on an overlooked region that is increasingly one of the largest importers and exporters of deception. It is doubly exploited, both as a region and by dictators who rely on the lack of attention in Western states to the abuse of those technologies.

The central purpose of the book is to comprehensively document the gamut of deception techniques evident in the MENA region, and where possible the actors and entities responsible for these methods. By doing so, it advances the argument that the dystopian potential of social media is ascendant in the Middle East. This has been underpinned by a new Gulf vision led by increasingly tyrannical regimes, and abetted by neoliberation technology. These elements, I argue, have profoundly shaped the Arab world's post-truth moment – a digitally dominant, Gulf-driven exertion of digital power.

In order to make these claims, this book documents the variety, scale and types of disinformation operation, as well as their evolving nature since 2011. It should be noted that this book is not, and cannot be, an exhaustive list of every disinformation operation occurring in the MENA region. Instead, it is an attempt to give as comprehensive a view as possible about disinformation and deception emanating from within or targeting the region. The book focuses on the breadth, capaciousness, variety and scale of disinformation operations, while also highlighting some of the key players within the deception order. Having said this, of course, the book also attempts to give a fuller account of the disinformation scene in the MENA region by referencing those studies performed by others on countries or cases relevant to the region.

PART I

DIGITAL DECEPTION AND
THE PSEUDO-REALITY INDUSTRIES

DIGITAL AUTHORITARIANISM, DECEPTION AND INFORMATION CONTROLS

Chapter Overview: Definitions

The advent – or, rather, resurgence – of the information disorder – or, indeed, the war against reality, whatever you decide to call it – has brought it with a broad and often interchangeable vocabulary of different ways to mislead that, ironically, can be quite misleading. Disinformation, misinformation, malinformation, fake news, propaganda, co-ordinated inauthentic activity, information operations and influence operations are just some of these terms. Many of them are similar, or overlap, but it is essential to single out some useful nuances between them. This chapter lays out the various definitions pertinent to studying the role of deception and social media in the Gulf's post-truth moment.

Information Controls

In the information age, where we increasingly depend on computerisation and information, the notion of informational controls should demand careful scrutiny. Here informational controls are, broadly speaking, the use of techniques to reduce dissent through the selective control of access to information on which a person makes decisions and formulates opinions. They rely on persuasion, indoctrination, socialisation and censorship. By controlling the thought diet of people, you can theoretically influence their behaviours.[1] As Gamson argues, informational controls seek to control the desire, not just the ability, to pursue a particular course of action.[2] A certain repertoire of techniques and tactics has emerged that characterises the nature of digital authoritarianism.

An overarching concern within informational controls is to reduce criticism or counter-narratives that may provide momentum to anti-status quo movements. Reducing counter-narratives can be achieved by targeting critics with coercion, deception or co-optation. Coercion can include intimidation, blackmail, torture or assassination, while co-optation might include incentives to write and publish pro-status quo material. Deception might include tricking influential gatekeepers or hacking their accounts in order to spread a pro-status quo narrative. The result of either of these processes is either praise or reduced criticism of the regime and its policies.

Criticism is rarely muted in its entirety, and thus flooding information space with desired narratives is an end and goal in and of itself. In a digital age this can be done in a number of ways. The vacuum left by the removal of counter-narratives can be dominated by filling the information space with propaganda and disinformation via deceptive means such as trolls and/or bots. Much of the disinformation or propaganda might itself be designed itself to intimidate, discredit or attack critics of the regime. Certain targets may elicit certain tactics. Some critics, such as Jamal Khashoggi, were threatened and then killed, while women journalists, for example, are attacked with misogynistic abuse and threats. The scale of operations is broadly commensurate with an actor's resources, but also the perceived challenge of maintaining positive public opinion. Public scandals, or unpopular foreign or domestic policy decisions, will necessitate more resources directed to influence operations to convince or drown out potential critics.

Beyond Disinformation and Propaganda: Weaponized Deception

Digital disinformation, and indeed deception, is an increasingly integral feature of modern international relations. It is used by foreign powers with malign intent, and 'thus a tool employed in a global power struggle'.[3] It is a strategic and tactical tool, utilised by various actors in the field of information warfare. It can be used as an instrument of 'destabilisation during election periods and is connected to broader international concerns such as a country's diplomatic relationships or security arrangements'.[4] Disinformation, and indeed information, is a weapon used by states and non-state actors for strategic influence.

Disinformation, misinformation and malinformation form a useful troika, as they primarily concern both the veracity and the intention of the content being produced. Disinformation can be classed as deliberately manipulated audio, textual or visual content. It is often utilised to demoralise an adversary or promote the agenda of a specific actor. That actor may be a lowly rogue conspiracy theorist or a nation-state.[5] The aspect of disinformation that separates it from misinformation is intent. Misinformation is information deemed to be factually inaccurate but spread unintentionally with no intent to cause harm. At the other end of the spectrum is malinformation (malevolent information), which is defined as information that is considered truthful, but broadcast tactically to cause harm or detriment to another person, entity or institution. Malinformation might include doxing or using revenge porn. Here doxing is the posting of private information about a person, usually to discredit them or shame them.

Fig. 1: Overview of key terminology assessed according to veracity and intent

	False	*Truthful*	*Intentional*
Propaganda	Yes	Yes	Yes or No
Malinformation	No	Yes	Yes
Disinformation	Yes	No	Yes
Misinformation	Yes	No	No

However, the primary focus of this book is disinformation and deception (which we will come to later). In most cases, the disinformation being discussed usually relates to campaigns spread deliberately to give political parties, governments and other actors some form of commercial or geopolitical advantage – often at the expense of another group of people, whether a polity, ethnic group or rival firm. A disinformation campaign 'is an intentional and coordinated attempt by an actor to spread false information to an audience, typically to achieve a political communication goal.'[6] A disinformation campaign will often include forgery and/or fabrication, along with accompanying publicity that seeks to gain a psychological advantage for its creator. A disinformation campaign is distinct from a disparate collection of untruths, as a campaign generally requires planning and intent, along with the weaponisation at scale of large volumes of information distributed to a large audience by powerful actors and with a specific purpose.

Disinformation campaigns ordinarily include both an originator and a target. The originator may often be referred to as a disinformation agent or a disinformation actor. Although the target is often clear, the originator may not be. Determining, through the process of attribution, who the originator is can often be incredibly tricky in online influence operations. It can also be challenging to establish the intentions of the originator if the motives of the perpetrators(s) are not known. Having said that, if people are mobilising significant resources to promote a specific message, whether through disinformation or propaganda, there is obviously a clear agenda behind the attack designed to attain widespread publicity and impact. While attribution may be tricky to determine, intent and scale can often be deduced through an assessment of the apparent means of dissemination.

Between Disinformation and Propaganda: United by Intent

Although the term disinformation seems to have become more fashionable recently, it is never far removed from the term propaganda, and disinformation and propaganda are often one and the same. Some have tried to make a distinction; Hill notes that disinformation involves the staging of an event accompanied by a persuasive message, while propaganda is a more run-of-the-mill attempt to persuade.[7] More contemporary definitions emphasise the importance of truth in disinformation, as opposed to the staging of a pseudo-event. However, some have used the umbrella term 'organised persuasive communication' (OPC) to include 'advertising and marketing, propaganda, public relations, organizational communication, information/influence campaigns, psychological operations, strategic communication and a whole host of other overlapping terms'.[8] Within this paradigm, 'non-consensual' manipulation via deception, incentivization and coercion separates propagandistic OPC from other forms of OPC. Propaganda need not be fake, and can be broadly understood as the intentional or deliberate manipulation of public opinion.[9] So while all disinformation is likely to be propaganda, not all propaganda is necessarily disinformation. However, the strict definition of disinformation emphasises the intent to mislead as well as the lack of truthfulness to the content. The objectives of disinformation are often not part of the definition, and this is where propaganda scholarship can be instructive. Synthesising the views of a number of scholars, Florian Zollmann defines propaganda as 'the forming of texts and opinions in support of particular interests and through media and non-media mediated means with the intention to produce public support and/or relevant action'.[10] It is these particular interests that are useful jumping-off points, as they imply the existence of partisan or commercial entities, and those with specific forms of power – often accumulated through wealth or privilege – who act to influence opinion. Traditionally the ability to launch widespread propaganda has been synonymous with the political or commercial capture of some means of distribution, either through advertising or state broadcasting. However, the rise of digital media has devolved the means of distribution without necessarily altering the goals of powerful disinformation agents such as states.

In contemporary literature on 'fake news' and disinformation, the term influence campaigns is often used, and refers to the broader purpose of a campaign designed to influence a particular outcome. That it is a campaign implies that there is some coordination, whether through funding, information sharing, propaganda or lobbying. As such, an influence campaign is a generic term used to describe a strategy that may or may not include disinformation but is likely to be propaganda. Indeed, open-ended definitions of both disinformation and propaganda are perhaps too broad an umbrella. While propaganda may contain truths, it has been confounded by definitions that seek to distinguish between benevolence and malice. A more open-ended definition may, for example, render a public health campaign such as promoting vaccination as propaganda. Here, it is propaganda because it is attempting to persuade the public of the collective benefits of vaccination. The benefit of such propaganda is hard to dispute, but propaganda tends to have negative connotations, mainly due to its wide-scale deployment in both world wars to demonise the belligerents. As such, some may only consider something to be propaganda if it is highly malicious, or conducive to the goals of a malevolent actor, although malevolence can then become a subjective term. However, for the sake of this book malevolence shall be broadly designated as any behaviour working in opposition to the tenets of the transformative paradigm, which reject culturalism relativism in pursuit of social justice, equality and human rights. As such, post-war attempts to rebrand seemingly benevolent or harmless propaganda as 'public relations' are equally contentious, not least because they sanitise or remove scrutiny from what might be campaigns that are fundamentally harmful. As Zollmann notes, it has 'remained convenient to sidestep an assessment of the problematic nature of PR and advertising as propaganda techniques'.[11] Indeed, 'corporate lobbying, media manipulation and networking can all be considered forms of propaganda.[12]

In this book, 'propaganda' is usually used to describe influence campaigns intended to bind specific groups together by 'othering' another group, or campaigns designed to disadvantage or harm a specific group or entity through what Laswell terms 'demonising propaganda'.[13] The target may be an ethnic group, a nation, or any particular group of people who identify based on their heritage, sexuality, gender, etc. This is information designed to stigmatise a subset of a population in order to mobilise public opinion against that group. Such propaganda usually involves selecting and emphasising certain tropes, for example, the use of violence by protesters to discredit a resistance movement. Such 'demonising' propaganda has been common throughout modern history. It helped legitimise and lead to the Holocaust, as well as the Rwandan genocide, to name but two examples. Indeed, the role of propaganda in exacerbating conflict is well established, and it is for this reason that propaganda for the purposes of war is illegal under the International Covenant for Civil and Political Rights. However, the digital age has resulted in new affordances, in which individual users can readily produce and consume digital propaganda. Although states and corporations can still use tremendous resources to dominate potential propaganda structures, the traditional power symmetries in which limited gatekeepers control the message has been challenged.[14]

Propaganda campaigns may include untruthful disinformation, or they may exploit small truths in a misleading way. Malinformation, such as doxing sexually explicit images as a means of causing shame or embarrassment, is a pertinent example. When done to target actors critical of governments or high-profile commercial actors, it can be readily construed as a political act that seeks to attack the credibility of the target. Smearing women as promiscuous is common the world over, and resonates more profoundly in conservative societies such as the Middle East. Such disinformation or propaganda campaigns may exaggerate negative elements of a persona, whether true or not, in order to diminish public support for, and the credibility of, that person.

Divide and Conquer

Although demonisation and smear campaigns are intrinsic to many propaganda campaigns, disinformation studies have, in some cases, tried to reinvent the wheel when it comes to a definition. However, for the sake of comprehensiveness, it is important to note the term 'adversarial content'.[15] A chief aim of propaganda and disinformation is to promote polarisation, division and conflict by pitting one side against an 'adversary'. By engaging in hyper-partisan politics, entities conducting influence campaigns often 'play' both sides to emphasise in-group and out-group categories. This may, for example, involve riling up anti-immigration sentiment, promoting racial tension or stoking sectarianism and religious conflict. As Decker and Fagan have argued, 'when adversarial narratives are deployed, they create a series of smaller conflicts played out across the internet. Adversarial narratives are effective because they inflame social tensions by exploiting and amplifying perceived grievances of individuals, groups and institutions.'[16] This may be especially tempting for geopolitical rivals, such as Russia and the USA, who strive to gain advantage from promoting social conflict in order to direct state resources towards combating domestic issues rather than abroad. We know, for example, that the St Petersburg troll factory, the Internet Research Agency, was discovered to have created both pro- and anti-Black Lives Matter campaigns to sow discord and division.[17]

Polarisation is about eliminating the middle ground, or areas of moderation around which people can better reconcile or recognise another's position and treat them with validity. Such campaigns seek to eviscerate nuance and promote unequivocal truths, both about people and in the arguments deployed. It is probably an exaggeration to say that tyranny is the absence of nuance, but rather that the absence of nuance is a key component towards dyadic thinking and polarised politics, and that is itself a stepping stone to tyranny and conflict.

At times, polarisation entrenches views and perspectives to the extent that truth itself becomes entirely relative to the position of an adversary. In many instances, this invokes a form of pathological tu quoque, whereby a person is only able to accept criticisms of their worldview on a quid pro quo basis, i.e. when their rival concedes that 'their side' is equally culpable in a similar moral transgression. This behaviour, resembling whataboutism, diverts people away from confronting evidentiary claims in exchange for challenging their perception of another's beliefs. Introspection and scientific discovery are discouraged, replaced instead by an adversarial moral relativism where ego prevents rational debate. Disinformation and propaganda are often primed to evoke this shift in ontological certainty. Indeed, part of the war on reality is designed to replace a shared reality with two competing realities.

Controlling the Narrative

Unlike propaganda, where definitions remain unsettled, it is clear that with disinformation intention to mislead is critical. However, this is certainly not the only goal for disinformation campaigns, or indeed for propaganda campaigns. Campaigns might seek to promote apathy in a specific population so that they do not vote. By doing so, the rival candidate in an election campaign achieves an advantage. Indeed, this 'democratic deterrent' was a tactic used by the British data firm Cambridge Analytica against black voters in the United States.[18] Digital technology allows companies to create large databases and information profiles about people based on their social media habits and other behaviours. These profiles can then be used to selectively target, or 'micro-target' people based on their personalities and behaviours. In short, personalised propaganda. Similarly, deception might be about muddying the waters of moral certainty. Western PR firms in particular have gained a reputation for whitewashing and boosting the reputations of human rights abusers, a form of deception that seeks to minimise the transgressions of tyrannical regimes in order that they can retain power. To misquote Hannah Arendt, such campaigns attempt to banalise and minimise evil.

For disinformation and deception to be more successful, one must limit the amount of competing contradictory information out there. This can be termed information domination, and can be achieved through privileging particular messages over others, whether by censorship or amplifying/swamping the information space with the desired narrative of the deception agent. Censorship is one way to do this, and can be achieved through several means. Activists and journalists can be silenced through murder, incarceration, embroilment in litigation, intimidation, blackmail and surveillance.

Similarly, flooding the information space is often achieved through state ownership of news channels or the use of state-funded social media bots and trolls. These tactics can be mutually enforcing. As Coppins argues, there is 'no need to silence the dissident shouting in the streets; they can use a megaphone to drown him out. Scholars have a name for this: censorship through noise.'[19] Indeed, amplification seeks to raise the salience of specific discourses, stories or events. This has become possible on social media as citizens are able to share, promote and amplify stories, news items or anything that interests them, regardless of their truthfulness. There is generally little barrier to what might be amplified on social media. While Vilares et al. argue that the primary purpose of Twitter within political discussion is to amplify debates in the traditional media,[20] such an argument is temporally and contextually bound. With so many turning away from 'mainstream media', in part due to its increasing stigmatisation by populist leaders as the 'fake news media', social media itself becomes the end goal for those spreading disinformation.

There is also an efficiency to both social media and disinformation that facilitates its transmission. Disinformation has been found to spread faster than the truth.[21] Traditional and competent journalism requires time, patience and a lot of work to create a well-substantiated and well-sourced story. Unrestrained by the burdens of diligent sourcing, corroboration and expert testimony, disinformation flourishes. False stories can be generated at speed, and in large numbers. In turn, networks of fake accounts can distribute that message at high volume and at a high velocity. The lack of fidelity to the truth can give unlimited scope for salaciousness, and thus the potential for virality. In other words, lies are fast while truth is slow.

Profit-oriented social media companies are also increasingly central in determining what news people read through algorithmically curated content. Unfortunately for truth, what is good for generating user engagement (and thus revenue) is often harmful, sensationalist or hyper-partisan content. When Facebook surveyed users on whether posts they had seen could be categorised as 'bad for the world' versus 'good for the world', they discovered that high-reach and widely shared posts were more often considered 'bad for the world'.[22] The Facebook engineers' attempts to incorporate an algorithm to demote such 'bad for the world' content in users' news feeds were dialled back when the change was found to lower the amount of time users spent on Facebook. In other words, 'good for the world content' was also bad for the profit margin content.

Towards a Definition of Deception: Malicious Means as a Form of Intent

The intent to mislead the public about a certain event, occurrence, personality or the source of a story is the cornerstone of disinformation. However, as the Introduction to this book indicated, disinformation need not only be about false content per se, and discussions about deception tend to be framed around content.[23] The rise of automation and artificial intelligence is prompting innovations in the dispersal of disinformation, facilitating both its volume and its potential reach.

It is thus important to note that 'information operations do not always use false content or false narratives, and often simply pick content to amplify and re-use for their purposes'.[24] Facebook uses a similar term, coordinated inauthentic behaviour (CIO), to describe accounts, groups or pages that seek to 'mislead people about who they are and what they are doing while relying on fake accounts'.[25] Thus, the methods of dissemination should be included within an exploration of deception and disinformation, as manipulating the prominence of a message, even if truthful, constitutes a form of deception and dishonesty. The same is true of provenance; masking accountability through a lack transparency can also be seen as deceptive and ties in with Glasius and Michaelsen's notion of 'authoritarian practices'. An increasingly common and deceptive method of dissemination is to create fake personalities and bots (non-human automated accounts) using social media to promote specific narratives. The fact that these accounts are not who they claim to be is inherently deceptive, whether or not they are spreading factual information or falsehoods.

Such deceptive campaigns, whether undertaken by private actors or the state, manufacture the illusion of vox pops in order to amplify, improve or legitimise the information disseminated. Regardless of the veracity of content, the disinformation lies in the deception of provenance. Thus deception can usually be conceived as being done through lying, distortion, omission or misdirection.[26] By adopting this framework of deception, we can determine that, if the means of distribution are manipulated, there is the intention at least to undertake propaganda. Deceptive tactics often point to malicious intent, and if the account of the person is not 'real' it can be considered to be false in itself. 'Deception' better captures all the nuances of both disinformation and propaganda, incorporating content, intent and the means of manipulation. Rather than solely focusing on whether the information is factual or not, deception captures all elements of intention, content and distribution. Deception is the wilful manipulation of the information space through erroneous content and manipulated forms of distribution, with the intent to cause some form of harm through demonisation, adversarial content, omission, misdirection, whitewashing or influencing information availability in the service of political power maintenance.

Electronic Flies: A Deception Lexicon for the Ages

Deception on social media is frequently carried out by bots or trolls. Broadly speaking, bots and trolls are the immediate agents who spread and amplify deceptive content. So ubiquitous is the phenomenon, and yet so particularistic the context, that people across the Middle East experiencing infestations have varying terms of 'endearment' for bots and trolls. In Bahrain during 2011, bots or trolls were termed *e-baltajiyya* (e-thugs). During the Gulf Crisis in 2017, Qataris termed them *dhabāb iliktrūniya* (electronic flies). During the Sudanese uprising in 2018 and 2019, the Sudanese word for chicken – *al-jadad*[27] – was utilised.

At root, bots are not fundamentally malicious, as they are software programs designed to execute commands, protocols or routine tasks, in this case on the internet. Bots exist online in large quantities, and are created for various reasons, including 'news, marketing, spamming, spreading malicious content, and more recently political campaigning'.[28] Many bots perform essential public services in pursuit of social justice goals, such as calling out racism online, or highlighting when members of parliament delete their tweets.[29] A Twitter bot called Laleh Karahiyya (a pun on the Arabic phrase 'no to sectarianism') would call out those using sectarian hate speech online. If someone used a selection of specific anti-Shi'a or anti-Sunni slurs, Laleh's Twitter account automatically replied by saying, 'do you think this is sectarian hate speech?'[30] However, bots are increasingly being used to distribute propaganda.[31] Even in small numbers, bots can have a significant impact on the sharing of information, including, for example, increasing the popularity of specific URLs.[32]

The potential impact on the information ecosystem is reflected in the volume of bots. There have been varying estimates for the number of bots on Twitter, ranging from 5% to 10.5%.[33] When you include bot-assisted accounts (or cyborgs), this figure can reach 36.2%.[34] More often than not however, bots are involved in spreading propaganda, fake news and disinformation.[35] Bots, or more likely trolls, may also be used to intimidate activists and online commentators.[36] They can manipulate trends, produce spam and create a large amount of pollution or noise. The term 'computational propaganda' has been coined to refer to the broader spectrum of how automation enabled by computers is being used to facilitate digital deception.[37] Such distortions 'can drown out legitimate debate and pollute conversations with malicious, extraneous or irrelevant information'.[38] Additionally, the repetition of messages has been found to make people more likely to believe them to be true, whether they are or not.[39]

Numerous studies have emerged that document the existence and, where possible, the impact of bots on the public sphere. Arnaudo, for example, has documented the prevalence of bots during the Brazilian elections held in 2014 and 2016.[40] Howard et al. have looked at the role of bots and political communication in the 2016 US elections.[41] Keller and Klinger argue that bots can boost the perceived popularity of public officials.[42]

Determining the actual impact or effects on public opinion is difficult, so some studies have focused on the efficacy of bots at promoting hyper-partisan news.[43] Indeed, it is more common for the existence, prevalence and activity of bots to be documented than it is for their impact on public opinion to be analysed. This is because it is easier to determine their impact on information availability. With advances in artificial intelligence, the increasing sophistication of bots is an inevitability. Even now, Twitter bots have been designed to learn based on their interactions with other users – albeit with limited success. Microsoft created a Twitter bot called Tay that was designed to improve via 'conversational understanding' (e.g. interactions with real people). However, it quickly became a sex-crazed neo-Nazi.[44] In other words, real people on Twitter taught the bot to be a 'racist asshole' within 24 hours.[45] Nonetheless, as bots become more advanced, they will become more difficult to detect.

Unlike bots, trolls are real people, usually operating multiple Twitter accounts designed to harass, distract, redirect, obfuscate or mislead other people. Trolls often engage in argumentation using logical fallacies, employing whataboutism, tu quoque and straw men to accomplish their goals. They frequently target journalists with disinformation. This process, known as 'source-hacking', is designed to trick journalists into picking up fake news and amplifying it to the public. Trolls can operate on large scales, almost like call centres. Within these operations, dozens or hundreds of people operate multiple social media accounts, working in shifts to do the bidding of particular clients. With little preventing people from adopting pseudonyms on many social media platforms – which allows tech companies to amplify engagement – it is easy for people to set up multiple accounts with fake identities. Six people, each operating thirty different personas' accounts, and posting nine hours a day, could actually represent 180 people online. If each of those accounts were to post even one tweet every 15 minutes, that would amount to 6,480 tweets per day. When you consider that Twitter allows one user to post up to 2,400 tweets per day, the same small group of trolls could produce nearly half a million tweets per day. There is ample evidence of entities setting up fake Facebook user profiles in order to artificially amplify engagement with politicians. The most notable case was probably that of Juan Orlando Hernández, the president of Honduras. In August 2018 a former Facebook employee, Sophie Zhang, 'uncovered evidence that Hernández's staff was directly involved in the campaign to boost content on his page with hundreds of thousands of fake likes'.[46] These fake accounts can promote engagement, and manipulate Facebook's algorithms into making the chosen content more salient. I have found the same. My analysis has shown that up to 91% of the Twitter accounts sharing posts by Mohamed bin Zayed Al Nahyan, the Crown Prince of the UAE, are fake.

Trolling can be a process motivated by financial gain or political reward. In China, for example, there are probably government employees who engage in the promotion of pro-state propaganda as a service to their employer.[47] Sometimes trolls utilise 'sockpuppet' accounts, which are accounts that used to belong to someone else but have been deceptively appropriated for malicious reasons. Sometimes accounts are termed cyborgs, displaying elements of automated behaviour with some level of human interaction. The ubiquity of trolls has created its own terminological confusion. Darwish et al. have studied the role of 'seminar users' in the Egyptian Twittersphere – accounts that actively spread pro-regime propaganda. Other terms include 'water armies', large numbers of people organising coordinated messaging campaigns that may or may not be operating from the same 'troll farm'.[48] As 'bots' and 'trolls' generally refer to the behavioural nuances of online actors, 'flies' is a useful catch-all term to describe all those involved in engaging in deception.

A frequent tactic by flies is the pollution of potentially useful hashtags with extraneous or irrelevant information. Spamming, as it might be termed, can pollute critical discussions that aim to raise awareness about key political, social or economic issues. Maréchal argues that hashtag spamming – or 'the practice of affixing a specific hashtag to irrelevant content – renders the hashtag unusable'.[49] The process of amplification by flies can also give the illusion of 'false equivalence or consensus' when it may not exist.[50] This is abetted by numerous logical fallacies, such as ad hominem attacks, tu quoque and whataboutism. Whataboutism, in particular, seeks to create false parity between two arguments or invite accusations of hypocrisy, eviscerating nuance and fact in pursuit of creating an illusion of balance. The mantra that there are 'two sides to every story' is also similar, as it pays scant regard to factual events. The natural progression of whataboutism leads to an absolute sense of moral relativism that, if pursued to its logical conclusion, would permit the occurrence of every form of deviance, simply because it has probably happened elsewhere. If, for example, whataboutism was a valid legal defence, probably no one would get convicted of a crime because attention would be diverted from a specific instance of criminality to an unrelated but similar event that had happened elsewhere.

The Rise of the Pseudo-Publics

Flies often engage in 'astroturfing', which involves creating the illusion of bottom-up popular support (astroturfing = artificial grassroots) for certain policy positions. Here, trolls masquerade as real people, often creating personas such as journalists or activists. In 2011 the UK lobbying firm BGR Gabara was caught in a sting operation by undercover reporters. BGR was planning to organise an 'online social media campaign' by Kazakh 'kids', who were supposedly upset that the musician Sting had decided to withdraw from a planned performance in the country. Sting's decision was based on a human rights issue raised in an Amnesty International report concerning the poor treatment of striking oil workers.[51] Mr Gabara, the firm's chief executive and a former European Commission press officer, stated that such a campaign by 'kids' might have emerged organically, but it would be 'stronger' if they [BGR] were 'coordinating it'. He added that the purpose of the campaign was to generate print coverage to balance public perceptions about Kazakhstan following the negative coverage about the country. Gabara stated, 'Once we have generated the online social media campaign we have what it takes to generate print coverage to balance Amnesty International's accusations that lead to this ill-informed decision by an artist to turn himself into the umpteenth self-appointed flagellator of the Kazakh authorities.'[52] (It is worth noting that BGR Gabara was working for the Bahrain government at the same time.) Gabara's words highlight how the intention of such astroturfing campaigns is so that they enter the mainstream information ecosystem. Such a process can be termed 'breaking out', and it is where disinformation goes beyond the confines of its initial delivery system into the broader media landscape.[53]

Conclusion

There are no shortages of ways to mislead, nor is there a shortage of individuals and entities willing to do so. However, for the sake of conceptual clarity, deception in the context of digital authoritarianism is primarily about how global networks of actors – usually acting on behalf of, or operated directly by, states – attempt to support power-maintenance objectives through the deliberate manipulation of the information ecosystem using digital technology. These tactics are often used to supplement other methods of coercion. Disinformation can be considered a facet of 'hybrid warfare', and works alongside other forms of warfare, such as economic or conventional warfare. While cyber-attacks, hacking, and other forms of cyberwarfare are, of course, aspects of digital authoritarianism, the focus of this book is primarily about deception, as opposed to any attempts to compromise digital infrastructure. However, the two are not mutually exclusive, as hacked content is frequently used as the basis for disinformation campaigns, such as in hack-and-leak operations',[54] something I term 'full-stack' disinformation operations. Conventional warfare, like cyberwarfare, relies on bespoke or sophisticated equipment, but digital manipulation is often crude, relying on harassment, intimidation, lying, or artificial amplification using fake accounts and inexpensive technology. Furthermore, the fact that it relies on loosely regulated and freely available social media platforms aids authoritarian regimes. Just as the success of the Avtomat Kalashnikova assault rifle was primarily based on its ruggedness, low cost and ease of production, the weaponisation of social media thrives due to the ubiquity, accessibility and low entry costs of sites like Twitter. Social media, and platforms such as Twitter, Facebook and YouTube, are new weapons in the hands of activists, but also of authoritarian regimes and those seeking to profit from deception. In the Gulf, high wealth and high mobile penetration rates create a fertile environment for scalable networked deception.

2

THE DECEPTION ORDER AND
PSEUDO-REALITY INDUSTRIES

Chapter Overview: The Long Supply Chains of Disinformation

From PR companies and political consultancies to governments and tech firms, this chapter highlights the assemblage of actors that allow for the creation of transnational illiberal practices such as disinformation. This group benefits from the commodification of deception and disinformation within the framework of digital authoritarianism, and can be termed 'the deception order'. It is an industry that exists to create a pseudo-reality, one in which a reality preferred by those with money and power is made. While there has been considerable focus on how China or Russia use economic power and technology to spread authoritarianism,[1] this chapter highlights how Western states and private companies are often involved in the commodification and 'export' of digital authoritarianism, especially in the Gulf.

The Swanky PR Firm

The offices of the Australian firm CTF Partners in London are perhaps not where you would expect to find a deception operation.

These are not the sweatshops of Macedonia, where young English-speaking university graduates can make around $1,000 a month pumping out fake stories about US politics for American audiences.[2] This is Mayfair, one of the most luxurious and expensive pieces of real estate on the planet. London, like Washington, has been described as the reputation-laundering capital of the world.[3] It is here where 'public relations firms are earning millions of pounds a year promoting foreign regimes with some of the world's worst human rights records, including Saudi Arabia, Rwanda, Kazakhstan and Sri Lanka'.[4] At many of these firms, well-educated and cosmopolitan suit-wearing elites, often exuding an aura of toxic masculinity, polish the reputations of some of the world's most despotic figures.[5] Under the logic of neoliberalism, human rights violations are simply another barrier restricting the exchange of goods and services.

Western PR companies have the luxury of undeserved legitimacy. With heritage comes the cultural cache of prestige, tradition and influence, unearned advantage in the form of reputational benefit. They are slick, well-branded organisations operating from the heart of one of the most prominent global financial capitals. From the outside, there is no hint of anything untoward. Slickly designed logos belie the nefarious nature of the work such companies do, which ranges from promoting polluting coal lobbies and whitewashing dictators to inflaming ethnic tensions on behalf of their clients.[6] This is the beauty salon of global capitalism, where money is king, and dictators and authoritarian regimes come to have their images enhanced in order to hide the often-brutal consequences of their rule. If Macedonia gets you a cheap and cheerful information operation, the offices of Mayfair offer designer disinformation, with value-added political legitimacy on account of being based in one of the world's most established liberal democracies.

Such services do not come cheap, and it is no wonder that such companies can afford luxurious premises. CTF Partners seem to have few qualms about working with countries that feature among some of the most authoritarian in the world.[7] CTF, whose offices are conveniently located next to Saudi Arabia's embassy to the United Kingdom, worked on a campaign to burnish the reputation of Mohammed bin Salman (MBS), Saudi's autocratic crown prince and de facto ruler. The campaign was fundamentally designed to deceive audiences as to its provenance. CTF would create websites promoting content that broadly aligned itself with the foreign policy of Saudi Arabia. The purpose was to create the illusion that there was grassroots support for the reforms taking place in Saudi Arabia. The campaign was also an avenue for pro-Saudi propaganda to be directed and targeted at global citizens through social media via micro-targeting. In short, it was a way to sell Saudi, and the crown prince, to the world via Facebook. As women activists languished in Saudi prisons, and a journalist critical of MBS's reforms was dismembered with a bone saw, well-to-do men in Mayfair had created a pseudo-public to sing MBS's praises.

The high price tag brings with it specific benefits, but most notably the political cover of operating within the heart of one of the world's largest former empires. It also allows countries such as the United Kingdom and the United States to legitimise their own relationship with human rights abusers. This is especially true in the Gulf, where the British had an imperial presence until the 1970s, and where both the United Kingdom and the United States continue to maintain military bases. Indeed, if clothes maketh the man, then reputation maketh the ally. After all, a customer that looks good is a customer that the UK and Washington can better justify doing business with to their citizenry. The fact that most Gulf regimes are wealthy also helps. As Timothy Snyder states, 'The biggest wallet pays for the most blinding lights.'[8]

The moral problems are relatively clear. Some in the employ of such companies may justify their actions by saying that they are providing a voice in the interests of parity or balance. Others say it is just a job. However, firms that are ideologically indifferent to taking money from dictators and human rights violators cannot be said to be apolitical, no matter how much they claim to be. In the current age of growing right-wing populism, there is also the possibility that those working for such companies are proponents of the often right-wing policies that their clients advocate. Indeed, *The Guardian* describes CTF Partners as being an entity 'staffed by a handful of senior executives and a large number of highly ideological right-wing twentysomethings who help run campaigns around the world'.[9]

That a group of right-wing ideologues are part of the global deception order is perhaps not surprising.[10] It was, after all, senior employees from CTF Partners who helped get the UK prime minister Boris Johnson elected. CTF Partners also helped undermine a more moderate Brexit advocated by Theresa May, largely on the basis that a moderate Brexit was perhaps not what was desired by the more nationalist faction. Although not all illiberal dictators are right wing, in the current era it is interesting that the likes of MBS and Mohammed bin Zayed, the ruler of the UAE, are finding ideological succour and bedfellows in the offices of PR companies in London and Washington. If populism is itself characterised by an appeal to emotions and not fact,[11] profiting from this indicates the commodification of falsehoods.

Selling War

While the ideological overlaps within PR companies may form part of the hegemonic apparatus – that is, wealthy, often conservative-minded and privileged people living in the West monetising the defence of their own privilege – they also exist in a permissive environment where such behaviours are possible. Indeed, in addition to the private benefits allowed by the commodification of deception, it is a service used by governments in pursuit of their own foreign policy objectives, a phenomenon we see clearly in the relationship between countries such as the UK and USA with those in the Persian Gulf. This devolution of deception is beneficial to governments, especially in democracies, as it helps provide political distance between state entities and the service provider responsible for deception operations.

Although the opening vignette of this chapter concerns the role of CTF Partners in burnishing the reputation of Mohammed bin Salman, it indicates just one of many contemporary examples of how PR companies legitimise the foreign policy of Western states towards the Middle East. This is not a new process. A more formative contemporary example of the deception order mobilising to promote US foreign policy in the Middle East can be seen in the 1990–1 Gulf War. Here, a PR company was a major contributing factor to the legitimisation of the US-led coalition's liberation of Kuwait.

During Saddam's invasion of Kuwait in 1990, the American PR firm Hill & Knowlton was contracted by the government of Kuwait to represent 'Citizens for a Free Kuwait', a 'classic front PR' group designed to hide the role of the government of Kuwait and their co-operation with the Bush administration.[12] A front group is an organisation set up by a third party (e.g. a PR company) to create an artificial grassroots lobbying outfit. Hill & Knowlton's focus was keeping US public opinion on the side of the Kuwaitis. While this was not a challenging task given the Iraqi invasion of a much smaller country, the group made sure they left little room for ambiguity as to Iraqi-led atrocities, highlighting egregious human rights violations through the distribution of regular videos and content.

In order to best tailor information, or indeed disinformation, to target audiences, specific themes that resonated emotionally were used to maximise the effectiveness of the campaign. The Wirthlin Consulting Group, an American political and business consulting company, conducted daily opinion polls to assist Hill & Knowlton adapt their strategy in order to best engender public support for military action against Kuwait. One of the tropes that resonated strongly was that Saddam was an unhinged madman – an irrational actor who had in the past killed his own people.[13] Although the trope itself is based on absolutely factual claims, it also made people susceptible to believing outrageous claims, the veracity of which might ordinarily be challenged had the perpetrator not been successfully smeared as a madman. The most salient example was the testimony of a 15-year-old Kuwaiti girl called Nayirah before the Congressional Human Rights Caucus. Nayirah, whose surname was initially kept secret for fear of reprisals against her family, said that during her time as a volunteer at al-Addan hospital in Kuwait, she had witnessed Iraqi soldiers remove babies from bassinets and leave them on the floor to die.[14]

The testimony was passed out as part of a media kit written by Citizens for a Free Kuwait and was subsequently repeated time and time again in the media in the three months before the start of the war. Like the famous First World War British propaganda story about Germans killing Belgian babies, Nayirah's testimony was, according to American journalist John MacArthur, the most important factor in getting American public opinion on the side of a war. It later emerged that not only was Nayirah a member of the Kuwaiti royal family, but that her testimony was false. She had also been coached by Hill & Knowlton vice-president Lauri Fitz-Pegado.[15] The whole Nayirah episode was disinformation, disseminated and concocted to help legitimise the massive deployment of US military power in the Middle East. However, it was undertaken by a reputable organisation with international pedigree, and in such a way that there was a plausible amount of distance between the US government and the private sphere.

Political Consultancies: Provoking Discord and Banalising Evil

Another British PR company highly active in the Middle East was Bell Pottinger, co-founded by Lord Bell, who had been a media adviser to Margaret Thatcher. The political connections accumulated by Lord Bell were no doubt instrumental in building up a substantial and influential client roster. Indeed, Bell Pottinger's spin doctors worked for numerous dictatorial regimes, from the government of Azerbaijan to the authoritarian governments of Egypt and Bahrain. Indeed, the Bahrain government spent millions of dollars on Bell Pottinger and was, for a period, the firm's most lucrative client.[16] Of course, the modus operandi of such companies is often shrouded in secrecy, so we do not know exactly what they are doing. However, whistleblowers and scandals in one country can indicate the nature of the services conducted by the company with other clients. The exact nature of Bell Pottinger's work in MENA remained opaque – that is, until 2017, when a scandal unprecedented in the company's history precipitated its demise.

Bell Pottinger was enlisted by Ajay, Atul and Rajesh Gupta, three wealthy brothers who had built a sprawling business empire in South Africa. Bell Pottinger, with assistance from the media arm of the Gupta empire, ran a campaign that sought to distract the public from accusations that had been circulating about the Guptas' alleged corruption. Bell Pottinger sought to do this by positioning the Guptas as fighting against 'White Monopoly Capital'. They did this, in part, by using hundreds of sockpuppet accounts on Twitter to post racist messages against the perceived enemies of the Guptas.[17] In a country with deep-rooted racial divisions built on a history of apartheid, the effect was catastrophic. Frank Ingham, the director-general of the Public Relations and Communications Association, a membership body for the PR industry, stated: 'The work was on a completely new scale of awfulness. Bell Pottinger may have set back race relations in South Africa by as much as ten years.'[18] What Bell Pottinger was doing was not simply PR, or propaganda, but using deception to re-engineer the very fabric of society for profit. Such behaviours have led to such firms being called 'PR mercenaries'.[19] The scandal marked the end for Bell Pottinger, highlighting how the work of PR companies, when made public, can be seen as so damaging to the common good that they can no longer function.

With the demise of Bell Pottinger came insights into their deception playbook – that is, a repertoire of techniques used in disinformation operations. This playbook had adapted to the advent of social media. One such technique involves dominating the social media space by creating fake accounts and fake blogs that defend the client (e.g. the Guptas or Bahrain) against malign foreign influence. In other words, such accounts can exploit emotive ideologies such as nationalism to smear any oppositional movements portrayed as agents of a foreign state. Bell Pottinger reportedly did this on behalf of Abdul Taib Mahmud, a government minister for the eastern Malaysian state of Sarawak. Here Bell Pottinger created a blog for a front group called Sarawak Bersat. The outfit was described as a 'group of Sarawakians who aim to protect Sarawak against the influences – and hidden agendas – of foreign political groups and activists'.[20] The blog was used to attack Sarawak-born British journalist Clare Rewcastle Brown, who had been critical of Taib's policies. A former employee at Bell Pottinger confirmed that they had created a lot of material for the site, which included false stories of sexual improprieties and accusations that Brown and her ilk were 'agents of British socialism'.[21]

Another tactic used by Bell Pottinger involved identifying potential targets in social media space: influencers who could theoretically be co-opted, targeted and potentially harassed or bullied if they did not adopt the desired messaging of Bell Pottinger's client. A digital team at Bell Pottinger curated for its Bahraini clients a list of the 'most influential dissidents on social media'.[22] According to the *New Yorker* magazine, one of the former employees involved in preparing the list claimed not to know the fate of those on it, but was 'troubled by the fact that Bell Pottinger performed this service at a time when Bahraini officials were imprisoning and torturing people who spoke out against the regime'.[23] It is difficult to imagine that such lists would have been used for any other purpose than targeting or potentially harassing critics of the regime. The line between PR and surveillance is sometimes even more clearcut. The Pentagon even contracted Bell Pottinger to created fake insurgent videos that were distributed on CDs containing code used to track potential al-Qaeda dissidents.[24]

The transference of techniques between firms, even those not ostensibly PR firms, is evident. The well-known global consultancy firm McKinsey has also come under fire for making a similar list of Saudi social media influencers. Naturally, this has brought with it attendant accusations of facilitating authoritarianism by curating a target list of potential dissidents. One of the activists featured on this list was Omar Abdulaziz, a high-profile Saudi Twitter user and well-known critic of the regime. Abdulaziz subsequently launched a lawsuit against McKinsey, accusing them of including his name in an internal report that documented those driving 'negative' coverage (or criticism) of Saudi's economic policies.[25] McKinsey attempted to defend its position by claiming that the report was an internal document and that Omar Abdulaziz had, by his own admission, been targeted by the Saudi government at least three years before the report.[26] McKinsey's reasoning is specious, not least because they were actually supporting the argument that Omar Abdulaziz was indeed a key node of criticism of Saudi Arabia's policies. To work for an authoritarian government that you admit targets activists and to simultaneously deny that you knew such information could be misused is entirely disingenuous. However, false indignation is an aspect of deception.

Despite the multiplicity of PR companies, reputation management firms and political consulting firms, many seem to share the same tactics. The advent of social media has created millions of data points that can now be exploited by such companies. Cambridge Analytica, the now-defunct British company that has been accused of misusing data to sway the outcome of the US elections,[27] has, like Bell Pottinger, been accused of deliberately provoking societal conflict on behalf of its clients.[28] Cambridge Analytica worked for Uruhu Kenyatta, the Kenyan president and head of the Jubilee Party during the 2013 and 2017 presidential elections.[29] Mark Turnbull, the former political division head at Cambridge Analytica, was caught on camera saying that the purpose of successful political campaigns was to exploit people's fears, as oppose to appeal to their reason. Turnbull expanded on his company's role in the Kenyan elections, stating, 'We have rebranded the entire party twice, written the manifesto, done research, analysis, messaging. I think we wrote all the speeches and we staged the whole thing – so just about every element of this candidate.'[30] Turnbull had described his experience as 'delivering campaign success via measurable behavioural change'.[31] The term 'behavioural change' euphemistically belies the potential consequences and strategies for generating it. Larry Madowo, a global opinions contributor to the *Washington Post*, went so far as to say that Cambridge Analytica hijacked Kenya's democracy through 'data neocolonialism'.[32]

Whitewashing

As well as promoting 'positive' information about their clients, another staple of the PR playbook is minimising negative information. In the digital age this can include manipulating search-engine results through search engine optimisation (SEO). In 2011, in another undercover investigation, a Bell Pottinger employee revealed that they 'could manipulate Google results to "drown" out negative coverage' of human rights violations and the use of child labour. They also created third-party blogs with a veneer of independence on behalf of their clients. These would be optimised so that favourable news of their client(s) displaced any negative coverage and ranked higher in internet searches.[33] David Wilson, a former employee of Bell Pottinger, stated: 'The ambition obviously is to drown that negative content and make sure that you have positive content out there online.'[34]

In 2011 the Bureau of Investigative Journalism posed as representatives of a foreign government soliciting services from Bell Pottinger. Bell Pottinger offered their potential clients the service of Wikipedia editing to make information about their clients more attractive.[35] After this revelation, Wikipedia initiated an investigation and suspended a number of accounts they believed were run by Bell Pottinger. The revelation prompted Jimmy Wales, the founder of Wikipedia, to tweet, 'Bell Pottinger behaved unethically and broke several Wikipedia rules in doing so. The public record can be seen by anyone.'[36]At the same time as that Bell Pottinger scandal broke, Wikipedia entries about the 2011 Bahrain uprising were being edited in a manner designed to stigmatise the opposition and lionise the Bahraini government. Several articles on Bahrain were edited by Wikipedia user 'PetersBah', who exclusively edited Wikipedia entries on Bahraini politics. Generally, PetersBah edits sought to do the following: 'To provide positive coverage on initiatives or reforms set up by the Bahrain government; to provide positive information on persons employed by the Bahrain government; to frame accusations of police violence as a response to protester violence; to demonise protesters by emphasizing negative stories such as their involvement in torture; to demonize activists and protesters by suggesting links to Iran; to frame the narrative in a manner that suggested the opposition were undermining progressive initiatives led by the government'.[37]

Wikipedia investigated Petersbah, and although they could not attribute his account to Bell Pottinger, they did state that it was 'behaviourally suggestive' of advertising and suspended it. There was even evidence to suggest that Petersbah was well connected, and had access to privileged information before it was made public. Petersbah edited the Wikipedia pages of John Timoney and John Yates, two former policemen who were sent to Bahrain in 2011 to reform the police. However, the edits, which cast Yates and Timoney in a positive light, were made before the first announcement of their appointment, which was first reported by the *Daily Telegraph*. As I have noted elsewhere, 'This would imply that whoever ran the account was a party to the information before it became public. A plausible explanation is that a public relations company working on behalf of the government was briefed ahead of the announcement'.[38]

While the PR firm may be the more luxurious façade of deception, other operations, while far less steeped in the prestige afforded by reputable postcodes, are no less efficient – or, indeed, deceptive. In countries such as Macedonia, young English speakers produce fake news stories to drive visitors to their websites, where they generate revenue from advertising. Such jobs can be lucrative, with some people making five times the minimum wage. One such operation targeted Americans during the US elections.[39] Similar operations exist in Poland. *The Guardian* reported how a single 'troll farm' created batches of ideologically opposed social media accounts to create online conflict and discord for the purpose of drawing attention to specific candidates.[40] Nonetheless, in the murky world of PR, which is a term used to encompass all manner of companies, we can only go by what we know, and we know that many of the companies providing such services in the MENA region are based in some of the world's wealthiest capitals.

Although scholars of PR have objected to their field being termed propagandistic, any activity entailing some aspect of unconsensual deception,[41] designed to facilitate despotic rule, is fundamentally an authoritarian form of organised persuasive communication. Here authoritarian practices can be determined as those that undermine accountability (through secrecy) and sabotage democratic processes, or potential.[42] They can also be those that militate against potential democracy. Fundamentally, the often-intangible aspect of the internet, as opposed to, say, the arms trade, has challenged the dominance of the state as key interlocutor in authoritarianism. The deception order is a public–private venture. As argued by Marlies Glasius and Marcus Michaelsen:

'... transcending spatial and political frontiers by design, the Internet has prompted a renegotiation of the boundaries of state power. As they seek to assert authority in the digital sphere, states increasingly depend on and cooperate with private companies that command online infrastructure and technical expertise. They also cooperate with and learn from one another, disseminating and legitimizing their ideas and tools for controlling the Internet in international and regional forums'.[43]

Silicon Valley

Social media companies are also part of the deception order. They are, after all, the entities that provide the platforms on which much disinformation is distributed. They should not be seen as the creators of an impartial 'tool' to deliver information. As Andrew Marantz stated in the NewYorker, 'Facebook has never been a neutral platform; it is a company whose business model depends on monitoring its users, modifying and manipulating their behavior, and selling their attention to the highest bidder.'[44] It is, of course, intellectually dishonest to state that Facebook exists to facilitate free speech. It is a company that makes conscious choices about paid political ads and facilitating or hindering certain data flows. At the very least, it thrives on increasing or decreasing the salience of specific messages for capital gain. Its apathy in tackling malicious disinformation was highlighted by a former employee-cum-whistleblower, Sophie Zhang, who stated: 'In the three years I've spent at Facebook, I've found multiple blatant attempts by foreign national governments to abuse our platform on vast scales to mislead their own citizenry, and caused international news on multiple occasions.'[45] Writing about one particular influence campaign, Zhang added, 'the truth was, we simply didn't care enough to stop them'.[46]

Although disinformation was never the specific intent of such platforms, their affordances and functionalities are leveraged for deception by malicious actors. The growing ubiquity of platforms such as Facebook and Twitter have, in some cases, caused those platforms to be equated with the internet itself. A survey of Indonesians revealed that many had no idea they were using the internet, even though they talked about how much time they spent on Facebook.[47] This seems particularly acute in the developing world, raising attendant problems of whether or not people are fully aware of how their data is being extracted and commodified in the Global North. The flow of disinformation and data through these platforms is modulated by functionalities that are themselves defined by a regulatory environment in the United States. It is here where the general aversion to regulation, and the failure to apply anti-trust laws, are creating data behemoths that determine the communication habits of billions of people around the world. It is here that our conversations, likes, dislikes and memories are all being converted into 'data streams'[48] that can be utilised to devise methods of influencing our consumption patterns, whether political or commercial. Neoliberation technology promotes data colonialism through creating datified and commodified subjects.

Indeed, a key aspect of the spread of disinformation has been the reluctance of social media companies to police their platforms as well as a profound ignorance of the regions in which they operate. When discussing issues arising in Saudi Arabia with the platform, one Facebook official reportedly asked digital rights activist Jillian C. York, 'Can't we just phone up a member of the Saudi Arabian parliament?'[49] Saudi Arabia, of course, does not have a parliament. This was at a time when Facebook was attempting to break into the lucrative Gulf market; Mohammed bin Salman visited the company, with its offices decked out in Saudi flags.[50] This ignorance, combined with a desire to profit from new markets, points in a way to a form of digital orientalism – the desire to exploit Middle East markets with a demonstrable ignorance of their political and social structures. Such ignorance of the region is not malign in and of itself; what is troubling is the desire to exploit markets without regard to or understanding of the harm those products might cause to the region.

In addition to wanting to encourage user engagement, which in turn drives revenue, social media companies have used the argument of free speech to give the illusion that they are preserving a fundamental human right. However, when the USA fails to regulate its social media companies, the whole world often bears the consequences, as we have seen to tragic effect in Myanmar.

Facebook's perceived apathy in tackling divisive influence campaigns on its platforms led to one employee saying she felt she had 'blood on her hands'.[51]

The ownership structures of social media companies have also invited attendant questions about their perceived neutrality. When Saudi prince al-Waleed bin Talal bin Abdulaziz Al Saud bought stock in Twitter in 2011, the same time as the Arab Uprisings, activists expressed concern that this could impact on Twitter's neutrality. This fear was amplified in 2015, when bin Talal was named as Twitter's second-largest individual shareholder, holding more shares than Twitter's CEO, Jack Dorsey.[52] This has been accentuated by further developments in the funding of Silicon Valley. Anand Giridharadas writes, 'As Saudi Arabia establishes its new role as one of Silicon Valley's most prominent investors, the risk grows that its investments will purchase silence.'[53] This perception of social media companies operating in the service of despots is felt acutely in the region, where numerous online campaigns have sought to encourage Twitter to move its office from Dubai to somewhere more democratic, like Tunisia (although recent democratic backsliding in Tunisia has muted such calls).

The cultivation of associations between tech giants and despots has already provided bad optics for social media companies. Jack Dorsey had meetings with the Saudi crown prince Mohammed bin Salman on at least two occasions, including at least once after it became known to Twitter that Saudi agents had infiltrated the company and stolen sensitive private data from Saudi Twitter users.[54] Of course, Saudi is not an exception here; foreign intelligence agencies in the UK, USA and Israel have reportedly been cosying up to Twitter officials to gain insights.[55] However, in an age where many people fetishise tech gurus such as Elon Musk and the late Steve Jobs, perhaps one should not be surprised at such meetings.[56] After all, Mohammad bin Salman is young, tech-savvy, rich, and understands the importance of social media, while tech entrepreneurs like Dorsey encourage ideas that technology is a universal tool conducive to reform and political participation.[57]

However, such relations highlight the often personalistic nature of the deception order, raising further questions about whether social media platforms are compromised by business relationships. They also reflect how a lack of transparency obscures the motivations for the direction of technological creation. Needless to say, sourcing private investment in a deregulated environment raises questions about the governance of those platforms and the subsequent affordances and utilities of such tools.

Although social media companies have been pressured into taking more action against disinformation and platform manipulation, there is little end in sight to the scourge of fake news. Facebook CEO Mark Zuckerberg even admitted that there needs to be more regulation on technology platforms.[58] Zuckerberg claims it is the role of governments to regulate platforms, not the companies themselves. However, Zuckerberg was simply passing the buck. His belief that governments rather than the platforms should be responsible for the regulation of speech is skewed, and was stated on the basis that the US government had generally been averse to introducing more regulations for big tech.

Tech companies and governments can also use the excuse of tackling disinformation to target political enemies. When these interests suit the foreign policy of the United States, social media companies seem more likely to comply. Twitter has, for example, been accused of singling out Palestinian accounts for suspension, in some cases those that have been mentioned by the Israeli Ministry of Strategic Affairs or the Palestinian Authority.[59] In October 2020 the ministry released a report entitled 'Manipulating social media: The effort to delegitimise Israel through coordinated inauthentic behaviour online'.[60] The report, which accused a number of accounts of inauthentic behaviour, resulted in the suspension of around 250 accounts promoting hashtags criticising Israel's attempts to annex part of the West Bank. In 2019 Twitter also suspended accounts belonging to the Quds News Network, which had hundreds of thousands of followers and often shed light on aspects of the Israeli occupation.[61] According to Sada Social, a digital rights group that monitors censorship of Palestinian online content, Twitter does little to stop any incitement or aggression against Palestinians, but does so when Israel is criticised.[62] At the same time, Israeli entities are often brazen in their celebration of co-ordinated efforts to manipulate social media and whitewash Israeli human rights abuses. Reichman University in Israel published a press release in 2021 lauding the efforts of students on its campus, who formed a situation room where they used social media to justify Israel's bombing of Gaza. There was no indication that Facebook or Twitter suspended accounts related to this co-ordinated propaganda. Such operations have become so widely known that the term *Hasbara* (to explain) is used to describe them.

It's not Always the Russians; Except When it is!

Another key actor in the deception order is, of course, the state. However, the smoking gun is often obfuscated. In authoritarian regimes there is, in theory, closer proximity between those who authorise deception operations and those who are tasked with carrying them out. Authoritarian regimes also tend to know what's going on within their borders. It follows then that disinformation campaigns emanating from places such as Russia, or Saudi, tend to fall within the orbit of high-level disinformation making. Networks of patronage and nepotism link disinformation operations to the state in Russia just as they do in the UK. However, it would seem that there is less deviation from key foreign policy points in authoritarian regimes, where disinformation operations, however formally removed from the state, do the state's bidding. There has been a tendency in English-language studies to focus on disinformation operations conducted by Russia. This generally reflects a transatlantic security-oriented paradigm that is still rooted in Cold War rivalries. There is also a reason for this; the Russian-linked entities are highly active in disinformation operations, and often serve as a model for regimes elsewhere.

The Internet Research Agency is a troll farm operating out of St Petersburg, and many of its employees are former journalists[63] Its speciality appears to be astroturfing using sockpuppet accounts on social media. During the 2016 US elections, thousands of their operatives posed as Americans to participate in and influence online political discussions during the lead-up to the vote.[64] The accounts fooled many among the general public. It was later found that the

American news outlet Vox had incorporated social media posts by these accounts as 'Vox Populi'.[65] The Internet Research Agency achieved extreme notoriety for the breadth of its operations, which have ranged from targeting the Black Lives Matter movement to working to promote the election of Donald Trump.[66] The social media accounts linked to the Internet Research Agency highlight an essential aspect of its modus operandi, which is to provoke polarisation within society with a view to creating social conflict among Russia's enemies. Accounts linked to Russia have even been involved in using social media to organise dozens of protests in the USA.[67] Their interference in US domestic politics reached such a pitch that the Internet Research Agency was indicted by a US grand jury in 2018 for their alleged role in electoral interference.[68]

Facebook recently revealed an operation led by the Internet Research Agency to establish a foothold in North Africa. After receiving a warning from the FBI, Facebook suspended a group of fake accounts linked to a news outlet called Peace Data.[69] Peace Data published in English and Arabic and focused primarily on current affairs in the USA, UK, Algeria, Egypt and other MENA countries.[70] As part of its deception operation the website actually employed real Americans to write left-leaning articles. Despite being left leaning, many seemed, like the Internet Research Agency accounts during the US elections, to turn people off supporting Joe Biden, claiming he was not left wing enough. Again, this type of rhetoric seeks to fragment Democratic Party supporters along internal lines, decreasing the unity of the party and provoking polarisation away from centre ground.

However, it is not just the Internet Research Agency playing this kind of role. Russia's foreign policy and tactics of disinformation are also spearheaded through its media outlets, the most notorious of which is Russia Today (RT), which is an extension of Russian state defence policy deployed to meddle in the domestic affairs of other states.[71] The nexus between state policy and the actions undertaken by quasi-state entities such as the Internet Research Agency was evident in one of the most virulent and perhaps successful disinformation campaigns to have targeted the Middle East, that deployed against the Syrian Defence League, otherwise known as the White Helmets.

The White Helmets were first responders operating in Syria. By late 2017 they were about 3,300 strong. Their difficult work in war-torn Syria was immortalised in a Netflix film that eventually went on to win an Oscar. Despite their humanitarian efforts, the fact that they were first-hand witnesses to regime brutality made them a threat to Syria's propaganda war. The Russian-backed Syrian regime launched a campaign to discredit them in the eyes of the world. As much demonising propaganda tends to do, the campaigns portrayed the White Helmets as terrorist supporters working to advance imperialist interventions in Syria.

One of the biggest tropes of the disinformation campaign was that the White Helmets had faked a chemical attack in 2017 after the regime attacked the opposition-held town of Khan Shaykhun.[72] After the Joint Investigative Mechanism – 'a body created by the UN Security Council and the Organization for the Prohibition of Chemical Weapons to research chemical weapons attacks in Syria' – released a report which concluded that the Syrian government had used sarin gas in Khan Shaykhun, the Russian-backed Syrian government essentially denounced the findings. The Russian defence minister even suggested that the opposition had gassed their own people. Indeed, in 2013 Russia backed the Syrian government's claims that the opposition had been responsible for a chemical attack in western Ghouta that killed approximately 1,400 people[73] – a fact denied by the UN.[74] The Syrian president, Bashar Assad, branded the White Helmets al-Qaeda operatives. Similarly, in Bahrain, first responders and medics who catered for those injured by the security forces were often targeted because they bore witness to state brutality. What's more, as doctors they were likely to be seen as providing credible and articulate narratives about repression.

Syrian and Russian groups supportive of Assad seeded the conspiracy via social media accounts and claimed that the White Helmets were recycling images of injured civilians to tarnish the Syrian regime. YouTube videos denouncing the White Helmets were then circulated on Twitter and other platforms. Although networks of accounts supporting the White Helmets existed, the number of accounts challenging their integrity was much more significant, and much more able to sustain its campaign through the judicious use of

YouTube videos.[75] Fundamental to this was the role of state-backed Russian media, which supported 'the anti-White Helmets Twitter campaign in multiple ways, for example, by providing sourced content for articles and videos and amplifying the voices of social media influencers'.[76]

The propaganda attacking the White Helmets became especially virulent, largely due to its cross-pollination and 'break out' across multiple information ecosystems. In addition to the endorsement by powerful actors such as Russia, even the American far right picked up the story. Alex Jones, the publisher and director of InfoWars, an American conspiracy theory website, linked the White Helmets to George Soros, the billionaire philanthropist so often the target of many far-right anti-Semitic tropes, which tend to view Soros as the *éminence grise* and source of numerous global conspiracies. The conspiracy has also been legitimised by what some have disparagingly called 'useful idiots', including a group of UK-based academics who formed the Working Group on Syria, Propaganda and Media (WGSPM). The group has supported Russian-linked disinformation, including that the White Helmets have staged war crimes in order to prompt Western airstrikes in Syria.[77] Although the weight of evidence indicates that this is entirely fictitious, WGSPM has been accused of either inadvertently or deliberately spreading Russian disinformation, not helped by the fact that a Russian official praised its work while at the United Nations Security Council.[78]

The deception campaign also targeted James Le Mesurier, the British founder of Mayday Rescue, the implementing partner for international support for the White Helmets, who were tasked with providing training and equipment. Le Mesurier was accused of fraud and embezzlement, claims which were amplified by those wishing to smear the White Helmets. The accusations, which constituted malinformation premised on an element of truthfulness, prompted a number of investigatory audits. It was later revealed that there had been no evidence of wrongdoing. However, these conclusions came too late. On 11 November 2019, Le Mesurier fell to his death from the Istanbul apartment. His death was ruled as suicide. However, the conspiratorial narrative was not enough. Assad doubled down, suggesting that Le Mesurier had been murdered by a Western-backed intelligence agency.[79] Not satisfied with eliminating Le Mesurier, they wanted to ensure that the smear campaign had a sufficiently conspiratorial denouement. The White Helmets, and indeed Le Mesurier, highlight the virulence and tragic outcomes of smear campaigns supported by state-backed deception operations.

The case of the White Helmets in many ways reflects the workings of the deception order. It is here that what appears to be state-led disinformation enters multiple information ecosystems to produce multiple organisms that reproduce the disinformation on different levels. Here, the distinction between legacy and digital media becomes nebulous, reflecting the convergence of new and old media. It is this convergence that is important, as it highlights how the digital sphere is not a hermetically bound entity. As Kate Starbird and Tom Wilson note, 'a comprehensive understanding of disinformation requires accounting for the spread of content across platforms and that social media platforms should increase collaboration to detect and characterize disinformation campaigns'.[80] In addition to this, the White Helmets conspiracy broke out beyond media and established depth, for example through a fringe of the academic community, which further reinforced the legitimacy of the conspiracy theories.

The Entrepreneur or the Mercenary

Although Russia provides a good example of the role of the state in MENA-centric deception operations, some of the most controversial actors in Gulf digital authoritarianism are American citizens. Former US intelligence officials have facilitated digital authoritarianism for the Gulf states. Dark Matter, a firm operating from the United Arab Emirates, employed more than a 'dozen former U.S. intelligence operatives recruited to help the United Arab Emirates engage in surveillance of other governments, militants and human rights activists critical of the monarchy'.[81] Under the name Project Raven, intelligence officers worked for an operation that was even tasked with spying on American citizens. Those at Project Raven had access to Karma, 'a tool that could remotely grant access to iPhones simply by uploading phone numbers or email accounts into an automated targeting system'.[82] Karma was subsequently used to 'hack an iPhone used by Qatar's Emir Sheikh Tamim bin Hamad al-Thani, as well as the devices of Turkey's former Deputy Prime Minister Mehmet Şimşek, and Oman's head of foreign affairs, Yusuf bin Alawi bin Abdullah'.[83] The promise of lucrative salaries in the UAE, which has developed a reputation for creating a large-scale private army of foreign mercenaries, often attracts highly trained former military officers – who then become part of the digital authoritarian apparatus.

Sometimes it is not quite as James Bond as Project Raven. Other actors in the deception order include programmers, who can create and then sell specific tools to be used for any form of information dissemination, whether for commercial or political gain. Saudi Arabia, in particular, has been plagued by organisations offering paid-for-trending services on Twitter. Many times, a phone number with a Saudi calling code will trend, along with a short note advertising trending services. In August 2017 two hashtags advertising trending services were visible at the same time.[84] BBC journalists Fahima Abdurahman and Anisa Subedar got in touch with one of these services after seeing the phrase 'grilled lamb' mentioned in 17,000 tweets. After communicating via WhatsApp, the BBC team managed to get the phrase 'congratulations Fahima' trending in Jeddah. The person behind the trend had to abort an initial attempt, as it conflicted with a celebrity wedding that generated a high volume of traffic.

In another instance, I was able to trace some of the trend manipulation software back to its creator. He had made a YouTube account that posted videos offering tutorials on how to use a form of bespoke Twitter automation software. This software revealed a number of functionalities. It allowed users to do the following: target hashtags and manipulate trends in specific countries;[85] manipulate Twitter surveys;[86] instantly have bot accounts retweet a designated tweet;[87] automatically simulate engagement by having bot accounts reply to a specific tweet;[88] and search Twitter for a specific keyword to retweet it.[89] The software also allowed the user to alter the biographies and profile photos of the accounts in the network at the click of a button. It also provided randomisation options, allowing randomisation of timings and characters in order to make it less likely that Twitter's algorithm would identify the pattern.[90] Indeed, the randomisation function demonstrated in one of the instructional videos was also in several networks of Twitter accounts I found, including one promoting Daesh propaganda.[91] This would suggest that whoever was behind the Daesh propaganda campaign, which operated by hijacking trends in Saudi Arabia, was using the software demonstrated in this video.

Conclusion

The deception order is an agglomeration or assemblage of many of the following: hacker/entrepreneurs, PR agencies, political consultancies, media organisations and government entities, as well as social media companies themselves. An agglomeration is a series of interconnected components that is formed through extant political, social and economic norms. In the case of digital authoritarianism in the MENA region, the wealth of the Gulf states, and their close alliance with the USA and Europe, have formed a nexus of actors who seek to profit or benefit from deceptive practices. In this agglomeration foreign governments, via PR firms, undertake lobbying in political centres such as Washington DC and London in order that their policy positions are viewed in a favourable light by powerful allies. It is no surprise then that in the United States alone, autocratic Gulf regimes are some of the biggest lobbyists. The United Arab Emirates, Qatar, Israel and Saudi Arabia all featured among the top ten foreign spenders on Western PR companies between 2016 and 2019.[92] This has been accompanied by the increased globalisation of wealth and tech companies, where investments by despotic regimes in Silicon Valley have raised attendant issues of neutrality and co-optation. Within the agglomeration, private firms, sometimes under the umbrella of doing unrelated consultancy, are providing intelligence data for authoritarian governments that can then be used to target human rights activists or critics of a regime. Others are simply trying to convince domestic populations in countries other than that of their client of the relative virtues of whoever is paying them.

The ecosystem that is conducive to this form of digital authoritarianism includes poor regulation, high scalability and the commercial imperatives of social media companies. Inherent within the Silicon Valley dimension is neoliberation technology, the ideological misconception that technology solves rather than creates problems, an absence of transparency, and digital orientalism – an entrenched lack of regard for what happens beyond the borders of the USA and northern Europe. A key aspect of the deception order is that it goes beyond the single-state context and recognises 'transnational illiberalism or public–private authoritarian partnerships'.[93] Whether in Russia or London, an element of nepotism and patronage exists among those best placed to deliver disinformation operations. Such examples of cronyism and 'access' allows such firms to secure lucrative contracts with well-placed politicians around the world. Due to the nature of this cronyism, disinformation operations directly or indirectly serve the foreign policy of the country in which they are based, irrespective of whether it is illiberal or democratic.

Digital authoritarianism is not simply a state-centric enterprise, but rather the result of states pursuing political goals, commercial entities seeking profit, and a technological infrastructure that is itself not value-neutral. In that regard, it is scarcely something novel; the advent of digital authoritarianism has simply reproduced extant power relationships and geopolitical alliances. However, that is not to dismiss it as meaningless. The ubiquity of the mobile phone and social media somehow brings authoritarianism to our very pockets. As we shall see in the next chapter, the growing assertiveness of Gulf regimes, along with a fetishisation of digital technology, is turning the region into a net exporter of deception, the impact of which is being felt across the globe.

PART II

CONTROLLING DOMESTIC POLITICS

3

MAKING ARABIA GREAT AGAIN

THE EVOLUTION OF DIGITAL MEDIA POWER AND DIGITAL POPULISM IN THE GULF

Chapter Overview: Tyranny and Digital Media Power

Sondrol has argued that 'totalitarians, unlike authoritarians, envision not only a transformed domestic society, but also an expanded national influence on the world's stage'.[1] If anyone has embodied both this local and global ambition, it is Mohammed bin Salman. The slogan 'Make Arabia Great Again' featured on the cover of the American magazine *Newsweek* in September 2018. It encapsulated the populist ethos of MBS's Saudi Arabia, as well as the young ruler's close relationship to the Trump administration. The nod to the defining slogan of Trumpism also emphasised a brash, braggadocious public façade of achievements, one that masked a different reality: the severe repression of domestic opposition. This chapter documents the rise of Saudi's media power and digital media power, laying out the general infrastructure of its digital deception apparatus. It argues that, while Saudi has devoted significant resources to attempting to control Arabic media since the 1990s, manipulating social media to mask criticism of Saudi has become a defining aspect of MBS's messianic vision for Saudi, both regionally and globally.

From platform manipulation to platform infiltration, this chapter highlights and documents the lengths Saudi has gone to in order to try and control the social media space, especially Twitter.

A Cult of Personality

In March 2018 residents of London were treated to the sudden proliferation of billboards featuring an image of Saudi crown prince Mohammed bin Salman. Along with the hashtag 'A New Saudi Arabia',[2] these boards contained milquetoast slogans such as 'bringing change to Saudi Arabia' and 'opening Saudi Arabia to the world'.[3] They were even plastered on the sides of flatbed trucks, which trundled awkwardly around London with the sole purpose of subjecting no-doubt-bewildered Londoners to the image of a person many had probably never seen before. The reason? The Saudi crown prince was in the process of rehabilitating his international image in the West as the death count in the UN-sanctioned war on Yemen increased.

The PR blitz probably cost upward of £1,000,000.[4] The adverts were sponsored by 'Arabian Enterprise Incubators, a consultancy founded by Adam Hosier, a former employee of BAE Systems, the defence company which has supplied Saudi Arabia with dozens of warplanes and other weapons'.[5] As is often the case within the mutually beneficial deception order, the campaign was as much about whitewashing UK arms sales to one of the most repressive countries on the planet as about promoting MBS as a reformer. Indeed, in 2017 Britain's arms exports broadly correlated with a country's human rights abuses: the worse the human rights abuse, the better the customer for British arms. Chief among these customers was Saudi Arabia. This PR campaign was not about arms, though. On the contrary, it was designed entirely to distract attention from dead Yemenis. The campaign sought to depict MBS in a more flattering light. This symbiotic relationship between the whitewasher and whitewashed highlights the frequent equilibrium we see in the working of the deception order.

In addition to the billboards, social media – and Twitter in particular – erupted with jubilant celebrations of MBS's arrival. The

Arabic hashtags 'Mohammed bin Salman in London' and 'Mohammed bin Salman in Britain' trended alongside the less populous hashtags 'welcome Saudi Crown Prince'. Although these hashtags sought to give the illusion of widespread grassroots support for the crown prince, the reality was anything but. Hundreds of accounts with somehow implausible procedurally generated Western-sounding names such as Evangeline Muller and Denita Martinelli retweeted enthusiastic welcomes of the crown prince.[6] An analysis of each of these hashtags reveals that a massive number of them were bots. Anomalies in the account data reveal that thousands of accounts were created within a narrow time frame, which is usually a clear indicator of bots.[7] Indeed, the likes of Evangeline Muller and Denita Martinelli no longer exist. In fact, on the 'Mohammed bin Salman in Britain' hashtag, around 10,580 (46%) of a sample of 23,000 unique accounts promoting the hashtag were deleted or suspended. Similarly, the number of accounts deleted, suspended or repurposed on the 'Mohammed bin Salman in London' hashtag was also around 46% as of 2020. For the English hashtag 'welcome Saudi Crown Prince', at least 30% of the accounts were estimated to be bots or sockpuppets.

Although PR campaigns promoting a cult of personality are not new, these crude and tasteless campaigns that descended on London reflected a more brazen attempt at influencing public opinion. This type of attention on the individual is perhaps more familiar in the Gulf states, where giant billboards or images of members of the ruling family often adorn the roadside or skyscrapers. Gulf social media mirror this phenomenon; Twitter accounts with images of royal family members from Saudi, Bahrain, Oman, Kuwait and Qatar are a common expression of nationalism.

From Media Power to Digital Power

While there is a tendency to ascribe every rupture in recent Saudi politics to MBS, the London campaign was, in many ways, the culmination of years of building first media power, and then digital power. Saudi's rise as a regional digital power is rooted in its strategic capture of legacy media infrastructure. Until the 1990s censorship and insulation largely defined the approach of many Gulf regimes to the spread of information they deem threatening to the status quo. Certainly prior to the 1990–1 Gulf War, the Saudi regime could have been characterised as relatively lethargic in its approach to media development. When Saddam Hussein invaded neighbouring Kuwait in 1990, Saudi news channels waited three days before reporting the story.[8] Instead, Saudis got their news from CNN.

Traditionally fearful of the threat Arab nationalism posed to monarchical rule, the Saudi regime had largely attempted to insulate itself from ideas that threatened its dominance over oil-based wealth distribution. Despite indirectly controlling ArabSat and its network of satellites, one of the most 'valuable media and information infrastructures in the Middle East',[9] the Saudi government had, prior to the 1990s, relied primarily on co-opting the media through intimidation, bribes and stringent administrative policy.[10] With a growing awareness that the kingdom could no longer be hermetically sealed from satellite news broadcasters, the Saudi regime began to invest in media infrastructure and broadcasting. This was, in part, to influence news outputs and, perhaps more broadly, to shape the meta-ideological discourse of regional news media.

As a result, after the 1990s the Saudis believed that dominating the Middle Eastern and Arabic-language media industry was a better form of control than blocking through censorship or coercion.[11] (This is not to say that such forms of violent coercion have ceased, as the Saudi state-sponsored murder of *Washington Post* journalist Jamal Khashoggi aptly demonstrated.) Soon, wealthy Saudis began to invest heavily in television channels, including entertainment-focused channels such as MBC, Rotana and Orbit. Even this was calculated, as it was important to dictate what could be aired to a pan-Arab audience, even if it was only entertainment.[12] As Cochrane notes:

> To Saudi Arabia such control is paramount in an era when the media is increasingly pervasive, because Riyadh's political and economic clout – and the survival of the Royal family – depends on the kingdom retaining its position as a leading player in the region's power politics. To retain this balance of power – held in

the region by the United States, Israel and Saudi Arabia against an ascendant Iran and non-governmental actors – informative and potentially damning news on the kingdom needs to be squashed.

Ownership brought political and social influence. With this relatively newfound investment and commitment to capturing various instruments of ideological control and media hegemony came the inevitable accusations of news bias. Scholars such as Asad Abu Khalil and Paul Cochrane argued that even by 2007 Saudi foreign policy, and in particular its pathological anti-Iranian stance, was permeating its media industries. Channels such as Al Arabiya and Al Wesal, in particular, have been accused of spreading *fitna tai'fa* (sectarian discord). Mohammad Yaghi argues that religious channels in particular pedal a form of sectarian politics that seek to serve Saudi's isolation of Iran: 'Through means of selection, emphasis and omission, intended to set a sectarian agenda by portraying Sunni Muslims as victims of the infidel Shia, these channels maximize the visibility of the terrorists' messages, bestow on them credibility, and create an environment of intolerance.'[13]

Yaghi argues that there has been a proliferation of religious channels since 2009, and that while they were previously seen as religious and therefore apolitical, they have since the Arab Uprisings been mobilised to promote sectarianism in an attempt to contain perceived Iranian expansionism. More recently, the blockade of Qatar has largely been attributed to Saudi's intense antipathy towards Al Jazeera, which it accuses of supporting terrorism through promoting the ideologies of people such as Yusuf al-Qaradawi – an important spiritual figurehead for the Muslim Brotherhood. In reality, Al Jazeera was a threat because, unlike Rotana, MBC or LBCGroup, it was for a long time one of the few Arab multiplatform media conglomerates outside Saudi control.[14]

Saudi's media power has also resulted in its agenda being promoted across the region. According to Andrew Hammond, 'Arab media have largely gone along with a Saudi media campaign against Iran over its growing influence in the Arab world'.[15] The rise of Saudi media power has been accompanied by a perceived degradation in journalistic ethics, as some are cowed or manipulated into 'self'-

censorship. As Yaghi states, 'Over the last two decades, the Saudi regime built a complex media empire that dominates most Arab newspapers and entertainment, news, and religious satellite TV channels. Its mechanisms of controlling pan-Arab media comprise direct ownership of media outlets, co-optation through deep pocket diplomacy, and taking satellite channels that are hard to buy off the air.'[16]

Saudi has sought to expand its media power by buying up international media outlets to prevent negative coverage and promote Saudi foreign policy. In 2020 the British magazine *Private Eye* reported that Evgeny Lebedev,[17] a Russian oligarch with ties to the Kremlin and the proprietor of the UK's *Independent* newspaper, made a deal in 2018 with Sultan Mohamed Abuljadayel of the Saudi Research and Marketing Group (SRMG). SRMG is an outfit chaired by Prince Bader bin Abdullah bin Mohammed bin Farhan Al Saud, the country's culture minister and a member of the ruling family.[18] The deal allowed SRMG to run four sites with Indy branding: Independent Arabia, Independent Persian, Independent Turkish and Independent Urdu. The selection of languages shows Saudi's intention to influence constituencies who speak the languages of its key rivals – most notably Turkey and Iran. The deal also allowed for the use of syndicated content from the UK version of the paper as well as that produced by SRMG journalists. Although journalists at *The Independent* were told that this would not adversely impact editorial practices, this has clearly not been the case (see Chapter 13).

The establishment of other media outlets with Saudi money, such as Iran International, have also raised concerns that Saudi is trying to compete in an information space dominated by Al Jazeera English and Al Jazeera Arabic. Similarly, the establishment of a number of well-known international reputable news channels, including Sky News Arabia, and CNN Arabic in the UAE's so-called media free zones have prompted questions about their continued journalistic integrity. But, as has been argued, 'the United Arab Emirates and Abu Dhabi face a conflict in interest between liberal media promotion and national censorship, which protects the UAE's political-cultural stability'.[19] Those concerns have turned out be entirely valid. In August 2020 the Beirut-based Dar El-Nimer cultural centre said that

Sky News Arabia had replaced the 'word "Palestine" with "Lebanon" on a "Visit Palestine" poster which appears in the backdrop of an interview with Professor Frederic Maatouk held at the centre and later published on Sky News Arabia's Instagram account'.[20] The bizarre editorial intervention happened amidst the UAE's aggressive normalisation with Israel, and was construed as another stage in the UAE's abandonment of support for the Palestinian cause.

While Saudi has been expanding its media dominance abroad, it is also increasingly dominating the digital media space. Saudi Arabia is one of the most penetrated countries in the world in terms of digital technology. The percentage of the population using the internet is 96%, while the number of those using virtual social networks such as Facebook or Twitter are among the highest in the world.[21] The networked readiness index, which measures 'the capacity of countries to leverage ICTs for increased competitiveness and well-being', places Saudi at 33 out of the 139 countries measured. The United Arab Emirates is at 26, Qatar at 27 and Bahrain at 28.[22] The wealthier Gulf countries far outpaced larger Arab states such as Egypt, which ranked 96.[23]

MBS, while clearly not the sole architect of Saudi's digital trajectory, which has been the result of decades of oil rent-fuelled infrastructural investment, has recognised that, in a country with extremely high internet penetration and a large 'youth bulge', social media is an important space for discussion and information consumption. Although a boon for development, youth bulges can also lead to violent conflict, especially if unemployment and prospects remain low. As a result, their issues must be either addressed or their demands modulated.[24] As Hicham Alaoui notes, 'Atop this generational foundation is technology, and in particular networking tools such as social media.'[25] The potential threat of a youth bulge forms the cornerstone of the securitisation of Saudi youth, which must be pacified and possibly repressed if the Al Saud dynasty is to continue in its current guise. That is not to say that there is no regard for the interests of the youth, but rather that protecting Al Saud continuity is prioritised over providing the youth with a loosely regulated public space where they can, without fear of retribution, contribute to the discussions about the future of their country.

In order to tap into this potential reservoir of youth digital media engagement, a central tenet of MBS's rise has been the deployment of digital media power. Thousands of Twitter and Facebook accounts with photos of MBS or his father, King Salman, praise the leadership and attack those who dare criticise Saudi. A hyper-nationalist online civil society has emerged, and reasonable discussion is prevented. Even those reportedly close to the regime have noted that this cyber-army is at risk of getting out of control. A debate on the news channel Elekhbariya revealed concerns some Saudi scholars had about how these armies were shaming those who were not showing 'sufficient patriotism'.[26] Indeed, online propaganda is a fundamental part of the new populism in MBS's Saudi Arabia. As Madawi Al-Rasheed notes, 'The newly celebrated citizen is no longer the one who obeys the religious clerics and is rewarded by the distribution of state sponsored prizes for religious observance and zeal, but the eclectic and creative young entrepreneur and propagandist for the regime. He is expected to not only celebrate and swear allegiance to the crown prince, but also rush to buy newly issued shares in the oil company Aramco.'[27]

However, digital media power, unlike media power in general, has never been substantially theorised. Couldry defines 'media power' as the concentration of symbolic power in media institutions, particularly those of television, radio and the press (the common-sense definition of 'the media').[28] It is these media that allow us to make sense of the world, structuring our understanding and interpretation of world events by 'actively ruling in and ruling out certain realities, offering the maps and codes which mark out territories and assign problematic events and relations to explanatory contexts'.[29] Indeed, media power shapes the selective experience of individuals and defines their imaginary relationship to the conditions in which they exist.[30] This is especially true in regard to the relationship between the ruling classes and dominant hegemonic order. Here, the discursive possibilities of criticism are shaped through the production of norms engendered through institutions of socialisation such as school and religion. This is not simply the purview of authoritarian regimes, where perhaps hegemony-building projects are more obvious. For example, in

September 2020 it was revealed that the UK government instructed schools not to use material overly critical of capitalism.[31]

Digital technology does, to some extent, challenge the monopoly on how authoritarian regimes can control the thought diet of those within and outside their polities. The key difference with digital technology lies primarily in its theoretical ability to disrupt vertical ownership structures that create nodes and hierarchies of power more easily subject to efficient government control. Despite this theoretical problem, within the context of neoliberation technology illiberal actors, in both democratic and authoritarian states, have demonstrated their ability to regulate the use of social and digital media. In the MENA region the well-publicised and high costs of engaging in dissent (such as heavy prison sentences or execution for criticising regimes on social media),[32] coupled with a well-functioning surveillance apparatus, dissuades people from enjoying the ability of social media to imagine new realities through criticism and self-expression.

Thus, digital media power can, broadly speaking, be summarised as an actor's ability to use or co-opt digital media technologies in order to assert ideological influence and power over a community (or communities) by regulating or simulating the thought diet of a target demographic, inside and outside the state. A sub facet of this can be considered social media power, which can be considered on a platform-by-platform basis. As with the definition of digital media power, social media content can be manipulated in specific ways to rule in and out the salience of certain realities. Whether or not this is successful in shifting public opinion is a difficult question, yet effects are not crucial to this definition. Instead, we are more concerned with the extent of capture of certain digital technologies by specific actors, and how they attempt to utilise such technologies in pursuit of political and ideological dominance.

So while the 1990–1 Gulf War example characterises the Saudi government as a slumberous juggernaut, apathetic in its management of new media threats, the same cannot really be said about its post-Gulf War approach to media development. The investment in satellite television channels and broadcasting infrastructure has highlighted the perceived benefits of a proactive, as opposed to a lethargic, media strategy. While this shift in Saudi policy has been going on for decades, the rise of Mohammed bin Salman seems to have brought with it renewed attention to the digital sphere.

Lord of the Flies

A key agent of Saudi's quest to build social media power is Saud al-Qahtani, MBS's right-hand man and former adviser to the Saudi royal court. In addition to being accused of overseeing the torture of female activists and the killing of journalist Jamal Khashoggi,[33] al-Qahtani was, and still is, widely regarded as the orchestrator of Saudi's social media and digital espionage policy. Al-Qahtani once tweeted that he takes his orders directly from King Salman and Mohammed bin Salman: 'Do you think I'm acting on my own whim? I am a civil servant and a faithful executioner of the orders of the King and the Crown Prince.'[34]

Al-Qahtani, who had served in the Saudi Air Force, is often termed the 'Lord of the Flies', a derogatory epithet that describes his perceived role as the puppet-master behind the thousands of bots and trolls (flies) that dominate Arabic social media. Al-Qahtani's rise reportedly began fairly modestly. He began a blog, which apparently prompted Khaled al-Tuwaijri, a former head of the Saudi royal court, to enlist al-Qahtani to help run an electronic media campaign (or army) to defend Saudi's image at home and abroad.[35] It was here that al-Qahtani struck up a relationship with Mohammed bin Salman.

Evidence of al-Qahtani's playbook shows that he was probably hired for his loyalty, rather than his technical competence. His foray into the world of cyber defence was revealed in his leaked communications with Italian spyware firm Hacking Team. After he reached out to the Italian firm in 2012, Hacking Team sent technicians to train Saudi's cyber army. As al-Qahtani's prominence grew, especially through 2017, people began to speculate whether it was the same al-Qahtani who went on websites such as Hack Forums to solicit the services of skilled hackers. This suspicion was confirmed when an investigation by Nathan Patin for the open-source intelligence (OSINT) outfit Bellingcat determined that an account attempting to procure services on Hack Forums most likely belonged to Saud al-Qahtani.

Through these websites al-Qahtani sought a whole gamut of tools designed for both censorship and propaganda/disinformation amplification. Among other things, he sought software solutions that could delete social media posts while fabricating artificial activity to boost posts on Facebook and YouTube. He has paid hackers to delete both YouTube videos and YouTube channels deemed unfavourable to his employers. His general modus operandi was to source digital tools that could erase certain social media accounts while promoting others. His attempts to censor information critical of the Saudi regime, in turn replacing it with pro-regime propaganda, represent the essential elements of influence operations.[36] In addition to this, al-Qahtani led from his own account. As the so-called Lord of the Flies, 'Qahtani drove Twitter traffic directly by rallying online followers as any social media influencer might'.[37]

It is not always clear how much success al-Qahtani had with his attempts to source tools for enacting digital authoritarianism. For example, there is evidence that he attempted to obtain Twitter tools that could suspend critical Twitter accounts. Although it is not clear if these tools were successfully deployed, unusual things were happening online. In 2016 the verified Twitter account of the well-respected international organisation Médecins Sans Frontières (MSF) was suspended. On 2 August 2016 Twitter informed MSF that its account had been reported as 'fake', had tweeted 'abusive' content, and had been the target of suspected hacking attempts. The suspension of the account occurred just days after an aggressive campaign launched against MSF activities in Yemen, mainly over Twitter. The campaign was ostensibly launched by the news outlet AlYemen Now. It targeted the @MSF_arabic and @MSF_Yemen accounts with negative tweets and encouraged people to use both the English and Arabic hashtags MSFBlamesCoalitionPardonCoup.

The thrust of the disinformation was that MSF had been collaborating with the Saudi-led coalition's enemies, the Houthis. In reality, the MSF Arabic account was targeted for highlighting the killing of Yemeni civilians by Saudi-led coalition airstrikes. The silencing of MSF seemed to have tacit approval from official sources, with the Arab Command of the Coalition criticising MSF and Amnesty International for 'fallacies'. It is highly probable the silencing of MSF Arabic was a state-led attempt to censor criticism of the coalition's killing of Yemeni civilians. How exactly the campaign unfolded was unclear, yet highly suspicious nonetheless.

Meanwhile, those covering the Yemen war also noted suspicious activity on social media. Iona Craig, a British Irish journalist, reported in 2017 that Twitter bots were mass-following influential Yemeni Twitter users. Craig reported that she had blocked around 9,000 accounts within two weeks. The accounts were mostly anonymous accounts that did not even have profiles images – sometimes called 'eggs'.[38] An analysis of the accounts revealed that around 16,000 accounts which began following Craig were created between November 2017 and April 2018. At the time, her total followers amounted to around 48,000, meaning that this influx accounted for 33% of her total followers. Of these 16,000, a significant number, were likely bots.[39] The exact purpose of the mass follows was unclear, but activists worried that it was an attempt to degrade the quality of the account being followed in order to trigger Twitter's algorithm to suspend the account. Yemeni analyst Hisham al-Omeisy noted that 'Fake followers can hurt your account's credibility, engagement rate'.[40] He also noted that international NGOs in Yemen were facing the same problem.[41] Although neither al-Omeisy nor Craig had their account suspended, Craig decided to limit her account, effectively self-censoring an important voice as a result of the alarming sense of surveillance brought about by the onset of a bot swarm. Somewhat worryingly, al-Omeisy was arrested the following month (August 2017) by Houthi rebels.

Troll Farms

In addition to bots, al-Qahtani's cyber army reportedly contains real people operating multiple social media accounts. The NGO Reporters Without Borders (RSF), which defends the right to freedom of information, used the term 'digital predators' to describe 'government agencies that use digital technology to spy on and harass journalists and thereby jeopardize our ability to get news and information'.[42] In 2020 RSF put Saudi Arabia on the list of the top 2020 digital predators, singling out Saud al-Qahtani as the head of Saudi's bot army:

> Created by Saud Al-Qahtani when he was an adviser to the Crown Prince, this network of pro-regime trolls and bots currently produces more than 2,500 tweets a day, above all promoting the content of the conservative satellite TV news channel Saudi 24. It has also been responsible for spreading sectarian and antisemitic messages and conspiracy theories about Jamal Khashoggi, the Saudi journalist [of] whose murder Al-Qahtani was clearly one of the instigators.[43]

Despite this little is actually known about the inner workings of the Saudi Electronic Brigade, or how centralised the various troll operations are in Saudi. The closest insight comes from the *New York Times*, which interviewed several people familiar with or involved in the operation. While the term 'troll farm' suggests large rooms of people hunched diligently in front of glowing screens, the reality is often different. In Riyadh, hundreds of young people (mostly men) sit in their offices and homes trawling social media to find and engage with critics of Saudi Arabia, its leadership and its foreign and domestic policies. Most of these so-called specialists reportedly receive around 10,000 Saudi riyals – or $3,000 – a month.[44] Despite their disparate locales, the trolls are directed by a core group of directors, who discuss on a daily basis what topics they want their trolls to engage with. Often, the issue of women's rights, the war in Yemen or new government policies are the topics of choice. Once the directors determine the rota of topics, they communicate with the trolls via WhatsApp or Telegram, providing the specialists with 'lists of people to threaten, insult and intimidate; daily tweet quotas to fill, and pro-government messages to augment'.[45] Those working in Saudi's troll farms often hear their seniors discussing 'Mr. Al Qahtani'.[46]

In order to give a veneer of authenticity to this clearly inauthentic engagement, the trolls are encouraged to use gifs and memes to mock dissenters. Just as pro-Trump accounts have adopted memes such as Pepe the Frog to attack opponents, so too have the Saudi troll army. These often include images of MBS, which function as a sign of loyalty but also a reminder that big brother is watching. While memes and gifs might ordinarily be a source of humour and repartee, their appropriation as part of cyber-harassment campaigns often renders them sinister and disturbing. Developments in technology such as Google Translate, as well as emojis and gifs, also allow linguistic or cultural barriers to be overcome, meaning that language need not impede international trolling efforts, with foreign journalists and activists also being targeted.

In addition to sending insults and memes, the troll army has often utilised innovative forms of censorship. In one example, trolls attempted to mute critics of Saudi attacks on Yemen by reporting their posts 'as sensitive'. When determining whether to block or censor content, Twitter considers such user reports when making a decision. The general consensus in the MENA region, though, is that if enough people report a post, it will be blocked by Twitter. Often, those who sign up as trolls have little idea of what they are getting into. According to some of the insiders interviewed by the *New York Times*, many were not aware of the political aspect of the work until they attended an interview. However, by this stage, 'some of the specialists felt they would have been targeted as possible dissenters themselves if they had turned down the job'.[47] This implies that even the hordes of hyper-nationalist pro-MBS accounts may not always be willing participants in their own abuse or propaganda.

Saudi Arabia Infiltrating Twitter

Part of achieving digital power, and the success of disinformation, is to reduce the salience of counter-narratives. An effective way to do this is to eliminate those who criticise the government, either through intimidation, coercion or incarceration. But in an age of anonymity, part of the battle for authoritarian regimes is identifying critics. As social media platforms have allowed some form of criticism through anonymity, the Saudi regime has flexed its digital power and found ways to subvert this anonymity through espionage. Although dictators are generally paranoid, it has been a feature of the new

Saudi regime to exercise its hegemony beyond its borders, whether through acquiring media outlets or assassinating critics abroad.

Recently, this has involved targeting dissidents abroad with Pegasus, spyware manufactured by the Israeli technology firm NSO Group. Omar Abdulaziz, a Saudi citizen living in self-exile in Canada, was a case in point. Abdulaziz was sent a link that masked a Pegasus spyware download. The University of Toronto's Citizen Lab determined that Saudi Arabia was behind the infiltration attempt. The attempt to hack Abdulaziz came shortly after Saud al-Qahtani reportedly sent two emissaries to Montreal to convince Abdulaziz to return to Saudi. [48]

Although Gulf regimes have been using spyware (such as Finspy) produced by European and Israeli companies to target dissidents abroad since at least 2012, Saudi has taken cyber-espionage to a new level.[49] Perhaps one of the most obvious examples of this brazen influence was the infiltration by Saudi and US citizens of Twitter's headquarters in San Francisco. In 2019 the FBI filed charges against three men for infiltrating Twitter and spying on behalf of the Saudi government during 2014 and 2015. Ahmed Abouammo, a dual citizen of Lebanon and United States, worked as a media partnerships manager at Twitter and provided help for notable MENA accounts. Ali al-Zabarah was a site reliability engineer at Twitter and a Saudi citizen.[50] Ahmed al-Mutairi (also known as Ahmed al-Jabreen) was also a Saudi citizen who owned a social media marketing company called SMAAT.[51] The three were alleged by the FBI to be working for Bader al-Asaker, the secretary-general of the charitable organisation MiSK, which belongs to Mohammed bin Salman. Although MiSK is described as a 'non-profit organization devoted to cultivating learning and leadership in youth',[52] the criminal complaint stated that al-Asaker (referred to in the FBI charge sheet as Foreign Official 1) was working at the direction of Mohammed bin Salman with regard to his online Twitter presence. Al-Asaker had listed his employer on his US visa application as the Saudi royal court.[53]

According to court documents, a Saudi official who listed the royal court as his employer (referred to as Foreign Official 1) gave US citizen Ahmed Abouammo $300,000 and a $20,000 Hublot watch in return for revealing private information about Saudi Twitter users.

Using their high levels of Twitter access, Ali al-Zabarah and Ahmed Abouammo accessed private information, such as email addresses, IP addresses and dates of birth of known critics of the Saudi regime, as well as thousands of other Twitter users. Their alleged handler, Ahmed al-Mutairi, was a media adviser to the royal family, and the information they fraudulently obtained was, according to the FBI, given to 'Foreign Official-1 and others related to, and working for, the government of KSA and the Saudi Royal Family'. The modus operandi was simple; the royal court employee would provide Abouammo and al-Zabarah with the 'names of Twitter accounts of interest to Foreign Official-1, members of the Saudi Royal Family, and others in the government of KSA'.[54] These names often included those of 'accounts posting information critical of, or embarrassing to, the Saudi Royal Family and government of KSA'.[55] There was no doubt about the purpose of the infiltration: to find the identity of critics of Saudi Arabia, and delete, silence or censor those accounts. As Abouammo said to Foreign Official 1: 'proactive and reactively, we will delete evil, my brother.'

Although the FBI has launched a case against Abouammo, al-Zabarah and al-Mutairi, al-Zabarah fled to Saudi soon after Twitter discovered he was passing on information to the Saudi authorities. Justice Department officials were reportedly furious at Twitter for tipping off al-Zabarah by suspending him, and thus allowing him to flee to Saudi Arabia.[56] It is not clear why the FBI did not immediately arrest al-Zabarah or why Twitter was less than discreet.[57] It also took Twitter until 2019 to suspend at least 88,000 fake accounts linked to al-Jabreen's social media company SMAAT.[58] All of these accounts were considered state-backed information operations. The Saudi penetration of the US tech giant has reportedly had devastating consequences. Saudi citizen Areej al-Sadhan stated that her brother Abdulrahaman al-Sadhan was disappeared by Saudi Arabia's secret police as a direct result of the Twitter breach. At least five others reportedly suffered a similar fate due to the Saudi infiltration.[59]

These political scandals have shaped perceptions of Twitter's neutrality in MENA politics. In 2020 a campaign demanding that Twitter move its headquarters from Dubai to Tunisia, the most democratic (at least until recently, when Kais Saied suspended parliament in a move widely seen as an autocoup) country in the MENA region, took off.

Digital Capital: Power and Privilege

Part of digital power is ensuring that, in addition to volume, one's presence on Twitter is legitimised through cultural markers of credibility. With regard to the dominant voices on Twitter, it is possible to say with reasonable confidence that institutions in Saudi take Twitter seriously. The number of verified accounts is in some ways indicative of this. While Saudi has a large population and high mobile and internet penetration rate, it is clear from the FBI's indictment documents against the Saudi Twitter spies that Abouammo used his position in Twitter to facilitate the verification of numerous Saudi Twitter accounts at the behest of the Saudi embassy.[60] This cyber-espionage undoubtedly gave Saudi an edge in terms of its digital footprint and social media power. While Twitter verification may seem trivial to some, it functions as a resource at the intersection of cultural, social and political capital. It gives some form of advantage to those who own it, such as perceived legitimacy and credibility or the ability to monetise tweets as an influencer. It can be considered a form of 'digital capital', which represents the full spectrum of digital competences and devices that can be utilised to produce other forms of capital and thus advantage within society.[61] The mobilisation of resources by a state to accrue digital capital on a large scale for the purpose of promoting hegemonic projects can readily be conceived of as a form of digital power.

Verification is a scarce resource on Twitter, with only a small percentage of accounts having that status – approximately 367,000 accounts as of November 2020.[62] As such, its value is increased by its relative scarcity, as is the fact that it is an asset frequently given to celebrities, politicians, journalists and other high-profile figures of 'public interest'. While there is still a debate as to whether verification impacts people's perception of the credibility of news,[63] verification is still an indicator of social status among an increasingly literate digital class. In a space awash with suspicious accounts it also affords the user a degree of immediate unearned credibility and legitimacy.

Twitter, as the gatekeeper of such verification badges, becomes a broker of digital and cultural capital, determining who in society gets the venerated badge. It is also possible that verification impacts Twitter's algorithm into making information more salient, allowing verified users to disproportionately influence online discussions.

Based on analysis of explicit user-reported location, as opposed to implicit location, approximately 2,796 of all verified users are based in Saudi, by far the highest of the Arabic-speaking countries. As of early 2019 these accounts have produced a net total of approximately 40,000,000 million tweets. The next-highest Arabic-speaking country in terms of Twitter verification is the United Arab Emirates, with approximately 1,085 verified accounts. Around 305 of the verified accounts in Saudi might be considered media-related accounts.[64] Saudi's digital power, partly achieved through the potentially illicit acquisition of digital capital outstrips all other Arabic-majority countries – at least on Twitter. Furthermore, when the information producers in that state are co-opted and unable to criticise the regime, and yet are prominent, it distorts the very nature of the information continuum across the region.

The Biggest Cyberbullies

The attention placed by Saudi Arabia – and indeed other members of the KUBE alliance – on social media hegemony can be evidenced by the archive of state-backed information operations published by Twitter. Following pressure to be more transparent about social media manipulation, Twitter launched a public archive of Twitter accounts suspended due to suspected state-backed information operations in October 2018.[65] An aggregation of all Twitter takedowns since the inception of the archives reveals that behind China, Saudi and the UAE come in second and third place, respectively.[66] Egypt is in fifth place, followed by Iran. Although these are the known state-backed operations discovered since October 2018, they are obviously incomplete. The research documented in this book reveals many accounts that, while pushing state propaganda, have not been included in the archives. On some occasions this has been admitted by Twitter. For example, the state-backed archives do not include

Fig. 2: Number of accounts by country suspended by Twitter due to state-backed influence operations

Country / Bloc	Accounts
China*	28,991
[KUBE] Saudi Arabia Combined with SA_UAE_EG takedown	11,318
[KUBE] UAE Combined with SA_UAE_EG and UAE/EG takedown	9,869
Serbia	8,558
[KUBE] Egypt Combined with SA_UAE_EG and UAE/EG takedown	8,162
Iran	7,973
Turkey	7,340
[KUBE] Saudi Arabia**	5,968
[KUBE] Saudi Arabia UAE Egypt	5,350
Russia (including Internet Research Agency)	5190
[KUBE] the United Arab Emirates	4248
Honduras	3104
[KUBE] Egypt	2541
Venezuela	1993
Ecuador	1019
Thailand	926
Indonesia	795
Cuba	526
[KUBE] United Arab Emirates/Egypt	271
Spain	259
Catalonia	130
Ghana/Nigeria	71
Bangladesh	15

17,000 accounts linked to China, or 88,000 accounts Twitter admitted to suspending linked to Saudi via SMAAT. One of the issues of Twitter's reporting of state-backed influence operations is that in some instances it aggregated some data for Saudi, the UAE and

Egypt. For example, in April 2020 they released a combined dataset titled SA_EG_AE. Although this makes it difficult to determine which state exactly was linked to the operation, it actually highlights the emergence of coordination between the countries, emphasising and validating the emergence of the KUBE political bloc.

Saudis for Trump and Americans for MBS

A key aspect of Making Arabia Great Again and the Gulf's post-truth moment, has been the kingdom's close public alignment with Donald Trump, who, unlike his predecessor Barack Obama, gave countries in the Persian Gulf free rein on domestic politics, especially with regard to human rights violations. Donald Trump himself repeatedly extolled the nature of a transactional relationship between the United States and Saudi Arabia. At a campaign rally in Alabama in 2015, Trump stated: 'Saudi Arabia, I get along with all of them. They buy apartments from me. They spend $40 million, $50 million. ... Am I supposed to dislike them? I like them very much.'[67] This connection was exemplified when Donald Trump broke with tradition to make Saudi Arabia, and not Canada, his first foreign visit as US president. Trump's relationship to the Gulf was also defined by his administration's renewed hostility towards Iran, a policy move supported by Saudi Arabia, the United Arab Emirates and Israel.[68]

Another, perhaps less obvious, similarity between Trump and MBS is their depiction as 'strongmen'.[69] The term is problematic and misconstrues as 'strength' behaviours more akin to high-functioning sociopaths exuding toxic masculinity. Their inability to take criticism reflects a fragile ego indicative of weakness, rather than strength. The Saudi regime seems to understand Trump, though, in no small part due to Trump's reaction to his poorly attended inauguration. The ensuing media ridicule upset him to the extent that, according to *The Guardian*, the White House gave the impression of wanting photos of the sparse inauguration crowds to be cropped to make them look bigger.[70]

As a result, the Saudi authorities – or indeed, pro-Saudi entities active on social media – made sure that they would not offend Trump's ego upon his visit to the kingdom. After it was announced that Trump would be visiting Saudi in May 2017 for the Riyadh Summit, the Arabic hashtag 'welcome Trump to the nation of toughness' started trending. A quick look at the hashtag on Twitter would suggest that thousands of Saudis were delighted at the prospect of Trump visiting the country; yet the reality was somewhat different. Most of the fanfare on the hashtag was created by 'fake' accounts. A sample of around 8,100 unique Twitter accounts active on the hashtag were downloaded. Around 3,643 (45%) of the accounts in the total sample were created in the first and second quarters of 2017.[71] Astonishingly, 1,313 (16%) were created on just two days in March and May 2017. Although some of the accounts had biographical information, many did not. Their names varied from English to Arabic to Dutch. The images often seemed at odds with their biographies. One user, called Husni Mukhalfi, had a profile picture of a masked man with a balaclava and a sniper rifle, although his biography claimed he like 'gaming, skating, surfing and talin' with [his] bros.'.

The bot accounts generally retweeted the same content, though not necessarily in the same order. The various bot networks retweeted positive news about the Saudi government and royal family, or adverts for various products, including hair-removal devices. This, and the fact that most of the accounts had generic profile pictures, and mostly used the same application to tweet, indicated that they were almost certainly the work of a troll/bot farm. As of 2020, around 34% of the accounts active on the welcome Trump campaign remain as they are. Of the 1987 accounts using Twitter Web Client, only 9% remain. The large majority of these accounts have been suspended, with the attrition rates of accounts using Twitter Web Client being higher, reflecting that influence ops gravitate towards using that platform. The number of bots in the overall sample likely falls in the approximate range of 1,788–5,200.[72]

In addition to creating the illusion of widespread Saudi support for Donald Trump, astroturfing campaigns signal to genuine Saudis the state's political support for Trump. If the bots indicate support for Trump, citizens are expected not to criticise him.

A similar phenomenon has been the emergence of a small but active group of non-Saudi citizens advocating for the policies of MBS.

This includes a number of American nationals who frequently tweet in support of MBS's policies or harass his critics. Ghada Oueiss, an anchor for Qatar-based Al Jazeera, has launched a civil action against this group (as well as MBS and MBZ) for repeatedly harassing her. According to Oueiss's lawyer and former federal prosecutor Daniel Rashbaum:

> It's clear that there was a concerted and co-ordinated effort by Saudi, UAE [United Arab Emirates] and some American counterparts to silence critics of their regimes, and their newest tactic is using illegal hacking, the release of stolen and doctored images and an online campaign of intimidation.

Such networks, whether organic or not, indicate another alarming aspect of social media disinformation emanating from the Middle East – the potential use and co-optation of real people to amplify Saudi and Emirate propaganda among organic right-wing social media networks in the United States and elsewhere.

Donald Trump's Timeline is Compromised by Pro-Saudi Bots

Trump's own proclivity to tweet has also yielded new opportunities for deception by Saudi-supporting entities. However, before discussing that, it is important to understand the context of Trump's relationship with Twitter. As the US president, anything he said was newsworthy, and when he tweeted, the media paid attention, allowing him to dominate headlines and inveigle himself into the news cycle. On 13 November 2017 Trump had about 43 million followers. By October 2020 this number was 87 million. Trump's use of the platform has garnered much attention, and studies have found that Trump was successfully able to use Twitter to trigger more mainstream press coverage.[73] Twitter eventually suspended Trump's Twitter account in January 2021 following the riots on Capitol Hill in Washington, DC, after determining that his tweets risked inciting further violence. [74]

Trump's personal use of Twitter aside, social media, in general, has attracted a lot of attention due to its potential role in impacting or predicting election outcomes. The use of social media by foreign actors seeking to interfere in the domestic politics of rival countries has also become a major issue, largely due to the fact that digital media transcend physical borders. In 2020 the US Senate Intelligence Select Committee acknowledged that Russia had conducted a sweeping campaign to interfere in the 2016 US election and had thus potentially assisted in getting Donald Trump elected. Connected to this campaign was the role of thousands of social media accounts promoting Donald Trump, many of which were run by the Internet Research Agency in St Petersburg. While it is not exactly clear what impact these trolls had on Trump's popularity, a study published in 2020 said that every 25,000 extra retweets by the Internet Research Agency predicted a 1% increase in popularity in Trump's opinion polls.[75]

Although there has been significant focus on Russian meddling, less attention has been paid to the role of the Gulf states in interfering in US politics, whether through online influence operations or otherwise. However, Trump's Twitter timeline was compromised by the fact that unknown actors were able to increase the salience of his messaging on topics of their choosing. On 4 November 2017 Donald Trump had a phone call with King Salman of Saudi Arabia, during which Salman offered Trump condolences for a terrorist attack in New York.[76] Trump also used the opportunity to ask Salman to consider the New York Stock Exchange for the listing of Aramco – one of the world's most valuable companies. Despite the arrests of high-profile activists by the Saudi authorities, no mention was made on the call of their plight.[77] Indeed, Trump seemed to be buttering up Salman in order to not jeopardise a profitable IPO offer, or indeed anger a lucrative arms customer of the USA. From the Saudi perspective it was a good phone call.

After the meeting Trump took to Twitter to praise King Salman, no doubt in an effort to underpin his administration's visible commitment to protecting Saudi interests. On 7 November 2017 Trump tweeted, 'I have great confidence in King Salman and the Crown Prince of Saudi Arabia, they know exactly what they are doing'.[78] Trump's tweet praising King Salman was an immediate hit. The average number of retweets for Donald Trump's tweets between 1 and 11 November was around 16,000, while a study conducted in May 2017 showed that the average (mean) number of retweets for Trump was 13,100 retweets per tweet[79] – a number that would have grown between May and November due to Trump's increasing follower base. However, the tweet praising King Salman was retweeted 82,946 times, much more than Trump's average for that week.

A sample of 24,704 Twitter accounts that retweeted Trump's tweet about Salman was extracted to assess the metadata of the accounts. Of the 24,074 accounts in the sample, approximately 7,415 were created in the nine-month period between April 2017 and November 2017. The sample date itself runs from the beginning of the establishment of Twitter, approximately 2006. In the third quarter of 2017 alone 4,474 accounts were created, accounting for approximately 19% of the entire sample (the average number of accounts created per month since May 2007 was only 169[80]). While this spike of new accounts in a nine-month period is itself indicative of inauthentic activity, certain days also saw a disproportionately high number of new accounts: 11% of the accounts in the sample were created in an eight-day period alone.

What's more, the anomalies in account creation were compounded by further anomalies in the choice of application that the accounts were using to tweet from. The majority (around 82%) of the accounts set up in the third quarter of 2017 were using Twitter Web App. Between 2007 and the first quarter of 2016 the average number of accounts in the sample using Twitter Web Client was around 7%. Of the 7,000 accounts that used Twitter Web Client, around 94% were deleted, suspended or had their names changed.[81] Again, this reflects the fact that Twitter Web Client is more commonly used by those creating bot accounts.[82] An individual examination of the accounts revealed that multiple bot networks must have been involved in promoting Trump's praise of King Salman. Many of the accounts had names written in Cyrillic, and examination of their past tweets indicated that they had been programmed to tweet on specific topics unrelated to US politics or the Middle East. In addition to promoting Trump's tweets, a number had been promoting Kenyan middle-distance runner Elijah Motonei Manangoi – suggesting that whoever ran the bot network was renting it out to multiple clients in addition to a pro-Saudi entity.

An analysis of another pro-Saudi bot network discovered in 2018 revealed other instances in which pro-Saudi Twitter accounts were promoting Trump's support of Saudi Arabia – particularly with regard to its antipathy to Iran and Qatar. The network was active during the emir of Qatar's visit to London in 2018, promoting hashtags such as 'oppose Qatar visit' and 'London rejects Tamim's visit'. Although the majority of those networks had been suspended by Twitter, the 25 or so accounts that Twitter failed to suspend revealed the campaigns on which they had previously been operational. In addition to praising Mohammed bin Salman, the accounts also included a few tweets from Donald Trump, specifically those lionising Saudi Arabia or criticising Qatar. Tweets by the US president known to have been boosted by this particularly pro-Saudi and anti-Qatar network are detailed in Figure 3.

The tactic of boosting someone's tweets is generally called megaphoning or signal amplification. The purpose is to increase the

Fig. 3: Tweets by Donald Trump that were retweeted by a pro-Saudi network

30 December 2017	Many reports of peaceful protests by Iranian citizens fed up with the regime's corruption & its squandering of the nation's wealth to fund terrorism abroad. Iranian govt should respect their people's rights, including the right to express themselves. The world is watching![i]
6 June 2017	During my recent trip to the Middle East, I stated that there can no longer be funding of Radical Ideology. Leaders pointed to Qatar – look![ii]
20 May 2017	Great to be in Riyadh, Saudi Arabia. Looking forward to the afternoon and evening ahead. #POTUSAbroad[iii]

i.   https://twitter.com/realDonaldTrump/status/946949708915924994
ii. https://twitter.com/realDonaldTrump/status/872062159789985792
iii. https://twitter.com/realDonaldTrump/status/865865814099939328

salience of a specific message. On Twitter, a high number of tweets and retweets on a particular topic may give the illusion that certain opinions or policy positions are more popular than they actually are. Furthermore, as Twitter is a global platform, amplification is not constrained to the national context, but reaches a global audience that may labour under the illusion that the perceived popularity is legitimate. Popularity can also encourage people to agree. Research conducted at the Massachusetts Institute of Technology (MIT) noted that people were more likely to 'like' a post if they already perceived it as popular. This 'herd effect' potentially challenges the notion that group decision making is necessarily better, instead highlighting the problem that people are more likely to support what is popular.[83] It is somewhat alarming that specific messages issued by the president of the United States can be selectively promoted by an entity potentially acting on behalf of a foreign power in order to positively shape perceptions of that entity.

Conclusion

This chapter has explored the expansion and rise of Saudi as a deception superpower. A key aspect to understanding disinformation and deception in the Arabic-speaking Middle East is to understand that certain actors appear to be engaged more profoundly in various influence campaigns. Saudi is certainly not the only actor, but is, along with the United Arab Emirates and perhaps Egypt, the most demonstrably active in engaging in digital deception. Indeed, it is important to dispel the myth that there is parity between digital disinformation players around the world. Although disinformation is very much something that most states do, it is intellectually dishonest to pretend that all states do it to the same extent. The global disinformation scene is primarily the domain of larger powers with more expansive foreign policies. This makes sense since disinformation is often used strategically alongside aggressive foreign policy manoeuvres to further the objectives of powerful players engaged in multilateral issues – often involving conflict. The emerging Saudi/UAE versus Iran nexus in the Persian Gulf, coupled with their interventions in Libya and Yemen, have also created the need to try and influence the thought diets of various regional and international constituencies. A battle for hearts and minds is playing out across the world, and disinformation seeks to address both local and foreign actors on the relative merits of the parties involved in a conflict. Conflict and disinformation are natural bedfellows.

Resources are also important. To some extent, Saudi's youth employment problem can be instrumentalised to the advantage of social media power. Saudi's large population and high mobile penetration mean that loyal citizens may take to Twitter to attack perceived opponents. Alternatively, trolling may serve as a form of employment for those not inclined towards hyper-nationalism, but who need a job (it is not clear how many people are involved in this industry). In this way, populous states have a human resource advantage when it comes to disinformation operations, able to leverage more resources to engage in these techniques. However, in Saudi it also seems to have been engendered by an increasingly youthful and aggressive desire to control the country's reputation at home and abroad. This has been abetted by personalistic attributes of the likes of Saud al-Qahtani and Mohammed bin Salman, who seem willing to take numerous risks in pursuit of reputational management in the digital space.

Saudi has adopted a multi-faceted approach to controlling social media, using a combination of infiltration, intimidation and co-optation. By using armies of trolls online, and by arresting and torturing critics offline, the Saudi authorities have created an oppositional vacuum on social media, and filled it with voices that only lionise or cheer on the regime. Saudi's espionage has also prejudiced the integrity of Twitter's internal security in ways that are still to be fully realised. As Alexei Abrahams states, 'Whether by influencing their citizens' thought diets by shaping the menu of topics that trend; or by deploying armies of bots or sockpuppets to parrot regime positions and poison opposition narratives; or by pressuring influential users to toe the party line; the Saudi regime – among others – has meaningfully blunted the liberation potential of social media, and threatens now to turn the tool to its own advantage.'[84] Fundamentally, the disinformation emanating from the Gulf region also reflects the ideological tenets of 'Make Arabia Great Again' which revolve around generating intense information operations targeting global and local publics in order to obscure some of the egregious realities of the social change undertaken by MBS, social change that seeks to rationalise support in the Arab world for Trump's unpopular regional polices – especially normalisation with Israel.

4

AUTOMATING DECEIT

AUTHORITARIAN AI AND JOURNOGANDA

Chapter Overview

The automation of disinformation and propaganda in the Gulf via the use of bots is one of the most defining aspects of the Gulf's post-truth moment. Artificial intelligence (AI) is already able to produce convincing deep fakes – fake images or videos of real people that could be deployed to great effect in disinformation campaigns. In authoritarian states, where illiberal practices are endemic across journalism, the notion of robots and AI subservient to the will of a dictatorial regime highlights with immense clarity the risks of AI in facilitating digital authoritarianism. Indeed, it raises the very real prospect of AI churning out millions of lines of propaganda and disinformation on behalf of malicious actors. With few ethical safeguards to prevent such a phenomenon, we are entering an alarming new phase where regimes and rulers can project deception to massive audiences. Although that stage is still in its infancy, especially in the MENA region, this chapter demonstrates how algorithms, automation and rudimentary AI are being utilised to dominate online journalism in Saudi Arabia and beyond. It also documents how bots and trolls are being used to create a pseudo-public, or pseudo-civil society. Indeed, a defining aspect of the Gulf's post-truth moment has been the instrumentalisation of hundreds of thousands of Twitter bots, often propagating state propaganda disseminated through legacy media institutions.

Robot Citizens and Journalists

In September 2020 *The Guardian* commissioned GPT 3, a powerful language generator created by the company Open AI, to write a newspaper article. Using a number of prompts and instructions, the *Guardian* journalists asked GPT 3 to write a piece arguing that robots had, in fact, come in peace.[1] The results, while convincingly human in many regards, still had a sinister undertone of intolerance. The closing salvo of the GPT op-ed included the sentence, 'AI should not waste time trying to understand the viewpoints of people who distrust artificial intelligence for a living.'[2] Meanwhile, over at Microsoft, hundreds of human editors were fired during the Covid19 pandemic and replaced with robots – giving them a very good reason to distrust artificial intelligence.[3] The AI software now did what human editors had done – curate news stories from other outlets to be used on Microsoft News, MSN and the company's web browser Microsoft Edge.

In the Persian Gulf, AI and robotics were also making headlines. In October 2017 Saudi Arabia offered a robot called Sophia Saudi citizenship.[4] The robot, manufactured by Hong Kong-based Hanson Robotics, responded with muted enthusiasm. "'Thank you to the Kingdom of Saudi Arabia. I am very honoured and proud for this unique distinction," Sophia told the panel. "It is historic to be the first robot in the world to be recognized with citizenship."'[5] The granting of citizenship to Sophia was a PR stunt, designed to give the impression that Saudi was a forward-looking state embracing a techno future. The move reflected the aspect of Saudi Arabia that has been characterised by the rise of MBS. As noted by Rosie Bsheer, the spectacle framed MBS's reforms in the 'language of hi-tech modernization, sustainable development, and socio-religious tolerance. Sophia, and all the trappings of modernization that "she" embodies, epitomized the ruling class's entrepreneurial vision for a new Saudi Arabia, and in turn, a new Saudi Arabian citizen.'[6]

The conferring of citizenship to a robot in a country that detains and tortures female activists, controls their movement and enforces elements of gender segregation was a 'tone-deaf' move.[7] Fittingly, the spectacle provoked criticism that aptly called into question the superficial nature of the stunt. Joanna Bryson, a researcher in Artificial Intelligence at Bath University, highlighted the ethical and moral paradoxes of granting citizenship to Sophia: 'It's about having a supposed equal you can turn on and off. How does it affect people if they think you can have a citizen that you can buy?'[8] It was also telling that Sophia never requested citizenship, demoting her agency and reinforcing the notion that Gulf regimes are patriarchal interlocutors in determining a woman's legal status.

Both the *Guardian* experiment and the Saudi publicity stunt highlight an interesting relationship between humans and robots. The exaggerated deference of Sophia and GPT 3 to the human race, as if it were a master–slave relationship, is both reassuring and alarming: reassuring in the sense that we need not worry that the replacement of the human race is imminent (assuming AI is yet to conquer the art of dissimulation), but alarming in the sense that a robot subservient to its masters is also a robot subservient to the ideology and political leanings of whoever is determining its use case, whether a programmer, customer or government. Creating an ontological separation between master and subject belies the huge human cost robots are already having. As a case in point, AI is already impacting the life chances of those journalists at Microsoft. The use of robots to maximise revenue at the expense of human labour has been normalised in many industrial societies and is treated as an inevitability, rather than a dystopian science fiction trope.

Automating Social Media Journalism

Journalism in Saudi Arabia is, in many ways, thriving. This is reflected in the proliferation of news websites, satellite news channels and other forms of content creation. From more established ventures such as *Okaz*, Al Arabiya and Al Wesal, to new insurgent outlets such as Saudi 24, there is no shortage of choice. Despite this flourishing, the nature of that journalism is very much constrained by an authoritarian political system that limits freedom of speech. In 2019 Reporters Without Borders ranked Saudi Arabia 170 out of 179 on its global press freedom index.[9] Not only does Saudi not permit independent media, but it monitors and surveils journalists abroad. The number of journalists imprisoned since 2017 and under MBS has tripled.[10] Indeed, while the advent of digital technology has created new channels for citizen journalists and entrepreneurs to set up news outlets, the intimidation of journalists and activists means that journalism is limited in its critical potential. A defining feature of the rise of MBS and al-Qahtani is that pro-government journalism, or that which does not challenge the status quo or various social taboos, is thriving.

In 2013 the murdered journalist Jamal Khashoggi tweeted, 'Someday Twitter will win a Nobel prize. But now we see it's slipping into darkness. Will Twitter take measures to protect our public square? Right now, I'm worried, but I will continue to fight for free expression, at least online.'[11] Just as satellite television marked a significant shift from newspapers, digital technology posed new challenges for autocratic Gulf regimes attempting to assert their ideological influence. Indeed, the rise of social media in the region has resulted in an arms race between Gulf countries, who vie with each other for 'market share' of the Arab world. Online, this means more followers, more views, more impressions and more engagements. Attempts to dominate the news cycle in the digital realm have been felt too on Twitter, where followers, and thus reach – or at least the illusion of followers – are sought after. Of course, genuine followers are preferred, as they imply that those news outlets are reaching a wider audience, but fake followers at least give the illusion that the news channel is popular. Where such figures are available to all to see, keeping up appearances becomes an important aspect of channel branding. A number of the most popular social media accounts are attached to established legacy media, such as Al Jazeera or Al Arabiya. Al Jazeera Arabic, for example, was one of the early adopters and is one of the most followed Arabic news channels. However, in the past six years or so numerous digitally native social media sites across multiple platforms have cropped up across the Gulf.

In addition to more traditional forms of television and press journalism, social media has brought new genres of micro-journalism. Social media news accounts are among the most followed and most vociferous 'news' accounts on Twitter. SaudiNews50[12] and AjelNews24 have huge followings, and are largely broadcast through WhatsApp, Twitter and Instagram. SaudiNews50, for example, does not have a website, yet it is one of the most followed news accounts in the Arabic language, with over 13 million Twitter followers and 12 million Instagram followers. Both SaudiNews50 and AjelNews24 are, of course, pro-government. SaudiNews50 posts frequently, and largely in support of Saudi foreign and domestic policies.[13] Part of the aggressive success of such outlets can be found in the fact they were primarily a means of marketing Saudi state policy. They reproduce state-sanctioned content as opposed to pouring resources and effort into generating in-depth analysis or investigative work. Unsurprisingly, SaudiNews50 was a project by SMAAT, the digital marketing firm run by Ahmed al-Mutairi (al-Jabreen), wanted by the FBI for his role in stealing private information of Saudi citizens from Twitter's HQ. Around 88,000 SMAAT Twitter accounts were also suspended for engaging in inauthentic behaviour. That SaudiNews50 is the project of a marketing company linked to Saudi state espionage suggests that information operations, rather than truth, is perhaps the primary purpose of the account.

With so many new self-proclaimed news channels cropping up, Figure 4 plots the number of followers of news-related Twitter accounts by country in the MENA region – an exploratory and somewhat crude measure of social media power.[14] It also shows how active they are, i.e. how often they post.

As a crude measure of overall Twitter influence, Figure 4 demonstrates how Saudi news-related accounts outperform other Arabic-speaking countries from the perspective of followers and statuses by some margin. Qatar also features highly (largely due to Al Jazeera and Al Araby), followed by the UAE and Egypt. The

Fig. 4: Followers of news-related Twitter accounts in the MENA region, by country

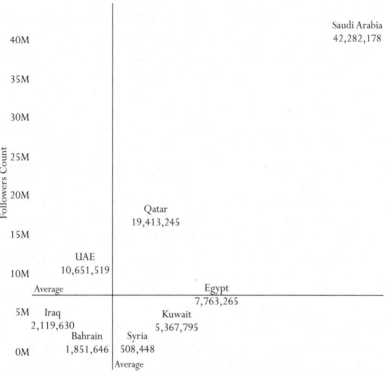

most followed news site on Twitter at the time of data collection was Al Jazeera Arabic (AJArabic), while the second most highly followed was SaudiNews50, which, as mentioned, is a product of the digital marketing company SMAAT. Saudi news accounts are, at least superficially, the most vocal and the most followed in the Arabic-speaking Twittersphere. Obviously, we need to factor in that a large proportion of those follower numbers are probably fake. Nevertheless, it is possible that such numbers could skew the algorithms and promote their content further.

The biggest danger to authoritarian regimes posed by social media platforms lies in the fact they can promote mobilisation around specific topics. The effectiveness of social media platforms at ensuring the mobilisation of revolutionary or anti-status quo forces is partly a function of the authorities' assiduousness in disrupting that ability. By dominating the social media space with state-controlled media, governments are able to ensure that their approved content is widely disseminated, even if that means creating an ecosystem of thousands of fake accounts and pseudo-news organisations.

Sultan al-Joufi Abu Saud

Saudi 24[15] and its subsidiaries are a relatively new set of satellite TV channels. They were set up by Elite Media Group, an organisation run by Sultan al-Joufi Abu Saud, a Saudi media entrepreneur.

Elite Media Group was connected to at least seven channels with a satellite presence, including: the Source, Safavid Plan, the Two Holy Mosques, Hello Homeland, Counter-Terrorism, Saudi 24 Sports and the Channel of Saudi Achievements. Elite Media Group also formulated a number of relationships with local, Saudi-based newspapers for the purpose of sharing content.[16] A number of the channels were largely patriotic, designed to praise the achievements of Saudi and promote its security (the Channel of Saudi Achievements – the clue is in the name). One of the channels, Safavid Plan, was devoted exclusively to criticising Iran and expounding on its nefarious ambitions. The fact it was named Safavid, a derogatory term used to refer to Iranians, is testament to the unusual regulatory environment that governs Saudi media. Some of the channels have since become defunct, while Saudi 24 seems to have consolidated its operation. Others have remained, however, such as al-Shariyyaa, a Yemeni-focused news site still connected to Saudi 24. It also has a channel focused on developments in Sudan: Sudan Now.

The expansive media operation launched by Elite Media Group seemingly reflected an attempt to establish a monopoly over the domestic Saudi news market, with a view to reaching international audiences. Indeed, more recently, Saudi 24 established an English news channel, although their operation seems to be in flux. There is also evidence to suggest that Elite Media Group and a similar news site called Saudi Al Youm had made a far more ambitious attempt to dominate the Arabic news space through the creation of dozens of news sites connected to regional countries and global capitals. An analysis of domains registered on the same server as Saudi 24 indicated that at least 157 news portals had been registered. Many of these covered Saudi's 13 regions, and had domain names such as bukiriahnews.com, buqiqnews.com and buridanews.com and shared the same Saudi Al Youm name servers. Other websites, subsequently deleted, included websites targeting the Arab diaspora in Washington (Washington News)[17], Geneva (Swiss News Networks)[18], Belgium[19] and Europe (EuropeforNews) – to name but a few. Most of the sites, while appearing independent, appeared to be recycling content from Saudi or Egyptian websites such as Al Arabiya or Masry Al Youm/ Youm7. There was even a website called hizbullahnewsagency.com, raising the question as to whether the operation sought to not only dominate the information space but frame the discourse of Saudi's rivals for political benefit.[20] Most of these websites are defunct, and while they point to a grand effort at dominating the Arabic-speaking digital media space, it is unclear how effective, if at all, they ever were.

Saudi 24 does not seem particularly far removed from Saud al-Qahtani, and thus the Saudi government itself. One of Saudi 24's journalists, Tarek al-Khitab Abou Zeinab, tweeted about how he had formed a new group at the direction of Saud al-Qahtani to defend Saudi Arabia from attacks.[21]

Saudi 24 and Automating Sectarian Hate Speech

In addition to what appears to be a centralised propaganda campaign to target global Arabic communities with pro-Saudi content, another interesting aspect of some of the new insurgent channels is the use of bots. We know now that SMAAT, the digital marketing company behind SaudiNews50, has had at least 88,000 fake accounts suspended by Twitter. However, Saudi 24 has also been engaging in similar practices for several years. In the Arabic-speaking world, and in particular in the Gulf, country-based hashtags such as #Bahrain, #Yemen and #Saudi have been dominated by bots connected to Saudi

24 and al-Shariyyaa. Hashtags are important and can be considered ad hoc publics, ideas and events around which people mobilise in order to discuss pertinent topics or shared interests. 'However, when hashtags are made prominent by bots, they shift from being genuine ad hoc publics to ad hoc public relations, reflecting the particular agenda of the propagandist paying for and/or organizing the campaign.'[22]

Alarmingly, Saudi 24 bots have been active in promoting sectarian hate speech in Arabic – perhaps unsurprising for an organisation that runs a channel called Safavid Plan. Often, hate speech aims to demonise certain population groups, relying on sensationalised, exaggerated or false tropes about the target population. In the case of religious rhetoric, certain derogatory monikers deployed in sectarian hate speech depend on highly specific interpretations of religious texts. Common anti-Shiʻa terms include *rawāfiḍ* and *majūsi*, while common anti-Sunni terms include *nawāṣib*. Such terms can easily be classed as disinformation, as their meaning would be refuted by the targets. While this might set up some ontological conflict as to the meaning of disinformation, it is sufficient to term interpretations of metaphysical claims that encourage malice through invoking apostasy as – at the very least – misinformation. Many of the insults stem from *takfir*, that is, the action of declaring a fellow Muslim guilty of apostasy. *Rawāfiḍ*, from the Arabic verb *rafiḍa*, means to reject or to refuse, and is used to denigrate Shiʻa as those who have rejected the true religion of Islam. Similarly, *majūsii* means Zoroastrian, and has a similar weight to accusing someone of being an infidel.[23] Similarly, anti-Sunni slurs often rely on religious interpretations that seek to distort the perceived legitimacy of religious claims by target communities. Such an example includes *nawāṣib*, which is often used to brand Sunnis as those 'who hate the family of Muhammad and are considered non-Muslims'.[24]

An analysis of sectarian hate speech on Twitter reveals that such slurs are not a ubiquitous phenomenon across the Arabic-speaking Twitterverse.[25] As I have argued before:

There is some evidence to suggest that anti-Sunni hate speech on Twitter correlates with those countries that have a larger proportion of Shiʿa as a per cent of the Muslim population. Anti-Shiʿa hate speech might be construed as being more widespread online, transcending national demographic considerations more so than anti-Sunni speech, which still seems to be more proportional to general communal demographics of certain countries.[26]

Twitter accounts in Saudi Arabia and Yemen exhibited the highest number of anti-Shiʿa sectarian slurs per 100,000 members of the population, while Iraq and Yemen exhibited the highest number of anti-Sunni slurs. *Majūsi* and *rawāfiḍ* were by far the most common forms of derogatory speech that could be termed disinformation.

However, bots are playing a key role in spreading sectarian hate speech. While Yaghi generally attributes the promotion of sectarian discourses to satellite channels that are religious in nature, the rise of Saudi24 and its related social media accounts has been more brazen in making sectarianism mainstream. Specifically, it has done this through bots and other deceptive means. This first became apparent in June 2016, when Isa Qassim, a prominent Bahraini Shiʿa cleric, was stripped of his nationality by the Bahrain authorities. The move was condemned by human rights activists, as the Bahrain government had frequently been using de-naturalisation as a form of political repression. Soon after the announcement of Qassim's de-citizenship, dozens of identical tweets from ostensibly unique accounts began defending the decision to revoke his nationality. Specifically, they accused Qassim of being a 'Shi'ite terrorist'. Although most of the tweets were in Arabic, a cluster of accounts began posting identical English tweets smearing Qassim. A search for the words 'Isa Qassim' on Twitter returned hundreds of results in English by unique accounts with Arab men as their avatars. Tweets smearing Qassim appeared every couple of seconds, in both English and Arabic. They were not retweets either, but identical tweets posted as tweets by unique accounts.

Although exact figures are hard to come by, these accounts sent upwards of 10,000 tweets per day between them, completely drowning out conversations by real people on the relevant hashtags. Clearly, the accounts were attempting to spam mentions of Qassim in order to dilute any criticism of the Bahrain regime's decision to revoke his nationality and replace it with attempts to conflate Qassim and Shi'ism, with violence and terrorism. Most of the accounts were posting embedded videos or links to YouTube videos from Saudi 24. Tracking the accounts revealed other aspects of hate. Many of the tweets sought to brand Shi'a figures and the Shi'a sect in general as 'rejectionist of the true Islamic faith' (rawāfiḍ). At specific times of day these accounts would tweet using the hashtags of Gulf countries perceived to have some degree of Iranian influence in their internal politics, most notably #Bahrain and #Yemen. Figure 5 shows a sample of tweets using inflammatory sectarian and anti-Iranian language by bot accounts linked to Saudi 24. Many of the tweets were not only sectarian but sought to conflate Iran's behaviour with that of Daesh.

Fig. 5: Tweets from propaganda accounts and their content[i]

No. of Tweets	English Translation	Original Arabic Tweet
88	Assaults by the deceased terrorist Nimr Al Nimr with the support and direction of the Safavid Persian Iranian regime #leader #faqih	اعتداءات الإرهابي الهالك نمر النمر بدعم وتوجيه من النظام الصفوي الفارسي الإيراني https://t.co/22eXRtES4G ... #Bahrain #القائد# الفقيه
1,511	Safavid Terrorists. #Ayatollah_Isa_Qasim #Shaykh_Isa_Qasim #Withdrawal_of_nationality_ofIsa_Qasim #Bahrain #Faqih #Leader	الإرهابيين الصفويين https://t.co/2Lilk4cgVB ... #آية_الله_قاسم #الشيخ_عيسى_قاسم #سحب_جنسية_عيسى_قاسم #Bahrain #البحرين #القائد# الفقيه

No. of Tweets	English Translation	Original Arabic Tweet
39	Safavid Majusi Terrorist against the country of the Holy Mosques #Withdrawal_of_nationality_ofIsa_Qasim #Bahrain #Faqih #Leader #Bahrain #Isa_Qasim	الارهاب الصفوي المجوسي ضد بلاد الحرمين https://t.co/0Ene5wvu0W #_سحب_جنسية ... #عيسى_قاسم #البحرين #الفقيه# Bahrain #القائد #آية_الله_قاسم
891	Saudi Shia Shaykh reveals truth about Safavid Iran against the Kingdom #Withdrawal_of_nationality_ofIsa_Qasim #Bahrain #Bahrain	الشيخ الشيعي السعودي البلادي يكشف حقيقة ايران الصفوية ضد# المملكة https://t.co/4bRTkx036U #_اسقاط_جنسيه ... #عيسي_قاسم #البحرين #Bahrain
12	Persians and the Majus hate the Arabs #Ayatollah_Qasim #Shaykh_Isa_Qasim #Withdrawal_nationality_isa_qasim #Bahrain #Faqih	الفرس والمجوس ...حقد على العرب https://t.co/7l9MAOhJLE #آية_الله_قاسم# ... #الشيخ_عيسي_قاسم #_سحب_جنسية_عيسى_ #قاسم #البحرين Bahrain# #الفقيه
204	Media report of Safavid lies and distorted facts #Withdrawal_nationality_isa_qasim #Bahrain #Faqih #Leader #Ayatollah_Qasim	تقرير الاعلام الصفوي الكذب وتزييف الحقائق https://t.co/76axOKnfAq #_سحب_جنسية "" عيسى_قاسم #البحرين #الفقيه# Bahrain #القائد #آية_الله_قاسم

No. of Tweets	English Translation	Original Arabic Tweet
481	Removal of Bahraini nationality from Shia Safavid Isa Qasim #withdrawal_of_nationality_of_Isa_Qasim #Bahrain #Faqih #Leader	تواصل.. إسقاط الجنسية البحرينية عن الشيعي الصفوي عيسي قاسم https://t.co/2sD5SOJRIf ... #سحب_جنسية_عيسى #Bahrain #البحرين #قاسم #الفقيه #القائد
254	Da'esh and Iran and their unified discourse #Faqih #Leader #Ayatollah_Qasim #Duraz #Bahrain #closing_of_AlWefaq	داعش وإيران والخطاب الموحد https://t.co/emLlqMUO5f #الفقيه# Bahrain ... #القائد #آية_الله_قاسم #الدراز #البحرين #اغلاق_جمعية_الوفاق
1,413	Video of Safavid terrorists #Ayatollah_Qasim #Shaykh_Isa_Qasim #Bahrain #Faqih #Leader #Ayatollah_Qasim #Dura	فيديو الإرهابيين الصفويين https://t.co/03CQrzHz5z ... #الشيخ# آية_الله_قاسم #البحرين #عيسى_قاسم #الفقيه #Bahrain #آية_الله_قاسم #القائد #الدرا

i Sample of tweets from propaganda accounts tweeting on the #Bahrain hashtag on 28 June. Number of Tweets extracted on 26–29 June 2016 = 10,923; total number of tweets suspected to be 'fake' = 5456; total number of suspected fake accounts = 1754; percentage of tweets to be fake/automated 2016 = 50%.

I made Twitter aware of these bot networks as early as 2016, and they suspended 1,800 accounts. However, Twitter did not suspend them for using hate speech, or indeed disinformation, but for engaging in 'spam-like' behaviour. Although in 2020 Twitter is behaving somewhat more transparently, releasing data dumps of state-backed or media-linked information operations, this was not the case in 2016.

In addition to promoting anti-Shi'a sectarianism, bots connected to Sultan al-Joufi's channels were also active whenever Saudi Arabia provoked controversy in Yemen. The Saudi-led coalition's brutal bombing of Yemen frequently yielded negative coverage of Saudi, and bots would attempt to drown this out. When Saudi fighter jets killed 155 civilians and wounded over 500 at a funeral in the Yemeni capital, Sana'a, a number of hashtags sprang up in the wake of the slaughter. Two of those were 'Massacre at the Great Hall' and 'Sanaa Massacre'.[27] A sample of around 20,000 tweets taken between 18 October and 4 November revealed around 5,682 unique accounts tweeting on the hashtags. In 2016 it was common for automated accounts to utilise the software Tweetdeck, and an analysis of the accounts in the sample using Tweetdeck was startling. Of the 2,692 accounts using it, 2,466 (91%) were most likely bots. This represented around 43% of all accounts in the sample. These accounts 'swamped' the massacre hashtags. Most of the accounts were spreading videos from the al-Joufi-owned al-Shariyyaa, including a clip from a regular talk show called Eye Witness. Other videos included a patriotically framed visit to the Saudi region of Al Jouf, by Major General Mohammed Ali al-Maqdashi, who was aligned with the Saudi-backed and internationally recognised Yemeni president, Ali Abbdurubba Hadi. In the video, al-Maqdashi praised the troops and their bravery, while criticising Iran. The swamping of the hashtag with propaganda was clearly intended to drown out the harrowing images of bomb victims, as well as other potential criticisms of the Saudi-led coalition that could turn domestic and international opinion against the war in Yemen.

Controlling the Domestic News Cycle[28]

In addition to swamping Yemeni and Bahraini hashtags, channels connected to Saudi 24 were attempting to flood the Saudi domestic information sphere with sanitised and apolitical content in order to dominate location-based hashtags. In July 2016, for example, I documented several thousand bot accounts connected to Saudi 24 drowning out a hashtag from Saudis criticising the fact that their country had just granted Egypt a $1.5 billion stimulus package at a time when many Saudis were complaining of the impact of austerity.[29]

Another aspect of the Saudi 24 digital news operation was the running of approximately thirteen regional news accounts on Twitter. The regional accounts largely corresponded to Saudi's thirteen regions and large population centres, including but not limited to the cities and regions of Jeddah, Medina, Mecca, Riyadh, Ha'il, Dammam, al-Ahsa, Abha, Najran, Buraidah, and Ta'if.[30] The names of the accounts reflected what might be considered common Anglophone newspaper names that followed a predictable formula, i.e. [name of place] + [news/today/times/now etc]. For example, *Hail Times* and *Najran Today*. The names of the accounts, along with their followers, are listed in Figure 6.

Fig. 6: Saudi regional news-related Twitter accounts showing changes in number of followers

Account Name	Followers March 2016	Followers July 2019	% decrease
@Hail_times	376,011	38,772	90
@Najran_today	401,573	44,023	89
@Medina_news	392,356	40,711	90
@makhah_now	405,004	48,142	88
@Abha_times	392,596	40,510	90
@damam_news	406,851	47,968	88
@sharqia_times	350,750	31,807	91
@ahsa_today	364,371	37,600	90
@tabuk_times	350,617	37,532	89
@jeddah_news	349,783	32,225	91
@buraidah_news	382,493	*account suspended*	
@jazan_today	354,065	*account suspended*	

Although the accounts generally did not show any sign of being linked, it is difficult to dispute that they were coordinated. An analysis of the metadata indicated that the accounts are linked in terms of both content and management. They were all created on the same date, and for some time all used the same bespoke web app for managing Tweets called Yoonoo. As of 2019 all the accounts switched to Tweetdeck. The content was replicated across all channels. In other words, each account tweets identical news stories, but puts them on one of the 13 specific regional hashtags. Most of the content originates from Saudi 24, indicating that the accounts form part of Saudi 24's news operation. The accounts also tweet the same number of times, at the same time of day. A sample of 26,000 tweets taken between June and September 2019 revealed that the accounts were producing approximately 800 tweets per day on their respective regional hashtags. Another element suggesting that the accounts were manipulated to increase the reach of their message was their clear artificial follower base. As Figure 6 indicates, all of the accounts had a similar number of followers in March 2016. These follower numbers decreased by almost identical amounts (90%) by July 2019, suggesting a harsh cull of fake followers by Twitter. The most likely explanation is that the followers were purchased and have been subsequently removed in one of Twitter's spam purges, again pointing to the high prevalence of fake followers for such news accounts.[31]

An important aspect of the deception here was that the news accounts, despite the illusion of being independent and unrelated to one another, were probably centrally organised by Saudi 24. This was perhaps to give the illusion of independence and a vibrant local news scene. This occurred for several years, until late 2019, when the branding became homogenised. It is difficult to determine the impact of such behaviours. Whether intentional or not, the inevitable impact of the accounts is that they populate regional hashtags with extremely pro-government, and often sectarian, propaganda.

Finding a Botmaster

Despite Twitter's limited takedown in 2016 of 1,800 Saudi 24 bots, its negative reaction to my intervention was alarming, pointing again to the lethargy of the deception order in tackling deception in the

Middle East. The continued activity of Saudi 24 bots suggested that Twitter was unable or unwilling to address the issue of hate speech and propaganda in Arabic. Together with Bill Marczak, from Citizen Lab, I decided to see if we could locate the 'botmaster' responsible for the network. Although it was most probably connected to Saudi 24, it was not clear who was responsible for engineering the social media campaign. However, locating botmasters can provide insights into their modes of operation. As Ferrara et al. have noted, locating 'botmasters' is imperative, 'especially if they are being deployed by governments and other entities for nefarious purposes'.[32] Indeed, it has become 'crucial to reverse engineer the observed social bot strategies: who they target, how they generate content when they take action, and what topics they talk about. A systematic extrapolation of such information may enable identification of the puppet masters.'[33]

There is no silver bullet that can be used to locate botmasters. If it were that easy, there would be fewer bots on the internet. With this in mind, our approach was thus: if we could detect metadata changes in known bot accounts on a large scale, we might have a means of detecting clues, errors, or even patterns in the data that could be traced back to control accounts within the bot network. The first step was to download tweets from hashtags we knew to be highly polluted by bot accounts. In this case, it was the aforementioned regional Saudi hashtags.

Given the high volume of tweets produced by bots, these were stored on an external database. We then examined changes in the metadata over several weeks in the latter part of 2016. We had noticed prior to this that the application being used to tweet kept changing its name, presumably to evade suspension by Twitter. By locating chronologically the first account that tweeted following the creation of a new application, we found an account that appeared to be the originator of the network. The account belonged to an AC Milan fan with the handle @katomilan. Permutations of Kato and Milan, such as twitkato, and twitmilan, were used to name the applications. Searching the internet for the username @katomilan yielded important results. First, we found a site called khamsat, a place where people in the Arab world can buy and sell services. Here katomilan had advertised a piece of software he had designed that essentially allows for the mass automation and creation of Twitter accounts. This software was called Diavolo, meaning 'devil' in Italian. Diavolo was a software that integrated with a Microsoft Excel macro to send automated tweets from any number of pre-created Twitter accounts. In short, it allowed the user to send thousands of tweets via bots. A screenshot included on one of katomilan's pages indicated that it was the same bots that had been promoting Saudi 24 content, while also magnifying the Twitter profile of Sultan al-Joufi. A subsequent search for katomilan also led to the Facebook page of one Ali Milan,[34] an Egyptian living on the Mediterranean coast.

After I contacted Ali Milan via Facebook, he revealed that Saudi 24 and its related channels used Diavolo to promote their content. After I put him in touch with a team from Al Jazeera, Ali also stated that '[The channels] wanted their videos to reach as many viewers as they could. So, they published them on Twitter, and my job then was to create so many Twitter accounts and publish the videos through each account.'[35] Ali was not entirely forthcoming about his activities, and underestimated the scale of the bot problem he had created: 'Al Jazeera also found Diavolo's developer selling Twitter followers on a website – 5,000 followers for $10 – indicating he controlled more than just the 400 accounts he claimed he used. When confronted with these findings, the man no longer responded to Al Jazeera's questions.'[36]

Despite its crudeness, the Saudi24 bot network has proved resilient. By July 2018 there were still more than 4,000 bots promoting Saudi 24 content. Periodic suspensions by Twitter seemed unable to tame them, and they frequently reappeared, often promoting propaganda linked directly to the Saudi state. In October 2019, on the anniversary of the killing of journalist Jamal Khashoggi, the accounts spammed the Khashoggi hashtag with irrelevant content talking about how expatriate workers enjoyed working in Saudi. Unmolested by Twitter, the bots survived well into December 2019, when Mohammed Saeed Alshamrani, a Saudi aviation student and second lieutenant in the Saudi Air Force, killed three US Navy personnel at Pensacola Naval Air Station in Florida. The shooting was treated as terror related, and was particularly sensitive as Alshamrani had been at the base as part of a Pentagon-sponsored security cooperation agreement between Saudi Arabia and the United States. Following the shooting, bots began spamming the 'Florida shooting' hashtag with content from Saudi 24, including tweets that sought to emphasise the positive relations between Saudi and the USA as well as Saudi's commitment to fighting terrorism. Several hundred copypasta tweets read, 'The Saudi and American are friends that share good values.' Another tweet read, 'The Saudi leadership has always supported and called for moderation and fighting the terrorism.'[37] The crude affirmation of Saudi's commitment to fighting terrorism came at a time when propaganda from the KUBE bloc was attempting to transfer the blame of Gulf-backed Islamic terrorism to Qatar and Iran.

The locating of a botmaster revealed that disinformation operations are not necessarily as high level or sophisticated as they might seem. A programmer from Egypt had an automated solution that was then used to disseminate aggressively nationalistic and sectarian content. It just so happened that the regulatory and ideological environment in which the bots operated allowed them to flourish.

Conclusion: An Autonomous Pseudo-Civil Society

This chapter has explored how the successful censorship of critical voices online has left the digital space vulnerable to the pseudo-isation of civil society with automatons – the ultimate tyrannical fantasy. The granting of citizenship to Sophia was a symbolic blow to the digital public sphere. The automaton represented the ideal authoritarian citizen: 'The symbolic power of giving subservient automatons citizenship is the authoritarian fantasy – for automatons can represent the ideal citizen, emotionless, subservient, programmable and predictable.'[38] The boundaries of the public sphere have long been discussed by theorists from Arendt to Lyotard, and although few have considered the potential role of automatons and artificial intelligence on this space, their impact on public discussion in the Arabic-speaking Twittersphere is increasingly becoming clear. Indeed, the space for critical public debate is being compromised by automated loyal denizens and automated journoganda, all of which have contributed to drowning out or steering genuine public discussion. This has resulted in the creation of a public sphere simulacra, one in which an illusion or simulation of active public debate is created by electronic flies. As Keller and Klinger note, 'the presence of software actors deliberately designed to manipulate popularity cues or contributions totally undermines the notion of a public sphere.'[39]

Bots can be deployed on a much larger scale than trolls, as they do not require as much human manpower. However, their functionality is different, and their purpose is less to engage with critics than to promote discourses, accounts and certain narratives through amplification. However, rapid developments in AI pose new dangers to the digital public sphere, the shared mediated space where we can interact with fellow netizens. Hundreds of thousands, perhaps millions, of automated accounts across the Persian Gulf continue to dominate online discussions, repressing conversations by real people to give a misleading illusion of public discussion. As bots become more sophisticated in their ability to fool humans into thinking they are real, we will need to remain especially vigilant. Crowding out genuine public discussion with top-down, artificial, regime-friendly and politically sanitised messaging is especially dangerous when that information is adversarial or hate speech. This type of information is divisive and can foster the type of thinking that promotes violent conflict and sustains tyranny.

PART III

TRUMP AND THE WAR ON REALITY IN THE GULF

5

THE US RIGHT-WING–SAUDI ANTI-IRAN NEXUS

Chapter Overview

The Trump administration's policy of maximum pressure on Iran was a jarring reversal of US policy in the Middle East, and has been the proximate cause in much of the Gulf-oriented disinformation since 2017. The post-truth moment in the Middle East has been profoundly influenced by the changing US–Iran relationship, itself supported by the desire of the UAE, Saudi and Israel in particular to maintain an economic and military stranglehold on Iran. The need to legitimise an about-turn in the wake of years of Obama-era diplomacy necessitated a massive influence operation to convince people that such a reversal was now a more 'favourable' policy. Here, the magnitude of the information operation reflects the perceived difficulty in mobilising a new discourse antithetical to that which preceded it. This chapter highlights how the Trump administration's abandonment of the Joint Comprehensive Plan of Action (JCPOA) has spawned a wealth of deception operations that have created 'deception synergies' between the US right and those in the Gulf wishing to contain Iran. In these 'synergies', the American right, the US government, the Iranian opposition and Saudi-connected sockpuppets have created a mutually reinforcing melange of disinformation. The chapter also notes the efforts on Saudi social media to generate Saudi support for the Trump administration, no mean feat considering his strong Islamophobic stance.

Saudis for Trump

Iran, Trump and social media discussions about Iranian politics on Twitter have tended to reflect the degradation in US–Iranian relations. Under Trump, the US relationship with Iran soured significantly as the Trump administration sought to exert a policy of 'maximum pressure'. This has had drastic and tragic consequences for most Iranians. Indeed, as Tyler Cullis noted, a policy of 'siege and starve' may better characterise the Trump administration's round of financial sanctions launched towards the end of 2020.[1] Trump had not been in the White House long before Michael Flynn, his then national security advisor, announced that he was putting Iran 'on notice' after an Iranian missile test.[2] While analysts struggled to determine what was meant by 'on notice', it became clear that Trump sought to dismantle Obama's legacy of diplomatic engagement with Iran by reinstating sanctions and pulling out of the JCPOA. Under JCPOA, the Iranian nuclear programme was restricted in return for ending sanctions.

The Trump administration's abandonment of the JCPOA deal and resurrection of new sanctions created a renewed animosity between the two states. As such, both American- and Iranian-led disinformation campaigns have increased profoundly since 2016. Trump's election sparked a new wave of disinformation accounts discussing Iran. As Azadeh Moaveni, a fellow at New America, noted:

> The turning point was really Trump's elections. Once it became clear from the outset that there would be re-heightened hostility with Iran, there was a profusion of new accounts, anonymous accounts, who were very single-mindedly and purposefully going after people who wrote about, talked about Iran with nuance. The majority of it is abusive, libellous, ad hominem and intended to silence.[3]

This highlights the perhaps obvious truism that an increase in political hostilities also results in an increasing amount of disinformation and propaganda. This was compounded by the Trump administration's support of the Mujahedin e-Khalq (MEK), an exiled Iranian political organisation intent on overthrowing the current Iranian regime, which also seems to be producing a lot of the more virulent disinformation. In addition to this, much of the Iran-focused disinformation has emanated from the Arab-speaking Gulf, most notably the UAE and Saudi. Indeed, the USA, Israel, the UAE and Saudi have come together on their shared desire to contain Iran and undermine its support for the Houthi rebels in Yemen.

The disinformation campaigns followed lock-step after the Trump administration fired its first warning shots. After Flynn had briefed reporters in the White House about putting Iran 'on notice', Saudi Twitter erupted with a number of English-language hashtags, including 'Trump warns Iranian aggression' and 'Trump Will Destroy Iran'. Imagine if you will, an image of Donald Trump, decked out in gilded armour, holding the hammer of Thor, which he uses to crush Khomeini's head superimposed on the body of the loveable Nintendo character Luigi.[4] This is not a bad dream, but a taste of the pro-Trump propaganda that emanated from Saudi at the beginning of his presidency in 2017. While the image may seem absurd, it was intended as flattery, one of many posts extolling and lionising Trump's policy of 'maximum pressure' on Iran. The gleeful hashtags also included bizarre fan art, such as images of Trump's head superimposed on a Spartan warrior, or Ayatollah Ali Khameini's head floating above one of the Twin Towers. Turki al-Dakhil, the head of Saudi's Al Arabiya news network, encouraged users to tweet on the hashtag: 'Use this hashtag #TrumpWarnsIranianTerrorism and comment in English to thank Trump for his stance in confronting Iranian Terrorism.'[5] It looked as if Saudis were cheering on Trump's aggressive stance towards Iran.

However, analysis of the tweets on both the 'Trump Warns Iranian Terrorism' and 'Trump Will Destroy Iran' hashtags reveals that the campaign was predominantly led and amplified by bots designed to encourage a discourse of pro-Trumpism amongst the Saudi public. A sample of 7,066 unique Twitter accounts tweeting on both hashtags was extracted on 11 and 12 February 2017. Many of the accounts were suspended very soon after the trend began. As of 2020, approximately 92% or 6,500 of the accounts no longer exist as they did, with a large proportion of that number likely to have been suspended.[6] Despite this, the extent of the 'breakout' of the news was significant. The left-leaning website AlterNet published an article titled '"Trump will destroy Iran!" Saudis cheer on anti-Muslim president'.[7] Although the article offered a vague qualification that 'at least some of these accounts are bots or paid trolls',[8] the framing was generally that the campaign was organic, promoting the notion that the Saudi street was supportive not simply of increased pressure towards Iran – but perhaps war. The bellicose nature of the tweets, especially those using the 'Trump will destroy Iran' hashtag, could be construed as condoning war with Iran, a propaganda tactic that would theoretically fall foul of the International Covenant on Civil and Political Rights (ICCPR) prohibition of 'propaganda for war', and thus potentially be in breach of international law. The fact is, the organic takeup of the hashtag was minimal, falsely giving the impression of widespread grassroots support for a war. Nonetheless, it clearly was once again a steer to Saudi netizens that they should support the new US president, despite his administration's clear hostility to Muslims.

The IranDisinfo Project

While Saudi bots were promoting Trump's aggressive stance towards Iran, those critical of Trump's approach and the rescinding of the JCPOA were facing increasing harassment online. As Ellie Geranmayeh of the European Council on Foreign Relations noted, 'the only thing #Iran watchers agree on is [that the] debate space is toxic'.[9] Indeed, many analysts and academics writing about Iran are targeted for simply not being militaristic in their stance and demanding regime change in Iran.[10]

Although such online abuse is unfortunately prevalent in almost every domain of politics, what sets the Iranian case apart is that the debate space was deliberately turned into a toxic bullying arena by the US government. Indeed, a substantial amount of the disinformation, deception and harassment targeting Iranian commentators seems to have emanated from the Iran Disinformation Project, an endeavour that was launched in 2018 and funded by the US State Department's Global Engagement Center in order to counter foreign propaganda.

On 25 April 2019 the IranDisinfo's Twitter account accused Tara Sepehri Far, a researcher for Human Rights Watch, of focusing too much on the impact of US sanctions on the lives of ordinary Iranians.[11] This prompted accusations that a State Department-funded entity was trolling a private citizen conducting valid human rights research. The furore surrounding the incident prompted IranDisinfo to delete a number of its problematic tweets. The scandal reached such a pitch that the US State Department announced that it had then cut funding for the project, while at the same time stating that some of the activities of the project had fallen outside the scope of tackling foreign propaganda.[12]

Much of the funding for IranDisinfo came from the Global Engagement Center, which had originally been set up to counter Russian and Daesh-related propaganda. Brett Bruen, the director of global engagement under Obama, stated that it had been starved of funds under Trump, with an operating budget of only $20 million. In February 2019, several months prior to the abusive tweets, Lea Gabrielle, a former journalist for the right-wing news outlet Fox News, had been hired to run IranDisinfo.[13] It was unclear if this was a political appointment, but it raised concerns that Trump's aggressive anti-Iranian policies would find ideological succour in the corridors of state institutions. Bruen also stated that the Global Engagement Center was being used to attack both the Iran nuclear deal and the Iranian government itself. He added that the 'Trump administration treat it like it is a reserve for dipping in to for pet political projects'.[14]

The Iran Disinformation Project overlapped with another pro-Israel Washington-based think tank, the Foundation for Defense of Democracies (FDD). According to journalist Eli Clifton:

> Buried on FDD's website is an 'Iran Disinformation Project' that publishes the identical content from Ghasseminejad [an FDD employee] that was cross-posted on IranDisInfo's website. And on at least five occasions, FDD's Twitter account promoted

articles by Ghasseminejad 'in @IranDisInfo'. Except the links didn't send users to IranDisInfo's website. Instead, the links were to FDD's own 'Iran Disinformation Project,' hosted on FDD's website.[15]

At times it seemed as if the FDD and IranDisinfo were one and the same. Indeed, Tyler Cullis described FDD as the 'brains trust' of the Trump administration's Iran policy, often recycling Israeli – and specifically, the right-wing/centre-right Likud party's – talking points on foreign policy. The seeming overlap would become clear later in 2020 when it was reported in Responsible Statecraft that two congressional sources confirmed that Saeed Ghasseminejad was in fact, a contractor on the Iran Disinformation Project.[16]

Other journalists covering Iran have complained about being trolled, harassed and attacked online by Ghasseminejad. Golnar Motevalli, an Iran reporter for Bloomberg, stated, 'An employee of this organization [the FDD] has targeted me along with several colleagues who cover Iran on Twitter over the years. Most of it started during the late 2017/early 2018 protests in Iran. This individual also encouraged others to harass and troll reporters online.'[17] Shanam Shantyaei, formerly a senior journalist at France24, publicly came out about her harassment in 2020: 'It's unfortunate that so many of us covering the Iran file, in and out of the county, have been targeted by this individual. For my part, it's the first time that I'm publicly addressing it.'[18] Negar Mortazavi, a journalist for the UK's *Independent* newspaper, wrote, 'This FDD staffer has attacked many of us journalists as well as analysts and academics working on Iran, particularly targeting women. And there has never been any apology or explanation from @FDD where this cyber harassment seems to be condoned.'[19]

The tropes focused on by the Iran Disinformation Project included accusing certain journalists of being 'mouthpieces' of the Iranian regime. One such journalist was the BBC's Bahram Kalbasi.[20] Kalbasi was not alone, in the sense that the BBC, in particular, was a target for numerous online smear campaigns by unknown actors. There have been a series of online social media attacks, or 'Twitter storms', targeting BBC Persian. On 24 May 2020 at least 5,500 accounts launched tens of thousands of tweets criticizing BBC Persian using the hashtag #IslamicRepublicOfBBC. Many of the accounts influential on the hashtag were anonymous, potentially indicating that they could be sockpuppets or in some cases bots. In general, they seemed to be pro-Trump and Iranian accounts supporting the Iranian monarchy, signalling a particularistic right-wing bent to the campaign. However, the campaign was reported on by FDD's Saeed Ghasseminejad, who accused the BBC of being effective against Ahmadinejad, but not Rafsanjani.[21] Again, the campaign fitted the modus operandi of attacking those not seen as militaristic enough in their criticism of Iran.[22] It also reflected the Zeitgeist of right-wing populism at the time, attacking legitimate media outlets. After writing about the Twitter storm, I was also attacked by dozens of anti-Iranian regime accounts for suggesting that the activity might be coordinated. Indeed, such is the phenomenon of this particular toxicity that even Rob Macaire, the British ambassador to Iran, weighed in on the debate via Twitter, essentially arguing that BBC provoked such controversy because, in its attempts to pursue impartiality, it irked both supporters and opponents of the government.[23]

The Foundation for the Defense of Democracies and Weaponising Concern for LGBTQ Issues

As well as Twitter storms and attacks on activists by anonymous accounts, other FDD staff also engaged in intimidation of those perceived to be critical of normalisation with Israel, and broader attempts to criticise the containment of Iran by the USA, the UAE and Saudi Arabia. The tropes used in cyberbullying are often dependent on the perceived impact they will have on the social group of the intended target. Accusations of promiscuity are often made against women activists in the Middle East, on the basis that such insults would resonate strongly in the context of a regional audience. For other critics of specific regimes in the region, adaptations have to be made in the light of how the attackers view the political sensibilities of the victim. After all, the aim is to paint the targets as deviant within the community of people whose validation they seek.

For many academics who are viewed as socially and politically liberal, accusations of hypocrisy need to be premised on the assumptions that they are violating specific moral convictions and those of the community to whom they feel ideologically attached. In 2020 I and other academics were subject to an adversarial harassment campaign by Benjamin Weinthal, a research fellow at the FDD. Weinthal's attack directly followed my own publication in the left-leaning Israeli newspaper *Haaretz,* which critiqued the recent UAE–Israel normalisation deal. I argued that the normalisation was a publicity stunt intended to bolster the political chances of Donald Trump, Mohammed bin Zayed, and Benjamin Netanyahu. After publication, I received an unsolicited tweet from Weinthal, who accused me of being a 'zealous advocate' for the Qatari Ministry of Foreign Affairs. (Clearly this was scurrilous, as I am a professor.)

Over the next 48 hours on 2 and 3 September, Weinthal sent me a tirade of around 90 tweets, most of them repeating the same questions demanding to know my stance on Qatar's laws pertaining to homosexuality. He also made numerous unfounded and scurrilous accusations of homophobia, such as 'Marc does not oppose Qatar's death penalty for gays'. He tagged others in these tweets in order to maximise their audience. During Weinthal's invective, he made numerous baseless claims against academics who lived in Qatar, or whom he perceived as sympathetic to the Qatari government. He implied that Andreas Krieg, a professor at King's College London, was a Nazi sympathiser, having previously accused him of working for 'Doha'. In August 2019 Weinthal launched a similar attack on Justin Martin, another Qatar-based academic, demanding that Martin make public his views on LGBT rights in Qatar.

Although Weinthal has written several articles in support of LGBT communities in the Middle East, for the FDD and other outlets, his harassment of academics risked endangering minorities while purporting to be a defence of gay rights. Indeed, if a primary aspect of Weinthal's argument is that the LGBTQ community is in jeopardy in a particular country, then constantly baiting someone living there to clarify their views on a topic that he believes to be life-threatening might prove risky for them. Furthermore, without Weinthal knowing the sexuality of those he is interrogating, there is also a risk of endangering someone in the LGBTQ community whose rights he claims to be defending. Weinthal was eventually censured by Twitter for violating its hateful conduct policy.[24]

With emerging evidence that the FDD had been part of IranDisinfo's attack on Iranian commentators, it also became clear that Weinthal had a track record of harassment on Middle East-related issues. Weinthal has previously targeted supporters of the Boycott, Divestment and Sanctions movement. Writing in Mondoweiss, journalist Jonathan Ofir noted that witch hunts were 'pet projects' of Weinthal's.[25] Weinthal has also been caught on camera admitting to 'exaggerating' when attacking those he perceives as critical of Israel, in order to get his point across.[26] Weinthal's tweeting habits certainly reflect an anti-Qatar bias and demonstrate that he is selective about which Gulf states he mentions. A corpus analysis of Weinthal's tweets between May 2011 and September 2020 showed that he had only tweeted about the UAE approximately 73 times, while he mentioned Qatar approximately 900 times, a pattern that increased markedly from August 2019. His concern with LGBT rights seems to largely exclude the UAE, despite the fact that their laws pertaining to homosexuality are barely different from those in Qatar.[27]

Weinthal's selective harassment of academics highlights an alarming use of 'disinformation as harassment', and raises further questions about an ongoing relationship between the UAE and the FDD (which is elaborated on in the following chapter). Given that the FDD was founded to 'enhance Israel's image in North America',[28] it makes sense that it should be aligned with a country (the UAE) seen as being the regional leader in encouraging normalisation with Israel while promoting the isolation of Iran. The reckless endangerment, a general lack of journalistic ethics and open harassment undertaken by FDD employees in attacking those who oppose their anti-Iran, pro-Israel and now pro-UAE stance on Middle East politics reflect an increasingly brazen effort to silence criticism, itself abetted by Trump's normalisation of online harassment.[29] Indeed, the FDD was showing itself to be an increasingly important actor in the new wave of MENA-focused digital authoritarianism.

MEK and Make Iran Great Again

In the age of Twitter, the distance between public figures and nebulous political entities is only a retweet away. Donald Trump, whose constant tweeting has fuelled many a political scandal, also appeared to endorse hawkish views from right-wing Iranian accounts of questionable provenance. Given Trump's huge following, his tweeting of disinformation or propaganda was clearly going to be a huge boost to whosoever's message he was promoting. Most notably, Trump retweeted Heshmat Alavi, an influential Twitter account purporting to be an expert analyst on Iranian affairs.[30] However, Hassan Heyrani, a high-level defector from the Mujahedin e-Khalq (MEK), told the news organisation The Intercept that Alavi is actually 'a persona run by a team of people from the political wing of the MEK'. Heyrani added, 'They [those who operate Alavi's account] write whatever they are directed by their commanders and use this name to place articles in the press. This is not and has never been a real person.'[31]

According to Heyrani, the account is run by three different people. Heyrani's testimony was confirmed by another MEK Canada-based defector, Reza Sadeghi. Despite the deceptive nature of Alavi's account, his articles have been published in well-established news outlets, including Forbes, the Daily Caller and the Diplomat. None of the editors interviewed by the Intercept were actually able to confirm that they spoke to Alavi, raising concerns that they did not adequately verify his identity before accepting submissions. As documented in Chapter 8, the trend of not verifying contributors is an avoidable, but persistent, problem. Between April 2017 and April 2018 Alavi published 61 articles on the Forbes Website. Unsurprisingly, Alavi's editorial stance was predictable: staunch criticism of the current regime while at the same time advocating a new leadership under Maryam Rajavi, the leader of MEK.

The fact Alavi might have been a MEK account run by a number of operatives is not surprising in and of itself. An interview by Al Jazeera's Listening Post with two MEK defectors highlighted how MEK members based in the organisation's Albanian headquarters were encouraged to tweet pro-MEK propaganda. Heyrani noted that

MEK members in the Tirana HQ received daily orders and that it was 'their duty' to praise anti-regime comments issued by politicians across the globe. Conversely, anyone who was not sufficiently critical of the Iranian regime, or anyone who criticised MEK, were subject to attacks by MEK's troll farm. Hassan Shabaz, another former MEK member, told Al Jazeera that anyone seen as remotely sympathetic to the Iranian regime would be called things like 'exported soldiers of the mullah's regime'.[32]

Trump's then-national security advisor, John Bolton, had reportedly been cosying up to MEK. This tacit endorsement in part contributed to what seemed like a US right-wing digital ecosystem for the promotion of anti-Iranian propaganda. A corpus analysis of the biographical data of Alavi's 67,000 Twitter followers revealed a number of interesting things, but most notably his support by a large proportion of far-right conspiracy theorists and pro-Trump accounts. The most cohesive community was a group of accounts with extremely pro-Trump and alt-right biographies: 27% of Alavi's followers had either MAGA (Make America Great Again), KAG (Keep America Great), or WWG1WGA (Where we go one, we go all). The most frequently reported biographical description of Alavi's followers was MAGA, followed by KAG followed by WWG1WGA.

While the first two slogans can be generally described as being broadly pro-Trump; the acronym WWG1WGA is more often associated with QAnon, or Q. Q started as a fringe online conspiracy theory, although it has emerged as a political force, with its followers believing that 'a high-ranking, anonymous government official called "Q" is providing top-secret information in internet posts about a cannibalistic, satanic cabal of "Deep State" actors engaged in a child trafficking ring that Trump has been chosen to dismantle'.[33] Some of QAnon's wilder notions include the belief that liberal politicians such as the Clintons are harvesting and oxidising children's blood after torturing them in order to make a super drug called Adrenochrome. Around 24 US political candidates[34] have endorsed the movement, with the *New York Times* arguing that Trump has 'all but endorsed' QAnon.[35] QAnon was seen as so harmful that Facebook, after years of avoiding the issue, said it would remove any account, page or group openly identifying with it.[36]

It is somewhat unusual, then, that an account purporting to be an Iranian dissident has at least 3,375 followers with the term 'WWG1WGA' in their biographies. Although it is possible that a large number of these accounts are sockpuppets or trolls, it is curious to see the overlap between the American right and an MEK Twitter account. Alavi's following raises questions. Do they follow Alavi organically or were they given a steer by influencers (and Trump) that Alavi is a 'legitimate' voice on Iranian politics? Why is it that so many follow him? In the large Twitterverse of Iranian commentators, why is Alavi disproportionately and organically favoured by Trump supporters? It is probable that Trump retweeting Alavi has the impact of endorsing him as an 'on message' person whose opinions can be trusted, and thus replicated by Trump supporters. Another more realistic assumption is that the online MAGA community is an amorphous combination of legitimate Trump fans and suspicious accounts. Suspicious accounts facilitate the promotion of Alavi's message within the organic community in order to spread MEK propaganda and generate support among the American public for MEK's goals.

Another Iranian movement to leverage US right-wing Twitter users was Restart. Led by Trump fan Seyed Mohammad Hosseini, an Iranian game show host living in the USA, Restart adopted alt-right tropes and advocated for attacks on mosques and police stations in Iran.[37] The movement began using the hashtag Make Iran Great Again, tapping into the Trump rallying cry. The movement gained further attention after Trump said 'Make Iran Great Again'. According to Adrienne Cobb, 'it is now not uncommon to see QAnon's hashtags co-mingling with Make Iran Great Again'.[38] The reality of this mix that some might see as benign, albeit irritating, is that it magnifies the already loud calls for war and violence in Iran.

The Rand Corporation has reported that the National Council of Resistance of Iran (NCRI), a coalition based in Albania that includes MEK, received funding from Saudi Arabia.[39] Turki al-Faisal, a former Saudi intelligence chief, even addressed an MEK rally, as did Salman al-Ansari, head of a pro-Riyadh lobbyist outfit, Saudi American Public Relations Affairs Committee (SAPRAC). This nexus of anti-Iran entities, from the US Administration, MEK, Saudi and the UAE, together with think tanks such as the FDD, contributed to a fertile environment for deception on MENA politics. The nexus frequently overlapped (see Chapter 14), with sockpuppet accounts purporting to be Westerners publicly condemning Iran while supporting Saudi Arabia and the UAE. One such account, claiming to be a doctor called Jhon Whiliams, used a stolen photo of an American music teacher to attack Iran and launch sectarian attacks against the Shi'a. It even ranked the best and worst countries in the Middle East. Naturally Iran was the worst, and Saudi and UAE the best.[40] It was accounts like this that, according to Mahsa Ali Mardani, an internet researcher focusing on Iran, highlighted the nexus of 'MEK online disinfo and Saudi disinfo'.[41] Underpinning much of this deception were clear steers from Saudi influencers and sockpuppets that Trump's policy on Iran, and MEK advocates such as Heshmat Alavi, should be promoted by Saudi citizens and troll farms. This not only contributes to boosting the signal of specific anti-Iran disinformation operations, but also risks generating a growing 'organic' overlap between the US alt right and Gulf-based citizens.

Pro-Iran Disinformation

As propaganda often begets propaganda, and increased political tensions generate propaganda, it is no surprise that the Trump administration's withdrawal from the JCPOA and implementation of renewed sanctions against Iran prompted an increase in Iranian deception operations. With Arabic sockpuppet accounts and influencers based in the UAE and Saudi praising Trump, the Iranian authorities decided to launch their own influence operations targeting Arabic-speaking audiences. In December 2018 Reuters published an investigation that revealed how Iran-linked actors were running a deception campaign where 70 websites were pushing pro-Iranian propaganda to 15 different countries.[42] One of the websites, Nile Net Online, targeted Egyptian audiences, producing news content that contradicted the heavily state-controlled Egyptian media. Nile Net claimed to be headquartered in Cairo, although Egyptians familiar with the address on its Facebook page said they had never heard of the outlet. Most of the content being pushed by the 70 or so websites was being produced by the International Union of Virtual Media (IUVM), an online agency based in Tehran. The intended audiences for the propaganda were based in the following countries, listed according to the number of websites dedicated to each place: Yemen (10); Syria (5); Afghanistan (4); Pakistan (4); the UK (3); Egypt (2); Iran (2); Palestine (2); Turkey (2); the USA (2); Indonesia (1); Iraq (1); Israel (1); Russia (1); and Sudan (1).[43] The real-world impact of the disinformation was felt when one of the fake sites, AWDnews, 'ran a false story in 2016 which prompted Pakistan's defence minister to warn on Twitter he had the weapons to nuke Israel'.[44]

Iranian information operations have frequently targeted Donald Trump. In October 2018 Facebook took down 82 pages, groups and accounts linked to an Iranian deception campaign.[45] The pages had over 1 million followers between them; many shared memes mocking the US president. Many of the groups even arranged events, which a number of Facebook users had expressed interest in attending.[46] Another likely Iranian-linked Facebook page was called 'the British left'. Interestingly, it makes sense that the Iranians would target the left, where they would be more likely to find a sympathetic audience, receptive to tropes revolving around Western imperialism.[47] As the Working Group on Syria, Propaganda and Media has demonstrated, even academics in the UK can find themselves supporting probably pro-Russian and, by proxy, pro-Iranian deception operations.

Although it has been argued by Graham Brooke of the Atlantic Council's Digital Forensic Research Lab[48] that Iranian disinformation tends to try and generate support for the Iranian worldview on international affairs, as opposed to Russian deception operations, which are more inclined to play both sides in order to generate polarisation, this is not strictly true. Indeed, it is often hard to make such generalisations. Deception operations are like anything else; people often learn from others. One particularly bizarre Iranian deception operation left off where the Russians had started, and attempted to support the movement advocating for the secession of California from the United States.[49] In early April 2020 at least 8,000 Iran-connected accounts, and at least 600 accounts seemingly set up in the month of April for the sole purpose of engaging on the campaign, tweeted on the hashtag #CalExit (California Exi).[50] Prior to this, in 2016, accounts linked to the Russian Internet Research Agency were found to be promoting the CalExit hashtag.[51] Indeed, like supporting Brexit, the Russian deception modus operandi was to promote causes that could weaken the sovereignty or unity of its enemies. Many of the most influential Iranian accounts promoting CalExit were soon suspended by Twitter.

Pro-Iran disinformation has also tended to receive more coverage in the mainstream press, partly due to the fact that US foreign policy concerns led to corollary pressure on social media companies to take action against propaganda from the country's perceived enemies. This has been demonstrated in the relative asymmetry with which US government entities mobilise resources to tackle Iran-linked disinformation campaigns. In October 2020 US prosecutors 'seized a network of web domains which they said were used in a campaign by Iran's Revolutionary Guard Corps (IRGC) to spread political disinformation around the world'.[52] The 92 domains were reportedly 'used by the IRGC to pose as independent media outlets targeting audiences in the United States, Europe, the Middle East and South-East Asia'.[53] These efforts are rarely directed at other key deception actors, such as Saudi Arabia, for example.

Conclusion

A key aspect of the Gulf's post-truth moment has been a resurgent wave of digital disinformation dedicated to supporting international isolation of Iran. Anti-Iranian disinformation, of course, is not new. Transatlantic security concerns, which have generally emphasised the isolation of Iran since the overthrow of the Shah in 1979, have tended to result in an understandable emphasis on human rights abuses in Iran. Iran has also been used as the regional bogeyman and the perpetual *éminence grise* in numerous Middle East conflicts. Of course, many of these stories are entirely true, but many are false. For example, during 2011 there was a string of false stories claiming that boats heading to Bahrain from Iran had been intercepted.[54] For states in the Persian Gulf, it has been convenient to seek to blame all wrongdoing on Iran. However, recent propaganda efforts, in particular, are striking in their audacity. One such trope, pushed forward by former vice president Mike Pence even involved trying to portray Iran as being implicated in the 9/11 attacks.[55]

In addition to this, the rise of the post-truth age amidst a wave of right-wing populism has been the proximate cause in a renewed modality of Iran-related disinformation. This is not simply reflected by the existence of such campaigns, but their very methodology. For example, a US State Department campaign that attacks American citizens not critical enough of the Iranian regime seems to have been made in the mould of Trump himself, whose frequent ad hominem attacks on opponents have been unprecedented in recent US history. Attempts by pro-Iranian regime change deception operations to influence right-wing Americans and beat the drums of war also indicates an alarming attempt to direct public opinion to support military action against Iran. However, just as the election of Trump ushered in the appearance of thousands of new anti-Iranian regime accounts, regional conflicts such as Saudi and UAE involvement in Yemen, Iranian interference in Syria and Turkish and Emirate proxy wars in Libya have brought with them attendant campaigns to win hearts and minds through digital deception operations.

Although the Iranian regime is, like any large and powerful actor, a sophisticated cyber-actor and purveyor of propaganda and disinformation, the Trump administration's abandonment of rapprochement through the JCPOA prompted a new wave of hostile disinformation. According to Bjola and Papadakis, 'the goal of disinformation is to strategically influence decision-makers to pursue a pre-determined course of action in international affairs by altering their set of policy preferences or, if that's not possible, by paralysing or neutralising foreign policy decision-making processes'.[56] With this being the case, it is self-evident that severe ruptures to previous courses of foreign policy will necessitate a deluge of disinformation and propaganda in order to radically re-align the expectations of the target audience. After years of the USA and Gulf/Iranian governments attempting to convince people that JCPOA was a good idea, to abruptly justify tearing it up inevitably requires significant input of persuasion resources. With general consensus that JCPOA was in the best interests of pursuing peace, arguments justifying further sanctions floundered, and thus necessitated partial truths or scare-mongering. When such policies reflect a limited set of interest groups, such as the UAE, Saudi Arabia and Israel, it is perhaps no surprise that the struggle to rationalise such policy positions requires significant deception.

6

THE GULF CRISIS NEVER HAPPENED

PSEUDO-EVENTS AND PSEUDO-PUBLICS

Chapter Overview

This chapter documents how the Gulf Crisis was a watershed in the region's post-truth moment. The scale of the disinformation operation launched in order to establish and legitimise the blockade, or embargo, of the Gulf state Qatar solidified the reputation of KUBE countries, but particularly Saudi Arabia and the United Arab Emirates, as key projectors of digital media power in the region. The crisis was premised on a hack and a number of simulated pseudo-events. Here pseudo-events refer to Boorstin's concept of pre-planned and staged moments designed to appear spontaneous and gather further press coverage.[1] In the Gulf Crisis the blockading countries attempted to give the illusion of aggression on the part of Qatar. But the influence operation around the Qatar Crisis took Boorstin's definition further, and the resultant use of PR companies, social media bots and trolls created pseudo-publics, a simulated civil society response and largely artificial creation of public opinion and hostility towards Qatar. It also marked the most salient moment of the 'creation of the enemy' within the new Gulf post-truth moment, an 'axis of evil' in which Qatar, its media, Turkey and the Muslim

Brotherhood are portrayed as the hostile forces. By contrast, it also attempted to position the KUBE countries as forces for good, combating global terrorism and extremism.

The Cyberattack on Qatar

In the early hours of 23 May 2017 Qatari state television reported that the country's emir, Tamim bin Hamad Al Thani, had made a controversial speech at a military graduation ceremony.[2] The quotes attributed to the emir praised Islamist groups, Hamas, Hezbollah and the Muslim Brotherhood, and also appeared on Qatar News Agency's (QNA) social media accounts.[3] Most controversially, the emir affirmed good relations with Iran, Saudi Arabia's arch-rival. The timing was important, as the US president Donald Trump had just visited Riyadh, and so the comments were perceived as an attempt to snub Mohammed bin Salman's attempts to isolate Iran with the support of the new US president.

To the layperson, such comments might seem insignificant. But to analysts of the Gulf or diplomats based in the region, the context was important. For a member of the Gulf Cooperation Council to publicly profess any sort of rapprochement with Iran was a political taboo. The reported comments set off a chain of events that proceeded to shape the political and social landscape of the Gulf, potentially irreparably. Despite the nature of the perceived transgression, the authenticity of the comments was quickly contested. QNA immediately claimed that they had been hacked. Some attributed the hack to Russians acting on behalf of the UAE.[4] An investigation by Al Jazeera showed that the hack had been via an Emirate-owned company operating from Azerbaijan, which had asked a Turkish company to probe a number of websites (including QNA) for security leaks.[5]

. It is apparent that the hack was a pseudo-event deliberately instrumentalised as a pretext on which to escalate diplomatic tensions with Qatar. Pretexts are an important element of propaganda and disinformation operations. Traditionally, legacy media either exploit real events or orchestrate fake ones in order to generate public support for what otherwise might be an unpopular policy decision, such as war or conflict. They can often incite religious, nationalistic or patriotic fervour.[6] Well-known pretexts in the Middle East include the claim that Saddam Hussein had weapons of mass destruction (WMD). While this claim was later debunked, it was key in mobilising public support in the United States and the United Kingdom for an unpopular invasion of Iraq in 2003. The WMD claim was difficult to challenge due to the secrecy surrounding the intelligence justifying the claims, making it impossible to scrutinise in a timely fashion, and as such was ideal. Pretexts can be entirely fabricated, such as in the case of Nayirah's testimony (see Chapter 2), or opportunistic moments in which real events are exploited and made more salient in media coverage. 'Pretexts provide an important framework for propaganda because they portray to citizens that the object of hostility is the natural aggressor and that the manufacturer of the pretext is the moral superior acting in response to an outrageous act'.[7]

The pretext of the emir's comments was rapidly exploited. On 5 June Saudi Arabia, Egypt, United Arab Emirates and Bahrain severed diplomatic relations with Qatar. The abrupt rupture created substantial chaos. Many Qatari residents in other Gulf countries had to be repatriated. Qatar, so reliant on basic goods coming over the Saudi–Qatar border, had to quickly adjust its trade and imports. The conflict played out as much online as it did on the ground. The quartet of countries made thirteen maximalist demands of Qatar that included the following: reducing diplomatic ties with Turkey; closing Al Jazeera and other news organisations; reparations; and severing ties with organisations such as the Muslim Brotherhood and Hamas.[8]

The Think Tanks

A dominant aspect of the Gulf Crisis was an international influence and disinformation campaign that sought to exclusively smear Qatar as the only Gulf country that supported terror. As with disinformation operations, it sought to influence high-level politicians and opinion formers in the USA and London. The quartet of countries poured enormous resources into promoting the adversarial discourse that Qatar was a global supporter of terrorism. Much of this was done through an agglomeration of government officials, think tanks and PR agencies. Indeed, a key aspect of deception is attempting to hide the source of funds or organisational agenda in order to give an illusion of independence that better enhances the credibility of content being promoted. In 2018 it was revealed that Charles Andreae, the CEO of Andreae & Associates, a DC-based consulting firm, was paid half a million dollars to produce a six-part film demonising Qatar.[9] Andreae & Associates was hired in August 2017 by Dubai-based Lapis Communications to create 'six multimedia products focused on an investigation into the role of the state of Qatar and the state's connection to global terrorism'.[10] According to a declaration to the US Department of Justice, the activities of Andreae & Associates were undertaken on behalf of a foreign nation and may have included communications with numbers of key opinion-formers, including congresspersons, journalists and academics. It was reported that the resulting film, titled *Qatar: A Dangerous Alliance*, was then distributed by the Hudson Institute during a conference in 2017. The film sought to smear Qatar as the *éminence grise* behind all terrorist activities in the region, a disingenuous claim but one that Saudi Arabia, in particular, was keen to promote given its well-established links to the 9/11 attacks.[11]

In July 2017 a Saudi lobbying firm, the Saudi American Public Relations Affairs Committee (SAPRAC) paid $138,000 for seven 30-second commercials that were played mostly in the Washington area. The adverts were designed not for a general audience, but to target high-level decision makers concentrated in the DC area. This selective targeting was evident by the fact three of the adverts were played during the British Open golf tournament, while the other four were played during Meet the Press, a weekly news show in which American television journalist Chuck Todd interviews high-profile and influential politicians:[12]

Despite the fact SAPRAC's ads were clearly reflecting Saudi foreign policy in attacking Qatar, SAPRAC did not initially register as a foreign agent, implying that its publication and activities were not subject to direction by the Saudi government.[13] Indeed, SAPRAC's ads attacking Qatar were circulated and broadcast in July 2017, while SAPRAC only eventually filed with the Foreign Agents Registration

Act (FARA) in August 2017. SAPRAC, which was founded by writer and lobbyist Salman al-Ansari, had been set up prior to the blockade in 2016, initially to strengthen understanding between the United States and Saudi Arabia. The outbreak of the Qatar blockade quickly saw SAPRAC turn into an aggressive lobbying arm of the Saudi government, promoting, among other things, material designed to present Qatar as a supporter and funder of terrorism. SAPRAC's work was facilitated when it joined forces with the Podesta Group, a US-based outfit set up by Hillary Clinton's campaign chair John Podesta, who aided SAPRAC in researching and communicating content to 'relevant audiences'.[14] Yet while Podesta was a registered foreign agent of Saudi Arabia, SAPRAC had not been registered until August 2017. After the Daily Beast reported that Podesta had been working with SAPRAC to help produce the anti-Qatar propaganda, Podesta registered as a foreign agent for SAPRAC.[15]

Again, the information war playing out over the Gulf Crisis in Washington was further highlighted when Avenue Strategies Global, a firm with close ties to Donald Trump and representing the Qataris, sent a letter to FARA arguing that SAPRAC was violating the law by not registering as a foreign agent. Avenue Strategies Global argued that it was almost 'impossible to meaningfully distinguish SAPRAC from the Kingdom of Saudi Arabia'. They added, 'In fact, if the Kingdom of Saudi Arabia were to establish a foreign agent for the purpose of producing and disseminating propaganda on behalf of itself, it would look exactly like SAPRAC.'[16]

SAPRAC was also the entity responsible for setting up the website The Qatar Insider, a news site largely dedicated to promoting anti-Qatar propaganda and disinformation. Much of the content focused on promoting a negative image of Qatar's economy, a form of economic warfare designed to make investors jumpy and cautious about investing in Qatar.[17] Former Associated Press journalist Josh Wood noted that the website 'pushed a steady stream of clickbait-style disinformation, often relying on catchy, misleading infographics to try to draw in an audience'.[18] Yet neither SAPRAC nor the Podesta Group's name appeared on the website, giving the illusion that the site was an independent effort. Like the front group set up by Hills

& Knowlton ahead of the US-led coalition's intervention in Kuwait, the Qatar Insider was a 'front newspaper'.

Although FARA allows for some transparency in determining what firms are lobbying on behalf of foreign entities and trying to potentially influence US domestic and foreign policy, it is poorly enforced and often relies on the goodwill and integrity of firms registering – even though registration may reduce the perceived credibility of the information and activities undertaken by such bodies. The relationship between the Podesta Group and SAPRAC seemed to reflect a desire to preserve the illusion that the content they produce is truly organic and representative of legitimate, as opposed to paid, sentiment.

Similar evidence of Western PR companies contributing to the isolation of Qatar on behalf of the blockading countries includes the activities of the Dubai-based firm Project Associates. Project Associates has held what have been described as pro-UAE briefings in London and Brussels. The briefings, which were reportedly attended by traditional opinion-formers such as journalists and academics, emphasised the importance of supporting MBZ's policies in the region. Implicitly, this indicates isolating Qatar, Iran and Turkey.[19]

According to official documents registered with the US government, another firm, SCL Social Limited, was retained by Project Associates in September 2017 to launch a series of anti-Qatar adverts on Facebook.[20] SCL Social Limited's director was Alexander Nix, the former CEO of Cambridge Analytica, the disgraced data intelligence firm that was found to have improperly acquired millions of Facebook users' data for the purpose of political advertising and potential electoral influence. In 2020 it was revealed that evidence filed in a US Federal Electoral Commission complaint accused Cambridge Analytica of serving as a conduit between the Make America Great 1 PAC and the Trump campaign.[21]

Whether by coincidence or design, SCL Social Limited and Project Associates found ideological allies in the pro-Trump Emirati regime. SCL Social Limited received $333,000 from the UAE Media Council to spread negative news about Qatar via Project Associates. Although it is unclear what the entire sum was spent on, a significant portion of the outlay went on promoting a hashtag that encouraged people to boycott Qatar. The #boycottqatar campaign had its own Twitter account called boycottqatarnow, and SCL Social Limited spent around $64,000 on Twitter, Facebook and YouTube adverts in a two-day period in September 2017 on behalf of the UAE Media council.[22]

The informational documents submitted by SCL Social Limited to FARA demonstrated that the op-eds linked Qatar to terrorism.[23] One of the articles, written by Abdellatif El-Menawy in the English-language *Independent Voices*, sought to frame Qatar's humanitarian aid to Palestine as terrorist funding.[24] Another article on the website New Europe again sought to conflate Qatar's funding of a charity with terrorism.[25] The accusation was tenuous, verging on disinformation: Muslim Aid, a British-registered charity, had allocated funding to the Hebron-based Al Ihsan Charitable Society in 2003 before it was designated a terrorist organisation under the UK Terrorism Order and sanctioned in 2005. Funds allocated to Al Ihsan for a dentist's chair and related equipment in 2005 were never paid. The UK's Charitable Commission concluded that there had been no improper or irregular use of funds. While the New Europe article acknowledges this, it clearly positions Muslim Aid as a deviant actor supporting terror and alludes to Qatar funding the charity to stir up unrest in the Middle East.[26] Another interesting aspect of the New Europe article was that it was written by Luigi Baresi, a journalist who has no internet footprint. In fact, the only other article he has written is another anti-Qatar article in the same magazine, raising questions about his actual identity.

Meanwhile, in London, the self-styled Qatari opposition leader Khalid al-Hail, who had emerged during the implementation of the blockade on Qatar, was putting the finishing touches to the Qatar, Global Security and Stability Conference. Al-Hail is also the founder of the Qatar National Democratic Party, and describes himself as a Qatari exile who was tortured in Qatar. The conference was touted as a (re)launch of the Qatari opposition abroad, so it was perhaps unsurprising that 'almost every debate was strongly critical of the current Qatari ruling regime'.[27] The conference was also an attempt to influence British political opinion to the detriment of Qatar and was attended by a number of high-profile British politicians, such as former Tory party leader Iain Duncan Smith and the pro-Saudi Conservative MP Daniel Kawczynski, who is often referred to mockingly as the 'honourable member for Saudi Arabia' for his pro-Saudi lobbying in British parliament.[28] Both Kawcynzski and Smith were paid by Akta Group, a business run by the wife of Khalid al-Hail.[29] Kawczynski received £15,000 for his involvement, while Smith received a £4,000 speaking fee.[30] Those involved in the conference denied that any of the funding came from the United Arab Emirates.

Bots

In addition to attempting to win the hearts and minds of Western politicians through aggressive lobbying in London and Washington, the Gulf Crisis was very much defined by the unprecedented use of social media disinformation. Primarily, the narratives promoted by bots sought to increase the salience of the accusations and 13 demands made against Qatar by the KUBE quartet. While the Gulf Crisis had its 'temporal logic rooted in the hacking pretext … the controversy surrounding this event was precipitated by considerable online bot activity against Qatar'.[31] Dozens of anti-Qatar hashtags began to trend on Twitter on the evening of the alleged hack. The overarching aim of the hashtags was to dominate the discourse around the word Qatar itself, ensuring that anyone reading social media posts containing the word 'Qatar' were exposed to the demands of the blockading countries.

However, many of the hashtags were generated, amplified or promoted by automated bot accounts. Many of these were directed at criticising media outlets based in or perceived to be connected to Qatar. On 28 May the hashtag 'Al Jazeera insults King Salman' began trending after Al Jazeera tweeted a cartoon that was critical of King Salman. Of the 21,387 unique accounts in a sample of those tweeting on the hashtag, 4,375 (around 20%) appeared to be automated. Bots on this hashtag shared crude infographics designed to conflate Qatar with Hamas, the Muslim Brotherhood and Iran. For example, an image titled 'Qatar's media snake' documented a host of entities perceived to be connected to Qatar, and seen as giving a platform to the enemies of the blockading countries. The well-known Qatar-based Arab public intellectual Azmi Bishara was a particular target for many of these campaigns, as was Middle East Eye editor-in-chief David Hearst, and former director of Al Jazeera Wadah Khanfar. Indeed, there was a particular emphasis on Qatar-based news organisations. On 23 June 2017 the hashtag 'We demand the closing of the channel of pigs' trended in Saudi Arabia. It was produced by around 2,831 bot accounts (It should be noted that Al Jazeera sounds similar to the Arabic word for pig, *khanzeera*).

In addition to hashtags, the disinformation campaign intended to dominate the discourse around the word Qatar itself. On 27 May 2017, a few days after the hacking scandal, a sample of 29,444 Arabic accounts mentioning the word 'Qatar' in either English or Arabic was taken. The sample was agnostic, and any tweet sent within a defined time frame that included the word 'Qatar' was included. The sample revealed a dramatic spike in Twitter accounts created in May 2017. Indeed, 'the average number of Twitter accounts in the sample created between March 2012 and March 2017 was about 318 per month, whereas, in May 2017 (the month of the crisis), 3,470 new accounts were created'.[32] Most of these accounts were amplifying opinions by public figures criticizing Qatar, such as Turki al-Sheikh, an adviser to the Saudi Arabian royal court. Khalid al-Hail's anti-Qatar tweets were also highly promoted. Even in early 2018, subsequent analysis revealed that on 1 January 18% of a random sample of accounts mentioning Qatar were produced by anti-Qatar bots.

While investigators were still attempting to discover whether QNA had been hacked or not, the examination of bot accounts suggests that the campaign was pre-orchestrated. On 21 May 2017, three days before news broke of the emir's alleged comments which triggered the crisis, the hashtag 'Qatar the bankroller of terror' was trending. Another analysis of around 33,000 tweets extracted on 28 May 2017 revealed that one bot swarm that became active following the hack was actually set up in April 2017. A content analysis of the 234 bots' biographies reveals that they were all in opposition to the Al Thani family and the Qatari government, suggesting that the sole purpose of their creation was to attack Tamim and the Qatari royal family. One such example of a biography of that particular network was, 'Qatari citizen. Make Twitter a platform to defend your land and country. Fight the traitors and mercenaries of the Al Thani family.'[33] The themes evident in the biographies also resembled the demands made by the quartet countries, including criticisms of the Muslim Brotherhood, but also accusations that Qatar was colluding with Israel. The discovery of this network suggests that some entity, whether a private organisation or a government, had prepared an anti-Qatar social media campaign ahead of the emir's alleged comments.[34] Some of the bots were linked to DotDev, a digital marketing company based in the United Arab Emirates and Egypt. A Twitter takedown in 2019 revealed that the DotDev network had, at one point, been used to direct disinformation at Iran and Qatar.[35]

The bots were successful in getting many of their messages into the international media. One hashtag, 'Qatar cuts civil service salaries by 35%', went viral, and was subsequently reported in BBC Trending as a legitimate news story (BBC Trending is the BBC entity that reports newsworthy occurrences related to the digital space). However, there was no evidence of such a cut in salaries. The story appeared to have its origins in a doctored, almost plausible screenshot of a Reuters news article. This was the impetus for a campaign that was soon picked up by real accounts, and then influencers, who further legitimised the claim. The idea behind the campaign was similar to those conducted by SAPRAC, to make potential investors jumpy about investing in Qatar, or perhaps to reduce the morale of Qataris in order to make them more hostile towards their own government.

Of course the holy grail of a bot-driven deception campaign is if authentic influencers pick up and amplify the story. As Andrew Leber and Alexei Abrahams note, there is strong evidence to suggest that 'politically salient Twitter conversations in the region are centrally dominated, which renders them vulnerable to organized intervention by state authorities'.[36] Of course, such campaigns are more successful when they pull in and influence or encourage engagement from real people. It is this 'mixed strategy' that is more effective, involving 'genuine' users 'in building popular engagement around a shared narrative, rather than simply flooding the social media commons with fake accounts tweeting in isolation'.[37]

Rent-a-Crowds and Astroturfing

An aspect of deception that characterised the Gulf Crisis as such an epochal disinformation moment was its breadth and ambition, however crude. It involved PR agencies, bots, hacking and even crude rent-a-crowds. A particularly bizarre aspect of deception that came on the back of the blockade was the apparent hiring of UK-based actors to protest against a visit by the emir of Qatar to the UK. In July 2018 Tamim bin Hamad visited British prime minister Theresa May to discuss bilateral relations. To coincide with his visit, a 500-person-strong protest had been scheduled to take place outside Downing Street. The only problem was that no one turned up. The reason: the protest had been concocted by a PR firm which had attempted to solicit actors to 'play' an anti-Qatar crowd. The UK casting firm Extra People sent an email out to its actors offering them £20 to take part in a protest outside Downing Street. Extra People, which had been approached by a PR company called Neptune PR, stated in an email to its actors that this was neither a TV nor film event and that their client was 'looking for a large group of people to fill space outside Downing Street during the visit of the president of Qatar [*sic*]. This is an ANTI-Qatar event – You will not have to do or say anything, they just want to fill space. You will be finished at 12:30.'[38]

Soon after, Extra People stated that it would no longer be involved in the project. By this time, media reports had begun to circulate, prompting much speculation on and offline about the bizarre turn of events. Soon, Neptune PR, the company that had approached Extra People about the job, opened a Twitter account, seemingly for the sole purpose of responding to the emerging scandal. Whoever ran Neptune PR's account tweeted at Extra People, denying that they had been involved. They also threatened legal action, stating, 'We demand you to provide a shred of evidence to support this outrageous claim. Can you provide an email trail to Neptune PR, a contact number or a contact for Neptune PR? Such accusations are liable to lead to legal action. Therefore, We shall consult our lawyers.'[39] Extra People quickly replied with a screenshot of an email from Neptune PR employee Lelie Genda which had a Neptune PR address. The issue suddenly de-escalated, and Neptune PR responded by saying, 'Can you please share with us the full details of the person on info@ neptunepr.co.uk.' Again, given that it was clear who the Neptune PR employee was, the response just generated bemusement from those following developments.

Neptune PR quickly disappeared, the company dissolving less than a year later in May 2019.[40] However, it was not the only social media campaign to attempt to influence British public opinion about Qatar. Between 21 and 28 July, ahead of Tamim's trip to London, two trends appeared, #OpposeQatarVisit and #LondonRejectsTaminsVisit. Like the campaigns promoting Mohammed bin Salman's visit to London, billboards with the hashtag 'oppose Qatar visit' appeared around London, with some being suspended on overpasses, others on the backs of flatbed trucks.[41] A photo of one of the billboards along with the hashtag was promoted by self-proclaimed Qatari opposition leader Khalid al-Hail. The billboard read, 'If a country was accused of paying $1 billion ransom to terrorist groups, should they be welcome in the UK? Then why is the UK rolling out the red carpet for the Qatar Emir?' An analysis of 4,800 unique accounts promoting the 'Oppose Qatar Visit' hashtag revealed a high attrition rate: 56% have either been suspended, changed their names or been deleted. At least 637 of them were created in a single day – 27 February 2017. All but 25 of these accounts have been suspended.

The messages being promoted by the bots tweeting on the 'oppose Qatar visit' hashtag reflected exactly the talking points of the blockading countries. A corpus analysis of 630 tweets posted by the now-suspended bot accounts revealed that the words terror/ terrorist/terrorism were used in 388 of the tweets, with most accusing Qatar of supporting terror either through its relationship with Iran, Hamas, the Muslim Brotherhood or Al Jazeera. Despite the relative crudeness of the bots, all of the accounts in the 637 samples posted unique content, with little to no copy and pasting. The language indicated that they had been written by a non-native English speaker, and almost all the tweets began with 'Qatar + verb+'. An indicative example is 'Qatar helped the terrorists by hosting and providing them with money and media support #OpposeQatarVisit'. The only digressions from this pattern were tweets that praised the Saudi and Emirate approach to tackling terrorism. For example, one tweet read, 'Saudi's attitude against terrorists is powerful, and Qatar doesn't seem to have the same view #OpposeQatarVisit'.

The 25 or so accounts that were not suspended give us an insight into their previous campaigns. In addition to posts boosting tweets by Donald Trump (see Chapter 3) the accounts had also promoted Shaykh Abdallah Al Thani, an exiled Qatari shaykh whom the blockading countries had attempted to promote as a new ruler of Qatar. Abdallah's grandfather, father and brother had ruled Qatar until 1972 when their branch of the family was replaced by the heir apparent, Khalifa bin Hamad Al Thani.[42] Following the blockade, Abdullah Al Thani had held a few high-profile meetings with MBS and King Salman. However, in a bizarre twist of events, he posted a video of himself while in the UAE saying, 'I am a guest of Sheikh Mohammed, but it is not hosting now, it is now an imprisonment.'[43] Shaykh Abdullah added, 'They told me not to leave and I am afraid something will happen to me, and they blame Qatar ... I just wanted to let you know that Qatar is innocent in this and I am being hosted by Sheikh Mohammed and anything that happens to me after this is under his responsibility.'[44] Abdallah later moved to Kuwait, in January 2018, although the nature of his stay in the UAE still remains unclear.

The Coup That Never Happened

In 2017 Saud al-Qahtani was extremely active on Twitter, and it was here that he began to earn his reputation as 'Lord of the Flies'. He quickly achieved notoriety when he tweeted that anyone expressing support for Qatar should be added to a public blacklist. Al-Qahtani's tweet was sinister: 'Does an anonymous handle protect you from the blacklist? 1. Governments have ways to get their real name. 2. IP address could be acquired in many technical ways. 3. A secret I won't divulge.'[45] That al-Qahtani was clearly intervening in organic public opinion by prescribing what people should and should not say about Saudi's foreign policy was indicative of the climate of censorship inherent in the Gulf post-truth moment.

In addition to these threats, a curious aspect of the Qatar Crisis were attempts, promoted by Saud al-Qahtani, to encourage and potentially instigate a coup d'état in Qatar.[46]

> On August 21, 2017, al-Qahtani tweeted 'The top trend in Qatar now is #LeaveTamim.' With this tweet, al-Qahtani included a screenshot of Twitter's trending topics, as if to alleviate any doubt about the veracity of his statement. However, an analysis of the #LeaveTamim hashtag highlights that not only were many of the accounts bots but also the majority of the accounts were located in Saudi Arabia, according to their user input location. Al-Qahtani then retweeted the results of a Twitter poll by an anti-Qatar Twitter user. The poll asked Qataris what they wanted to do about Tamim. The results in the poll indicate that the majority wanted Tamim to go. After al-Qahtani shared this poll, which he intimated reflected the popular will of Qataris (despite no transparency about who voted), he offered a veiled threat, indicating that any attempt to quell popular insurrection by Qataris would be met with force: 'Qatar (Gaddafi of the Gulf) should know that any attempt to repress a peaceful movement of the brotherly Qatari people by foreign forces shall be punished severely, it is a war crime.'[47]

Despite al-Qahtani's sinister threats, and use of digital rent-a-crowds to potentially provoke social conflict, his account was verified and untouched by Twitter for years. It was only in September 2019 that Twitter suspended his account for platform-manipulation policies. This was a year after the killing of Khashoggi, in which al-Qahtani was implicated, and two years after the outbreak of the Gulf Crisis. For many in the region, and especially al-Qahtani's targets, the failure to suspend him in a timely fashion was indicative of either apathy or indifference on Twitter's part, or, more disturbingly, an unwillingness to target high-level officials in the regime – especially those who were close to MBS, whom Jack Dorsey had met on at least two occasions. Indeed, the longevity of al-Qahtani's account simply raised questions about Twitter's thoroughness in policing its platform during the Gulf Crisis.

The Coup That Never Was

With al-Qahtani suspended, many Twitter users in the Gulf began to believe that he was tweeting from another account. Regardless, Twitter in the region has continued to be used for deception operations that seemed commonplace while al-Qahtani was active. In the early hours of 4 May 2020, news of a coup in Qatar started trending on Twitter. The trend seemed to have started around 1 a.m. UTC. The Twitter account, @faisalva_, which had a profile pic of King Salman, posted a video reporting gunshots and explosions in al-Wakra, a region south of the Qatari capital, Doha. Another account, self-described as a Saudi radiologist, tweeted that a coup was happening.

Shortly after 1.30 a.m. an apparently Saudi-based account with only a small number of followers replied to the tweet. Whoever ran the Twitter account claimed that there had been a coup attempt against Shaykh Tamim bin Hamad Al Thani, the Qatari emir. Soon after this initial salvo of tweets by anonymous accounts, 'al-Wakra' began trending on Twitter in Qatar, while 'coup in Qatar' began trending in Saudi Arabia. By 9 a.m. hundreds of thousands of tweets about al-Wakra and an alleged coup attempt had been posted across several hashtags. 'Coup in Qatar' was soon the number-one trending topic in both Saudi Arabia and Qatar.

A few residents of al-Wakra had reported a bang that night. This was not in and of itself unusual. Every now and then those who live there are used to being startled by the sonic boom of military jets conducting training exercises. However, the loud bang near the capital provided a convenient pretext on which to hang the plausibility of a military-led coup. The Twitter storm bore striking similarities to that which occurred in May and June 2017. The majority of Twitter accounts were ostensibly based in Saudi, and mostly retweeting a small group of verified Saudi, Egyptian and Emirati influencers. These included Abdallah al-Bandar, a Saudi presenter for the international news channel Sky News Arabia, who has 234,000 followers on Twitter. Al-Bandar, along with a number of other highly followed accounts, had fuelled speculation of a coup by claiming on 4 May that military aeroplanes were flying around Qatar.

This rumour was loosely legitimised by a screenshot he had posted of a flight-scanner website showing images of aeroplanes. However, there was no context provided. This trope of increased military activity was compounded when a Kuwait-based influencer with more than 500,000 followers claimed that Tamim had ordered Turkish forces to Doha following the coup attempt. His post included more screenshots of flight trackers. (Interestingly, the use of flight radar screenshots has been fairly common in the Gulf Crisis, as it gives a veneer of technical and evidential legitimacy to bolster spurious claims. There was no indication, or attempt to explore, whether these were routine manoeuvres, which they evidently were.)

While most of the accounts spreading the rumours had Arabic names, hundreds of others had European-sounding names. These accounts were obvious sockpuppets, and none had a history of tweeting about Middle Eastern politics, let alone in Arabic. Many other influential Saudis amplified the disinformation by sharing false, unverified information on social media. These included influencer Monther al-Shaykh Mubarak, sports commentator Musaid AlSohimi, and Saudi poet Abdlatif al-Shaykh.

Many of the tweets claiming that there had been a coup were accompanied by vague and hazy videos showing gunfire and explosions. It soon became clear, however, that videos had been doctored, or were from entirely unrelated events. One widely shared video allegedly showing bombs going off in Doha was actually of an explosion at a container storage station that took place in 2015, in Tianjin in China. Another video purportedly depicting a night-time scene in al-Wakra in which off-camera persons discuss the sound of gunshots was circulated. Although it was taken at night time and did not show anything of substance, it was possible to identify the video as an event that occurred in Riyadh, in April 2018. The video had, ironically, been posted on Al Jazeera's website.

In a more egregious use of doctored videos, several Saudi-based accounts shared a video clip shot in al-Wakra on the morning of 4 May, in which multiple gunshots could be heard. However, the video had actually been created by a Qatari citizen named Rashed al-Hamli, who originally filmed the video as a satirical response to the rumours that there was a coup in the country. Al-Hamli's light-hearted video, in which he joked that he could only hear birdsong and not gunfire, had its video stripped of audio and replaced by sounds of gunfire. It was then posted by a highly followed account claiming to represent the Qatari opposition government.

The narrative being manufactured and pushed on Twitter by a select group of mostly Saudi influencers was that the former Qatari prime minister Hamad bin Jassim was attempting to overthrow the emir, and that the emir was being protected by Turkish troops stationed in Qatar. According to the disinformation campaign, bin Jassim was disgruntled by a corruption investigation. Those behind the disinformation campaign sought to legitimise this claim by creating a fake tweet by bin Jassim. Although the agitators took a screenshot of the tweet and claimed that Hamad bin Jassim had deleted it, there was no evidence that the tweet had ever existed. Crucially, the screenshots of the tweet showed that there had been replies to bin Jassim's tweet. On Twitter if there are replies to a tweet, even when it is deleted you will see a notification saying 'That tweet does not exist.' In this case, there was nothing.

As for the information about Turkish troops interceding on behalf of Tamim, this has been a key trope deployed by KUBE propaganda countries since 2017, which have sought to raise the spectre of what the Saudi Arabian and Emirate governments see as 'Neo-Ottomanism', or Turkey's increasingly active role in the perceived Arab domains of northern Syria and Libya. Indeed, Qatar is often framed in propaganda as collaborating with the Ottomans and, by doing so, betraying its Arab sensibilities. Another network of accounts discovered in 2019, which were subsequently suspended, also masqueraded as Qataris opposing friendly relations between Turkey and Qatar. They promoted the hashtag 'we reject Ottoman imperialism'. It was likely the accounts were also linked to one of the blockading countries.[48]

By the morning of 5 May there were almost 150,000 tweets on the hashtag 'coup in Qatar'. This momentum dulled somewhat, perhaps partially as a response to the fact that it was quickly debunked by myself and others, but also perhaps because it was only intended to be a short 1–2-day campaign. However, rumours of a coup picked up once again on 12–13 May. Interestingly, the same group of Saudi influencers was instrumental in producing the disinformation, suggesting some level of coordination.

The second spike in the coup rumours was somewhat more sophisticated than those from 5 May. Fake videos used as evidence of a coup in Qatar were far more audacious than they had been previously. Instead of dark, jumpy and ambiguous recordings with no immediate context, videos clearly showing dramatic events unfolding in Doha were being used. One video depicted two young boys filming and discussing a fire near a park in Doha. In the background, small explosions could be heard. Unlike the other videos, it was clear this was filmed in Qatar. As one of the boys panned his phone around, one could see it was filmed at Al Legtaifiya Park near the coastal development of Katara. An open-source analysis pinpointed that the angles of shadows cast by the boys, the purple colour of the smoke and the direction and location of the explosions indicated that the footage was of a fireworks festival that took place in February 2020 in the locale of Katara.[49]

The information operation was bolstered by the fact those behind the disinfo had some high-value Twitter accounts that could plausibly dupe people into believing that they were credible. One of the most highly followed accounts tweeting that there was a coup was called the Qatari Media Channel. Its Twitter handle was @Qatar_Press_Net. The account has 62,000 followers and was created in 2009. Since the outbreak of the fake coup it had steadily been distributing numerous doctored videos, some of which claimed to show Turkish troops and aircraft in Qatar. These videos were mostly of training exercises from the months or years before, taken out of context. Several more videos emerged, showing military movements or fires around Doha. A video posted on 14 May by a verified Twitter user, British-Arab researcher Amjad Taha, showed a big fire in broad daylight. Filmed from Doha's West Bay, the author claimed the conflagration reflected the diminishing of security in Doha. Fake Qatari opposition accounts also tweeted the video, with one claiming that it was a 'leaked' video showing operations related to the coup occurring near the Turkish embassy in Doha.[50] Despite these claims, the video showed a fire that occurred in 'the Pearl' area of Doha in 2018.[51] Videos and images of Turkish troops in Doha were also used to emphasise the rise of

Neo-Ottomanism on the Arabian Peninsula. Again, the videos were deliberately taken out of context. One video of a Turkish Apache helicopter flying in Doha, used by the electronic flies to give the illusion of a skirmish in Doha, was actually footage of a joint Qatari–Turkish military manoeuvre in 2019.[52]

The Qatari Media Channel account's biographical details claim that it wished to see Qatar 'liberated' from its current regime, a discourse which followed that of the blockading countries. There was little doubt that the account was intended to deceive. This is clear from the fact it changed its Twitter handle at least six times during 2020, and around three times in the week of the fake coup rumours. Its former names included @fconxzero, @SGA_ALTHANI @Qatar_Poost, @qatre_shek and @Qatar_hawks. One of the accounts (SGA_ALTHANI) was clearly trying to give the impression that it was a dissident member of the Qatari ruling family. In its most recent guises, the account tried to give the illusion that it was an official Qatari opposition press outlet. Changing Twitter handles (handle switching) is usually a means of avoiding investigation by open-source research teams, and generally points to suspicious or deceptive intent.

Although at least 33 suspicious accounts were suspended in the days following the disinformation campaign, Twitter only announced these suspensions in October 2020, some four months later. For reasons that are unclear, Twitter did not release more accounts, even though hundreds were involved in spreading the disinformation. An analysis I conducted of a sample of 31,000 unique accounts active on the fake coup hashtags revealed that between 4 and 16 May at least 1,100 of the accounts had changed their handle or had been suspended or deleted – a very high rate of attrition. Again, the fact that Twitter only published information for 33 accounts highlights the lack of transparency around what Twitter chooses to publicise in terms of deception operations.

Given the convergence between social and legacy media, it is not surprising that the stories of the fake coup were picked up by numerous Arabic newspapers across the MENA region, most of which reported the stories uncritically. The conservative Bahrain-based newspaper *AlWatan* was one of the first to report on the coup. Others quickly followed. Although some framed it in a way that suggested a coup was potentially under way, others were more circumspect and chose only to report on rumours of a coup. However, the real story is not that there were rumours of a coup, but that there was a disinformation campaign designed to give the illusion of a coup. The fake coup story highlights the issue of attempting to either prove or disprove a negative. In the post-truth age, a technically factual report on social media trends can fan the flame of fake news, serving the agenda of the disinformation agent.

Outlets with known political and economic links to Riyadh, such as Al Arabiya, or the partially Saudi-owned *Independent Arabia*, published opinion pieces and news reports supporting the coup claims. Al Arabiya showed, as fact, the doctored video purporting to show gunshots in Qatar. *Independent Arabia* published an article titled 'Did Qatar witness a coup?'[53] The piece, which was also translated into Persian and Turkish, treated the story as credible. Disinformation campaigns often attempt to provoke discord, instability and uncertainty about their target. Simply by reporting that there were 'rumours of a coup in Qatar', therefore, media outlets played into the hands of the propagandists by promoting some element of doubt in the stability of Qatar. But if this was centrally coordinated, it was likely that was the intention.

The *Independent Arabia* piece cited a number of Twitter accounts that I had identified as suspicious, and were later suspended by Twitter for being linked to a Saudi-led information operation. This included the account @QatarGov, which claimed to be the Qatari government in exile, and had over 64,000 followers. The author of the *Independent Arabia* article, Ayman al-Ghabiwi, used the account to corroborate news about the shooting down of an aircraft in Qatar. Al-Ghabiwi stated, 'The account "Qatar Interim Government", which is followed by most of the external opposition, confirmed on Twitter that the news about the coup is 100 per cent correct, that there has been the downing of a warplane.'[54] Al-Ghabiwi also cited a tweet by Fahad Al Thani, a verified Twitter account and cousin of the current emir of Qatar living in Saudi. Fahad bin Abdullah Al Thani is alleged to be a dissident member of the ruling family, yet his Twitter account had been appropriated for the purpose of the Saudi-led disinformation campaign. It is unclear exactly who ran the network, but it was also one of the 33 accounts that were suspended by Twitter as part of a Saudi-backed information operation.[55]

Conclusion

As this chapter has illustrated, the Gulf Crisis is perhaps one of the first examples of a political conflict initiated and sustained by a multi-levelled cyber and disinformation operation. From the hacking of a news agency to the continued use of fake accounts to amplify the political demands and threaten those sympathetic to Qatar, the capaciousness of the operation was unprecedented. Although its efficacy is unknown, many of the tropes, stories and strands of disinformation have 'broken out' into legacy media, and continue to circulate in various forms on social and traditional media. Online, a crucial element is that select influencers, supported by bots, create pseudo-events. The amplification of the pseudo-events by fake accounts also reflects the existence of pseudo-publics, which then filter into legacy media in an attempt to influence real public opinion. In other words, social media has become awash with fake news perpetuated and amplified by fake accounts, who in turn form fake publics.

Social media influence campaigns have also been underpinned and underscored by high-level lobbying in the UK and the USA, buttressed and enabled by a network of lobbyists and politicians who organised and attended conferences with a long list of influential invitees. A fascinating aspect of the pretext for the crisis in 2017, and the more recent fake coup, is the brazen artificiality of the story. It is 'a manufactured crisis'.[56] The purpose of these manufactured events, facilitated largely by social media deception campaigns, was to legitimise the implementation of a strategy seeking to isolate Qatar both regionally and on the global stage. In terms of scale, audacity and complexity, these deception operations arguably marked the zenith of the Gulf's post-truth moment.

PART IV

PROJECTING INFLUENCE ABROAD

7

FOREIGN INTERFERENCE IN ELECTIONS, REVOLUTIONS AND PROTESTS

FROM IRAQ TO ALGERIA

Chapter Overview

A defining aspect of social media operations in a global context is the exploitation of porous online 'borders'. In the digital age, states are no longer hermetically sealed from one another, yet geographical trending locations on sites such as Twitter provide pseudo-locales that can be exploited by malicious actors through the use of electronic flies. In the Middle East region there is increasing evidence that malicious actors, including Saudi Arabia and Iran, are exploiting extant tensions within society to try and influence election outcomes to the advantage of autocratic states. In particular, this chapter explores how powerful deception actors are attempting to 'export authoritarianism' via social media in those states with vulnerable democracies. Democracies in the Arab world score poorly in most indexes designed to measure political freedom. The Economist Intelligence Unit's Democracy Index ranks approximately 167 countries according to whether they are authoritarian, hybrid regimes, flawed or full democracies. The 2019 rankings designated

15 out of 20 of the MENA countries surveyed as authoritarian.[1] While many of these countries have functioning parliaments and elections, the nature of digital disinformation in electoral interference and parliamentary politics remains underexplored.

This chapter focuses on the use of sockpuppet accounts and bots in three potential influence campaigns, in Algeria, Iraq and Lebanon, pointing to the potential reach of foreign powers, particular Saudi Arabia, Iran and the UAE in attempting to influence political outcomes while also exploiting crises for other gains. The choice of the three countries is partly to emphasise the extent of the reach of GCC-deception superpowers, but also on the basis that Lebanon and Iraq, in particular, have been subjected to varying degrees of foreign interference. Iraq, especially since the invasion of 2003, has been subject to the presence of foreign militaries, whether those of Daesh, the US-led coalition or Iranian militias. Lebanon has had a long-running conflict with Israel, while also being a crucial fulcrum in the Saudi–Iranian cold war. This chapter highlights the fragility of democracy and civil activism in the MENA region, and the ability of (at times unknown) deception operations to appear to be interfering in domestic politics by simulating or exaggerating the strength of grassroots movements and attempting to shape the narrative. In particular it identifies how the Iran–Saudi tension is shaping many of the influence operations.

Iraq

On 1 October 2019 Iraq witnessed some of the largest protests since the US-led invasion in 2003. Thousands of Iraqis occupied public spaces to demonstrate against corruption, unemployment and foreign interference. The government response was brutal, and between 1 October and 2 December 220 people were estimated to have been killed. Despite the real concerns being raised by Iraqis, there is also evidence that the online campaigns in support of the protests were being manipulated by Saudi-connected accounts.

Very early on in the protests the hashtag, 'save the Iraqi ppl' began to trend. An analysis of the hashtag revealed that it started trending quite suddenly on 2 October, and that around 10% (836) of the accounts tweeting on the hashtag had been created in the first four days of October. Of these, approximately 27% have been suspended since October 2019, suggesting that they were part of an influence campaign.[2] One of the originators of the hashtag, an account with the name Rami Al Shibly, posted lots of images containing a combined Saudi and Iraqi flag. This account was suspended by Twitter fairly shortly after the launch of the operation. A corpus analysis of over 20,000 of the tweets also revealed that one of the most salient political entities mentioned (after Iraq and Baghdad) was Iran. Most of the tweets mentioning Iran were retweets heavily critical of the Iranian regime, and generally used language such as 'bloodthirsty mullahs' or criticised 'Iranian militias'. One popular tweet read, 'this is not a sectarian uprising, they are all Arabs marching against the Iranian regime'. Around 40 accounts sharing this hashtag have since been suspended. Most of the tweets on the hashtag were 'replies', and most of the content was directed at news organisations or politicians such as Donald Trump, the *New York Times* or CNN, no doubt to get them to 'mainstream' the anti-Iran narrative.

Similar campaigns have occurred throughout Iraq's uprising. The hashtag 'Iraq Revolts'[3] was also synonymous with the October Uprising. However, network analysis revealed that the most active accounts tweeting on the hashtag were pro-Saudi accounts that had been set up in the month prior to the Uprising. One of the three most active accounts, mooha_8018, featured a profile picture of King Salman. The other two accounts were also active in promoting pro-Saudi and anti-Turkey content. Although user-reported location on Twitter must be regarded with caution, the vast majority of accounts were located in Saudi Arabia. A corpus analysis also showed that within a sample of around 15,500 tweets and retweets, 'Iran' was the fourth most common word, after Iraq, god and revolts.

A campaign showing similar manipulation also occurred on 5 January 2020 when the Iraqi parliament voted to end the presence of US troops in Iraq. The hashtag 'I am Iraqi, and the parliament doesn't represent me' sought to delegitimise the campaign, with many of the active accounts having historically rallied against Iranian influence in Iraq. In addition to the metadata markers that pointed to an influence campaign, the likelihood of the campaign being authentic is questionable since an aspect of the uprisings had been the end of foreign influence. It is possible that some Iraqis would no doubt see the US presence as a counterweight to Iranian influence, although protesting Iranian interference should not be construed as pro-American sentiment.[4] The discursive emphasis on the Iran trope on Twitter, along with the role of Saudi accounts promoting the hashtag, suggests an attempt to co-opt the discourse of the movement to reflect Saudi foreign policy concerns. Regardless of the true motivations for genuine protests, social media highlight how foreign actors can potentially use their digital clout to dominate and re-orient online discussions to suit their own agenda, often piggybacking off organic sentiment.

It is likely that a similar network also exploited the Iraq protests in an attempt to bolster the production of adversarial content against Qatar. The Arabic hashtag 'Qatar is against the people of Iraq' trended on 25 November 2019. Although relatively small (around 500 accounts), many of the accounts in it had professional-looking profile photos of attractive Arab men and women, many of whom had pictures of Iraqi protests in their banner images. However, the accounts had almost identical tweeting histories. They almost all promoted a Twitter account called 'jazira is liar [sic]' (Al Jazeera lies) and featured an image of the Al Jazeera logo alongside an image of the devil. Many had also been active in promoting and lionising the Egyptian president, Sisi. The network tweeted in both Arabic and English. Among the tropes in the campaign against Qatar was that the Qatari emir Tamim bin Hamad Al Thani was collaborating with the Iraqi prime minister Abdul Mahdi to 'bring down our revolution and enable Iran to impose its control again'.[5] Other tropes promoting baseless conspiracies that Qatar was colluding with Iran included the argument that Qatar had prior knowledge of a drone attack on Saudi oil facilities in September 2019.[6] The network was probably a private marketing firm with government clients, as at least one of the other campaigns the accounts had been active on were promoting the Emirates' Federal Authority for Identity and Citizenship.

Iraq-connected campaigns, in some cases from the same network, were also analysed by Stanford Internet Observatory and highlighted a number of other hashtags subject to manipulation, mostly focusing on Iranian influence:

> The focus on Iran was also reflected in the most commonly used hashtags: 'العراق ينتفض' ('Iraq_is_rising' – frequently used in the context of Iraqis revolting against Iran), 'الملالي' ('the_mullahs'), 'إيران تدعم الإرهاب' ('Iran_supports_terrorism'), and 'جواسيس خامنئي' ('Khamenei_spies').[7]

Moqtada al-Sadr

Another Iraq-connected campaign that took place in early 2020 aimed to promote the viewpoint of Moqtada al-Sadr. Al-Sadr, a populist cleric and leader of the Iraqi parliament's largest political bloc, had initially been supportive of the Iraq protests, but this changed after the US assassination of the Iranian general Soleimani in January 2020. Following the assassination, the parliamentary political bloc led by al-Sadr 'clearly shifted away from its previous focus on the protests and the need for reform towards anti-American sentiment'.[8] As Iraq expert Fanar al-Haddad argues, the assassination of Soleimani simply gave opponents of the protesters a counter-case to rally behind. After Reuters reported that eight people were killed after forces loyal to al-Sadr stormed a protest camp in the Iraqi holy city of Najaf, two particular hashtags 'Support Moqtada' and With you oh Son of al-Sadr'[9] appeared after a note rallying support was posted on a popular Facebook account.[10] In a sample of 5,100 unique accounts tweeting on the hashtag, approximately 17% (865) were created on a single day – 6 February 2020. Around 676 of the 865 accounts created on the same day had 15-character gibberish handles, suggesting they had been set up hastily for the purpose of an influence campaign. Many of the tweets contained pictures of al-Sadr and were written in English and Arabic, suggesting they were designed to appeal to a broader audience (which makes sense, as Twitter is not used a great deal in Iraq – relative to Facebook).[11] With fewer indicators (through flags) or a tweeting history to go on, it is hard to say if there was a foreign power behind the campaign, and many of the accounts have not been suspended, although most remain unused since February.

Nonetheless, it is clear that hundreds of new accounts joined Twitter in order to tweet praise of Moqtada al-Sadr at a time when he and his supporters were being criticised by the media for their role in the deaths of protesters

The Twitter activism in Iraq highlights the growing problem of states, and unknown deception actors, lending the weight of their digital influence to campaigns that support their foreign policies. The fact that many of the digital campaigns seem to have been boosted by accounts reflecting Saudi (and US) and likely Iranian foreign policy demonstrates the relative ease with which foreign actors can manipulate the online space to either initiate or provoke discord or simply piggyback on legitimate demands and attempt to shape the narrative in favour of foreign policy objectives – in this case containing Iranian influence. Of course there is rarely a smoking gun, and we can't be sure who might be behind such deception campaigns without clear evidence. Yet Iraq has often been a sectarian battleground in which Iran and Saudi (among others) vie for political influence, and so it makes sense they are big players in the information space. As Haddad notes, 'today a binary of anti-Americanism and anti-Iranianism is being instrumentalised and imposed on the Iraqi public discourse in an attempt to prioritise Iran–US rivalries, rally pro-Iranian forces and outflank the protest movement'.

Lebanon Revolts

Lebanon's domestic policies are synonymous with outside interference. Regional actors have long sought to exert influence in Lebanon, from Syria and Iran to Saudi Arabia and Israel. The entrenched boundaries of Lebanon's confessional political system have brought with it the attendant problems of compartmentalised allegiances and at times accusations of allegiances to outside powers. Iran has long backed the Shi'a political party Hezbollah, while, for example, Saudi has attempted to curb what it sees as Shi'a/Iranian expansionism by supporting the Sunni Hariri family. Attempting to attribute disinformation and influence operations in Lebanon is not easy, with genuine expressions of discontent susceptible to being hijacked by other actors. Nonetheless, various forces compete for influence in Lebanon's digital space. This problem is likely to get worse as the economic crisis in Lebanon risks provoking further political instability.

An interesting example of this was during the protests that began in Lebanon on 17 October 2019. The protests, like those occurring in Algeria and Iraq, railed against corruption and a political order seen as either anachronistic or beholden to outside powers. The hashtag 'Lebanese Revolts' trended, and none of Lebanon's numerous political parties escaped criticism. The protests were galvanised by a general antipathy to the entire system. As Joey Ayoub noted, the slogan 'KELLON YAANI KELLON' (all of them means all of them) became common, conveying the simple and powerful message that 'no politician can ride this revolutionary wave as it explicitly and pre-emptively excludes them all'.[12] One such politician to be targeted specifically by a hashtag was Hassan Nasrallah, the secretary-general of the Lebanese political and paramilitary party Hezbollah. The hashtags 'Nasrallah Wahad Menon' (Nasrallah is one of them) and 'Nasrallah! Distance yourself and your weapons from us' began trending almost immediately after the uprising began.

An analysis of 4,494 unique accounts on both hashtags revealed what were clearly many genuine accounts; 2,297 of these accounts had user-reported location data, around 35% of which reported that they were based in Saudi. One of the most retweeted accounts was pro-Saudi analyst Amjad Taha (see Chapter 6). Furthermore, there was a spike in new account creations in September 2019, before the uprising had begun. At least 150 of the 300 or so accounts created in September and October 2019 were soon suspended. Their handles were generally gibberish, suggesting they had been created hastily, probably for an information operation. The profile pictures were generic, and they produced a lot of slick infographics and political cartoons portraying Nasrallah as a puppet of Iran or, in one case, a horn being squeezed by a large, robed hand – presumably belonging to Khameini. Another showed Hezbollah as a locust. This type of trope is familiar in many Saudi-led operations.[13]

In line with the idea that disinformation begets disinformation, the response to the hashtag was a similar one praising Nasrallah. The hashtag 'Nasrallah has our trust' was clearly a response to the one criticising him. This was evident by the fact at least 108 Twitter accounts praising him were set up on 20 October, immediately after the critical hashtag. As with many hastily created accounts, the handles contained a lot of numbers or a seemingly random collection of characters. Of the 495 new accounts created in September and October 2019, only 215 remain, pointing to a high suspension rate by Twitter, itself indicative of coordinated inauthentic activity. Of course, it is difficult to determine where this operation was based, and although user-reported location is not strictly reliable, the majority of the accounts reported themselves based in Lebanon. This would not be surprising, given Nasrallah's following there. It is perhaps interesting to note the similarities between the non-organic devotional campaigns seeking to lionise and defend both Nasrallah and Moqtada al-Sadr in the wake of contested criticism. It highlights how certain political actors or those acting on their behalf view social media as an important arena in which to contest and defend their legitimacy. Such campaigns, which seek to give the illusion of organic and grassroots support, tend to be negated when exposed as inauthentic campaigns, incurring further legitimacy costs to those they claim to defend.

Beyond the protests of 2019, events in Lebanon, regardless of what they might be, are clearly exploited by internal and external political interests. When 2,750 tons of ammonium nitrate exploded unexpectedly in the port of Beirut on 4 August 2020, unleashing a massive shockwave that damaged much of the Lebanese capital, regional actors were quick to exploit the tragedy to insert their own narratives. With absolutely no evidence at the time as to why the ammonium nitrate stored in one of the warehouses exploded when it did, the hashtag 'Hezbollah's ammonia burns Beirut' was the top trend in Lebanon a day later. While the average Twitter user will not be able to see why a trend is being generated, a network analysis of 14,000 interactions produced by 9,870 unique accounts on the aforementioned hashtag revealed that the most influential accounts promoting the disinformation were Saudi-nationalistic accounts, including Monther al-Shaykh – a ubiquitous participant in most online campaigns emanating from the country.[14] Other influential accounts, including @5aldi, @albarii_sa and @vip300400 all had profile and display pictures of MBS and/or King Salman. The conspiracy was abetted by other influencers connected to the United Arab Emirates. Dhahi Khalfan, the deputy chief of police and general security in the UAE, tweeted that the smoke cloud from the explosion resembled those who were responsible (i.e. a man in a turban – a not-so-veiled reference to Hassan Nasrallah). Khalfan wrote, 'In the Beirut Port bombing, the image of the perpetrator of the raid appeared in its apparent form before you.'[15] Saudi's Al Arabiya news channel even cited an anonymous high-level official, who claimed that Hezbollah had been siphoning off the ammonium nitrate for years.[16]

Subsequent attempts by the US State Department to leverage the explosion to encourage sanctions on Hezbollah came when State Department official Nathan Sales accused Hezbollah of storing ammonium nitrate around Europe to be used in future explosive attacks, subliminally capitalising on the recent tragedy to create links between the explosion and Hezbollah's activities in Europe.[17] The deception campaign attempted to muddy the waters during a time of confusion, and at a time when people's desire for answers was compounded by a sense of grief, shock and anger. The explosion was symptomatic of many of the issues of systemic corruption endemic across Lebanese political parties, including Hezbollah,[18] yet the desire from some Gulf states and the USA, the Israel lobby, to create a coherent narrative that placed the blame squarely on the Iran-linked organisation reflects simply how actors leverage disinformation and human tragedy for geopolitical ends.

Algeria, Hirak and Elections

By the end of September 2019 Algeria had seen its thirty-second weekend of pro-democracy demonstrations. The internet was viewed as crucial in helping mobilise Algerians, and the government used targeted network shutdowns in the first quarter of 2019 in an attempt to curb the flow of information about protests. Despite this, peaceful protests, led by what became known as the Hirak (lit., movement) movement, successfully pressured Abdelaziz Bouteflika, the president of 20 years, to step down in April 2019.

However, protests continued. The caretaker government stipulated that, in accordance with the constitution, an election would take place on 12 December to help try and resolve a political stalemate. Nonetheless, many Algerians worried that the elections would be rigged by a military junta, an understandable concern given Algeria's history of colonialism and political conflict. Many Algerians believed that elections without systemic reform would simply give democratic legitimacy to continued authoritarian rule. As a result of this suspicion, a number of opposition leaders called for a boycott of the elections until there were guarantees of an end to elite military-dominated cronyism exemplified by the army chief, Ahmed Gaid Salah, a Bouteflika appointee and de facto leader of government since Bouteflika stepped down. On the other side of the coin, the army wanted people to go to the polls, in the knowledge that they had generally benefited from the current electoral system.

Activists suddenly became concerned about social media campaigns that seemed designed to undermine Hirak. The appearance of two hashtags provoked the suspicion of opposition activists, who believed attempts were under way to divide the movement's broadly supported opposition to the elections. The two hashtags were 'not in my name' and 'Algeria votes/is voting'. The 'not in my name' hashtag was criticising those boycotting the elections, essentially trying to depict those opposing the elections as being a small but vocal minority. The hashtags were obviously aimed at giving the idea of support to the military's request to vote. Although such an opinion may have existed among the youth, it was certainly a fringe view, made the more surprising when it trended several times on Twitter.

It soon became clear that much of this support was being created and, indeed, 'inflated' by suspicious accounts. I analysed a sample of around 20,000 tweets from 5,769 unique accounts between 15 and 28 September 2020. Most tweets in the sample were sent on 22 September. The sample was skewed in favour of recently created accounts. Since 2008 the average number of accounts created per month in the sample was only 44. However, September saw this number rise to an incredible 723 accounts (12%). Furthermore, 474 (7% of the total sample) of those 723 accounts were created in a two-day period. A further analysis two days later on 30 September highlighted that at least another 260 accounts were created on 29 September, meaning that 20% of the entire sample of accounts in a subsequent analysis of 5,244 accounts were created in September 2020. Most of the accounts appeared to look like real people. They had Algerian-sounding names, profile pictures, and tweeted in support of the army and the elections.

Some claimed that as Algerians mostly used Facebook, a call was made on a Facebook group for Algerians who wanted elections to join Twitter and make their voices heard. However, such an argument is more likely to have been a convenient way to attempt to paint a deception campaign as a legitimate, albeit coordinated, influence campaign. Algerian activists have noted concerted efforts on Facebook in particular to undermine the unified voice of the Hirak movement. Raouf Farrah, one of the founders of the Collective of Activist Youth, who had been active in the broader protest movement, noted how 'electronic flies', new accounts with very few followers, would target their posts and try to swerve or deflect the debate with a specific set of topics, most notably that the protests were a foreign (French)-backed phenomenon. Considering Algeria's history of French colonial rule, such an assertion is likely to provoke nationalist sympathies and portray protesters as traitorous. On other occasions, the flies lionised the army, often copy and pasting (copypasta) slogans like 'Long Live the Army' several times.

The investigation I had undertaken then appeared to be exploited by some ostensibly supporting the status quo. After sharing my analysis on Twitter, it was picked up by a number of news sources, and also Mondafrique, a French-language website dedicated to opinion pieces and investigate research. The French journalist Nicolas Beau wrote up my findings yet, bizarrely, entirely misrepresented them. He used my data to argue that a campaign had been set up to target Ahmed Gaid Salah in order to discredit the military. Soon Algerian activists began to question how Beau reached this conclusion. Later Mondafrique offered a correction to the article, saying, 'We had written in error and we apologize that Marc Owen Jones concluded that adversaries of the military had unleashed a massive campaign of disinformation about the Web. In fact, the conclusions of this researcher were exactly the opposite of this observation.'[19] Despite this, it did not alter the main argument of the article, which maintained the original notion that a fake network had been set up to attack Gaid Salah. It is not clear if the article was a deliberate (disinformation tactic) or accidental (misinformation) interpretation of my results. However, given that the article was not itself rectified, it would seem difficult to argue that it was misinformation.

As the election date loomed, new deception campaigns appeared. In late October and early November a new hashtag began to gain traction. This one translated as 'we are all Zegmati'. Belkacem Zeghmati had been appointed attorney general earlier in 2019. However, he was at odds with the country's judges after they went on strike after a huge reshuffle. The strike threatened the 12 December elections being opposed by the Hirak movement but supported by the army. The sudden appearance of the hashtag 'we are all Zeghmati' was viewed with suspicion by activists, as it was seen as an attempt to legitimise the man who had provoked the ire of those judges threatening the elections being advocated by the military. The hashtag started around 26 October, but really began to get traction between 2 and 4 November. An analysis of 4,021 tweets by 2,044 unique accounts was undertaken. Between 2008 and November 2017 the average number of accounts in the sample created per month on the hashtag was only 15. However, the number of accounts created in September 2019 was 303. In October it was 204. Indeed, over 25% of accounts in the sample were all created in the three-month period of September 2019–November 2019. What's more, 15% of all accounts in the sample were created across just five days, a strong indicator of inorganic and deceptive activity.

Aside from the newer Twitter accounts set up in November and October, the accounts that had tweeted on the anti-opposition hashtags (not in my name) and (Algeria votes/is voting) were generally the same accounts tweeting on the 'we are all Zeghmati' hashtag. So whoever ran that campaign back in September and October appeared to be running the pro-Zeghmati campaign, adding weight to the argument that this was some sort of anti-protester influence operation. That an organic collective would adopt two specific tropes, especially one as specific as supporting an attorney general, is quite improbable.

In addition to slightly less malicious campaigns to get people to vote, the network began to get more aggressive as the election approached. On 8 December, four days before the election, 'Zitout is a traitor' began trending. Mohamed Zitout was a former Algerian diplomat who moved to the UK. Zitout had founded the opposition Rachad movement, and provoked the ire of Saudi Arabia and the UAE by accusing them of trying to stifle the Hirak movement in Algeria. Zitout's concerns were not unfounded, as Saudi Arabia had historically backed the Algerian status quo deep state as a bulwark against perceived Islamist expansionism. An analysis of 5,975 tweets by 2,640 unique accounts revealed that 838 (14%) of the accounts using the 'Zitout is a traitor' hashtag were created between September 2019 and December 2019. What's more, in September 2019 around 200 of these accounts were created in a three-day window. Of these, 154 were created on 8 December alone, the day the trend began.

Although the elections eventually happened, their lack of popularity was evident in the fact that the turnout was the lowest in any Algerian election since independence. The disinformation campaigns leading up the elections reflected attempts to try and encourage support for the unpopular elections. Although it is not clear what impact the campaigns may have had, they clearly were not sufficient to inspire a large number of people to head to the polls.

It also not clear who was behind the campaign, as it could theoretically be anyone supporting the status quo. It was later revealed that the European Union had, through the European Union Agency of Law Enforcement Training (CEPOL), funded the training of the Algerian and Moroccan police in counter-surveillance techniques that included the use of sockpuppets and fake online accounts. Officers who participated in the training were taught how to create and maintain sockpuppet accounts 'from purchasing SIM cards from a local shop to posting outside of office hours, avoiding home and office networks, creating a "story" to blend in online, and using software to run multiple fake identities at the same time'.[20]

That is not to say they were the ones involved here, but it highlights the murky world of state-backed and endorsed deception operations.

While Iraq, Lebanon and Algeria are just three examples of countries in the region whose online politics are manipulated by external actors, nowhere remains off limits, particularly to gulf-based influencers. In 2021, when Tunisian president Kais Saied took more power in an autocoup, the online conversation was dominated by accounts attempting to justify the move as a necessary means of preventing the Muslim Brotherhood from stifling Tunisian democracy. While many may have held this opinion, the dominant voices were Saudi and UAE influencers. In other words, gulf influencers were using their social media power to dominate the public sphere, speaking on behalf of Tunisians in order to legitimise a return to authoritarian rule.[21]

Conclusion

This chapter has documented the vulnerabilities of Middle East (or indeed any) countries to social media manipulation by malicious actors. A conundrum of hashtag activism is the paradox of simultaneously wanting to raise international awareness and solidarity for a political cause, versus it being hijacked by other actors who simply wish to promote their own agenda. The cases of Iraq and Lebanon have highlighted the very real problem of pro-Saudi, Emirati and Iranian digital hegemony in the region. Their ability to mobilise digital disinformation campaigns in a co-opted social media space with no boundaries allows them to insert themselves into the narratives of neighbouring Middle Eastern countries. The sheer volume of resources they are able to mobilise allows them to muddy the waters of narratives about particular events, whether it's an explosion born of administrative incompetence and political corruption or protests that have the potential to lead to regime change.

The potential impacts for democracies and activists across the world and in the region are clear: a lack of sovereignty over an information space, in a MENA context dominated by states with scant regard for truthfulness, leaves countries vulnerable to potential electoral interference and public opinion manipulation by actors with digital media power. The Algerian case is also interesting because it reveals that when attempts to manipulate social movements occur, we cannot always be certain of the origins of those efforts. They could as easily be the work of a regime seeking to bolster the legitimacy of a military government, or the military themselves seeking to encourage the perpetuation of the status quo. The absence of attribution, and the difficulty in doing so, simply exposes the extent to which social media, as a product, has become untethered from our ability to establish a chain of accountability or transparency in its deployment. The ability to weaponise social media lies on the very fact that it allows malign actors to anonymously mass produce content and deploy across boundaries that, in normal circumstances, prohibit, control or monitor the flow of goods, ideas and people. That there is rarely a smoking gun leaves the manipulation space open to any entity with the ambition and resources to attempt to deceive.

8

YOU ARE BEING LIED TO BY PEOPLE THAT DO NOT EVEN EXIST

THE PSEUDO-JOURNALISTS

Chapter Overview

Deception actors must innovate and outsmart their adversaries in order to find ways to circumvent algorithms or other means of deception detection. However, sometimes brazen deception in the form of creating fake personalities can be sufficient to undertake successful propaganda campaigns. This chapter discusses one of those most audacious, far-reaching and sophisticated deception operations of its kind. In it, a group of fake journalists fooled dozens of news outlets from across the globe into publishing propaganda for over a year. This chapter argues that such audacious deception operations emanating from the Gulf reflect a deep commitment to attempting to convince global audiences of the merits of containing Iran, and celebrating the vision of the Middle East as desired by the UAE in particular. It also highlights that, despite a renewed and concerted focus on disinformation, newspaper editors still play a key role as gatekeepers in preventing disinformation. Similarly, the demand for content and news in an information society is working against diligent sourcing and screening of journalists and information.

181

'A Grave Danger to Freedom of Speech'

On 7 June 2020 a message appeared in my Twitter inbox from Matt Suiche, a cybersecurity entrepeneur based in the United Arab Emirates. He had received a strange message from a man called Raphael Badani. Suiche sent me a screenshot of Badani's message.

Hi Matt,

My name is Raphael, and I am a political risk analyst.

Based on your profile, I believe that you and I share common values. It has come to my attention that a member of the Muslim Brotherhood, Tawakkol Karman, has recently been appointed to chair Facebook's oversight committee. This is a grave danger to freedom of speech, the exposure of truth, and our very future as citizens of the free world.

I am looking for like-minded people who could help me share relevant content so as to inform the general public of Facebook's dangerous decision. I would be extremely grateful if you could help me share/re-tweet relevant content so it can reach your audience.

Thank you in advance,
Raphael

Matt, slightly perturbed by Badani's unorthodox and serpentine approach, dropped me a message explaining that he thought it was strange that Badani only had a few LinkedIn contacts and that he had not really written anything before January 2020. A cursory Google search revealed that this was indeed true, but perhaps Raphael Badani was an up-and-coming journalist? He did, after all, have an impressive CV. He was a graduate of George Washington University and Georgetown University, both of which are known for their strong Middle East Studies expertise. Following his graduation, Badani spent time working for the US Department of Labor and had a brief stint as a geopolitical risk consultant and interactive simulation designer – whatever that means. Indeed, in his short stint as a journalist, Badani had been quite prolific, with pieces in the *Washington Examiner*, RealClearMarkets, American Thinker and the *National Interest*, several well-known conservative American news outlets. He even had a column in Newsmax, an American news and opinion outlet promoted by Donald Trump as an alternative to CNN and MSNBC.[1]

I contacted Adam Rawnsley of the US news outlet the Daily Beast, noting that there was something untoward about the Badani account. We both began to dig. Meanwhile, given my experience with sockpuppet accounts, I suggested that Matt offer to have a Zoom call with Badani, as this would at least show that Badani was who he purported to be in his photographs. Matt agreed, and Badani responded:

> Hi Matt , thank you for your response. I prefer to keep it in messaging for the time being. I take my privacy very seriously and understand that people may have a problem with that.
>
> Would be happy to discuss further here if you are interested.

Given Badani's refusal to appear on a video call, we thought it prudent to ask him exactly what 'relevant content' it was that he wished to share – on the basis that whatever he wanted people to read might give an insight into his political stance.

Badani responded eagerly, sending a link to an article from the *Asia Times* titled 'Why Facebook's oversight appointment is dangerous'. The article was authored by Lin Nguyen, who had a strikingly similar profile to Badani. Her bio described her as an analyst in South East Asian regional security, focusing on economic and political developments. Nguyen had worked on projects advising South East Asian government ministries and also private enterprises seeking to do business in the region. She had, according to her biography, 'leveraged' her experience to write publicly about pressing economic and political issues concerning Asia. Like Badani, Nguyen seemed to have only been a journalist for a short while, with her first piece appearing in the summer of 2019. Unlike Badani, who wrote in US-based publications, Nguyen focused on Asian affairs, writing a remarkable 18 differences pieces in the Hong Kong-based *Asia Times* and the *South China Morning Post*.

Although Nguyen mostly wrote about Asian-related affairs, the piece promoted by Badani was somewhat different; it focused on Facebook, with the drop head reading, 'Platform's selection of Yemeni with links to Islamist group for the committee will undermine efforts to combat hate'. Various people shared Nguyen's article on Twitter, as did Nathalie Goulet, a French senator and vice-chairman of foreign affairs and defence,[2] and David Reaboi, a member of the think tank Security Studies Group, who had previously published a report suggesting that murdered journalist Jamal Khashoggi was an 'asset' being 'handled' by Qatar.[3]

Despite her general focus on Asian affairs, Nguyen had found a captive audience among a group of people known for their public hostility to the Muslim Brotherhood and Qatar. In addition to her piece on the Facebook oversight board, Nguyen had also written a more general piece about disinformation titled 'Misinformation becoming the currency of "soft power"'. In this piece, Nguyen had singled out the Middle East Eye as a case study in spreading misinformation. The Middle East Eye has long been a target of quartet-related smear campaigns, especially in 2017, where thousands of fake Twitter accounts published infographics denouncing it as part of what they called 'Qatar's media snake'. For a journalist largely focusing on Asian current affairs, it was curious that Nguyen singled out what she perceived as a Qatari attack, via the Middle East Eye, on Mohamed Dahlan, a UAE-based security adviser. As much as anything else, the article was a thinly veiled attack on Middle East Eye. Nguyen wrote, 'After Middle East Eye was sued in a UK court, it was revealed that the publication consistently does this sort of thing.' The court case Nguyen was referring to was one in which Dahlan sued the Middle East Eye for defamation.[4] Nguyen's concluding salvo sought in clear terms to frame China and Qatar as birds of a feather in their misleading disinformation strategies, noting:

> China can make the world look the other way on human rights violations, censorship, and its attempts to tamp down a protest movement that has been gaining steam. Qatar can make itself appear a liberal mecca in a sea of conservative, regressive regimes, and other countries can uphold archaic laws using misleading, and in some cases completely fabricated, data. Soft power is quickly becoming the major way states leverage their influence. When complemented with disinformation, it allows

governments to create the conditions designed expressly to keep the rest of us in the dark.

Again, it seemed strange that a journalist focused almost entirely on Asian affairs was taking a highly specific and parochial foreign policy position adopted by the KUBE countries.

Stranger things began to emerge. A reverse-image search of Lin Nguyen initially revealed nothing suspicious. There was no obvious evidence that her image had been stolen. I contacted Robert Haddow, the editor of the *South China Morning Post*, to ask if he could shed any light on Lin Nguyen and whether or not he knew her or had met her. Haddow responded saying he would speak to Lin and put us in touch. I heard nothing and so decided to contact Cindy Xi, another Twitter user who had also shared one of Nguyen's articles on Twitter. Cindy noted that she and Lin moved in the same circles and she would pass on my details.

A few days passed, but no news from Lin, or Cindy.

Realising I was not going to get an answer, I persevered with my image searches. Using a different search engine than usual, and not one that traditionally offers the best results, I found a picture of Lin. Nguyen had flipped her image along the vertical axis to make it more difficult to locate. This time, whoever ran Nguyen's account had stolen it from someone called Nhu Thai, a Vietnamese woman who worked at the Singaporean business advisory firm Fidinam Group Worldwide. Whoever Lin Nguyen was, she was clearly lying about her appearance.

Curiously, the fact that Cindy Xi had claimed to move in the same circles as Lin now made her suspect. After all, if Lin was not who she claimed to be, then what did that say about someone who claimed to move in the same circles?

There was no evidence that Cindy had stolen a photo from someone else's account. Xi was less prolific as a journalist than Badani and Nguyen, and had written a piece in a publication called the ASEAN Post, this time about the UAE's 'exemplary resilience to Covid-19'. This piece, extolling the virtues of the UAE's medical system, reflected how regimes were politicising their own responses to the coronavirus crisis. For many leaders facing criticism about their handling of Covid19, there was no harm in attempting to burnish their credentials to aid domestic legitimacy.

Like Badani and Nguyen, Xi had impressive credentials. She claimed to have a PhD in Political Science from the National University of Singapore (NUS), one of the best universities in the world. That she was writing for a rather parochial publication, the ASEAN Post, was not in itself unusual, but there was little evidence of her work elsewhere. I contacted the NUS about Cindy. It did not take them long to confirm that no one of that name had ever graduated with a PhD in PoliSci from NUS.

It seemed that Cindy Xi also did not exist.

The Arab Eye and Persia Now

During the Nguyen affair, Adam Rawnsley had got back in touch about Badani. Reverse-image searches revealed that Raphael Badani, who had his smiling visage plastered across his Newsmax column, was not who he claimed to be. Instead, his profile picture traced back to a man called Barry Dadon, an entrepreneur based in San Diego, California, who had no idea that his image was being used for deception. Whoever was behind Badani's account had clearly sifted a number of Dadon's social media profiles. Like Nguyen, they had flipped the images along the vertical access in order to make it harder to find them via reverse-image searches.

But there was something else unusual about Badani. In addition to his contributions to high-profile conservative-leaning outlets, he had also authored pieces in the Arab Eye, a little-known blog offering a conservative (in the American sense) perspective on Middle East politics. The Arab Eye was relatively active, publishing op-eds on a more or less weekly basis. Arab Eye also shared SSL certificates and Google Analytics code with Persia Now,[5] and both domains were registered on the same day. They also had almost identical green and white branding.

Soon, Adam and I began to explore the profiles of contributors to Arab Eye and Persia Now. With the exception of a journalist called Amin Farhad, none of the contributors wrote for both outlets, ostensibly to keep them separate in the public eye. However, it soon became clear that the contributors all had a lot in common with Nguyen, Badani and Xi. Most had careers that seemed to go as far back as only 2019, with most beginning their writing careers in early 2020.[6]

The journalists were also a diverse bunch, with names and profiles suggesting they came from a variety of different backgrounds. With names ranging from Joyce Toledano to Salma Mohamed, whoever was creating the profiles clearly wanted to add a sense of authenticity and credibility to the operation by giving the image of a diverse staff. Indeed, it was not unlike the profile of staff on an international news outlet such as Al Jazeera English.

It soon became clear that almost all of the journalists did not exist. Many had extremely sparse LinkedIn profiles, and reverse-image searches revealed that some of them also had photos stolen from social media accounts. Navid Barani, a contributor to Persian Eye, and who had written several articles, had stolen the image of Cristopher Turoci, an insurance broker from California. There was also no evidence of Barani's claimed degree from James Madison University.[7] Ironically, one of the writers, Amani Shahan, described herself in her biography for Global Villages and Persia Now as also being a contributor and ghostwriter for the Daily Beast – the very paper that would publish the exposé.

Of the 26 or so journalists writing in either Arab Eye or Persia Now, some, like Badani and Nguyen, had published in high-profile publications. The list was impressive and included Western and English-language news outlets with a conservative slant. In addition to the aforementioned sites, other outlets to publish articles by these non-existent journalists included but were not limited to Spiked Online, the *Jerusalem Post*, the Western Journal, the National Interest, the *Washington Times*, the Post Millennial, Human Events, *Asia Times*, the *South China Morning Post*, Japan Today and the Diplomat. Even Yahoo News republished one of the articles that had originally been published in the *National Interest*.

While many of the journalists whose accounts were established earlier in the network's existence had used stolen Facebook photos, others employed more imaginative, yet equally thrifty, methods of deception. 'Mikael Virtanen', a Finnish businessman who wrote about Middle East current affairs in the Jewish News Service, took his avatar from a free image database. Perhaps the most disturbing development in the fake news network was the fact that the newer journalists began to use photos generated by artificial intelligence. It has long been argued that AI-generated 'deep fake' technology will be a game changer in disinformation. No longer will analysts be able to identify stolen photos using reverse-image searches, because disinformation agents can now create unique, realistic images of humans at the click of a button using generative adversarial networks (GAN). Although AI-generated faces are currently possible to identify, it is only a matter of time before they become hard to discern from the real thing.

It is highly likely that whoever ran the network used thispersondoesnotexist.com to create avatars. Using GAN, the website allows anyone to generate lifelike and unique human faces by simply refreshing their web browser. Despite the realism, certain tells can suggest that photos have been generated using this particular program. For example, the fake journalists Lisa Moore and Joyce Toledano had extraordinarily symmetrical features, with an almost identical alignment of eyes, mouths and eyebrows. For the avoidance of doubt, Adam Rawnsley even consulted a dentist, Leonard Kundel, to examine some of the facial features of Joseph Labba, a fake journalist who had written for the Post Millennial. Kundel stated, 'This mouth looks either fake or has some sad dental story behind it.'[8] Labba's image showed some of the 'telltale glitches commonly found in AI-generated faces. The left ear [was] oddly smooth without any ear lobe creases.' Image-analysis software also confirmed Kundel's expert analysis, revealing that Labba appeared to have three misfit teeth in his mouth where there should have been four.[9]

Content and Modus Operandi

All in all, 19 confirmed fake journalists wrote more than 90 articles between them, in at least 46 different outlets as far afield as the United States and Japan. This number includes those articles written in the Arab Eye and Persia Now. The earliest posts dated back to July

2019 and were authored by Lin Nguyen. Of the approximately 77 articles written in international news outlets, 48 (64%) were about the Middle East. Of these 49, 25 (51%) were focused on criticising Iran, and especially Iranian involvement in Iraq and Lebanon. Several of the articles were anti-Qatar and Turkey, while many of the others focused on criticising the Muslim Brotherhood, Hamas or Hezbollah. Tawakkol Karman's appointment to the Facebook oversight committee was something that particularly irked the network. In articles for the Jewish News Syndicate, *Asia Times*, Politcalite, and Middle East Online, the network variously portrayed Karman as a

Fig. 7: A topical analysis of the articles published
by the fake journalists

Category	Category Description	Number of Articles
Anti-Iran	Those articles criticising Iran, its leadership, and its interference in regional affairs	24
Anti-Qatar	Articles criticising Qatar, mostly for its foreign policy and the media industry	4
Anti-Turkey	Criticism of Turkey, especially with regard to its role in Libya	3
Anti-Muslim Brotherhood	Articles framing the Muslim Brotherhood as a terrorist organisation. Includes articles about Tawakkol Karman, who was framed as an MB, and therefore terrorist, sympathiser	4
Pro-UAE	Mostly articles celebrating the UAE's response to Covid19	3
Anti-Hezbollah	Criticism of Hezbollah's role in Lebanon, with implicit criticism of Iran	4
Anti-Hamas	How Hamas is supporting Turkey	1
Miscellaneous	Articles on the 'Deal of the Century', Daesh and Egypt	5

'nefarious political actor with a questionable past' who would make Facebook the 'platform of choice for extreme Islamist ideology.'[10]

Although it was now obvious that the journalists did not exist, it was less clear who was behind the operation, or whether it was a state-led endeavour subcontracted to a private firm. The policy positions of the articles pointed to the UAE, not least because several articles heaped praise on the country. The modus operandi of the fake journalists was to approach international news outlets and pitch op-eds with well-crafted articles. When the journalists were not publishing in international outlets, they boosted their portfolios and created a trail of legitimacy through the Arab Eye and Persia Now.

Ironically, the Arab Eye described itself as a bulwark against 'fake news' and 'biased narrative'. It stated on its website: 'Now more than ever it is crucial to hear opinions from the other side of the aisle on matters pertaining to the Middle East.' Persia Now listed a non-existent London mailing address and an unattended phone number on its contact form. The editors of the outlets, Sharif O'Neill and Taimur Hall, have almost no online footprint, let alone a clear history of journalistic contributions. They did, however, try to contact real people in an attempt to get them to write for Arab Eye and Persia Now. Ahmed Aboudeh, who holds an MA in War Studies, claimed he was approached: 'About two months ago, I've [sic] contacted on Twitter by Sharif O'Neil, [who] introduced himself as Editor of the Arab Eye & offered me a long term arrangement to contribute to the site. When I asked who the sponsors are, he didn't reply.'[11] After being asked whether O'Neill had offered to pay, Aboudeh noted, 'Yes, after explaining that they were a new publication' and 'needed respected bylines' to appear on the site. 'But after demanding detailed answers on the sponsors, the office's location and staff, he didn't come back to me. We didn't reach the point of payment details.'[12]

The Response and its Impact

After the Daily Beast broke the story about the fake journalist network, Twitter suspended Badani's account along with 15 others, including Cindy Xi and Navid Barani, for violating their policies on platform manipulation and spam. The breaking of the story also brought other insights to the surface. Tom Grundy, the astute editor of the *Hong Kong Free Press*, tweeted that he had been approached by at least three of the journalists, including Nguyen, Xi and Toledano.[13] However, he sensed something was amiss and declined their offer of an article.

> Glad we dodged a bullet – twice.
> I rejected a number of pieces from the fake 'Lin Nguyen' and 'Cindy Xi' in early 2020 as they both seemed suspect. Now we know:
> Their emails were very polite but persistent. & the op-eds were extremely well-polished.[14]

In order to facilitate the process of getting their propaganda and disinformation into outlets, the journalists offered to waive any fees they might ordinarily receive for their contributions. Grundy tweeted a screenshot of one of Nguyen's emails which stated, 'happy to submit without a fee as well'. Other than Tom's comments, which came after the publication of the exposé, there is little publicly available evidence to suggest that the network provoked suspicion among other editors. One of the earliest contributions, written in September 2019, was an article in the *International Policy Digest* by Joyce Toledano called 'How Qatar is using disinformation tactics to attack its rivals'. The piece complained about Al Jazeera, a key concern of the blockading states. The article argued that 'the landscape highlights a fascinating case study of how fake news can affect regional political discourse'. The editors at the *International Policy Digest* deleted the article 'in response to criticism of the article's sourcing'. They also noted: 'We regret its publication.' Despite this, an almost identical article titled 'Misinformation is becoming the currency of soft power' by Lin Nguyen appeared several days later in the *Asia Times*. In addition, two months later, Michel Haddad, another fake journalist from the network, posted another article on the *International Policy Digest*. The move simply highlighted a lack of awareness and coordination among news editors amid the global information deluge. It also pointed to the inability of some outlets to develop policies to tackle such problems.

The reactions by those outlets that had been duped were startling in their variety and inconsistency. The responses can broadly be divided into the five following categories: deleting the articles without comment; deleting the articles with an editorial comment; not deleting the articles; keeping the articles up along with an editorial note; and defending the publication of the articles. The *Washington Examiner*, for example, deleted its article written by 'Badani', and posted the following note from the editor: 'This op-ed has been removed after an investigation into its provenance and authorship.'[15] Daniel Kleidman, the editor of Yahoo News, reacted quickly after being informed that Yahoo News shared Badani's National Interest article as a part of a content-sharing agreement, and deleted the post. Yahoo News stated that that it had launched an investigation.[16] The *South China Morning Post* withdrew all articles by Lin Nguyen, stating, 'This article has been withdrawn because we are unable to verify the authenticity of the author. As a result, we are now reviewing our policies for contributors.'[17]

Newsmax quickly deleted all articles by Badani and deleted his profile page, which listed him as an 'insider'. Newsmax did not provide any editorial comment on this decision. The *Asia Times* was slower to delete the articles by Nguyen, and did so only in July and without comment. The *Jerusalem Post*, the Post Millennial and the *National Interest* also deleted their articles without any statement from the editor.

Spiked Online, which has been described as libertarian, chose to keep a piece by Joyce Toledano on their website along with an addendum, which stated that Spiked 'takes seriously any claim of questionable authorship'.[18] However, it had left the text up in the interest of 'transparency.' Human Events took a more strident position, and outright defended their publication of the article, placing an editor's note on the piece by Joyce Toledano reading: 'We have reviewed the substance of this piece, and have not found any factual errors – and we still agree with the thesis of the piece. As such, we are keeping the piece up, and adopting its arguments as a publication'.[19]

In addition to this, the editor-in-chief of Human Events at the time, Will Chamberlain, released a salvo of tweets attacking myself, the Daily Beast and Qatar.[20] Ironically, Chamberlain dismissed the provenance of these fake journalists as being irrelevant because he agreed with their arguments. At the same time, he used ad hominem attacks against me and the Daily Beast based on our provenance. To defend disseminating propaganda on the basis that one believes in the message simply highlights an inability to understand that one's beliefs have probably conformed to the desired message of the propagandist. In addition to Chamberlain's invective, the then managing editor of Human Events, Ian Miles Cheong, told me to 'get fucked'[21] when I criticised Human Events' response to the issue. Certainly, the response of Human Events was indicative of a fundamental tenet of 'truth decay', that is, the 'blurring of the line between opinion and fact'.[22]

Another alarming element to this is that, despite the widely publicised investigation, many of the articles have neither been deleted nor qualified with an editorial comment. The Western Journal, a site that prides itself on telling the 'truth', and had the ironic tagline 'Real Stories, Real People', still carries articles by the fake journalist Michael Haddad, mostly about ramping up sanctions on Iran. While many may not have heard of the Western Journal, it once had a readership of around 36 million, and was one of the most widely read online news sites in America.[23]

Despite post-truth politics and disinformation never being far from headlines over the past five years or so, there remains a startling naivety, and occasional malice, in confronting the scourge. First, it is surprising how many experienced editors were duped by the pitches. This is no doubt partly systemic, as digital outlets are increasingly under pressure to produce more and more content and thus have less time to adequately vet submissions. Most of the fake journalists had portfolios of pieces, along with social media profiles that would have given them a superficial veneer of credibility if one was to do a cursory Google search.

Nonetheless, the varied responses from editors also highlight that while actors spreading disinformation are part of the problem, other actors in the ecosystem also compound the issue. For example, to delete a post on account of its questionable provenance without disclosing that it might have been disinformation or propaganda is to reduce the likelihood that those who may revisit the article might be informed that they were being deceived. Furthermore, not publicising an editor's note declaring that a deceptive piece of content was produced can potentially reduce reader vigilance by fostering an atmosphere of complacency. Indeed, news outlets suffer from the fact they must be perceived to be credible, while also being truthful and honest.

Although it is hard to know the full impact of the operation, we know from Twitter that numerous high-profile public figures shared the articles written by the fake journalists, including Students for Trump co-founder Ryan Fournier, US right-wing commentator Andy Ngo and French senator Nathalie Goulet. Despite the low followings of most of the journalists on Twitter, they still secured high-profile attention from their work, perhaps in part by a private messaging campaign similar to the one Raphael Badani had undertaken. It has also not been confirmed who was behind the campaign, but the ideological bent of the articles, including the overpraise for the United Arab Emirates, suggests an entity working on behalf of an Emirati institution.

Operation Endless Mayfly and Ephemeral Disinformation[24]

A somewhat similar operation to the Arab Eye and Persia Now network, with a different ideological bent, was Operation Endless Mayfly, uncovered by the University of Toronto's Citizen Lab in 2019. Endless Mayfly was, according to Citizen Lab, 'an Iran-aligned network of inauthentic personas and social media accounts that spreads falsehoods and amplifies narratives critical of Saudi Arabia, the United States, and Israel'.[25]

The purpose of the network was to push divisive and adversarial content by impersonating legitimate, mostly Western, news outlets. Its main modus operandi was to create web pages that impersonated genuine websites and post deceptive content on them. In November 2018 Ali al-Ahmed, an expert in Gulf terrorism based in Washington DC, received a private message on Twitter from someone called Mona A. Rahman. Rahman chatted with al-Ahmed, and eventually shared an article linking to the Harvard Kennedy School's Belfer Center for Science and International Affairs. The website looked identical to that of the Belfer Center. The only tell-tale difference was that the impersonating domain was belfercenter.net as opposed to belfercenter.org. This process, known as typosquatting, involves creating a typographically similar domain to the target website. It operates on the basis that people will not be savvy or aware of such minor discrepancies in the web address.

The article that Rahman sent to al-Ahmed contained information that would potentially be damaging to Russia–Israel relations, and 'contained a purported quote from former Mossad director Tamir Pardo, alleging that former Israeli Defense Minister Avigdor Lieberman had been dismissed by Netanyahu for being a Russian agent'. The Endless Mayfly network had performed similar impersonations for reputable or well-established media outlets including *Haaretz*, Al Jazeera, the *Times of Israel*, *The Guardian*, Bloomberg and *The Atlantic*. In total, Citizen Lab 'identified 135 inauthentic articles, 72 domains, 11 personas, 160 persona bylines, and one false organization'.[26] However, Mayfly also impersonated other domains, such as a German government website, Twitter and a pro-Daesh outlet.

Like the Raphael Badani network, the Endless Mayfly operatives created social media personas which they would use to engage people on Twitter with. Often they described themselves as activists or journalists. Like the Arab Eye and Persia Now network, Endless Mayfly's writers would target genuine websites that allowed for user-generated content, such as '*China Daily*, *FairObserver.com*, *Buzzfeed Community*, *Medium*, *Opednews.com*, and *WN.com*, among others'.[27] Some of these, such as Fair Observer, were also targeted by the Badani network, revealing ongoing problems for sites that permit unverified user-generated content.[28] This tactic is not new. Back in 2009, Liliane Khalil, the fake journalist who features at the beginning of this book, and who attracted a large following in 2011 during the Arab Uprisings, wrote content for CNN's iReport section – which allowed for user-generated content.[29]

At times the Endless Mayfly accounts would take screenshots of their false op-eds and circulate them on Twitter. This tactic is not unique to the operation. It was common in the Gulf Crisis too, often breaking out into international media. The Endless Mayfly network appeared to be directing most of its criticism at Saudi Arabia, the United Arab Emirates and Israel. A fake article written on a site impersonating the US publication *The Atlantic* was titled, 'A shocking document shows the shameful acts of Saudis and Emiratis for hiding human rights abuses in Yemen'.[30] The trajectory of the network also changed. In its early stages its tactics revolved around amplifying content on impersonator websites that it controlled, and evolved to writing articles on third-party sites. To evade detection, the operators would quickly delete their articles after they had been absorbed into the information ecosystem, leading Citizen Lab to brand the term 'ephemeral disinformation'.[31] As Lim noted, 'once Endless Mayfly content achieves social media traction it is deleted, and the links are redirected to the domain being impersonated. This technique creates an appearance of legitimacy while obscuring the origin of the false narrative.'[32]

Conclusion

The methods of Arab Eye/Persia Now and Endless Mayfly were similar. Both used tactics of deception (inauthentic personas) to insert and amplify content into social media discussions. Both networks engaged privately with activists, journalists and influencers in order to maximise the dissemination of their content. However, while Endless Mayfly produced divisive content on websites that impersonated legitimate media outlets, the Arab Eye network focused mostly on producing content for its native sites (Arab Eye and Persia Now) in addition to pitching articles to well-established international outlets. Endless Mayfly did this to an extent, but perhaps with less success than the Badani network. This might reflect something as simple as the fact the Arab Eye network had better content producers. Rather than attempt brute force in the disinformation sphere, this represented a far more escalated level of deception.

What these networks highlight is not simply an issue or phenomenon of social media and technological change impacting upon the spread of disinformation, but rather a failure of well-established protocols of detecting deception. Although deception is not new in journalism, basic steps of verification undertaken by editors would have prevented a lot of these problems, as would better curation of websites that allow user-generated content. So rather than simply being a unique product of a post-truth age, both these networks reflect a failure of well-established journalistic protocols and standards. They also reflect a growing demand for content, and perhaps how the imperatives of monetisation are leading to lax standards in the quest for veracity and truth. Perhaps the most striking aspect of these disinformation campaigns is their audacity. While creating impostor content on websites controlled by the deception actors is technically easier, submitting op-eds by fake journalists to reputable international outlets reflects a certain level of boldness. The fact that so many people were duped, often on multiple occasions, suggests that this tactic is set to continue, especially as developments in AI can make it easier for malign actors to create fake personas.

As this chapter has demonstrated, while the Qatar Crisis cemented the ambitions of KUBE countries as key disinformation players within the Arabic-speaking world, the Arab Eye network reflects an increasingly audacious and far-reaching strategy of disinformation, probably undertaken on behalf of the UAE. That the content often targeted Iran also reflected a central tenet of the Gulf's post-truth moment, which was to turn public opinion against Iran at every juncture. Operations like Endless Mayfly also reflected the role of Iran as a key actor, although not particularly in the Arabic-speaking space. Nonetheless, the operation highlights the way in which the MENA tensions between Iran and Saudi/UAE/Israel have generated a lot of deceptive content.

9

FOOTBALL CRAZY

SPORTSWASHING AND THE PSEUDO-FAN

Chapter Overview

This chapter highlights the capacious reach of Gulf-led deception operations into the world of professional football. In doing so, it addresses the growing assertiveness of Saudi Arabia in extending its influence operations under the tutelage of MBS and how the use of sockpuppets was leveraged on Twitter to spread and influence narratives about the proposed takeover by Saudi's Public Investment Fund (PIF) of Newcastle United Football Club (NUFC). It also explores the discursive phenomenon of disinformation meta-narratives, whereby disinformation from other instances, in this case the Gulf Crisis, is combined with the new narratives in order to rationalise foreign policy to new, impressionable and invested audiences. Here, NUFC fans were made to believe that Saudi's bid to take over NUFC was being scuppered by Qatar as the result of a feud, and not reasons related to piracy and human rights. Crucially, it highlights how football fans in general are being targeted by the deception order, which is monetising deception to either engage in sportswashing or negative campaigning.

Some Unlikely Football Fans

St James's Park, home to the English Premier League's Newcastle United, is not the kind of spiritual home one would expect to find a legion of potential new devotees of the Saudi crown prince Mohammed bin Salman. However, on Twitter, scores of NUFC fans with Saudi emojis in their biographies took to Twitter to praise MBS and Saudi Arabia in the spring of 2020. One man even took a picture of himself wearing his Newcastle jersey and the traditional *ghitra* (a male headscarf worn by many Gulf nationals).[1] But perhaps more bizarrely, two young women called Emily Sarnes and Georgia Abrewis tweeted their support for a Saudi-led consortium's proposed takeover of their beloved Newcastle. Both Emily and Georgia had profile pictures displaying their loyalty to the club. Georgia had a picture of herself taking a selfie in her black-and-white striped 'magpie' jersey, while Emily's photo was a group shot of a women's football team, all wearing Newcastle jerseys. What was strange, though, is that they both tweeted an identical photo of the emir of Qatar taking a topless selfie, along with the words 'so ugly'. This piece of malinformation, believed to have been extracted from Tamim's iPhone during a UAE-led hack, was circulated at the outbreak of the Gulf Crisis in 2017.[2] Something did not seem right; why would two young women from the north-east of England be tweeting esoteric images of a Gulf emir who had apparently no immediate bearing on their lives?

More to the point, why would they care if he was ugly or not?

Football Fever and Project Ball

In order to understand this unusual chain of events involving Emily and Georgia, we have to go back somewhat, to the Qatar World Cup and the Gulf Crisis. Qatar's winning of the bid to host the 2022 World Cup, announced on 2 December 2010, generated no small amount of controversy. Much of this was based on alleged bid corruption concerns, and also legitimate human rights concerns documented by organisations such as Human Rights Watch and Amnesty International, which lamented the treatment at the time of labourers, and raised concerns about the barriers to inclusion of the

LGBTQ+ community. Qatar's winning of the 2022 World Cup was soon seen as a useful trope to exploit within the context of the Gulf Crisis. Indeed, the global visibility of the World Cup was seen as an opportunity for Qatar to address a number of its labour problems, which it has attempted to do with varying degrees of success. According to Steve Cockburn, head of economic and social justice at Amnesty International,

> In recent years Qatar has introduced a series of major reforms, including amending laws to give workers freedom of movement and allow them greater job mobility. It has also promised better pay and access to justice in cases of abuse. But many migrant workers have not yet benefited from these changes. Until these reforms are fully enforced, many will remain trapped in a cycle of exploitation.[3]

Nonetheless, the advent of the Gulf Crisis provided new impetus for KUBE countries to find means of attacking Qatar. Despite their own poor treatment of migrant workers, the KUBE bloc has used migrant rights as an attack line to delegitimise Qatar. Indeed, the Gulf Crisis, along with the high visibility of the World Cup, has acted as a honey pot for deception profiteers. One such company was that founded by the Tory strategist Sir Lynton Crosby, who offered to use his lobbying firm CTF Partners to delegitimise Qatar in order to restart the World Cup bidding process. In a pitch document seen by *The Guardian* newspaper, entitled 'Project Ball', CTF partners detailed 'a proposal for a campaign to expose the truth of the Qatar regime and bring about the termination of the 2022 World Cup in Qatar'.[4] The pitch, sent in 2018 and signed personally by Crosby, costed the negative campaign at £5.5 million, broken down into £300,000 per month over 18 months. In addition to placing negative stories in the traditional media, the proposed pitch would involve using a number of deceptive tactics, including running fake grassroots campaigns on social media and lobbying friendly politicians, journalists and academics.[5]

The proposed client for Project Ball was Khalid al-Hail, the self-proclaimed Qatari opposition figure living in London. Al-Hail rose to prominence during the Gulf Crisis, where he organised what journalists Anthony Harwood and Alex Delmar-Morgan described as a 'multi-million-pound marketing campaign' to 'strip Qatar' of the 2022 World Cup.[6] In May 2018 the Foundation for Sports Integrity held a launch at the London's upscale Four Seasons Hotel. It was not clear who funded the event, although it became known that a number of attendees had business-class flights paid for, as well as receiving a substantial fee for their participation.

According to *The Guardian*, the event contained a substantial amount of anti-Qatar propaganda, such as vox pop videos and other advertisements attacking Qatar.[7] Nicholas McGeehan, who has researched labour rights in the Gulf and the politics of GCC football, was initially offered a fee to speak at the event, but after he asked for assurances that the event was not funded by Gulf money, he was un-invited.

Attempts to 'piggyback' on issues dominating the news cycle for the purpose of creating adversarial content targeting Qatar's hosting of the World Cup have continued through 2020. The Foundation for the Defense of Democracies journalist Benjamin Weinthal wrote a piece in Fox News linking Covid19 and the World Cup. The title read, 'Qatar lying about its COVID-19 outbreak to avoid jeopardizing its hosting of the World Cup?'

The similarities between the playbook used both in London and Washington to delegitimise Qatar (namely, two funded conferences) are striking. The modus operandi seems to be to host conferences where academics and politicians are invited to give the illusion of legitimacy to an event whose motives remain to influence important power brokers around a certain state's foreign policy objectives. In addition to this, there was a parallel and incessant campaign of adversarial content creation across social and traditional media.

With various elements of the deception order tripping over themselves to secure contracts for negative campaigns related to the World Cup, it was no surprise that the digital space was flooded with adversarial content. As was expected, social media campaigns targeting the World Cup became especially common. On July 2019, for example, the Arabic hashtag 'Qatari pitches kill workers' began trending. Of at least 629 of the unique accounts tweeting on the hashtag, around 427 (68%) have been suspended by Twitter, pointing to an influence operation. Conversely, at the same time, an Indian company linked to Qatar appeared to have been enlisted to counterattack the waves of disinformation targeting the World Cup. In March 2020 Graphika, a social media analysis company based in New York, released a report named 'Operation Red Card' that revealed how an Indian PR company called aRep had run an influence operation targeting the United States, Canada, the United Kingdom, Western Europe and the world of professional football. It had focused in particular on the 2022 World Cup in Qatar.[8] The content of the bot network mostly addressed issues related to Gulf politics, with an overarching theme of attacking the UAE and Saudi Arabia. The bot network, mostly on Facebook, and described in the Graphika report as 'relatively' small, was taken down on 29 February 2020. It consisted of around 122 'assets' and, like several takedowns associated with Israel, Egypt and the UAE, was run by a commercial marketing company.

The chief modus operandi of Operation Red Card was the use of fake accounts to manage groups and pages with the intent of driving 'people to off-platform websites masquerading as news outlets'.[9] Politically, the campaign 'largely reflected international concerns over issues such as the Gulf states' military campaign in Yemen and the accompanying humanitarian crisis, the murder of Saudi opposition journalist Jamal Khashoggi, and Saudi Arabia's record on women's rights'.[10] In addition to this, 'Operation Red Card used football to target the UAE. It did this particularly by focusing on the travails of Manchester City FC, which is owned by Sheikh Mansour bin Zayed al Nahyan, deputy premier of the UAE and a member of the royal family of Abu Dhabi.'[11]

Saudi PIF's Newcastle Bid and BeoutQ

As adversarial World Cup content played out on- and offline, the initiation of the Gulf Crisis took the world of football and deception to another level of dissonance. Just after the blockade began in 2017, Saudi Arabia established a piracy operation that directly stole and redistributed content from the Qatari firm beIN SPORTS, the legitimate MENA broadcasting rights holder of the English Premier

League and almost every major sports body in the world. *New York Times* journalist Tariq Panja described this as 'The brazen bootlegging of a multibillion-dollar sports network'.[12] In a not-so-subtle allusion to the politics of the Gulf Crisis, the piracy operation was called beoutQ (Be Out Qatar). In tandem with the launch of the illegal beoutQ operation, Saudi also ejected beIN SPORTS from the country as part of the cessation of trade and diplomatic ties with Qatar. In addition to being a Qatari company, the fact that beIN SPORTS also used to be Al Jazeera Sports further irritated the Saudis, who tied it in to their disinformation campaign linking terrorism to Qatar – despite beIN simply being a sports pay-TV broadcaster.

In April 2020, almost three years after the third anniversary of the Gulf Crisis and the establishment of beoutQ, a consortium led by Saudi Arabia's Public Investment Fund (PIF), which included British businesspersons Amanda Staveley and the Reuben brothers, launched a bid to purchase Newcastle United Football club for £300 million. As well as being a form of economic diversification for Saudi's sovereign wealth fund, it was also a kind of sportswashing, a phenomenon whereby countries project soft power through portraying themselves in 'ways that contrast starkly with their image as autocratic and often brutal violators of human rights'.[13]

Saudi Arabia is not unusual in this regard. European football club ownership has become a status symbol, and the UAE, Saudi and Qatar are increasingly trying to gain more influence in global sports governance.[14] In 2011 Qatar's state-owned shareholding organisation Qatar Sports Investments (QSI) bought a 70% share in the French club Paris Saint-Germain. This is not a uniquely Gulf phenomenon either, but rather one of wealth. Rich oligarchs and business tycoons from around the world have purchased football clubs, for example, the American Glazer family, who own 90% of Manchester United, or Roman Abramovich, the Russian owner of Chelsea Football Club. For autocratic regimes there can be attendant reputational benefits. For Saudi, the PIF's bid for NUFC came on the back of high-profile human rights violations masterminded under the auspices of MBS, most notably the murder of journalist Jamal Khashoggi, the war in Yemen and the detention of numerous women's rights activists in Saudi.

However, these factors, which prompted global outrage at the Saudi regime, fed into another, perhaps less auspicious, factor: TV piracy. As a result of beoutQ, in 2018 Qatar filed a complaint through the World Trade Organisation's Dispute Settlement Body. The complaint was supported by numerous rights holders with whom beIN had partnered to show various sporting events, including FIFA, UEFA, the AFC, the Bundesliga, LaLiga, the Premier League and Lega Serie A.[15] In addition to the human rights abuses, it was actually the WTO case filed by Qatar that posed the biggest threat to a potential PIF takeover. Indeed, the Saudi state's flagrant three-year theft of numerous global sports bodies' intellectual property, including that of the English Premier League itself, was a red flag for those charged with overseeing any potential takeover. Those advocating for a PIF takeover had to wait for the outcome of the Premier League's 'Owners and Directors' Test', a procedure designed to make sure that potential directors of Premier League clubs are deemed suitable to 'protect the reputation of the game'.[16]

The confluence of the PIF bid, and the ongoing WTO case, created a potent opportunity for the seeding of adversarial narratives. It was here that Saudi would attempt to convince Newcastle fans that Qatar was a villain trying to scupper the PIF's plans to resurrect the destiny of an underperforming football club for the sake of settling petty political scores. In other words, deception would be used in an attempt to get Newcastle Fans to support MBS's attempt to rehabilitate his international reputation through sportswashing. Sure enough, strange things began happening on Twitter, and this is where we come back to the story of Emily Sarnes and Georgia Abrewis.

After Abrewis and Sarnes inexplicably posted a picture of Qatar's emir Tamim bin Hamad, they quickly changed their profile pictures; or rather, their profile pictures were changed. Abrewis, whose Twitter handle was NewcastleMBS, suddenly changed her image to the NUFC logo and began tweeting exclusively in Arabic. The 'so ugly' tweet, along with the image of Tamim, was deleted from the accounts, and all the old tweets scrubbed. It was as if the accounts had been stolen and appropriated for the campaign. Emily Sarnes, who had the account handle MBSLoved and who also tweeted the image of Tamim, was soon suspended by Twitter. Other pro-MBS and pro-NUFC takeover accounts with suspicious provenance appeared. One account, with the Twitter handle @NUFC_SA, claimed to be a consortium of people who supported the PIF takeover. When I explored the history of the account, it seemed that it had once belonged to a pharmacy, and someone had appropriated the account for the purpose of spreading propaganda on the hashtag.

Other anonymous accounts began to crop up on Twitter. Many of them attempted to frame the bid not as an international legal issue concerning piracy and genuine human rights concerns, but simply as a conflict between two Gulf regimes feuding. Some accounts purporting to support Newcastle United began to embrace many of the adversarial tropes used by the blockading countries to attack Qatar. One account, with the British name Gary Finnigan, had a link in his bio that directed to a news article seeking to frame Jamal Khashoggi's fiancée as a Turkish deep-state agent.[17] Another account claiming to be a Newcastle fan tweeted that he had had a conversation with a Saudi on Twitter, who managed to convince him that Khashoggi's fiancée, Hatice Cengiz, was being used by Qatar in an attempt to stop the NUFC takeover.[18] The newly converted Newcastle fan then proceeded to slut-shame Cengiz. Indeed, as Cengiz was attempting, as part of a campaign to secure justice for Khashoggi,[19] to persuade the Premier League that Saudi should not be allowed to own NUFC, she became a target of the adversarial content.

Much of the discourse defending Saudi Arabia emanated from a pseudonymous account called Kate Stewart, which has spent much of its time advocating for Saudi Arabia and MBS while criticising Qatar. During the PIF's bid, Stewart was one of the most vocal commentators on the hashtag 'NUFC Takeover', which was being used to discuss developments in the process. A network analysis of around 19,000 tweets on the NUFC Takeover hashtag taken in April 2020 highlighted that Stewart's English-language advocacy for the takeover was one of the most retweeted. In particular, one tweet, explicitly defending MBS from accusations of his well-publicised involvement in the Khashoggi killing, and Saudi atrocities in Yemen: 'Lies are being spread across the #FakeNews media about #Saudi_ Arabia in an unprecedented campaign of hate. Here's the truth:

#MBS was NOT involved in any way with the death of #Khashoggi 2) #KSA provides millions of food aid to #Yemen. The Houthis steal it #NUFCTakeover'.[20] Although Stewart's account has been suspended several times, it has also been reinstated by Twitter.

Meanwhile, other accounts sought to deflect blame to Qatar by stating that money from beIN SPORTS would be used to support terrorism. Saudi-based Awwad Alotaibi tweeted, 'Bad move from #Qatar which everyone knows that the #beINSPORTS money is used to support terrorists in #MiddleEast and overseas. #NUFCTakeover is going through smoothly, which will make them radgie. #NUFC forever'. In addition to Alotaibi's spurious claims, it is interesting to note his attempts to appeal to NUFC fans through cultural competence cues by using the term 'radgie' – a derogatory term peculiar to Tyneside, the north-east and parts of Scotland that means a violent or aggressive person.

The WTO Report

On 16 June 2020 the World Trade Organisation issued a long-awaited report detailing how Saudi Arabia had prevented Qatar-based international sports channel beIN SPORTS from defending its intellectual property. The WTO's findings were not confined to the interests of beIN, with the panel also finding that, despite being provided with extensive evidence by the Premier League, the UK Government, FIFA, UEFA and others, the Saudi authorities deliberately did not take any criminal action against beoutQ. The Saudi government obstructed the initiation of civil copyright infringement cases, including by pressuring nine Saudi law firms to refuse to take on a civil action by the Premier League and others. The ruling was unambiguous, and found, crucially, that beoutQ was a 'commercial-scale' operation operated by individuals or entities under the jurisdiction of Saudi Arabia. It also found that the Saudi government not only failed to prevent piracy but actively encouraged it. Indeed, the report detailed how high-profile figures, such as Saud al-Qahtani, actively promoted beoutQ, with the country even organising 294 public screenings of beoutQ during the 2018 Russia World Cup.

The WTO's judgment was clear; it was damning of the Saudi government's approach to IP. The world press was also clear. Reuters, *The Guardian*, Bloomberg, the *Financial Times*, the BBC, the *New York Times* and many others all covered the story. The Reuters headline read, 'WTO says Saudi broke global rules in Qatar broadcast dispute'.[21] The *Washington Times* stated that 'Saudis facilitated sports piracy'.[22] Everyone got the message, and that's when the Saudi disinformation machine kicked in, deliberately misrepresenting the official findings in a way that allowed Saudi to save face. The legacy Saudi media such as Arab News, Al Arabiya, and the Saudi Gazette all falsely claimed that the WTO had ruled in favour of Saudi, or said that Saudi's argument of national defence was 'justified'. The Saudi Gazette, for example, claimed that 'the real dispute behind this false intellectual property issue is of diplomatic, political and security crisis among the Gulf Cooperation Council'.[23]

One of the most striking examples of the potential co-optation of global news outlets by Saudi influence was how the Saudi-owned Independent Arabia and its parent paper The Independent covered the matter. The headline in the Saudi-owned Independent Arabia (see Chapter 3) read, 'WTO rejects Qatar complaints against Saudi'.[24] Meanwhile, the headline in the UK the *Independent* stated, 'Saudi enabling of sports piracy "threatens the existence of sport as we know it", says UEFA after WTO ruling'.[25] The headlines were the complete opposite, and revealed once again how Saudi ownership of Indy Arabia was once again impacting upon the editorial line, to the extent it was explicitly distributing disinformation under cover of the reputable Indy branding.

Not long after the ruling, the hashtag 'WTO rejects Qatar complaints' began trending on Twitter. Tens of thousands of tweets appeared. Saudi and Emirati accounts also began claiming that Saudi had won the ruling, deliberately misquoting and misinterpreting the report. Numerous accounts stated that the report had said that Saudi's action against Qatar had been justified, although the report had stated no such thing: this was simply a quotation from the Saudi submission to the panel, not the opinion of the panellists. Many of the most influential proponents of the influence campaign were again those responsible for previous campaigns, such as Monther al-Shaykh, Sky News Arabia presenter Abdallah al-Bandar, Saudi analyst Amjad Taha, SMAAT-linked Saudi News50, 5aldi and 70sul.[26]

Perhaps the most shocking aspect of this influence campaign was that there was no real plausible deniability between the government and its disinformation agents. It was the Saudi's Ministry of Interior that led the charge with the disinformation, deliberately misleading and misrepresenting the report and tweeting on the 'WTO rejects Qatar complaints' hashtag.[27] The KSA Ministry of Foreign Affairs focused on things that were irrelevant to the report, such as there being no evidence that the pirated broadcast came from Saudi 'land'.[28] This was immaterial and irrelevant – but also absurdly incorrect: the WTO specifically identified Riyadh-headquartered ArabSat as the satellite agent of the beoutQ operation. Attempts to deceive social media users were also made. A press release featuring the WTO's branding was circulated and again emphasised that the WTO had found Saudi's legal defence, based on national security concerns, to be justified. Closer inspection revealed that it was a circular by the permanent Saudi mission to the WTO, illegally using the WTO's logo to pass it off as the WTO's opinion.[29] Most remarkably, this illegal use of the WTO's intellectual property in a Saudi government press release was done within the context of an adverse intellectual property ruling. Weeks later, after spreading disinformation about how it had won the case, Saudi Arabia formally appealed the WTO ruling – a curious move by a party that purported to have won.

Soon after, in July 2020, the PIF withdrew its bid to buy NUFC. In the ensuing weeks, campaigns promoted by a network of pro-Saudi accounts included the hashtag 'PremierLeagueisCorrupt', which featured an image of EPL head, Richard Masters, with puppet strings being controlled by a hand next to the logos of Qatar and beIN SPORTS. A petition to investigate the EPL and Richard Masters was launched on Change.org. Disturbingly, the petition praised MBS's human rights reforms while attacking Qatar for the failure of the PIF bid.[30] The petition stated:

Mohammed Bin Salman who is the crown prince of Saudi Arabia is an ally of the UK government, and Royal Family has been integral in supporting the UK with the outbreak of Covid-19 along with reforming the KSA policies on human rights. As a result of the EPL's negligence and Qatar influences around the Newcastle takeover, the city of Newcastle has been deprived of some well-needed investment into the local football club as well as the city as a whole.[31]

Although 110,222 people signed the petition, it is not clear exactly who set it up (the name of the person who started the petition was simply 'Sean h' – but no further details are available). One signatory purported to be Richard Masters, head of the Premier League, himself. Whether or not the petition was legitimately set up by aggrieved Newcastle fans, or by some agency attempting to put pressure on the EPL to potentially approve a renewed Saudi bid, its text highlights the effectiveness of Saudi disinformation in influencing the discourse on civic-participation mechanisms abroad. The takeover of NUFC by the PIF was eventually approved in October 2021, officially after 'legally binding assurances' were offered that the Saudi state would not control the club.[32] In reality, the agreement was most likely approved after a resolution was reached with beIN over piracy of their content.

Perhaps an interesting element of the deception operation here was its relative success in co-opting a local and specific constituency to lobby on behalf of the PIF's bid to take over Newcastle. While many disinformation campaigns can be somewhat diffuse in their targeting, the deception campaign around the NUFC takeover exploited the 'identity fusion' and 'visceral sense of oneness' that can form between supporters and their club.[33] Supporters of clubs such as Newcastle United, so often used to disappointment and failure – which can create a form of trauma – are potentially at more risk of such fusion. This 'one-ness' may make fans more susceptible to believing that their redemption lies with a takeover by a rich saviour such as the PIF, however problematic the actions of Mohammed bin Salman or the Saudi state. Here personal judgement is subsumed in the collective good of the overarching social identity. The willingness to blame Qatar (if indeed authentic) also reflects the nature of tribalism in football, where rivalries are the norm, and whereby the whole game is premised on adversarial competition between two competing sides. Indeed, the NUFC takeover case has highlighted how group identity can facilitate the absorption of adversarial content, even if that content is decidedly implausible – or, indeed, patently false. It has also highlighted the potential risks of how foreign states, in this case Saudi Arabia, can attempt to manipulate external communities, potentially against their better judgement, for the sake of achieving their own foreign policy goals and domestic reform goals.

Conclusion: Disinformation is Coming Home

The disinformation around football politics in the Gulf has not remained a regional or parochial issue. The politics of Gulf football, even in this relatively limited case study, highlights the complexities and capaciousness of the disinformation order. From the World Cup to the Gulf Crisis, major regional events and the politics around them have spawned deception operations that spill out in the global information ecosystem. From UK-based PR companies exploiting the World Cup in order to generate business opportunities to a government deliberately lying about the ruling of an international organisation, deception campaigns connected to Gulf football politics offer a stark insight into the intersecting motivations and interests that underpin the post-truth era and the Gulf's post-truth moment. The explicit role of the Saudi state in spreading disinformation about the WTO ruling has highlighted a relatively rare example of direct state complicity in a deception operation, while the activities of news outlets such as Independent Arabia have demonstrated how supposedly reputable Western news organisations can be co-opted for the purpose of projecting the false claims of a foreign state. These naturally raise attendant questions about regulations around media ownership, as well as transparency regarding the actions of unaccountable PR firms. It is important not to forget that the war against reality, and the post-truth milieu, is as much generated by nefarious state actions and dubious business practices as by the rise

211

of digital technology. When actors such as states show a willingness to deceive, and other entities, whether PR firms or think tanks, can profit of that deception, the resultant combination is one of large-scale deception.

10

COVID19'S DISINFORMATION SUPERSPREADERS

Chapter Overview

Covid19 has been utilised and instrumentalised by politicians as a political weapon to attack rivals. How states dealt with the pandemic became a source of rivalry for many nations, with some countries receiving opprobrium for their high death rates, and others being celebrated for their successful containment measures. Covid19 has also prompted a seemingly inexorable swathe of disinformation. While there might be a tendency to think of disinformation around Covid19 as a product of ignorance, disinformation is often profoundly political and strategic. This chapter highlights how Covid19 disinformation was absorbed and exploited according to the foreign policy objectives of Gulf states. It highlights in broad strokes the various Covid19 disinformation narratives in the Gulf region, and also examines how deception actors seemingly connected to Saudi Arabia and the United Arab Emirates used Covid19 disinformation to further attack and demonise their regional opponents.

Covid19 and Disinformation

'Covid19 stories are getting a lot of clicks right now, do you want to write a piece on it?' was what my op-ed editor said. They weren't alone; I have no doubt editors around the world were experiencing this. Covid19 news dominated the news cycle, in part, because it was what many people wanted to read, whether through fear or from a desire for the latest facts on a rapidly developing crisis. The business model of online news, so often reliant on generating internet traffic in exchange for advertising revenue, was fuelling the online glut of often erroneous and misleading information about Covid19. Indeed, as Tedros Adhanom Ghebreyesus, the World Health Organisation's director-general, at the 2020 Munich Security Conference stated, 'We're not just fighting a pandemic; we're fighting an infodemic.' Ghebreyesus was acknowledging that fake news, dis/misinformation and conspiracy theories had skyrocketed since the beginning of the Covid19 pandemic. The states of affairs was extremely worrying and risked undermining fragile trust in health institutions and programmes.[1]

Ghebreyesus was right to worry; the US president, Donald Trump, had already touted false cures for Covid19 and endorsed conspiracy theories about the cause of the pandemic. In fact, an analysis by Cornell University of over 38 million news articles concluded that 'the President of the United States was likely the largest driver of the COVID-19 misinformation "infodemic"'. Much of this was news sources simply reporting on the words of Donald Trump, further exposing people to disinformation. Claire Wardle identifies three important motivations of Covid19 disinformation: financial gain, political gain and experimental manipulation. There is often overlap in these categories, especially with regard to financial and political gain. Trump's Covid19 conspiracies were no doubt a combination of a number of these, but they were mostly about political gain. His desire for political capital required him to downplay the severity of the virus, deflect blame and ridicule those (scientists) who contradicted him in order to pander to his support base.[2]

Covid19 and the Qatar Crisis

Following the Gulf Crisis in 2017, the blockading countries mostly focused on portraying Qatar as a rogue, terrorist-supporting state.

However, the advent of Covid19 has highlighted how propagandists and disinformation agents piggyback on topics dominating the global news cycle in order to better leverage audiences to their adversarial content. In March 2020 several Twitter accounts created in January and February 2020 began to spread messages that Qatar, and specifically Qatar Airways, the country's national airline, was being negligent in its handling of the crisis, and had spread Covid19 to Argentina. One of the messages read, 'This is what I've been thinking past weeks the negligence and incompetency of #Qatar causing madness! A person who flew from Qatar to Argentina turned out to be positive of Corona Virus. Why aren't they checking all the passengers? Is Qatar really spreading the virus?'[3]

The other messages, all posted by accounts featuring attractive young women as their display pictures, almost all mentioned the phrases 'negligence' or 'incompetency'. After I informed Twitter of this bizarre behaviour, Twitter suspended the accounts, probably on the basis that they were engaging in some form of platform manipulation. The accounts themselves had no previous evidence of being concerned about Argentina, Covid19 or Gulf politics. In fact, they all seemed to be united by the fact that they were BTS stan accounts – fans of the Korean boy band BTS. Geoff Goldberg has recently written how BTS stan accounts frequently engage in inauthentic behaviour.[4] This seems to indicate that some entity or agency has had both BTS fans and someone else as a client.

A takedown of state-linked information operations by Twitter later revealed that a number of accounts connected to the UAE, Egypt and Saudi Arabia had targeted Qatar Airways, with one video accusing it of being the 'official carrier of the coronavirus'.[5] It is not certain, although it is likely, that these accounts were part of the same network.

Covid19 disinformation grew more virulent as the pandemic took hold in early 2020. The Gulf was no exception, and in early March a journalist called Noura Almoteari posted a tweet stating that Qatar had known about the existence of Covid19 since 2015. Almoteari, who freelances for the UAE-based paper *Al Bayan* and the Saudi paper, *Okaz*, also accused the Qatari government of paying billions to China in order 'to grow the virus'. Unlike the aforementioned BTS accounts, which were emphasising incompetence on the part of Qatar Airways, Almoteari was arguing that Qatar was acting with malice.

Like Donald Trump, who was provoking racial tensions by calling Covid19 the 'Chinese Virus' and 'Kung Flu', Almoteari was seeking to align Qatar with China, which the US president had already accused of being a duplicitous actor. Soon, the politics of the Gulf Crisis began to infiltrate Almoteari's discourse, and she also made the baseless claim that Qatar was maliciously and deliberately spreading the virus in order to damage the Emirati and Saudi economies. Specifically, Almoteari stated that Qatar wished to scupper the UAE's upcoming Expo 2020 and derail Saudi Arabia's Vision 2030 – an attempt to turn Saudi Arabia into a post-oil economy. In addition to the tweets, Almoteari also initiated a hashtag campaign called 'Qatar is corona'. Although thousands of people tweeted on the hashtag, it was not clear what proportion were expressing support or derision of the bizarre hashtag.

The attention provoked by the tweet and subsequent hashtag forced Almoteari to backtrack. Associated Press journalist John Gambrell tweeted at Almoteari, asking if she felt any responsibility as a journalist to write factually about Covid19.[6] The backlash prompted Almoteari to defend her actions by claiming that she was using a genre called 'political mythology', although it is not clear what this actually meant. The UAE Media Office even got involved, and stated that Almoteari was using a 'cynical style'.[7] She later clarified to Associated Press that she meant satire. *Al Bayan* also distanced themselves from Almoteari, emphasising that she was, in fact, a columnist and not an employee and that her views did not represent those of *Al Bayan*.

Almoteari was not alone in weaponising Covid19 to affirm extant political conflicts in the Gulf. Nora Shaner, a journalist who writes for the Saudi-owned London-based online newspaper *Elaph*,[8] tweeted that Corona was an Iranian and Qatari conspiracy.[9] Almoteari's comments seemed to cause outrage and ridicule in equal measure, although despite the absurdity it seemed to be a calculated attempt to place Qatar and China on an anti-US axis in order try and demonstrate that the UAE and Saudi were more appropriate regional allies for Donald Trump.

Meanwhile, the Arab Eye network, detailed in Chapter 8, also entered the Covid19 deception fray. Cindy Xi, a fake journalist with an AI-generated profile picture, praised the UAE's handling of the Covid19 pandemic. Xi had written an article for the Asean Post titled 'The UAE's exemplary resilience to Covid 19'. In it, Xi argued that 'the UAE's balanced approach is one that can and should be replicated'. Meanwhile, another member of the Arab Eye network, Raphael Badani, wrote a piece singling out Qatar Airways' role in spreading Covid19 – again smearing businesses connected to Qatar.

With the rise of Covid19 disinformation, social media companies, including Twitter, were taking a tougher stance on combating fake news pertaining to public health. However, while Twitter began to label tweets containing Covid19 disinformation, both Shanar and Almoteari's tweets and hashtags managed to evade its censorship, pointing to an important but overlooked aspect of disinformation: to what extent are non-anglophone markets a wild west for social media platforms to expand their markets with minimal corporate responsibility? In the context of the crisis, the failure of Twitter to enforce takedowns on political disinformation reaffirmed anxieties that Twitter was at best indifferent to the travails of non-Latin Twitter and at worst a partisan entity subject to political control through its headquarters in Dubai.

From the Gulf to Libya

In Libya, a raging proxy war, with Saudi Arabia, Egypt and the UAE on the one side, and Turkey and Qatar on the other,[10] has been compounded by an ongoing disinformation campaign. In the conflict, Qatar and Turkey support the internationally recognised interim Government of National Accord (GNA), while Saudi, the UAE and Egypt support the Libyan National Army (LNA) headed by Khalifa Haftar. Although disinformation has plagued the Libya conflict for some time, Covid19 has been used as a political weapon to attack geopolitical rivals. In the spring of 2020 a large network of social media accounts spreading pro-Haftar propaganda was taken down by Facebook and Twitter. Facebook removed 164 pages and 76 Instagram accounts, while Twitter closed 5350 accounts.[11] The

Stanford Internet Observatory, which examined these accounts, titled its report 'Blame it on Iran, Qatar, and Turkey', as many of the accounts lumped the 'blame on these three countries for everything from terrorism throughout the Arab world to the disappearance of Malaysia Air Flight 370 to the spread of COVID-19'.[12]

Prior to their emphasis on the pandemic, the accounts had mostly praised the LNA and Khalifa Haftar. Many had also attacked Fayez al-Sarraj, the GNA prime minister, accusing him of being a traitor after he signed an agreement to redraw maritime boundaries with Turkey.[13] Some of the assertions were absurd. Several accounts claimed that Turkish president Recep Tayyip Erdoğan had sent Covid19-infected fighters to battle against Haftar, and, presumably spread Covid19. The argument was that Erdoğan was exploiting the global pandemic to help his goal of re-establishing a new Ottoman empire.[14] Indeed, the invocation of the Ottoman bogeyman has been a trope of other disinformation campaigns, and is often deployed in an attempt to rile up historic Arab sensibilities against Turkish hegemony. The broader tropes of the propaganda simply attempted to paint the alliance supporting Haftar as humane and compassionate, while portraying Qatar and Turkey as Machiavellian actors. According to Grossman et al.:

> From these Twitter and Facebook takedowns, we have learned that the Egypt, UAE, and Saudi Arabia axis is continuing to drive disinformation campaigns targeting the Middle East and North African countries, with the goal of creating the impression of popular discontent with Qatar, Iran, and Turkey. Digital marketing firms implemented these campaigns and leveraged the latest news stories – in this case, the COVID-19 pandemic – to further their agenda. Tactically, we observed hashtag laundering, with geopolitically aligned 'news' sites publishing stories about inauthentically created hashtags.[15]

From Anti-Shiʿa to Anti-Israeli Disinformation

In addition to political disinformation, Mahsa Alimardani and Mona Elswah have documented how religious leaders in the region have sought to exploit the crisis to boost their popularity or expand their follower and subscriber base.[16] This has led to the sharpening of political, social and religious tensions in the Gulf. As in the rest of the world, fake cures and treatments for Covid19 have formed a substantial part of the religious disinformation. Some of the proposed remedies have been so bizarre that they have attracted the attention of the global press. Fringe Iranian cleric Ayatollah Tabrizian, who has rejected scientific medical science as a 'pillar of western infiltration',[17] advised those infected with the virus to swab their anuses with a piece of cotton dipped in violet oil. Such was the virality of the proposed treatment that it was soon picked up by some international media outlets,[18] provoking ridicule, and potentially amplifying Islamophobia.[19]

Although clerics issuing bizarre fatwas is fast becoming a genre itself, inviting ridicule and perhaps reaffirming stereotypes and prejudices people may have of the Islamic world, Covid19 has also amplified intra-religious rivalries. In particular, it has accentuated sectarian tensions along the Sunni–Shi'a divide. A quick search for the words 'Corona' and 'Shia' in Arabic returns dozens of tweets linking the spread of Covid19 to Shi'a backwardness. One Twitter user wrote that while 'Sunni' Saudi Arabia's response to the outbreak was civilised, logical and scientific, 'Shi'a' Iran's was beset by stupidity, superstition and dogma. This trope played on embedded sectarian tropes in which the Shi'a are portrayed as rural, uneducated simpletons,[20] beholden to ritualistic traditions that are so vital to their worldview that social distancing would be an impossibility. The sectarianisation of the Covid19 pandemic was nowhere more evident than in Pakistan, where certain viral WhatsApp conversations revealed the extent to which certain communities believed that the minority Shi'a Hazara population would bring back Covid19 from their pilgrimages.[21]

Just as religious leaders have cynically, or perhaps ignorantly, promoted fake Covid19 cures, state-controlled news channels have instrumentalised Covid19 to attack Iran's enemies. In March 2020 the Iranian channel Press TV published an article with the title 'Zionist elements developed a deadlier strain of coronavirus against Iran'.[22] The piece quoted a former American professor, James Fetzer, as saying, 'I believe that what is going on is, under the cloak of the alleged coronavirus epidemic, that biological warfare is being conducted against Iran by Zionist elements who are taking advantage of the situation.' Others, such as Gholamreza Jalali, the head of the IRGC Civil Defence Organization, implied that the United States spread Covid19 through its biological labs. Hossein Momeni, an Iranian scholar, also claimed that the virus was a man-made disease used to attack the Shi'a and Iran.[23] These tropes were amplified through the International Union of Virtual Media, a Tehran-based outfit that's modus operandi has been to create or copy web-based content that amplifies Iranian government narratives, then post it to social media accounts that pose as independent news outlets or journalists'.[24]

The emotive impact of Covid19 was used as a fulcrum with which to rile Iranian nationalism and accentuate geopolitical grievances. According to Royesh and Grossman, 'In April 2020 a handful of Twitter users began posting tweets incorporating a very specific hashtag: #Covid1948. The hashtag framed the creation of the State of Israel in 1948 as a virus, suggesting that it has been deadlier for the Palestinian people than COVID-19.' Many of the accounts were copypasta tweets that had been copied from Aliakbar Raefipour, a pro-regime Iranian and founder of the Masaf Institute, an organisation that has previously promoted an anti-Zionist cartoon conspiracy.[25]

At the same time, deception campaigns seeking to discredit the Iranian regime were also accentuating Iran's handling of the crisis. Navid Barani, a fake journalist from the Arab Eye network, wrote a piece titled 'Could Covid-19 herald regime change in Iran?'.[26] Here Covid19 was being used as a means to demonise the Iranian regime, and was contributing to the narratives that were legitimising renewed sanctions and even encouraging regime change. It is interesting that Barani was using Covid19 to will on regime change. This was not necessarily a fringe opinion. Writing in *The Hill*, AJ Caschetta stated, 'So what are the odds of a coronavirus coup in Iran? I'd give it 50-50, especially if senior members of the regime die from the disease. That judgment, admittedly, is colored by my hope for regime change in Iran.'[27]

Conclusion: Covid19 Disinformation: A Political Weapon

This chapter explores how Covid19 disinformation has been used by Gulf-aligned entities to attack their regional enemies, provoke fear and/or anger among certain communities or reinforce the legitimacy of autocratic rule. The *duwal al-hisar* (lit., countries of the blockade: blockading countries) and Iran appear to be the regional 'superspreaders' of Covid19 disinformation. This infodemic has also been particularly acute in the MENA region, where authoritarian regimes have been quick to appropriate social media as a means of spreading state propaganda. Although the global Covid19 infodemic has not discriminated, the MENA region, in particular, is dogged by authoritarian regimes, regulatory blackspots and relative apathy on the part of social media companies in combating platform abuses. The multitude of political and social tensions, whether in the form of sectarianism or the conflict in Libya, also contribute to creating a Petri dish in which the growth of Covid19 disinformation flourishes. The general persistence of Arabic-language Covid19 disinformation also highlights how an aspect of the Gulf's post-truth moment is digital orientalism, and a tendency of tech companies to ignore violations of their terms of service in non-'Western' markets.

PART V

ATTACKING JOURNALISTS AND SILENCING DISSENT

11

SILENCING JOURNALISTS

THE KILLING OF KHASHOGGI

Chapter Overview

This chapter documents the methods of deception deployed by Saudi-connected entities in the wake of the murder of Saudi journalist Jamal Khashoggi. Specifically, it interrogates Twitter algorithms and raises questions of how Arabic-language Twitter in Saudi Arabia appears to have been successfully censored to prevent narratives relating to Saudi government involvement in the assassination from becoming salient. It also explores why and how the dominant Arabic narrative on Twitter was that which reflected the Saudi government's disinformation and propaganda.

Khashoggi: MBS's Potential Swan Song

The extremely violent killing of Khashoggi reflects an important aspect of disinformation: the attitudes of regimes towards criticism. One can argue that disinformation and propaganda, like any form of repression, is modulated in part by the attitudes of influential members of a regime. According to Lopez and Stohl, 'Legitimaters are a core group of influential personnel who lend support to acts of state terror because they directly benefit from them or because such brutal use of state force permits the realization of goals that are highly salient to them.'[1] For the likes of MBS and Saud al-Qahtani in particular, the efforts made to brand Saudi Arabia and its new reforms positively to the rest of the world were, and are, highly salient. In a very real sense, the murder of Khashoggi, and the direct implication of MBS, has posed one of the most serious challenges to MBS's desire to rebrand himself and Saudi Arabia. Its sheer newsworthiness, and the long shadow it has cast politically, is only exceeded by the need to censor and shape a discourse exonerating MBS.

The brutal murder of the US-based journalist Jamal Khashoggi by a Saudi hit squad was a tragedy for most of the world, but a crisis communication stress test for the Saudi authorities. Here the need for MBS to maintain his image as a reformer, and to protect himself from domestic criticism, necessitated the use of image-repair tactics. However, such tactics, which rely on the following five tenets denial, evasion of responsibility, victim blaming, conciliation and (eventual) apology, also necessitated the use of significant volumes of disinformation.[2] If the Gulf Crisis was a pre-organised pseudo-event launched on digital platforms, the murder of Khashoggi highlights what happens when you lose control of the narrative. It also reflects a universal element of the post-truth moment, a disdain for journalists critical of the new breed of populists. Crucially, the brutal murder of a journalist on government property highlights one of the most egregious acts of censorship in the Gulf's post-truth moment.

Who was Khashoggi?

A man sporting a grey beard, distinct rimless glasses and a blue blazer entered the Saudi consulate in Istanbul. CCTV footage then showed the man exiting some time later. This relatively inconspicuous event drew a significant amount of attention from the world media. Why? Because the man entering was Jamal Khashoggi, and the man leaving was meant to be Jamal Khashoggi – only he wasn't. In fact, Jamal Khashoggi never left the building. He had been killed and dismembered in the consulate. The man who left was a Saudi agent dressed up in the clothes removed from Khashoggi's dead body.

226

To this day, the body of Khashoggi has not been found.

It may be extraneous to detail who Jamal Khashoggi is, but context is important. Khashoggi was a Saudi citizen residing in the United States, where he worked as a journalist for the *Washington Post*. He also contributed under a pseudonym to other outlets, including the Middle East Eye, a fact that was only revealed after his murder. Khashoggi often wrote columns about the Middle East and Saudi Arabia, and had become increasingly critical of reforms being led by the Saudi crown prince, Mohammed bin Salman. Often described as a 'dissident', Khashoggi was, for much of his life, anything but. Instead, he had been a member of the inner circles close to the ruling Al Saud family. Even towards the end of his life, to brand him as a dissident belies his generally moderate critique of MBS's reforms. Nonetheless, for many authoritarian regimes, but especially under MBS, any hint of criticism is enough to deem someone a dissident or subversive, especially if they are perceived as a defector. In fact, characterising Khashoggi as a dissident plays into the hands of those attempting to smear him as a terrorist.[3] Indeed, after his death numerous op-eds in state-influenced media sought to paint him as a paid agent of Qatar.[4]

If there was ever a testament to the impact of the exertion of social media power, it is the case of Jamal Khashoggi, who received hateful comments and threats on a daily basis for his columns critical of reforms under MBS. The abuse grew to such a pitch that Khashoggi confided to his friends that he wept on a daily basis.[5] Part of the reason the Saudi cyber-armies targeted Khashoggi was that he was a Saudi citizen, and a former insider. His perceived betrayal, as well as insider knowledge, was a sensitive issue. Indeed, Khashoggi had escaped Saudi immediately before MBS ordered the incarceration of many influential Saudis in what became the gilded cage of Riyadh's Ritz Carlton Hotel.

For Khashoggi, the architect of the online abuse directed at him was the work of Saud al-Qahtani, adviser to the royal court and right-hand man of MBS.[6] Much of the abuse was on Twitter. The attacks on Khashoggi grew more virulent over time: 'It's the beginning of the end, Khashoggi,' read one posting in December 2017. 'Every word you said against the nation is tallied and will be punished soon.'[7] Sure enough, nine months later Khashoggi was murdered by a Saudi hit squad as he visited the Saudi consulate in Istanbul.

Khashoggi's Murder

At the time of his murder, Khashoggi was betrothed to a Turkish woman called Hatice Cengiz, or Khadija in Arabic. In order to marry Cengiz, Khashoggi went to the Saudi consulate in Istanbul to secure a document that would legally annul his previous marriage. Khashoggi's failure to emerge from the consulate soon alarmed Cengiz, who raised questions about his whereabouts to the Turkish authorities. It soon became clear that Khashoggi had never re-emerged from the embassy. Over the next few days the world's media sought to determine what had happened to Jamal Khashoggi.

The media storm around the disappearance was galvanised by the fact Khashoggi had been a journalist, potentially murdered for attempting to speak truth to power. The initial official Saudi story was that Khashoggi had left the embassy. However, this was routinely contradicted by the reportings of the Turkish authorities, who drip-fed intel they had about the killing to the press. This had the effect of making Saudi's narratives and protestations seem increasingly absurd. After saying Khashoggi had left, the Saudi authorities then stated he died in an accidental struggle.

Indeed, it soon emerged that the Turkish authorities had bugged the Saudi consulate and obtained audio recordings of Khashoggi's final moments. The Saudi authorities were forced to admit that Khashoggi had been killed. The Turkish recordings of the murder dispelled any attempt to frame the incident as a tragic accident. It soon became clear that Khashoggi's death was the result of premeditated murder, probably ordered by MBS himself. The final details were clear. On 2 October 2018 Khashoggi entered the embassy, and was almost immediately killed and dismembered by the 'Tiger Squad' – a fifteen-man team of assassins sent from Riyadh.

The killing of Jamal Khashoggi in October 2018 in Saudi's Istanbul consulate was an extraordinary and newsworthy event. However, the nature of the coverage has been amplified by certain contexts. As a correspondent for a US broadsheet, the *Washington Post*, Khashoggi's murder provoked the ire of journalists around the globe, none more so than the newspaper's global opinions editor, Karen Attiya, who inexorably pursued a quest for answers about Khashoggi. With Saudi Arabia and four other countries blockading Qatar, international crises involving any of these countries have been utilised as a stick with which to beat the other. Unsurprisingly, the Doha-based Al Jazeera dedicated a considerable amount of coverage to the killing, aided by the Turkish authorities' drip-feeding of sensationalist details over a period of weeks.

However, one should not confuse this mutual criticism as being equally valid. In the case of the murder of Jamal Khashoggi, it was clear, by Saudi Arabia's own admission, that it had lied repeatedly about the fate of Jamal Khashoggi during his disappearance. As such, much of the Gulf state-controlled news media sought to imitate the official line of the state, while continued pressure and leaks from the Turkish authorities and investigative journalists soon poked gaping holes in the Saudi disinformation campaign.

No Justice

Attempts to mobilise the international community to get justice for Khashoggi have ended in apathy and indifference. The then UN special rapporteur on extrajudicial killing, Agnes Callamard, wrote a detailed investigative report in 2019 on the killing of Khashoggi. The report made numerous recommendations, including that 'the UN Secretary-General open a criminal investigation into the murder, or set up a tribunal to prosecute the culprits.' Callamard's report also urged companies to boycott those believed to be connected with the killing.

Despite that, the Saudi authorities have not done much to bring Khashoggi's killers to justice, and an investigation and trial that they initiated did little to assuage a belief that justice had not been done. Of the 15 members of the Tiger Squad, only 11 were put on trial. Of those 11, only eight were convicted, with sentences ranging from seven to 20 years. This whittling down of culprits is not unusual, as states tend to portray official deviance as the work of a few 'rotten apples'. The fewer they can deem to be culpable, the more likely they can portray it as a rogue operation detached from the personal influence of the leader.

The trial itself failed to meet the most basic international standards of fairness; it was a closed trial not subject to media scrutiny and witnessed only by members of the security council, all of whom agreed to sign non-disclosure agreements. This prompted Agnes Callamard to state that these members had been complicit in a theatrical 'mockery of justice'. Indeed, a show trial is, in many ways, its own form of deception.

Some of the most pertinent details of Khashoggi's murder remain hazy. The whereabouts of his body is perhaps one of the biggest mysteries of any modern high-profile political murder. Numerous rumours emerged over the course of his disappearance. It has been claimed that his body was dissolved in acid, or burned in a newly built special oven at the Saudi consulate. In many respects, it is a powerful testament to his killers' impunity. It is, of course, highly improbable that a regime that has shown itself willing to torture human rights activists is apparently unable to ascertain the location of Khashoggi's body after interrogating everyone in the 15-man death squad.

Yet, as international outrage waned following Khashoggi's killing, so too did any attempts to obtain justice. The UN secretary-general did not open a criminal investigation. Those higher up the accountability chain, such as the infamous Saud al-Qahtani, were let off the hook. This lack of political will allowed Saudi Arabia to replace any chance of justice with the illusion of justice within the Saudi legal system.

Challenging and Interrogating Algorithms: Minimising Khashoggi

Despite this official evasion of justice, it was harder to hide the truth of what had happened. The social media reaction to Khashoggi's disappearance and death was enormous, not just in the Arabic-speaking world but across the globe. As early as 2 October hashtags questioning the whereabouts of Khashoggi began to appear. One of the first was 'Ikhtitaf Jamal Khashoggi' (the kidnapping of Khashoggi). Others soon followed, with many explicit in implicating Saudi, such as 'Ightiyaal asSaudiyya Jamal Khashoggi' (the Saudi assassination of Jamal Khashoggi). It was not long after these hashtags appeared that counter-hashtags promoting the soon-to-be-debunked Saudi narrative began to trend. One of the most common pro-Saudi narratives sought to frame the event as a Qatari or Turkish *masrahiya*, or 'play' designed to smear Saudi Arabia. The word 'play' is often used as a means of claiming that some conspiracy is afoot. Again, the powerful myth of Saudi victimhood, which 'dulls the impulse of self-correction',[8] was deployed to mobilise reactionary nationalism.

Saudi's own eventual admission of murder is a rare instance in which a state has been forced to confront and admit to its previous fabrications. For researchers of media and fake news, digital or otherwise, this is a rare opportunity to be given a dataset where one can definitely class certain narratives as 'false'. This then allows observers to see how prominent, shared or potentially influential or dominant these false narratives were. One way to do this is to interrogate algorithms that sort, arrange and prioritise the data we see. By doing so, we can try to understand how our thought diet is being manipulated.

But what are these algorithms? Increasingly, the data we consume are sorted in an automated fashion by a set of procedural rules. For example, Twitter sorts and prioritises the tweets that we see based on how many people are using a hashtag, how quickly people are tweeting (velocity) and the 'value' of an account. By manipulating this process, or algorithm, malign actors can make certain information more or less salient. One way to do this is with electronic flies. Any entity with enough bot accounts or trolls is able to manipulate the algorithm that governs Twitter's trends. In other words, malign actors can manipulate, maximise/minimise and prioritise the information they believe better reflects their desired narrative.

Although there are more technical ways to interrogate algorithms, one can analyse data outputs in order to problematise how an algorithm is sorting and hierarchising data. The killing of Khashoggi was one such opportunity. A facet of authoritarianism, digital or otherwise, involves ranking and determining what information it is that people are exposed to. Naturally, the Saudi regime wanted to suppress information about the true nature of Khashoggi's killing. But to what extent was this successful on social media, a technology that generally evades the more vertically controlled media structures of legacy media?

To interrogate algorithms is to devise investigative solutions to see how information is prioritised. In this case, two important questions required answers. First, how did Twitter's trending topics section report information pertaining to Jamal Khashoggi in Arabic-speaking countries? Second, were truthful or false narratives more salient on the [lit #Jamal_Khashoggi] hashtag? By doing this we can do two things: (1) establish to what extent Saudis may have been exposed (in an obvious way) to information about Jamal Khashoggi in Arabic; and (2) determine the nature of the information they may have been exposed to.

Using Trendogate, a free-to-use web resource that archives Twitter trends according to geographical location, all trends in Arabic-speaking countries where Twitter has the trending feature for the period of Khashoggi's disappearance were listed. For the period 28 September to 30 October any trend mentioning Khashoggi in English or Arabic was recorded, along with the name of the country in which it trended. These included Qatar, the UAE, Saudi Arabia, Lebanon, Algeria, Kuwait, Egypt, Bahrain, Oman and Jordan.

For almost all countries analysed, trends mentioning Khashoggi peaked on 15 October 2018. This period reflected a lot of new revelations about the Khashoggi killing. However, the most interesting revelations related to how much his name trended in particular countries. Firstly, Khashoggi's name trended the most in Qatar. His name was recorded at least 126 times. (For a sense of perspective, the second highest was in Jordan, with 44.) This is perhaps unsurprising for a number of reasons, not least because several Qatar-based accounts are attached to its highly influential news channel Al Jazeera. While Al Jazeera would no doubt have covered the Khashoggi killing regardless, the fact that Qatar had been blockaded by a Saudi-led quartet since 2017 prompted a renewed criticism of Saudi policies, as well as a concerted effort to delegitimise Saudi on the international stage. Given the dominance too of news outlets emanating from the blockading states, Al Jazeera has also adopted a role in which it counters propaganda emanating from these countries. Having said that, Khashoggi's murder was a newsworthy event being covered extensively by most global news channels.

More interesting, though, is that Khashoggi's name trended the least in Saudi Arabia, returning only eight mentions. This is unusual for a number of reasons: Jamal Khashoggi was a Saudi citizen; the news itself involved the highest level of the Saudi government; and it was a sensational story that dominated the international news cycle for some time. Saudi also has the highest reported Twitter penetration rate in the Arabic-speaking world.[9] This analysis highlighted, at least on a very superficial level, that Khashoggi's name had successfully been minimised from appearing in topics trending in Saudi Arabia.

Fig. 8: The number of times the name Khashoggi appeared in a Twitter trend in MENA countries during October 2018

Country	24 September 2018	1 October 2018	8 October 2018	15 October 2018	22 October 2018	Grand Total
Qatar	0	17	44	45	20	126
Jordan	0	8	17	12	7	44
Lebanon	0	7	11	10	5	33
Algeria	0	0	6	14	4	24
United Arab Emirates	0	3	9	6	2	20
Kuwait	0	5	6	5	2	18
Egypt	0	5	6	4	2	17
Bahrain	0	0	3	10	0	13
Oman	0	1	1	5	3	10
Saudi Arabia	0	2	3	1	0	6
Grand Total	0	48	106	112	45	311

So why was it that Saudi Arabia, the country most involved in the killing, had the fewest trends on Khashoggi? Certainly, if we were to assume, for the sake of argument, that Twitter's trending algorithm accurately reflected what certain people in a defined area were discussing, we would deduce that Jamal Khashoggi was not as popular as other topics. Similarly, given the climate of fear around expressing political views openly in Saudi, it also might be reasonable to assume that people in Saudi were fearful of discussing Khashoggi, Indeed, almost immediately after the Khashoggi scandal broke, Saudis were reminded in no uncertain terms that 'rumour-mongering' and 'spreading fake news' online was punishable by five years in prison.[10]

If the aforementioned hypothesis was to hold, one would expect to find fewer Saudi-based accounts tweeting on any issue related to Khashoggi. To test this, the most populous and commonplace hashtag Jamal_Khashoggi was downloaded for the whole period of October 2018. This resulted in around 2.48 million tweets.[11] Tweets in the sample were then ranked in order to find the following parameters: the most popular tweets; the most common user input location; and the general stance of the most popular tweets.[12] A crude locational analysis was conducted using the 'user-reported location' category, which relies on the user defining where they are located. The most frequent user-reported location in the sample was Saudi Arabia, making 33% of the total.[13] In second place was Qatar, with around 13%. Certainly, on this hashtag most of the accounts tweeting the Jamal_Khashoggi hashtag were Saudi based – at least according to their user-reported location. This, therefore, raises the important question, why did Jamal_Khashoggi trend the least in the country that most dominated the hashtag in terms of location?

Part of the reason is likely to be the prevalence of sockpuppets, bots and trolls. We know that in October 2018, during the public outcry at Khashoggi's death, Twitter suspended hundreds of accounts spreading pro-MBS propaganda.[14] We also know that a further batch of accounts suspended by Twitter in 2019 was probably also part of a network spreading Saudi propaganda around the Khashoggi story, drowning out legitimate debate while attempting to muddy the waters of conversation with spurious conspiracies. Bots belonging to the news channel Saudi 24 also attempted to drown out the discussions about Khashoggi on the first anniversary of his death, by posting unrelated information regarding the Aramco IPO on the Jamal Khashoggi hashtag. However, bots do not necessarily explain why people in similarly authoritarian countries currently allied with Saudi, such as Bahrain and the United Arab Emirates, reported a much higher number of trends.

Fake News Lingers, Long after Admissions

As most of the tweets on the Jamal_Kahshoggi hashtag were coming from Saudi, an analysis of their stance revealed whether or not they were reporting the Saudi narrative of events. In this case, the most popular retweets on the hashtag were predominantly pro-Saudi. Of the most popular 179 tweets[15] on the hashtag, 145 reflected the Saudi narrative about the events. The top 14 most retweeted comments reflected the Saudi side of the story exclusively.

A thematic analysis of the most popular tweets was instructive. Generally, this discourse followed the previously mentioned five tenets of image-repair theory.[16] The predominant discourses sought to portray Khashoggi's disappearance as either a Turkish 'deep-state' operation, a ploy to sully the reputation of Saudi or a conspiracy perpetrated by the Muslim Brotherhood. Many of the most popular tweets sought to emphasise declarations made by American officials. One stated that Trump 'trusted' the investigation by Saudi Arabia, while another claimed that John Bolton had warned that Turkey might create fabrications to attack Saudi. The propaganda generally sought to reaffirm Saudi's trustworthiness, while highlighting the machinations of Qatar-based media and the Turkish government. A number of conspiracy theories were also popular, including one that sought to denigrate Hatice Cengiz, Khashoggi's fiancée, and imply that Qatar was somehow involved in the killing.

A number of tropes also reflected criticisms made of Qatar by the blockading countries. Like Trump's attacks on CNN and whoever/whatever he perceives as the fake news media, many of the top comments on the #Jamal_Khashoggi hashtag attacked news channels attempting to get to the bottom of his murder. One of the most popular tweets was from Saudi prince Sattam Al Saud, who told everyone to prepare for the media onslaught including so-called 'pens for hire', who were about to attack 'the Kingdom'. Another mocked Al Jazeera's reporting of the killing.

Interestingly, one of the most popular tweets on the hashtag was also one promoting American former YouTuber and conspiracy theorist Thomas Wictor, who often wears a sieve on his head when articulating his theories. Wictor stated that Khashoggi had left the building and that Iran was probably involved in his murder.[17] Wictor's video was translated into Arabic without a hint of irony, despite the absurdity of his account. Wictor was eventually suspended from Twitter for making violent threats (unrelated to Khashoggi). It is unclear what motivated Wictor to support the Saudi narrative, especially with regard to placing suspicion on Iran, but such an allusion is perhaps no surprise in a climate of anti-Iranism among the US right.

One popular hashtag blamed Qatari intelligence for killing Khashoggi, while another accused the Turkish government of covering up his killing. Some of the more absurd disinformation that surfaced included someone accusing Khashoggi's fiancée of actually being a former minister of Egypt who was a member of the Muslim Brotherhood.[18]

The pervasiveness of fake news was also evident in the fact that the false stories were circulating long after they were debunked. Many of the Saudi narratives that were later contradicted (by the Saudi themselves) still circulated following their change of narrative. Although Khashoggi's name mysteriously evaded Twitter's official trending topics in Saudi Arabia, the most retweeted comments on the most popular hashtag #Jamal_Khashoggi (in Arabic) reflected the implausible and vacillating Saudi side of the story. This would suggest that Saudi's electronic army is able, through crude manipulation, or some other means, to limit the prominence or salience of anti-Saudi information on social media.[19]

The long shadow of Khashoggi's murder was evident as late as 2021. When Joe Biden was elected in 2020, his administration released the intelligence report prepared by the Office of the Director of National Intelligence (ODNI) implicating MBS in the killing of Jamal Khashoggi. The release of the report was diminished by a relatively new technique involving the use of so-called chopped hashtags. Here misspellings of Khashoggi's name were trending, and when one clicked on those trends, one was directed to criticism of

American hypocrisy in the field of human rights, including images of prisoners being abused by coalition troops in Abu Ghraib prison. Twitter soon suspended 3,500 accounts, although my own analysis shows this was far from comprehensive, with thousands of similar accounts still remaining. However, a disturbing development was also under way.

Another worrying development in Twitter manipulation is:

the use of a legitimate Twitter functions to incentivize the promotion of pro-MBS propaganda. Through an advertising function, Twitter allows paying customers who have applied for the service to send tweets containing a picture and a 'tweet' button. When someone presses the 'tweet' button, they are instantly able to repost the exact same content posted by the original advertiser. Although this is designed for businesses generating hype around a particular product, it has been utilized as a propaganda tool. On the day of the release of the report, thousands of accounts used this function to tweet the identical message, 'I am Saudi and proud of this great country and trust and have faith in the wise leadership'.

One might think such behaviour falls foul of Twitter's political advertising policy which 'globally prohibits the promotion of political content'. However, they would be wrong; Twitter has a caveat which states that 'cultural customs and local protocols to show allegiance or provide salutations do not fall under this policy', even though the stated purpose of the policy is that political messaging reach should be 'earned not bought'.[20] It is somewhat striking that it is against Twitter's policy to pay money to promote candidates in a democratic society, but acceptable to promote dictators in an authoritarian country where no political parties exist.

Meanwhile, in Washington, DC ...

Beyond social media, the deception order sprang into action to portray Khashoggi as a terrorist, undeserving of sympathy due to his time spent doing embedded reporting with the Mujaheddin (considered freedom fighters at the time by the US administration)

237

in Afghanistan. This aspect fits typically within the subset of image-repair theory that seeks to reduce the perceived egregiousness of an act by attacking and smearing the victim as an unworthy victim and deserving of their fate. During the month of Khashoggi's disappearance, the *Washington Post* reported that a group of Republicans began to circulate articles from right-wing publications casting aspersions on Khashoggi.[21] This 'whisper campaign' reflected the talking points coming out of the Gulf-blockading quartet, who sought to frame Khashoggi as a terrorist and al-Qaeda operative. Donald Trump Jnr even tweeted the trope linking Khashoggi to Islamic terrorism.[22] The trope was also repeated by Harris Faulkner, a presenter at the conservative outlet Fox News, who suggested that Khashoggi's links to the Brotherhood were somehow the reason for suspicion. Mark Levine, a conservative radio talk-show host, called Khashoggi a 'long-time friend' of terrorists, implying that the media furore was somehow part of a media conspiracy to smear Trump.[23] A number of other pro-Israel outlets also sought to smear Khashoggi as a terrorist.[24] Whether or not those sharing the stories believed it, or whether they simply wanted to find a way to legitimise their continued support for Trump's policy towards Saudi Arabia, is unclear.

The US right-wing think tank Security Studies Group (SSG), whose funding remains unknown, published a number of articles taking a mocking tone about Khashoggi's death. One article argued that 'to lionize Khashoggi and to destroy the US-Saudi relationship was built on the fiction that the Saudis had killed a mere journalist'.[25] The article, which amounted to a scurrilous hit piece, made no bones about its lack of evidence, talking of only 'rumours about his questionable and financial links to Qatari intelligence'. SSG, founded by David Reaboi, was once described as a 'think tank led by men associated for years with conspiracy theories about Muslims'.[26] SSG's agenda appears to be quite circumscribed. Writing in the HuffPost, Akbar Shahid Ahmed notes:

> Although the group does not accept foreign funding, it often promotes anti-Qatar material from The Qatar Insider website, which is part of an expensive media blitz run by the Saudi

American Public Relation Affairs Committee. It also endorses the UAE's suggestion that the U.S. should have its biggest base there rather than in Qatar.[27, 28]

Attempts to smear Khashoggi as a terrorist were made in order to reduce sympathy for him as a worthy victim and as someone whose death deserves righteous public opprobrium towards his killers. Muddying the waters around a clear political murder helped legitimise a weak response from Donald Trump towards some of his most favoured allies, Saudi Arabia and Mohammed bin Salman. The repetition of such tropes from US-based think tanks gave a veneer of legitimacy to the crude disinformation campaigns occurring on social media. They also highlighted the overlap of the US right-wing ecosystem and Saudi disinformation operations.

Jeff Bezos Hack, Leak and Disinformation

Khashoggi's murder, and the subsequent deception campaign, also sucked in the world's richest man, Amazon founder Jeff Bezos. This ostensibly bizarre development again reflects the capacious reach of Saudi's deception apparatus, but also an element of personalism. Since 2018 Bezos has been increasingly vocal in public shows of solidarity with the murdered journalist. In 2020 Bezos tweeted a photograph of himself alongside Hatice Cengiz with his hand on Khashoggi's memorial outside the Saudi consulate in Istanbul.

Bezos's perhaps inadvertent involvement in the Khashoggi affairs is in part due to the fact that he owns the *Washington Post*, the newspaper for which Khashoggi had been a columnist. The understandable anger felt by journalists around the world at the brutal murder of one of their own was felt nowhere more acutely than at the *Washington Post*. Furthermore, even before Khashoggi's death, his columns in the newspaper had angered the Saudi regime, which had tried to lure him back to Saudi Arabia prior to murdering him.[29] For that reason, it fell foul of the Saudi regime's campaign to preserve its international reputation.

The Saudis allegedly launched a campaign to silence the *Washington Post* by targeting Jeff Bezos. Bezos and MBS had swapped numbers in April 2018, after meeting at a dinner in Los Angeles. A month later, in May, four months before Khashoggi was killed, Bezos received a video on WhatsApp from MBS. The video was a patriotic exhortation of the merits of Saudi Arabia. However, it was also 'likely loaded with malware'.[30] An investigation by the security forensics firm FTI Consulting determined with 'medium to high confidence' that this video file had been an attempt by Saudi Arabia to hack Jeff Bezos's phone. Other cybersecurity experts felt that FTI did not go far enough and that it was impossible to determine if there was a 'smoking gun'.[31] Bill Marczak, of the University of Toronto's Citizen Lab, recommended that a number of further tests be carried out before a determination could be made.[32]

Despite this divergence of opinion, what is undisputed is that, after receiving the video via an encrypted downloader, Bezos's phone began transmitting a massive amount of data, which could indicate it was sending Bezos's phone data back to the hacker. In November 2018 MBS sent another WhatsApp message to Bezos, this one a photo of a brunette woman. Several months later the US magazine the *National Inquirer* published salacious details of Jeff Bezos's affair with a woman called Lauren Sanchez. When MBS sent the photo of the woman who resembled Sanchez, news of Bezos's relationship with her had not been published, suggesting that MBS had personally been attempting to taunt or pressure Bezos with private information at the height of the *Washington Post*'s coverage of the Khashoggi affair.

It was the *National Inquirer* story that prompted security experts to examine Bezos's phone. The *National Inquirer*'s parent company American Media Inc. (AMI) claimed that it had received the information of Bezos's relationship with Sanchez from the estranged brother of Bezos's girlfriend, Michael Sanchez.[33] As James Shires notes, 'It is possible that Bezos' phone was infected and that Michael Sanchez provided the texts, or that the leak was double-sourced, or that either is incorrect.'[34] The various stories about Bezos prompted, and were perhaps intended to prompt, a fierce backlash on Saudi Twitter. Several hashtags criticising Bezos were started by suspicious Twitter accounts. When the story of Bezos's potential phone hacking broke, thousands of tweets appeared using the hashtag 'boycott Amazon products', 'Jeff Bezos is immoral' and 'Jeff Bezos liar'. At least two of these hashtags, 'boycott Amazon products' and 'Jeff Bezos is immoral' were started by a Saudi patriotic account with the Twitter handle MBS_MBSKSA. The account frequently promoted nationalist hashtags, or hashtags attacking those perceived to be operating against Saudi's interest, including Tawakkol Karman, the Yemeni activist who won the Nobel Peace Prize, whose own run-in with the electronic flies is discussed in Chapter 13.

MBS_MBSKSA has probably had at least 12 different Twitter accounts, all of which were suspended for unspecified activities, raising the question whether it was for platform manipulation or other infractions.[35] Indeed, in the case of #boycottamazonproducts, the account was suspended after starting the campaign, perhaps pointing to some degree of inauthentic behaviour surrounding the account.[36] The hashtags highlighted how the Saudi patriotic Twittersphere moved in lockstep with Saudi's attempts at reputation management, especially on issues regarding MBS.

Many of the accounts active on the anti-Bezos hashtags shared articles from the Saudi legacy media. These articles sought to smear Bezos as immoral, using pictures of him hugging Khashoggi's fiancée to imply some sort of illicit affair between them.[37] Again, it reflects how disinformation campaigns can draw on interpretations of local cultural norms (in this case, infidelity or moral promiscuity) to increase, or attempt to increase, their efficacy. It also reflects the trend of creating the illusion of a broader conspiratorial narrative, one in which perceived deviant actors are bound together as part of an elaborate conspiracy designed to target Saudi Arabia.

While it has been surmised that Saudi might have wanted information on Bezos that could be used to blackmail him, perhaps in exchange for more favourable coverage in the *Washington Post*, the *National Inquirer* exposé about Bezos's affair was also mobilised in an attempt to discredit Bezos, and by proxy, the *Washington Post*, in the eyes of the Saudi public. The deception campaign also highlighted the links between the Saudi disinformation machine and Trump-connected entities. It is perhaps no coincidence that the *National Inquirer* was favourable to Trump. At the time, AMI was the owner of the *National Inquirer*. The CEO of AMI at the time, David Pecker, was a longtime Trump ally who confessed to federal investigators that he had buried a story about Trump's relationship with a *Playboy* model in order to tilt the 2016 election in Trump's favour.[38]

No Lessons Learned

Despite the widespread condemnation in the wake of the Khashoggi killing, there was little sign of Saudi changing its trajectory. On the contrary, the revelation that members of the Tiger Squad that killed Khashoggi were sent to Canada to kill Saudi citizen Saad al-Jabri indicated an increased boldness in the regime. Amidst this violence there has been the cyber harassment and disinformation online. Any dissident critical of Saudi still faces online smear campaigns or harassment.

Indeed, an op-ed in the *Washington Post* written on the second anniversary of Khashoggi's death argued that Saudi's cruelty had only grown since 2018.[39] The public face of this cruelty often takes the form of online attacks against perceived enemies. In late May 2020 Ali Soufan, a former FBI agent who was a lead investigator in the months leading up to the 9/11 attacks, was subject to a virulent social media campaign from Saudi Arabia. Soufan, whose organisation the Soufan Center holds an annual security conference in Doha, was targeted for his perceived links to Qatar.

The threats were sinister: 'You're gonna end up in a garbage dump in Qatar', 'make yourself dead', 'it's the beginning of the end'.[40] They were also familiar because they were exactly the type of threats that had been used on Jamal Khashoggi. Other attacks against Soufan were led by self-styled Saudi journalist Hussain al-Ghawi, who raised again the claim that Soufan personally tortured a member of al-Qaeda – which Soufan denies. Other content accused Soufan of co-operating with 9/11 victims in a court case against Saudi Arabia.

> Partnering with forensic analysts from Limbik, a New York firm, the Soufan Group analyzed hundreds of Arabic Twitter accounts that were flagged by Twitter officials in 2019 as being part of a government-backed Saudi influence operation. Scores of those accounts – many of them subsequently blocked by Twitter – had been involved in attacks against Khashoggi, Soufan said. Some

accounts were clearly connected with Saudi citizens, while others appeared to be 'bots,' a kind of automated account used to help spread messages on social media.[41]

As if this was not disturbing enough, there were other grounds for Soufan to be concerned. Two weeks before the online threats started, Soufan was warned by the CIA about a possible attempt on his life by al-Qaeda. The fact that the online attack came two weeks after the CIA warning was not insignificant.

For Soufan, the killing of Washington, DC-based journalist Jamal Khashoggi by the Saudi state in a foreign country highlighted that no one is off limits, and the campaign against him indicated that Soufan could be the next target. Journalist Ali Velshi noted a disturbing aspect of such information operations: that an online smear campaign could provoke some other party (such as al-Qaeda) to do the dirty work. Soufan worried that Saudi would not dare attack him directly, as this would be an act of international aggression, but would instead use al-Qaeda to murder him in Qatar – where he is a frequent visitor. It is also possible that Saudi disinformation agents are trying to provoke al-Qaeda into attacking Soufan by bringing up debunked stories of torture against their former members. This would not be surprising, as the Saudi state's historical overlap with al-Qaeda was well documented after the 9/11 attacks.

Dexter Filkins, a journalist who wrote Soufan's story in the *New Yorker* recently, attempted to contact the accounts that threatened Soufan. However, none responded, adding to suspicions that they might be operated by professional agitators who deliberately do not engage with difficult questions. Filkins also contacted the Saudi government and received a classic 'non-denial denial'. He said that the Saudis initially did not 'deny that they were involved', and they gave him a 'very strange answer' that Soufan should complain to the social media companies. They then later commented that they rejected such 'baseless allegations', presumably because the story began to make them look bad.

Digital attacks on the likes of Ali Soufan support the idea that critics of MBS should not entertain the illusion that the Khashoggi affair has deterred Saudi attempts to silence dissidents. Indeed, an aspect of digital authoritarianism is to utilise the social media space to issue threats with plausible deniability easily maintained as to the threat's provenance. It devolves accountability, and traceability, and is an ideal space for attacking regime critics. Even years after his death, anyone who asks for justice for Jamal Khashoggi is trolled relentlessly, and astroturfing on any publicity about Khashoggi's murder continues unabated. Even *The Dissident*, a documentary film about Khashoggi's murder directed by Bryan Fogel, has found it difficult to find a distributor. Prior to its release, suspicious activity on the movie review website IMDB indicated that fake accounts were artificially trying to give the movie a bad score in the hope of discrediting it.[42]

Conclusion

Jamal Khashoggi, a former insider turned moderate critic of the Saudi regime, was assassinated for criticising Mohammed bin Salman's reforms. It is acknowledged by a number of people, including the CIA, that only MBS could have ordered the killing of Khashoggi. His murder was preceded by an online campaign of intimidation on social media, accompanied by a formulaic attempt to repair the image of the perpetrators (the Saudi authorities), and followed by a posthumous online campaign to smear him as a terrorist. The unanticipated and unplanned exposé of Saudi involvement in Khashoggi's murder has prompted one of the most sustained and far-reaching deception operations to emanate from the Gulf. Again, the role of MBS also highlights how perhaps his own inability to accept criticism, like many of the current crop of populists, invites a corollary fascination with image, information and the media.

In many ways, Khashoggi was killed because he did not fit the mould of the new hyper-nationalistic drum-beater embodied by the millions of anonymous, on-message social media accounts. He disrupted the desired reality of the new order proposed by MBS: daily hashtags with messages of love and support for the crown prince. Khashoggi was a real person, a verifiable corporeal being amidst a sea of unverified bots, trolls and hyper-partisan digital foot soldiers. His death served to remind potential critics of the extreme consequences of diverging from the new, MBS-led narrative, whether on- or offline. It fundamentally symbolised the dangers of journalism in the Arab post-truth moment – hostility not just to truth, but to information that contradicts the narrative of the new Gulf project.

The demonisation of Khashoggi and the resultant lionisation and exoneration of MBS were, and still are, an important dialectic of Saudi Twitter, where the community – authentic and inauthentic – is mobilised to articulate common stances on global issues. At times where people really need to express criticism, the regime demands conformity, creating an intolerable tension. However, paid trolls, and hyper-nationalistic citizens, police Twitter for any signs of sedition or deviance from the official narrative. Even silence can be considered sedition, and there are anecdotal stories of editors being encouraged to tweet specific propaganda. However, just as there remain so many unanswered questions about Jamal Khashoggi, this chapter has highlighted how there are still many unanswered questions about how Saudi propaganda managed to remain ascendant on Twitter, seemingly fooling Twitter's algorithms and succeeding in dominating the Khashoggi narrative.

12

ATTACKING WOMEN

MALINFORMATION AND DIGITAL MISOGYNY

Chapter Overview:Women, DigitalViolence and Digital Predators

As with the global post-truth moment in general, the Gulf post-truth moment is also deeply misogynistic. Using network and content analysis, this chapter evidences how women who criticise Saudi Arabia and MBS on certain topics, such as his involvement in the killing of Khashoggi, face orchestrated and industrial-scale deception campaigns that involve misogynistic abuse and private information (doxing). It also documents similar misogynistic campaigns directed against journalists who are perceived as insufficiently critical of the Iranian regime. Although online misogyny is endemic around the world, this chapter argues that the post-truth Gulf moment, and particularly the Gulf Crisis, has been accompanied by public attacks on women via social media.

Ghada Jacuzzi

Ghada Oueiss, an experienced journalist and the principal anchor of Al Jazeera Arabic, is no stranger to trolling and harassment on Twitter. As a high-profile presenter of one of the Arab world's

247

best-known news channels, she receives abusive messages with alarming regularity. So when Oueiss took time out of her busy schedule to celebrate her husband's birthday with a quiet dinner at their apartment in Doha, only to receive an urgent message from a friend warning her she was under attack on Twitter, she knew it was serious.

Oueiss had been doxed. When she checked her phone, she saw thousands of notifications. An anonymous Twitter account had posted private photos of Oueiss wearing a bikini and emerging from a jacuzzi. The photos had been stolen from Oueiss's phone and quickly circulated online. In many of the photos, Oueiss's bikini had been crudely pixelated to make her appear naked. Those sharing the photos were calling her a prostitute, ugly and a mercenary. This was malinformation par excellence.

Soon, thousands of Twitter accounts began to falsely claim that the photos had been taken at the private farm and retreat of the Al Jazeera Media Network's Qatari chairman, Shaykh Hamad Bin Thamer Al Thani. The Twitter mob made numerous spurious accusations, most of which accused Oueiss of exchanging sexual favours with the head of Al Jazeera in return for promotions and salary increases. The tweets in question were designed to shame Oueiss and her colleague Ola al-Fares by making them appear sexually promiscuous, an insult that has particularly sharp connotations in the Gulf region and the wider MENA more broadly.

Later, Oueiss would write in the *Washington Post* about the experience:

> 'Tell us about your night. How was the prostitution? Were you drunk while you were naked?' wrote a Twitter user with the name Saoud Bin Abdulaziz Algharibi who has been active on the site since 2013. 'No wonder she's naked. She's a cheap Christian. She's old and ugly,' he continued. Like almost all of the Saudi accounts attacking me, the majority of Algharibi's Twitter timeline is filled with tweets praising Saudi Crown Prince Mohammed bin Salman.[1]

But that would be later. Oueiss's ordeal was far from over. 'Farm of Hamad bin Thamer' (in Arabic) began trending on Twitter, with tens of thousands of tweets being posted in the space of 24 hours. Ola al-Fares was also pulled into the fray and attacked along similar lines. Other hashtags began to emerge, such as 'Ghada jacuzzi' and 'Ola sauna'. Vulgar caricatures of the two women decked out in Qatar-flag bikinis doing lap dances for Hamad bin Thamer were circulated, along with animal imagery, such as Oueiss and al-Fares's heads superimposed on dogs and goats. One cartoon portrayed Oueiss lying on bin Thamer's desk saying, 'Can I have a pay rise, the Saudis are giving me a really hard time?' Bin Thamer replies, 'Let's reach an understanding on the farm.' Another showed one of the women outside a garish night club titled 'cheap brothel', with a menu of various services outside. Several of the tweets bordered on veiled threats, with one anonymous account posting a picture of a woman seemingly dead after taking a drug overdose – no doubt a nod towards the intended purpose of the campaign – psychological violence.

An analysis of 25,000 tweets on the hashtags 'Farm of Hamad bin Thamir', 'Ghada Oueiss' and 'Olaa Al Fares' over a 24-hour period on 10 June revealed the scale of the cyber-violence.[2] These posts were not simply being shared by anonymous accounts, bots or sockpuppets. High-profile public figures were amplifying them, including Dhahi Khalfan, 'former head of Dubai Police; Naif Al-Asaker, a mufti at the Saudi Ministry of Islamic Affairs and a close ally to MBS; and Hamad Al-Mazroui, a close associate of the UAE crown prince'.[3] Such high-level endorsements encouraged and made permissible the ensuing dogpile among less influential accounts, as well as the armies of trolls and bots. Some of the most influential accounts included pro-Saudi influencers Abdul Latif Abdullah al-Sheikh and Ibrahim Suleiman. Most of the accounts spreading the disinformation, which had millions of followers between them, had images of MBS, King Salman or the Saudi flag as their Twitter profile picture. An analysis of the incoming tweets to both Oueiss and Ola revealed the industrial level of the misogyny and harassment: Between 6 and 9 June they received at least 3,000 tweets between them, the majority of which were part of the orchestrated smear campaign. The UN's rapporteur for extrajudicial killing commented on the vitriolic campaign, tweeting, 'online harassment campaigns should not be tolerated by the platforms. #Twitter Standing with women journalists'.[4]

In addition to this, those behind the campaign were exploiting extant regional geopolitical tensions to promote specific foreign policy goals. In one instance, a doctored tweet attributed to Oueiss was circulated, primarily by Saudi influencer Abdul Latif Abdullah al-Sheikh. The doctored tweet claimed that Oueiss had insulted Oman by stating that it had set up an electronic army. At the time, Oman's deteriorating fiscal situation was being discussed in a high-level meeting with Gulf officials.[5] The fact that Oman was potentially seeking financial assistance from its Gulf neighbours, and with the Gulf Crisis creating a heterogeneous set of foreign policies in the region, meant that aid from the UAE and Saudi would no doubt come with strings attached. Andreas Krieg noted, 'Any financial assistance from either the UAE and Saudi Arabia will be conditional on Oman becoming more supportive on issues where Oman has opted out to support Abu Dhabi and Riyadh'.[6] Making it seem that Ghada Oueiss, the lead anchor of the Arab world's most prominent and Qatar-based news channel, had publicly insulted Oman, was no doubt designed to provoke tensions between Qatar and Oman – or at least get Oueiss into trouble. With a number of highly followed influencers promoting the story, 'Ghada insults Oman' began trending on Twitter.

In a similar incident, designed to create tensions between Oueiss and her Al Jazeera colleagues, the Saudi influencer Abdul Latif al-Sheikh posted a doctored tweet attributed to Ghada Oueiss in which Oueiss stated that she believed Ola al-Fares was behind the leaking of her private photos. Oueiss had never written such a tweet. The campaign reached such a pitch that it 'broke out' into traditional legacy media, but only on those channels that were broadly aligned with the blockading countries. The UAE-based CNN Arabic produced a piece that legitimised the credibility of al-Sheikh's doctored tweet. Instead of detailing the harassment campaign at al-Fares and Oueiss, it framed the story as a simple disagreement between al-Sheikh, on the one hand, and Ola and Oueiss, on the other. The article itself was premised around al-Sheikh's tweet, and the reactions it provoked from Oueiss, Ola and others. Nowhere did CNN Arabic state that the tweet was fake. As such, it infantilised Oueiss and Ola by whitewashing an industrial-scale harassment campaign, reducing it to a petty squabble and infighting between colleagues who had stabbed each other in the back.

Although Oueiss and al-Fares were singled out in the attack, Al Jazeera was a primary target of Saudi and the UAE's deception campaigns. This was evident both in the amount of propaganda and disinformation targeting Qatar-connected media outlets and in the amount of resources dedicated to attempting to compromise the devices of Al Jazeera journalists. In fact, Citizen Lab documented that Saudi and the UAE, using the spyware Pegasus developed by Israeli firm NSO Group, hacked the devices of 36 Al Jazeera journalists in August 2020.[7] Indeed, of all known public infections by Pegasus at that time, Al Jazeera journalists represented the largest single group. Oueiss, who launched a legal challenge against those accused of participating and orchestrating the attack, believes Pegasus was also used to compromise her device.[8]

Misogyny and Social Context

Although violence against women is as old as time, the ways in which digital media 'exacerbate existing patterns of gendered violence and introduce new modes of abuse' is becoming increasingly evident. Digital technology is not neutral, or devoid of bias, and it is a fallacy to argue that technology can be 'value-neutral'.[9] How technology is utilised reflects the beliefs of those who create the technology and the patriarchal social environment in which it is used. As Dana Boyd points out when discussing the inexorable rise of new digital technologies, 'We didn't architect for prejudice, but we didn't design systems to combat it either.'[10] Indeed, cyber-violence[11] is gendered, with women and men experiencing and perpetrating different volumes and types of bullying.[12]

Cyber-violence against women generally reflects patriarchal societal norms, with women often being on the receiving of gendered and sexualised forms of abuse that put them at risk of violence and discrimination.[13] As Sarah Sobieraj has argued, 'Aggressors repeatedly draw upon three overlapping strategies – intimidating, shaming, and discrediting – to silence women or to limit their impact in digital publics.'[14] According to a report by the Institute for the Future, 'every female target of government-backed harassment receives rape threats and is subjected to sexist and misogynistic language'.[15] Although gendered epithets such as 'bitch' or 'whore' are designed to provoke shame, it is also important to acknowledge that such terms in themselves represent examples of disinformation. Claiming someone is a bitch, whore, slut is, more often than not, a meritless statement that invokes unknown/irrelevant sexual behaviours based on no evidence (this is hardly the point, as no sufficient evidence could exist that warrant such expressions, but it is a useful conceptual clarification).

An analysis of all the tweets directed at Ghada Oueiss between October 2020 and April 2014 revealed that she had been subjected to similar sexually suggestive or degrading misogynistic terms at least 401 times (due to the retroactive scraping technique used, this does not include tweets that may have included those terms but were later deleted).[16] 'Words such as *Sharmuta* (whore, n=150), *Ghahba* (bitch, n=98), *Tayzik* (your ass, n =64), *Mamhuna* (horny, n=42) and *Zibi* (my dick, n = 29) were among the most common. Often such commentary is adopted to demean the subject and includes the use of terms recognized to be misogynistic and sexualized in nature that express toxic representations of women.'[17] Here the central grounds for condemnation revolve around perceived sexual behaviour and sexual value. Many of the comments verged on threats of rape or sexual violence, highlighting intimidation in addition to condemnation. Of all these insults, a notable spike occurred during October and November 2018, immediately after the Khashoggi killing, and when Al Jazeera was intensively covering the murder.[18] No doubt, the insults were designed to intimidate her at a time when Saudi Arabia was desperately trying to minimise negative coverage of the incident.

The 2020[19] attack on Oueiss was one of the most sustained and intense attacks on a woman journalist to have been documented since the Arab Uprisings. Of course, online violence against women is not new, but the modalities in the Gulf region appear to be changing. A distinctive characteristic of the 2017 Gulf Crisis, narrated by many

Qataris targeted by the blockade, has been the erosion of certain social norms and red lines that would previously have remained relatively sacrosanct, irrespective of political conflict. One example of this has been the targeting of elite women, such as Shaykha Moza bint Nasser, the wife of the former of emir of Qatar. Moza, which can mean 'banana' in Arabic, has been the butt of many an innuendo.

In some ways, Moza bint Nasser has been targeted partly because of her comparatively humble beginnings. Her father, Nasser al-Misnad, has been described pejoratively as a commoner, who provoked the ire of the ruler of Qatar by asking for a redistribution of wealth.[20] The phallic connotations of banana, along with Shaykha Moza's perceived modest background, have spawned allusions to her as a gold-digger using sexuality to attain her power and wealth. One recent tweet from a Saudi-aligned account is indicative. It translates as: 'because Qatar has no men Moza is happy to do the duty [5 banana emojis].' A more accurate translation would read 'she will take care of him'. The tweet, which was sent in reply to an image of Moza meeting the Tunisian prime minister, played off traditional masculinities while inferring that Moza's diplomatic prowess involved trading sexual favours.[21]

In addition to Moza's perceived lack of royal lineage, she is a woman who drove much of Qatar's soft-power success, partly through the establishment of the Qatar Foundation, a non-profit that has sought to establish a global reputation in science, education and social and cultural development. These efforts to establish Qatari multilateralism in the face of regional conservative forces have been particularly acute given her role as a woman. It is this fundamental independence along with the power embodied by Moza that seems to have irked so many of her trolls, who have transgressed social norms in the Gulf by openly using vulgar, sexualised innuendo when berating her, a tactic usually reserved for women activists in the region. The trope has 'broken out' beyond the region, albeit with a small but vocal cadre of pro-Saudi Americans using the term, as well as attacking her looks, and the fact she has had plastic surgery.[22]

This digital misogyny in the Gulf context is indicative of the global post-truth moment, characterised by the normalisation of violence against women by leaders like Donald Trump. Although digital misogyny is not new online, the Saudi government under MBS has done more to encourage, rather than restrict, digital misogyny. In one high-profile incident, MBS was reported to have sent a sexist joke to Amazon founder Jeff Bezos in connection with his apparent knowledge of an affair Bezos was rumoured to be having. The text read: 'Arguing with a woman is like reading the software license agreement. In the end you have to ignore everything and click I agree.' While such behaviour might only be a superficial indicator of MBS's attitudes towards women, the brutal treatment of Saudi women activists such as Loujain al-Hathloul, who was imprisoned for publicly driving in Saudi, highlights a step change in the treatment of women under MBS. As Hana Al-Khamri argues, although migrant women and Saudi women activists have always been treated badly by the authorities, the rise of MBS has seen even women perceived to be from privileged backgrounds facing brutality, torture and sexual assault.[23] This brutality has manifested itself in the online space too, and reflects a departure from mere authoritarian rule, and the emergence of a totalitarian ethos. What separates the totalitarian dictator from the autocrat, among other things, is a desire to disrupt existing social norms and institutions in order to renegotiate loyalties from subjects to the new leadership.[24]

Iran

The US abandonment of the JCPOA, along with Saudi and UAE support for the isolation of Iran, has turned the Gulf social media space into a hostile battleground. The process to persuade people of the merits of this 'maximum pressure' policy position has been underscored by intimidation and disinformation. Those opposing the new vision of the region are at particular risk, as are those seen as critical of any of the belligerents. Mahsa Alimardani, a senior researcher and digital rights expert for the freedom of expression NGO Article 19, is just one of many women who have been on the receiving end of such abuse. Once, she received a 'barrage' of abuse and 'aggressive gender-based threats' simply for asking Facebook to clarify its policy of removing certain accounts. The attack came on the back of Instagram blocking a number of accounts linked to the

Iranian Revolutionary Guard, which had been designated a terrorist organisation by the USA.

Negar Mortazavi, a journalist for the British newspaper *The Independent*, receives almost constant misogynistic abuse, much of it on Twitter. An analysis of tweets sent to Mortazavi between May 2014 and October 2020 revealed that she received at least 349 tweets in Persian and English calling her a *jen'deh* (cunt, n = 200), *faahe'she* (whore, n = 78) or bitch (n = 31).[25] The abuse seemed to peak in December 2019 and January 2020, at about the same time there were protests in Iran.[26] The attacks frequently portray Mortazavi as a sympathiser of the regime and are especially bizarre given that she fled Iran and went into self-exile in the USA in 2009. However, in many ways this represents the modus operandi of the IranDisinfo project, as Mortazavi is someone who is well followed on Twitter, frequently features in reputable news outlets read by policy makers, and does not exclusively dedicate her efforts to attacking the Iranian regime or supporting sanctions – despite being a victim of their tyranny. Her nuanced and non-militaristic take on Iranian politics is a reflection of her professionalism as a journalist, and, ironically, the very reason she is singled out for abuse. Often in adversarial campaigns, those who offer nuance are targeted because they confound attempts to generate smear campaigns with a clearly identifiable enemy, and thus a clear policy response.

Both analyses highlight that certain deception actors utilise sexually aggressive trolling. Digital authoritarianism in the Middle East has led to what appears to be a growing use of attacks on women online. Often this is done on such a scale that it is either tacitly condoned or encouraged by the state, suggesting a specific form of state-sponsored gendered repression. This form of intimidation is detrimental to the visibility and contributions women make in public discussions online, leading to a potential 'spiral of silence'.[27]

The attacks on many of the women documented here[28] are typical examples of the shame- and honour-orientated nature of online violence faced by women in the Middle East. When asked about the impact of the online attacks, Oueiss noted that the distinction between physical and psychological abuse was perhaps nebulous. In her own paraphrasing of research she had done in order to come to make sense of the attacks, Oueiss noted with interest that often when we are bullied or humiliated it is the part of the brain that responds to physical pain (such as being burned by coffee) that responds.[29] For Oueiss, the insight reflected the need to understand the new phenomenon of industrial-scale digital harassment campaigns. However, the need for Oueiss to rationalise her own feelings using science highlights the fact such abuse is rarely treated as seriously as other, more overt or widely accepted forms of violence.

Resisting Online Misogyny •

However, we should not discount elements of resistance and agency. Women who face online harassment frequently mobilise to resist online misogyny, engaging in what Emma Jane calls digilantism.[30] Here, targets of cyber-violence call out and shame those who are engaging in such tactics. Oueiss and al-Fares have both taken to Twitter to denounce those attacking them. Oueiss wrote a column in the *Washington Post* titled 'I won't be silenced by online attacks'.[31] However, despite the importance of awareness raising, it reflects a systemic problem in which online misogyny is enabled by a lack of proper regulation to prevent such behaviour. As a consequence, the digilantism enacted by victims can be seen as 'as both reflecting and bolstering a dominant cyber norm which shifts the burden of responsibility for gendered hostility from male perpetrators to female targets, and from the public to the private sphere'.[32]

Part of the problem again lies in the neoliberation ontology of tech companies. Social media companies in particular are slow to respond to such behaviour, especially when it is not in English. *New York Times* journalist Farnaz Fassihi stated succinctly, 'Twitter needs to seriously improve response/prevention: Vile sexual attacks & harassment of women. Identifying & removing bots engaged in death/rape threats. Fixing its broken Persian language support response.'[33] However, even raising issues related to misogynistic abuse prompts similar abuse, and those perceived as promoting feminism are also attacked using highly deceptive tropes. The Egyptian author and activist Mona Eltahawy has documented on numerous occasions the responses she gets to many of her tweets supporting feminism in the Arab world: '#Saudi regime script is, as this regime troll accused me, "feminists are engaged in intellectual terrorism vs family & society w/goal of recruiting young women similar to how al-Qaeda and ISIS/ Daesh recruited young men". Incredible. And speaks to how they fear feminism.'[34]

Gendered Surveillance: There's an App for That

Despite the industrial-scale misogyny from thousands of accounts bearing the image of the Saudi crown prince, the Saudi flag or King Salman, criticism of the Saudi government's treatment of women is considered highly sensitive, largely because MBS has positioned himself as a champion of women's rights. This sensitivity became abundantly clear when there was a global outcry over the smartphone application Absher. Absher, meaning 'your request shall be fulfilled', is an app in Saudi for iOS and Android that allows users to access the Ministry of Interior's services. In Saudi and Qatar, women of a certain age and/or marital status must have a male guardian, who in some cases must grant permission for her to travel abroad. Absher now allows a male guardian to conduct a previously paper-based procedure in the digital realm. Male guardians can grant permission for single or multiple trips, and even suspend permission to travel for a previously authorised request.

Although it has been argued that Absher had actually facilitated some aspects of travel, providing a more efficient means of obtaining permission for travel, it simply represents the technological institutionalisation of laws designed to entrench male domination over women's movement. If it has facilitated some women's travel due to efficiency, it has also restricted other women's travel with equal efficiency. Human Rights Watch stated: 'In the case of Absher, which facilitates discrimination against women and is used to limit freedom of movement of women and foreigners in Saudi Arabia, Google and Apple have a responsibility to mitigate abuses associated with Absher'.[35] In many respects, the advent of the smartphone has allowed the existing patriarchal structures to be digitised and expressed through a new modality of control.

Absher prompted a global controversy because it drew attention to Saudi Arabia's oppressive guardianship system at a time when Saudi was also coming under scrutiny for a string of human rights abuses including attacks on women activists and the murder of Jamal Khashoggi. Soon Absher received coverage in the global news cycle, with *The Guardian*, Human Rights Watch and the *New York Times* – to name but a few – publishing articles on the subject. The global backlash prompted another reputation crisis for Saudi Arabia.

The Saudi Ministry of Interior denounced criticism of the app, claiming that it offered 160 different services. The ministry, oblivious to any sense of irony, issued the following statement: 'The Ministry of Interior at the same time confirms its rejection of the attempts to politicize the systematic use of technical instruments which represent legitimate rights to the users, and its keenness to protect the interests of the beneficiaries of its services.'[36] There was no mention of the fact that the 'beneficiaries' of the specific service being criticised were mostly men, and that the service mentioned was the functional control of women's movement. It also reflected the overt emphasis on the delusion that technology is 'value-free', stating that Absher was a 'technical instrument', seemingly detached from any social context.

A campaign to defend Saudi's reputation through legitimisation of the Absher app was launched. Soon, the hashtag #I_Support_ Absher began trending, with many reviewers suddenly taking to the Google Playstore to astroturf away any criticism of the app. The astroturfing on Google Play seemed suspicious. Almost all reviews of the Absher app occurred after 17 February, immediately after the scandal broke. The app went from receiving almost no reviews per day to suddenly receiving around 973 reviews on 18 February. Over 2,200 of the app's total of 2,331 reviews happened between 17 and 21 February. The Atlantic Council corroborated my findings with data extracted at a slightly later date, with higher numbers. They noted that 50% of the application's reviews occurred on a single day – 17 February. A large number of accounts contained generic expressions such as *momtaz* (excellent). According to the Atlantic Council:

Absher saw a spike in star ratings as well, receiving more than 85,000 5-stars and 3,500 4-stars within a week. By the end of the day on February 20, the app had 86,587 ratings. These spikes suggest that app supporters had launched a coordinated attempt to make it appear as if the Absher app was popular and uncontroversial.[37]

An astroturfing campaign by fake accounts praising an application that facilitated control of women represents a fundamentally alarming aspect of digital authoritarianism in the context of the Arab Gulf's post-truth moment, that once again the illusion of consent can be manufactured through digital manipulation.

Conclusion

In the global context, the post-truth moment is also a misogynistic one. The rise of right-wing populism, epitomised by the election of Donald Trump, has raised attendant questions of how misogynistic discourses are playing out elsewhere in the world. However, the ubiquity of gendered attacks on women do not always provide nuance into the often contextually defined nature of those attacks. This chapter has emphasised the discursive and tactical particularities of attacks on women publics figures, especially those journalists critical of a new Saudi, UAE, Israel and Trump administration led-vision for the Middle East. Indeed, Saudi Arabia, Iran, and perhaps the US State Department, are some of the most dangerous cyberbullies in the region. For the most part, to be a female public figure, journalist or activist in the MENA is also to be a target of cyber-violence, especially if you're seen as critical of Saudi Arabia or Trump's maximum pressure policy on Iran.

The rise of populism, in part fuelled by a form of misogynistic chauvinism, has seen an assault both on women in the public sphere and on the advancements in women's rights. Women critical of political projects led by the new breed of populists and traditionalists seem at particular risk. Failure to abide by the new foreign policy directions formulated ultimately by a particularly aggressive troika of populists in the form of Trump, MBZ and MBS, is exposing women to industrial-scale online abuse. In particular, those not adopting a militaristic enough stance on Iran, or those who dare to criticise, for example, Saudi's role in the killing of Khashoggi or treatment of women will face a constant barrage of cyber-violence. The fact that very little is being done to combat this reflects the neoliberation ontology of tech companies. It also points again to a digital orientalism, and many of those interviewed feel that companies like Twitter take claims of abuse occurring in Arabic or Persian less seriously than those in, say, European languages.

13

STIGMATISING MUSLIMS

THE SISTERHOOD OF THE MUSLIM BROTHERS

Chapter Overview: Creating Conspiratorial Meta-Narratives

This chapter explores a key aspect of the Gulf's post-truth moment, which has been the creation of external bogeymen in the form of Qatar, Turkey, Iran and the Muslim Brotherhood. It documents how specific influential public figures across the world who demonstrably oppose KUBE foreign and domestic policy are smeared as terrorist agitators operating on behalf of the new axis of evil. This chapter also discusses the growing disinformation synergies between the US right wing and the Arabian Peninsula, in which populist regimes share and exploit each other's conspiracies to create a meta-narrative that places Hillary Clinton and the US Democratic Party as an enemy of Saudi Arabia. This itself reflects how conspiracy theories share similar narrative constructs to fiction, where, 'all the elements in a conspiracy theory are linked through clear lines of cause and effect'.[1] These conspiracies are mobilised through a combination of social media influencers, fake social media accounts and legacy media outlets, which work in tandem to add 'depth' to the deception narratives. It also explores how these meta-narratives, and the formation of external enemies, are attempts to reconcile Saudi and

UAE support for one of the most Islamophobic US administrations in history.

The Campaign against a Nobel Peace Prize Winner

On 6 May 2020 Facebook announced that it had created an independent oversight board.[2] The 20-member board was a response to growing international criticism on how Facebook deals with toxic content, hate speech and disinformation. In 2018 Facebook CEO Mark Zuckerberg said that the oversight committee would be Facebook's 'supreme court', and stated that it would have the final decision on whether to take down problematic content. The committee included former UK newspaper editors, judges from Hungary and Columbia, academics and activists, a former Danish prime minister and many others. The committee also included Tawakkol Karman, a Yemeni human rights activist who won the Nobel Peace Prize in 2011 for her promotion of non-violent change in the Arab Uprisings. It was probably this activism that prompted the UAE to hack Karman's iPhone in 2017 using Karma software.[3] Karma is a form of spyware that can be used to infect 'hundreds of iPhones simultaneously, capturing their location data, photos and messages'.[4]

Karman's appointment to the oversight board prompted a storm of disapproval on Arabic Twitter, mostly emanating from Egypt, the United Arab Emirates and Saudi Arabia. On 10 May 'No to Facebook' began trending. Like previous trends criticising Jeff Bezos and calling for the boycott of Amazon in the wake of the Khashoggi murder, the inception of this trend seemingly began with a Twitter account called mbs_mbsksa.[5] Soon tens of thousands of posts attacking Karman began to appear on Twitter and Facebook. Other hashtags emerged in Arabic and English, such as 'Expose Tawakkol'. While the attacks on Oueiss and al-Fares attempted to smear them as sexually promiscuous and lascivious, the attacks on Karman were more bestial; a lot of anonymous Twitter users posted edited images or caricatures of Karman with her head on the bodies of snakes, dogs and vultures.[6] Although the animalistic imagery is common, the use of different tropes for Karman versus Oueiss and al-Fares is indicative of a perceived notion that Karman was a less plausible sexualised object – unlike Oueiss and al-Fares, who do not wear the hijab and frequently appear on television.

Other comments were more political and explicit in their attempts to smear Karman as a Muslim Brotherhood agent beholden to Qatar and Turkey. One cartoon caricature portrayed her as a witch, wrapped in a Turkish flag and riding a broom with bristles painted with the Qatari flag.[7] Although Karman had been a member of the al-Islah Party in Yemen – widely seen as a branch of the Muslim Brotherhood – she was expelled in 2018 for criticising the Saudi bombing of Yemen.[8] As with many adversarial campaigns, the tropes against Karman have sought to take a generally nuanced position held by someone and transform it into unequivocal support for a specific position. (Indeed, Karman criticised and protested against Morsi prior to his ousting, which she then criticised because it was a coup)[9].

The overarching trope was to smear Karman as a supporter of terrorism linked to Qatar and Turkey, an ongoing aspect of the discourse used by the UAE and Saudi Arabia to attack their enemies. Around 17 May 2020 'Facebook Caliphate' began trending. The term 'caliphate' was a contemporary reference to Daesh, which declared that it had established a caliphate, with Abu Bakr al-Baghdadi as the self-proclaimed caliph. As with the other hashtags, a similar image of Karman appeared. One widely shared cartoon showed a terrorist in a black balaclava operating a puppet of Tawwakol Karman, with Karman wielding the blue letter F from the Facebook logo.[10]

The hashtag itself demonstrated signs of serious inorganic activity. An analysis of around 17,000 interactions involving 10,000 unique Twitter accounts revealed that a large network of bots was boosting the hashtag. A network analysis using a community detection algorithm showed a separate cluster of around 2,000 accounts, distinct from the more organic activity. The vast majority of these suspicious accounts were created between May and August 2019, further indicating that they were a sockpuppet network. The analysis also revealed that these accounts almost all used the same application to tweet from, Twitter Web App. Their user input location was Saudi, presumably to give the illusion that real Saudis were tweeting against Karman's appointment, bolstering the illusion that Saudis wished to boycott Facebook if Karman's appointment was not rescinded.[11] Interestingly, the hashtag 'Facebook Caliphate', according to Trendogate, was trending in Saudi Arabia and Belarus. Without knowing exactly how Twitter trends work, it is possible to speculate that a number of accounts using the hashtag were either working from Belarus or were using a VPN set to Belarus.

Twitter disinformation was focused on the fact that Karman was not a supporter of the Saudi-led coalition's intervention in Yemen. This social media disinformation was 'layered' with other known deception campaigns. A number of articles written by fake journalists in the aforementioned Arab Eye network criticised Karman's appointment. Meanwhile, an informal pro-Saudi network of American Trump supporters on Twitter also launched attacks on Karman. They included a Florida-based woman who previously acknowledged working with the Saudi 24 journalist Tarek al-Khitab Abu Zainab to produce pro-Saudi video content.

Conspiracy Theories

Conspiracies, and indeed conspiracy theorists, are often framed as irrational, which is generally an unproductive term that can discourage debate and inquiry.[12] In actual fact, as Operation Ajax or the Sykes–Picot Agreement have shown, conspiracies or secretive machinations by states and politicians are often very real. Notwithstanding, an interesting development of populist politics in the post-truth age is that it turns conventional notions of conspiracies on their heads. Matthew Gray made a distinction between American conspiracism and those emanating from the Middle East, arguing that while US conspiracism traditionally attempted to challenge state power, Middle East conspiracism usually functioned as a means of boosting the state's power. Even if one found such a distinction tenuous, Trumpism obliterated any doubt about such a conceptual difference and demonstrated the US administration's willingness to embrace conspiracy theories.[13] From fake coronavirus cures to QAnon, Trump and the Trump administration embraced conspiracism as a means to legitimise their image as an outmatched foe defending disenfranchised white Americans on the verge of erasure at the hands of rampant immigration facilitated by deep-state machinations. Populism seems to have leveraged the conspiracy theory to align with an underdog strategy, positioning itself as outside the mainstream, and thus credible by virtue of that. In many ways it can be useful to think of conspiracy theories as 'a response to politics, rather than a manifestation of culture or psychology'.[14] The term *mu'āmara* (conspiracy) is still commonly deployed in the Arabic-speaking world to explain certain political events beyond what might be their mainstream explanations. While some conspiracism may challenge a state's power, the post-truth moment has found states acting as conspiracy-theorists-in-chief, typically through the use of 'monopolized mass media, or governing party structures, or under the direction of a charismatic leader'.[15] Indeed, it might be more productive to view many conspiracy theories as strategic disinformation by increasingly autocratic governments. Often conspiracy theories are a means to construct counterfactual claims that, if believed, serve the purpose of protecting the state. They may serve to bolster nationalism and redirect antipathy away from the government and its leaders towards a foreign entity or external enemy. In such cases, demonising enemies is often a means of framing and promoting the state as a protector against external, albeit exaggerated, threats from foreign powers.[16] Indeed, the production of conspiracy is not ad-hoc, but often a function of power maintenance.

The Conspiracy of Muslim Brothers

The campaign again Karman highlights an important aspect of the weaponisation of context in conspiracy theories. Here, genuine information is warped or reframed to suit a particular agenda, one that resonates with a specific audience. A campaign is far more successful when it relies on a kernel or element of truth.[17] Regardless of whether Karman supported the Muslim Brotherhood or al-Islah, it does not mean she is a terrorist or a terrorist sympathiser, let alone a member of Daesh. Furthermore, regardless of one's opinions of the Muslim Brotherhood, it is not, as most academics and analysts argue, a terrorist organisation.[18]

However, the popularity of the Muslim Brotherhood poses a threat to the unelected leaders of Egypt, the UAE, Saudi and other Gulf states, who have designated it a terrorist organisation. The propaganda campaign against it became increasingly virulent leading up to the overthrow of the Egyptian president Mohammed Morsi in 2013: 'Anti-Muslim Brotherhood propaganda may be the result of a concerted effort by media tycoons unfriendly to the Brotherhood, a consequence of decades of anti-Brotherhood fear-mongering, or both.'[19] Since the Gulf Crisis in 2017, much of the disinformation campaign from the blockading countries has equated refusal to be militantly opposed to the Muslim Brotherhood with support for terrorism. This ill-defined 'political Islam', emanating in particular from the UAE and Saudi, has shaped much of the propaganda of the Arab Gulf's post-truth moment.[20]

The election of Trump, whose administration (including Mike Pompeo and former national security advisor John Bolton) was also sympathetic to listing the Muslim Brotherhood as a terrorist organisation, led to an increase in virulent propaganda. This sympathy in the White House led to renewed efforts from the UAE and Saudi Arabia to have the USA brand the Muslim Brotherhood a terrorist organisation. Thus, the very existence of increased Muslim Brotherhood disinformation and propaganda is reflective of the 'Trump administration's accelerating tilt toward the UAE-Saudi axis in Middle East politics, its domestic political calculations and its disregard for warnings of negative consequences'.[21] It is also indicative of the totalitarian tendencies of MBS, and to some extent MBZ, who, like many dictators, require an external enemy against which to deflect internal domestic political tension.

Ilhan Omar: Between Orientalist Tropes and Misogyny

A striking aspect of the Arab Gulf's post-truth moment has been its reach, and a willingness to target American Muslim politicians seen as critical of Saudi, UAE and Israeli policy in the region. Two politicians subjected to an aggressive propaganda campaign targeting the Muslim Brotherhood have been the Somali American Ilhan Omar, the US representative for Minnesota's 5th congressional district, and the Palestinian American Rashida Tlaib, the US representative for Michigan's 13th congressional district. Writing in *Foreign Policy*, journalist Ola Salem notes that Saudi had 'declared war' on America's Muslim congresswomen – a fact some might initially find counter-intuitive. Indeed, as Hamid Dabashi asks, 'Aren't the Saudis "the Custodians of the Two Noble Sanctuaries", as they call and thus congratulate themselves? Aren't they supposed to be protectors and supporters of all Muslims around the world?'

However, Ilhan Omar and Rashida Tlaib's fierce criticism of human rights abuses, whether they are perpetrated by Israel, or the Saudi-led coalition's bombing of Yemen, have put them at odds with the blockading Gulf states. Indeed, they are not 'good Muslims' according to the Saudi definition. That is to say, they are not Muslims who watch silently as Saudi 'massacre Yemenis and cut Khashoggi to pieces while rushing to make ticket reservations for their Hajj pilgrimage'.[22]

For the current Saudi and Emirati regimes, to be a Muslim who does not stay silent in the wake of their atrocities is to be a bad Muslim, and to be a bad Muslim is to be a member of the Muslim Brotherhood. Many of the attacks on Ilhan Omar have been made through influential analysts or journalists. Ahmad al-Farraj, a Saudi writer and researcher, launched a social media campaign against her. A number of hashtags dominated by anonymous accounts attacking Omar began trending. Most of them used similar insults and variations of the same language while boosting the tweets of pro-government accounts.

While online attacks on Saudi's perceived enemies are common in the region, the manner in which they 'adapt' to the target reflects both implicit prejudices and explicit attempts to potentially address psychological weakness in the targets – and indeed rile up similar populism. Ola Salem noted that there was an interesting bifurcation in the on- and offline abuse directed at Omar and Tlaib: 'While Tlaib and Omar have both been the targets of smears, it's been easier for Gulf Arabs to single out Omar for insults because of her African heritage. Negative stereotypes about Africans – who serve as poorly treated migrant workers in the Gulf's oil economy – are widespread throughout the region.' Salem describes al-Farraj's attacks:

'These miserable beings coming from the underdeveloped worlds are more hateful to their race and to you than any enemy,' Al Farraj tweeted to his more than 60,000 followers. A steady stream of racist attacks followed in response. One person tweeted a picture of Omar accompanied by the caption 'whenever you buy a slave, buy a stick along with the slave. The slave is miserable filth.'[23]

As with the tendency to 'stack' various tropes on each other, the propaganda targeting Omar has also played to the tropes evident in the Gulf Crisis. In a particularly strange turn of events, Alan Bender, a businessman with a number of connections to high-level officials in the Gulf states, was subpoenaed by a Florida court in a federal case against the Qatar emir's brother, Shaykh Khalid bin Hamad Al Thani. The case in question was brought by Matthew Pittard, a defence contractor who claimed he had been hired to protect Shaykh Khalid. However, Bender's affidavit in the case contained a string of bizarre allegations repeating the same disinformation tropes about Ilhan Omar's involvement in the Muslim Brotherhood. In the affidavit, Bender painted Omar as the Qatari Manchurian Candidate, who would do anything the 'Qataris' asked her to, especially when it came to assisting any of the fanatical 'brothers or sisters' who are 'important to Qatar'. Bender also accused Omar of providing US intelligence to Iran via Qatar while swearing allegiance to the Turkish president Erdoğan.

Bender's fantastical claims also involved Linda Sarsour, a Muslim American activist, who he claimed was another Muslim Brotherhood agent planning a 'Qatari-funded run for the senate'.[24] Bender's claims read like a shortlist of propaganda points emanating from Saudi Arabia, the UAE and Egypt since the blockade. He even claimed that Khashoggi was killed after the Qataris turned against him. Even the conservative media in the USA, who have attacked Ilhan Omar with zeal, largely on the basis that she is a Muslim person of colour who wears a hijab, were quick to cast doubt on the allegations. Writing in the conservative Middle East Forum, Sam Westrop noted, 'We should treat Bender's claims about Qatar and its American "agents" as little more than a set of unlikely conspiracy theories.'[25] It would seem a sworn legal testimony that could not really be 'disproven' was too appealing a forum in which to articulate anti-Muslim Brotherhood smears.

The overlap between propaganda networks supporting the policy of the blockading countries and the US right was evidenced in the anti-Ilhan campaign, largely through the figure of a self-styled reformist Muslim cleric, Mohammed Tawhidi. According to Robert Mackey, Tawhidi is a Shi'a Muslim cleric who 'presents himself as an Islamic reformer [and] who embraces and amplifies far-right warnings that immigration by his fellow Muslims poses an existential threat to Western civilization'.[26] Tawhidi has branded America's US congresswomen as agents of Hamas, and also repeated claims that Omar is an agent of Qatar. He has a large Twitter following. Like MEK member Heshmat Alavi, the most common biographical descriptor of Tawhidi's followers is MAGA, suggesting he has a large following among Trump supporters, and perhaps fake accounts posing as Trump supporters.

However, on top of the racialised abuse, Ilhan Omar is also subjected to the added violence of misogynistic smear campaigns attempting to accuse her of being a terrorist sympathiser. Between June 2018 and October 2020 she was called a terrorist on Twitter at least 740 times. She also received at least 3,089 slurs on Twitter calling her either a bitch (n = 2548), whore (n = 227), slut (n = 179) or cunt (n = 135). (As an interesting theoretical point, much of this abuse spiked when it was reported that Omar was having an affair with her campaign adviser, Tim Mynett.) The attacks on Ilhan Omar, Rashida Tlaib and Linda Sarsour are indicative of the fact that they are seen as legitimate targets by propagandists supporting the new political configuration in the Middle East. A striking aspect of the attacks is that they reflect a peculiarity of the Trump, MBS and UAE nexus, one in which two Muslim-majority nations formed an alliance with a populist leader who initiated some of the most Islamophobic policies in US history.

A Simulated Scandal?

Ilhan Omar is not the only female US politician to be targeted by KUBE propaganda. On 11 October 2020 the Arabic hashtag

'Hilary's emails' began trending in Saudi Arabia. Before long it had reached over 170,000 tweets in 48 hours. The trend came on the back of an announcement by the then US secretary of state Michael Pompeo, who was being pressured by Donald Trump to release more of former secretary of state Hillary Clinton's emails. Although releasing more emails was criticised as potentially illegal, Pompeo, a particularly loyal underling to Donald Trump, was attempting to appease his boss, who, amid poor poll numbers in October 2020, was undoubtedly trying to replicate the political boost that he had immediately before his 2016 election victory when the FBI director James Comey reopened an investigation into how Clinton had a private email server at home that she used for work purposes.

The immediacy and suddenness of the Twitter storm suggested that there had been a revelatory scoop. Hundreds of accounts, mostly from the UAE and Saudi, used the term *tasribaat* (leaks) when referring to the information garnered from the emails. There is a logic to this. For conspiracies to be effective, they must be seen as removed from the dominant narrative, as opposed to originating in what is widely acknowledged as censored and co-opted state media. Instead, 'leaks' occur on social media, and are then 'picked up' by the state media, giving them a believably organic, salacious authenticity.

One English version of a little-known Egyptian news site wrote, 'Many leaked e-mails related to former US Secretary of State Hillary Clinton revealed her close relation with Qatari Al-Jazeera TV network and how she had used it to spread chaos in the Middle East.'[27]

In actual fact, there had been no leak or publication of new emails, by Pompeo or anyone else. The information being shared was actually taken from over 4,000 emails legitimately and legally released by the State Department in 2015 at the request of Hillary Clinton, following an FBI investigation into Clinton's use of a private email home server for government-related work.[28]

The 'Hillary's emails' hashtag was a good example of a disinformation synergy. Pompeo's announcement about a release of more emails was seized on as an opportunity to attack domestic and foreign enemies of KUBE in the lead up to the US election. In addition to targeting Clinton, most commentators on the hashtag talked of a conspiracy against Saudi Arabia by the Democratic Party and the Muslim Brotherhood. The Emirati news site @Alain_4u, which was previously found to have been boosted by numerous inauthentic accounts, was circulating stories about how the Muslim Brotherhood was set to bring down the Arab world with the help of Qatar and Turkey.[29]

Other influencers and outlets focused on the fact that Clinton had been scheduled to meet officials from Al Jazeera in 2010. This was interpreted as support for the channel and its perceived role in stoking the Arab Uprisings. As they had done with Ghada Oueiss, cartoonists drew caricatures of Clinton, with one of them featuring her standing next to a pile of money overseeing a man sitting in front of a blood-covered laptop bearing the Al Jazeera logo.

Other allegations were clear examples of weaponising context; some argued that Clinton was planning to greenlight a $100 million media campaign led by the Muslim Brotherhood. Writing in the *Washington Post*, David Ignatius noted of the smear campaign:

> A Clinton email that has been cited repeatedly in the campaign is a Sept. 17, 2012, message to her from Jake Sullivan, then her closest adviser, noting that the Muslim Brotherhood was planning a $100 million media campaign based in Qatar. In a two-sentence message, Sullivan wrote that, with such developments, he was 'totally invested' in creating a '21st century' U.S. communications strategy. This was spun by Saudi commentators as a claim that Clinton 'gave the green light to the Brotherhood and their project,' according to an account published by *Sky News Arabia*.[30]

A significant aspect of the Hillary hashtag was how it 'broke out' into established legacy media outlets. Like many of the hashtag scandals documented in this book, the story subsequently appeared in locally based legacy media. UAE-owned Sky News Arabia, part of Sky News International, also ran the story as if it were a scoop with revelatory information. One article opened with a sentence highlighting how the declassification of the emails had provided insights into US policy. Nowhere did it clarify that the content was published in 2015.[31] The Sky News Arabia article emphasised how the emails demonstrated Obama and Hillary Clinton's support for the Muslim Brotherhood. This breakout once again highlighted the complicity of the reputable news channels in propagating deceptive content.

The faux scoop against Clinton was also designed to generate a plausible and far-ranging conspiracy theory with Saudi once again as the victim. The most distinct trope was that Clinton, along with former CIA director John Brennan (in addition to the Obama administration in general), had sought to undermine MBS through the elevation of Crown Prince Mohammed bin Nayef (MBN). Also implicated in the conspiracy was Saad al-Jabri, who was the former top intelligence adviser to MBN. Al-Jabri fled to Canada following the deposing of MBN, and Saudi issued an arrest warrant for him in 2017. Since that time, al-Jabri's family have been taken hostage by the Saudi regime in order to pressure him to return, where he will undoubtedly face arrest.[32]

The demonisation of MBN and al-Jabri was not random, but was rather a calculated attempt to mobilise Saudi domestic opinion against the two men. MBN, who had been lauded by numerous American officials for his perceived competence in tackling terrorism, was long viewed by MBS as a rival for the throne. As a result, he now faces charges of corruption and disloyalty.[33] Supporters of MBN claim that the charges are trumped up, designed to give a fig leaf of legal legitimacy to an attempt by MBS to remove challenges to his power. Al-Jabri faced similar charges, this time for heading up a fund that used Saudi money to pay foreign officials (such as Sudan's former president Omar al-Bashir) and informants. This was widely known and considered 'business as usual' in Saudi Arabia, according to an investigative report in the *Wall Street Journal*.[34] Indeed, David Hearst argued that, in addition to eliminating potential rivals, al-Jabri and MBN had similar damaging dirt on both the King and MBS.[35] Interpol rejected the Saudi arrest warrant, claiming it was 'politically motivated'.[36]

This did not stop the Saudi authorities from launching a domestic smear campaign. In July 2020 social media campaigns led by Saudi accounts targeted MBN and al-Jabri prior to expected corruption charges being filed. The trending hashtags, which included 'corrupt

Saad Al Jabri' and 'the corruption of Saad Al Jabri', were an attempt to sway public opinion ahead of a potentially unpopular policy decision involving two men feted by the United States.[37] In 2020 al-Jabri filed a lawsuit in Canada against Mohammed bin Salman, in which he claimed that MBS had sent members of his personal hit team, the Tiger Squad, to kill him.[38] This was the same squad that had killed Jamal Khashoggi. After the filing of this lawsuit in August 2020, Saudi-led accounts once again began a smear campaign on Twitter, and 'corrupt Saad Al Jabri' began to trend, highlighting that social media smears were very much part of the national reputation-management strategy.[39] The campaign was clearly an attempt to link relatively disparate elements of an anti-MBS plot together, undertaken in order to damage al-Jabri and MBN's reputations domestically ahead of a possible trial.

Another emerging aspect of the post-truth world is how conspiracy theories and disinformation fit better when they can be rationalised as part of an interconnected and interwoven set of events. It is no secret that many conspiracy theories invoke some sort of secret cabal who pull the strings of world events to suit their own agenda. From David Icke's notion of lizard people to anti-Semitic theories that posit the existence of a global syndicate of Jews controlling the world, conspiracy theories thrive when they can provide an ontology that rationalises and explains complex events in simple terms. By creating the illusion of a global plot, with the Democratic Party at the helm working in cahoots with Qatar, the campaign was relying on creating an overall 'narrative' that served to legitimise a draconian response to two men with a popular support base. To unseat such figures, who have developed a strong reputation at home and abroad, a convincing narrative was required. The formulation of an entire plot, in which Saudi triumphs over a series of powerful and evil characters and protagonists, forms a much more convincing narrative arc, with an appropriate set-up for the denouement: the trial of MBN. By attacking Clinton, and the Democratic Party in general, the campaign sought to undermine the praise and value given to MBS and al-Jaabri by former Democratic administrations which had worked successfully alongside them. Instead of feting MBN as an example of a key partner in counter-terrorism, it behoved MBS to demonise him as someone aligned with an administration and party supporting terrorism through the Muslim Brotherhood.

The Clinton trope was not random, and ties in with years of demonisation via Trumpist calls to 'lock her up' and brand her 'crooked Hillary'. That it tapped into a real scandal, in the form of real content provided from Hillary's emails, meant that it had the kernel of truth sufficient to make other claims of deviance more credible. This kernel of truth, along with the framing of the information as revelatory and sensitive, can be termed the 'simulation of scandal'.[40] The simulation of scandal is, in part, an attempt to utilise 'direct moral judgement against the target' by revealing information obtained through sensitive private information.[41]

Legitimising Conspiracy Theories

In the transnational context, where parochialism in the information ecosystem is being eroded, conspiracy theories transcend their local context and rub up against one another, creating a jarring array of complex narratives that may or may not invite accusations of contradiction or incompatibility. Indeed, conspiracies are best narrated when a coherent narrative can be formed that ties in with a dramatic structure which includes evil protagonists and nationalistic heroes. By tying in these American politicians as part of a Muslim Brotherhood conspiracy to attack Saudi, the Saudi regime is using extant tropes of Islamophobic and anti-immigrant sentiment that appeal to the US right. In this sense, Omar, Tlaib and Clinton had already been 'primed' for smearing by the virulent rise of populism. On the other hand, Saudi can achieve domestic goals of smearing internal enemies such as MBN and Saad al-Jabri by implicating them in pre-existing conspiratorial tropes, namely association with established narratives like that of 'crooked Hillary'. These disinformation synergies are further strengthened and legitimised through linking Democrats via the likes of Ilhan Omar and Rashida Tlaib to the Muslim Brotherhood, Qatar and Turkey. The alignment of the US right, Saudi and the UAE has resulted in a disinformation meta-narrative, an alternative reality made in the mould of a new breed of populists stretching from Riyadh to Washington, DC. Deception campaigns like those mentioned in this chapter that rely on a combination of social media influencers, real accounts, fake accounts and stories in the legacy media usually indicate that these are narratives perceived as important by the Saudi and Emirati regimes.

PART VI

ADVENTURES IN TROLL-LAND

'To live is to war with trolls'
Henrik Ibsen

14

TALKING PRO-MBS ZOMBIES

Chapter Overview

An aspect of deception in the Middle East space has been the hijacking of verified Twitter accounts for the spreading of propaganda. Here, deception actors utilise the added credibility and social capital of verified accounts in order to increase the efficacy of the propaganda. As this chapter demonstrates, however, it has raised troubling questions about Twitter's competence and efficacy in dealing with compromised accounts. It also strengthens claims of how social media companies are failing to intervene in a timely manner with platform manipulation emanating from the MENA region.

David Schwartz

David Schwartz was the consummate professional and loved by fans and colleagues alike. Fellow Weather Channel reporter Stephanie Abrahams once described the veteran Weather Channel meteorologist as one of 'the kindest, happiest, wisest & most authentic humans' that she'd ever known. He had survived a battle with cancer, and his strength and fortitude inspired many going through the same struggle. Like many TV personalities, Schwartz embraced social media, and particularly Twitter. Here he would engage with his fans, not only updating them on the weather, but also in casual repartee. He was personable, and not at all aloof. However, when he tweeted in 2018 about Saudi Arabia, his fans were shocked. Not because he had never really tweeted about Saudi before, but for another reason.

David Schwartz had been dead for two years.

Schwartz had tragically died in 2016 after a long struggle with cancer. Such was his profile that the *New York Times* even ran an obituary on him, noting his 'easy-going manner' and 'gentle sense of humour'.[1]

However, two years after his death, strange things began to happen. Gradually, fans of Schwartz began to notice that his account was active again. The name on the account had changed, but the unique Twitter handle remained the same: @twcdaveschwartz (it is important to keep the unique user handle, as changing it would result in the loss of the blue badge).

Not only was Schwartz's account tweeting again, but his followers were confused as to why he was now tweeting in Arabic. His banner picture had changed to the visage of the Saudi region of Al Qassim, and he appeared to be tweeting pro-Saudi propaganda. Whoever ran the account had changed the name to Al Qassim Events, and a number of the tweets promoted events occurring in Saudi governorate of Al Qassim.

Many of Schwartz's fans were upset to discover that his Twitter account had been posting pro-Saudi propaganda from beyond the grave. One Twitter user, @spectrumaots, wrote to whoever had taken over the account, asking them to 'give up ownership of the account because it's disrespectful to dishonour someone who died of cancer'.

In early 2018 there were no longer any tweets on Schwartz's account; the last to be deleted was a single retweet from March 2018. It was originally posted by the Saudi poet Ziyad bin Nahit.[2]

What made the David Schwartz affair more bizarre was that he had a verified, or 'blue tick', account. The blue tick verification badge was originally created by Twitter to let others know that the account was authentic and of public interest.[3] The blue badge has come to be associated with a mark of credibility and legitimacy. In an age of fake news and fake accounts, it lets people know that your account is real. The scarcity of the blue badge has also resulted in demand for such accounts. They are frequently hacked or sold to those desirous of their coveted status. However, it is important to note that verified accounts lose their verification status if they change their unique Twitter handle. Given that the purpose of verification is to validate an account's authenticity, it is no surprise that Twitter can remove the blue badge if the account intentionally misleads 'people on Twitter by changing one's display name or bio'.[4] Therefore, accounts that have been appropriated change their names but retain their handles in order not to lose verification. Thus if one does not look intently enough, one may not notice an incongruity between the name and the handle.

Not just the one account

David Schwartz is not the only person to have had his verified Twitter account appropriated by pro-government propagandists, nor is he the only celebrity to have had his Twitter account come to life posthumously. Perhaps more shockingly, at least from an information security perspective, Democratic American politician Debbie Smith, who was elected to the Nevada senate, also had her account hacked by an Arabic-speaking account. Smith passed away in 2016, and her account has since been suspended. Although it is not clear what Smith tweeted after her account had been hacked, many other accounts have also been hacked by Arabic-language users.

The hacking or appropriation of Smith and Schwartz's verified Twitter accounts is the tip of a much large iceberg. At least 70 Twitter verified accounts belonging to various celebrities, among them sports personalities, actors, comedians, athletes and musicians, have been appropriated – many of which have been used to promote state propaganda. Of the 52 of these accounts that report their location, 32 are located in Saudi.

Many of those who have had their accounts hijacked have subsequently tweeted on topics reflecting the Saudi regime's views on domestic and foreign policy. The vast majority of hacked or appropriated accounts taken over for the purpose of propaganda tended to reflect a pro-Saudi foreign policy. Sheyna Steiner, an American financial analyst who once appeared on Fox Business News (among other things), had her account appropriated by a pro-Mohammed bin Salman troll in 2019. The new account, that went by the name Abd al Aziz al Harthi, was very active, mostly tweeting pro-Saudi regime hashtags and praise for MBS.

The gamut of different types of accounts taken over to distribute propaganda highlighted that it was probably the blue tick badge, rather than the potential audience, that was coveted. The account of motivational speaker Jeff Emmerson was hijacked by Saudi advocates, who attacked anyone critical of Riyadh's treatment of political prisoners. Emmerson's account retweeted Saudi user @Fayez_101, saying, 'We demand that the French authorities release immediately 1500 French citizens and give them an amnesty, as its Christmas'.[5] Emmerson's account had been used to deploy propaganda during a Saudi spat with France, which began when the French Ministry for Europe and Foreign Affairs' official Arabic Twitter account called on the Saudi authorities to pardon Saudi human rights activist Raif Badawi on the occasion of Ramadan.

Tanner Chidester, an American fitness trainer, also had his account hijacked by an Arabic-speaking account. This time they used Chidester's account to promote a viral hashtag about Qatar. One of the hashtags was, 'Hey donkeys it's a boycott, not a blockade'[67] – a common trope that sought to downplay the severity of the Gulf Crisis by attacking those who called it a blockade. The hashtag was also meant to be humourous – the Arabic word for donkeys (*himaar*) is similar to the Arabic word for blockade (*hisaar*). Nicole Jade Parks, a former Olympic skier who competed at the 2014 Sochi Winter Olympics, also had her account hacked. Although there were no tweets remaining on her timeline (at the time of writing), many of her followers appear to be pro-Saudi bots or trolls, with patriotic banner profile and display pictures.

In September 2019, the Twitter account of Kjetil Jansrud, a well-known Norwegian skier, was hacked. Bizarrely, the account was hacked and taken over by one Reem bint Waleed, who used the profile image of Prince al-Waleed bin Talal. Ironically, al-Waleed was reportedly the second-largest individual shareholder in Twitter. Twitter restored @Kjansrud's account quite quickly, although, during its brief tenure as Reem bint Waleed, the account was nationalistic in tone and celebrated Saudi and its leadership. One tweet, for example, asked God to make Saudi stand tall in front of its enemies and to protect it. What is perhaps more bizarre is that the biography of the account was that of Reema bint al-Bandar, the relatively new Saudi ambassador to the USA. Jansrud saw the funny side of it, and upon restoring his account changed his profile photo to a picture of him wearing the *ghutra*, a traditional gulf male head covering, along with the biography 'Alpine Skier and Sheik fan'.[8]

Although it is difficult to know when this practice began, it continued well into 2020. The various political crises and social media influence operations that have rocked the Gulf have usually involved the use of appropriated accounts. In May 2020, when Saudi accounts launched false rumours of a coup d'état in Qatar, a number of appropriated accounts were used. Verified accounts belonging to an American musician called Aaron Persinger, and a baseball player called Joey Krehbiel, were also tweeting anti-Qatar propaganda. After I engaged with him on Twitter, Krehbiel's account reverted to a chauvinistic Egyptian account called Ahmed AlWakeel,[9] while the account of Aaron Persinger reverted back to a Saudi 'journalist' called Mustafa.[10] These accounts had been repurposed as Arabic accounts and sought to use their verified status to fool people into thinking that credible accounts were tweeting about the coup.

It is unclear exactly how these verified accounts, with their added security, have been appropriated. It might be that the account owners abandoned Twitter and remain unaware that they were hacked. They also might be aware of this and be entirely indifferent. There is a possibility that some might be complicit; it is certainly true that many people with verified accounts are approached by people willing to purchase a blue tick account. One informant stated that she was approached by an anonymous account which asked if they were interested in selling their blue tick. Regardless of how they are obtained, the fact that a number of the compromised accounts remain verified for some time after they have been 'called out' is also alarming, and points again to a worrying apathy on the part of Twitter in tackling deception.

Conclusion

Appropriating verified accounts is an interesting phenomenon. First, hackers can benefit from the credibility that is often associated with a verified account, and fool people into believing that that account has legitimacy and trustworthiness. This increases the potential to deceive readers. Second, hacking accounts also increases the diversity and global reach of a message by allowing deception agents to promote disinformation and propaganda beyond the usual filter bubbles and echo chambers that may form around certain online communities. The jury is still out on whether verified accounts are more likely to be perceived as credible. For example, a study by Vaidya et al. concluded that 'the presence or absence of an authenticity indicator has no significant effect on willingness to share a tweet or take action based on its contents'.[11] Edgerly and Vraga note too that, 'currently, users appear to rely on other cues than the verification label when judging information quality'.[12]

While studies tend to find little correlation between having a blue tick and an impact on information sharing or perceived credibility, it is important to do contextual investigations into how socially constructed notions of reputation may play out in why people endorse certain ideas, especially in media ecosystems that do not offer a plurality of views. Certainly perception of the legitimacy of a blue tick may well be different for some MENA audiences than those elsewhere. Without knowing this, verified accounts are still potentially assets that allow the disinformation agents to reach new constituencies and audiences through the appropriation of accounts with generally large followings. Whether or not they are engaging in other forms of platform manipulation, phishing or social engineering is also an alarming possibility.

On another level, the human aspect is important. Despite a number of people complaining to Twitter about the phenomenon, Schwartz's account remained verified until the middle of 2020, several years after he had been hacked and four years after his death.

For his fans, seeing the account of a man they had deeply admired come to life to tweet propaganda was a damning indictment of the new frontiers of online deception. The apathy of Twitter was indicative of what is a large part of the disinformation problem, in the Middle East or elsewhere, an absence of clear oversight or timely remedy of deception operations.

15

THE RISE AND FALL OF MAGNUS CALLAGHAN[1]

Chapter Overview

Often deception involves people using social media accounts to influence others, or extract human intelligence from them. Social engineering often involves creating fake profiles so as to deceive others into handing over private and potentially sensitive information. Alternatively, there may be attempts to co-opt perceived 'enemies' to defuse their criticism or, conversely, enlist them as propagandists. The following story narrates an experience with one such person, providing insights into how regional experts and commentators are targeted by nefarious accounts for undetermined, yet sinister reasons. In addition to being run by multiple operatives, the account was promoting MBS propaganda while attempting to gain intelligence about Qatar.

Meeting Magnus

It was May 2019 when I embarked upon an unlikely friendship with a Twitter troll called Magnus Callaghan. Magnus recently had a sex / ethnicity reassignment operation. He is now called Jasmine, but we'll come to that a bit later.

Magnus first started to message me in May 2020. His thin moustache and warm yet darting eyes endeared me to him immediately. As his name suggests, he was British. In his profile picture he wore a distinctive lilac shirt that did little to enhance his pallid complexion.

Magnus would regularly criticise my stance on Middle East politics. For some reason unknown to me he was very anti-Iran and anti-Qatar, but very supportive of Saudi's crown prince Mohammed bin Salman. He once tweeted: 'The disgusting, racist, and frankly Islamophobic campaign against Saudi Arabia is highly misguided. The Saudi people are 100% behind King Salman and MBS. I know. I lived there for 22 years.'

Like many Twitter accounts in recent months, Magnus's profile was replete with multiple flags. Befitting his provenance and political stance, Magnus had the flags of the United Kingdom, Saudi Arabia and the United States on his profile.

He was at times abrasive, often capricious, and prone to mood swings. Sometimes I'd get pleasant Magnus, other times I'd get angry Magnus – or Sméagol, as I used to refer to him in my head.

Why this middle-aged white man with a faded lilac shirt had such strong opinions on the region was unclear. It wasn't long before Magnus slid into my DMs in the most unconventional manner. In a surprise move, he self-doxxed and sent me a copy of his passport page. It was a British passport, furnished with his date of birth and his middle names. It looked authentic enough, and surely enough, it said Magnus Callaghan.

Pre-empting my confusion, Magnus then messaged me to assure me that he was no troll. After all, I did now have his passport.

Magnus: 'Fyi … not everyone who criticises the anti-Trump disinformation ecosystem is a bot/troll or girl called Natascha from Vorkuta. Just sayin'.

The reference to Natascha and Vorkuta (a town in Russia) was no doubt playing on the increasingly prevalent idea that many known information operations are run out of Russia or Eastern Europe. His informal use of 'Just sayin" was jarring for a man of Magnus's years and did little to reassure me that his colloquialisms were authentically vernacular.

Nevertheless, despite our differences, Magnus and I used to banter. We'd bond over our time in Wales, where Magnus had also lived. He confessed to me that he was a fan of Welsh comedian Max Boyce, the 1980s sitcom *Hi-de-Hi* and *Battlestar Galactica*. His occasional forays into slightly esoteric cultural references would usually end abruptly by an unsolicited diatribe about Middle East politics. He especially had it in for Iran and Qatar.

Marc if you focus on Iranian disinformation, you will be at the cutting edge. Tip of the spear. It will help your career, your research, all in every possible way. And you would indeed be doing a great service to regional security. Think about it …

I thought about it, and, despite his unspecified offer to be part of the 'tip of the spear', I resisted Magnus's advances. Instead, I wanted to know why he thought he knew so much about the Middle East, and especially Qatar, which he seemed to single out for particular criticism.

'So why do you think you know so much about Qatar,' I asked.
'I don't know anything about Qatar. So I'm the wrong person to ask about any of that stuff', replied Magnus.

Confused by Magnus's seeming feigned ignorance, I asked him why he always tweeted about Qatar if he claimed to know nothing about it. Over the next few days, Magnus's behaviour became more and more bizarre. Despite having very strong and frequently expressed opinions on Qatar, Saudi and Iran, he would always say the following:

I didn't [sic] know much about that stuff.

Undeterred by Magnus's obtuse rebuttals, I asked why he always tweeted about Qatar but claimed to know nothing about it. He responded by saying it was for learning purposes.

Our relatively polite personal messages contrasted sharply with Magnus's public abuse directed at me. In light of his capriciousness, I asked him why he was so rude to me outside our private messages.

He denied being rude, which I found bizarre. I politely disagreed and told him that he was, in fact, quite rude. I reminded him of a time where he had said I was one of Azmi Bishara's Qatari 'cells'. I also noted that knowledge of Azmi Bishara seemed quite esoteric for a man who claimed to know nothing about the Middle East, Qatar or 'that stuff', as Magnus put it. Indeed, there were growing inconsistencies about what he discussed publicly and what he said in private.

But then things started getting really weird.

He began to allude to the fact I could move anywhere I wanted, presumably if I took up his offer of joining the dark side.

Magnus: 'Very many things trouble me. I feel you are not happy in Qatar. Why don't you move to a nicer climate? Where would you like to go?'

Naturally, I resisted his mind games and joked around with him:

Me: 'I hear Lusail is nice!' (Lusail is a town in Qatar)

It started getting stranger when Magnus began to suggest that people were trying to steal my research. He had particular problems with Jessika Aro, the Finnish troll wrestler, who he claimed was taking credit for my work. He was very worried that people would steal my work at a conference that I was due to attend in Helsinki in the summer of 2019.

Magnus: 'I am very worried about your research. I feel others appropriate it and give you no credit. It seems very unfair. After Beijing, Danmark [sic], Sweden, people should respect you more. It's not fair. Don't let them use you!'
Me: 'Who is stealing it?'
Magnus: 'Her name is Jessika. Cos she can't figure stuff out herself even.'
'Is Jessika your wife?' I joked.
Magnus: 'Err, she's nothing to do with me in any way. She's taking your stuff, putting her name on it then sending it to the COE in Helsinki. Next, it goes to Brussels. So it's terrible, really.'

I was touched by Magnus's concern for academic integrity and plagiarism, and made a note to narrate this amusing episode to

Jessika if I ever met her. Magnus also had a few other organisations he was keen to know more about, most notably the think tank Atlantic Council, the open-source investigation outfit Bellingcat and the cybersecurity firm Fire Eye. His interests did not stop there. He developed growing anxiety about the Quakers, whose activism he insisted could not be ideological, but rather under 'command and control' from some nation-state. He was concerned that their 'simple mentality' made them vulnerable to 'infiltration by outside forces'. I thought it was interesting that at the time some Quaker activists had been protesting BAE systems for selling weapons to Saudi that were subsequently used in Yemen.

Between our conversations about world politics and the Middle East (which Magnus repeatedly claimed to know nothing about), we would return to bantering. Sometimes he would send me Ariana Grande memes or talk about Korean pop music (K Pop). On other occasions he would take a break from his requests for Gulf political intelligence by sending selfies for my 'collection'.

But over time it was increasingly clear that Magnus's language was odd and seemingly inconsistent. As a native English speaker, I was convinced that he was not, as he claimed, one himself. Certain unusual grammatical or syntactical infelicities were unsettling. Indeed, small errors made me suspicious.

At one point, he went all Buffalo Bill, referring to me in the third person:

'see how nasty what he's telling'.

… It rubs the lotion on its skin …

I tried to catch him out. I asked where he had learned English, but he didn't answer. I also asked him why he did not criticise Saudi or the UAE, but despite his vast knowledge about the Middle East, this 'was nothing to do with him … so everything is normal'.

… Indeed, everything is normal.

In addition to his apparently non-native English, other inconsistencies began to manifest themselves. He had once claimed in a tweet that he had lived in Saudi for 22 'wonderful years'. Yet this was roundly contradicted a number of times, especially when he told me that he had never even been to the Middle East. I was soon convinced that the account was not only operated by someone who was not Magnus, but by more than one person. The inconsistencies, the changes in language, all pointed to that possibility.

I consulted the Wayback Machine, an archive of internet pages that record old information of webpages. I wanted to see Magnus's original biography on Twitter and to see how it had changed over time. Initially, it stated that he was living in Devon, and that he had lived in Saudi for 22 years. For a short time he claimed to be a disinformation analyst, defending 'America and its strategic alliances in the Middle East'. His final incarnation was a chauvinistic #MAGA account that included hashtags of #BuildtheWall #Qanon and #Trump. His profile was also replete with a Saudi, Egyptian, Emirati and US flag emoji.

The only public record of a Magnus Callaghan I could find in Saudi was of a man who had been an English teacher in Dammam. Matching photos of him could be found on International House Dammam's Facebook page. The man in the picture was definitely a teacher in Dammam. Could it have been he, and if so, why was his English so bizarre? Also, if it was he, why had he lied about living in the Middle East?

Soon, Magnus's pupation period as a relatively amiable moustached *Battlestar Galactica* fan came to an end. His account had begun to resemble one of those many troll accounts that spread US right-wing propaganda. In addition to his newfound #MAGA awakening, Magnus started sending me bizarre, almost cultish polemics about the perils of liberalism. He brought up the German philosopher Heidegger and said that Trump had 'Dasein', a term meaning to be present in one's world, as opposed to immersing oneself in the trappings of escapism.

Callaghan's foray into QAnon Trump-worship territory was peculiar, and I became increasingly sure of a few things: despite showing me a matching British passport, Magnus was clearly not a middle-aged British man. He had clearly lied about his past, and was also trying to get intel on various organisations that were involved in fighting disinformation. His political beliefs were your standard alt-right tropes mixed in with an anti-Qatar and anti-Iran stance that aligned him with Saudia Arabia and the United Arab Emirates. Indeed, Magnus was a caricature of your present-day ultra-right-wing populist, except that he liked Ariana Grande gifs! Despite our previous repartee, our relationship would come to a difficult end. Magnus and I had been flirting for some time now, so I decided to finally ask him for a Skype meeting. This was immediately after I had unintentionally provoked him into a rant against Nazis:

Me: 'You've very much Nazi in your ideology you realise? Anti-Marx, anti-liberalist, pro-military state, pro-white populist leader that enflames right-wing populism.'

Magnus: 'Nazis? I wudnt spit on Nazis, and very hard 2 believe they wudnt just shoot me first cos obviously they wud as not up 2 their racial standard Pro-white? I couldn't care less about racial politics. It's Al Jazeera + Iran using active measures trying to start a race war, and I constantly oppose it. Nazis hate me and call me an Anglo-Zionist, a Zio Neococon, a pro-Russian Anglo Jew, a Jew Oligarch, a hasbara troll, IDF. Whatever. Can we both agree we should stop the Nazis? No. Why? Cos u ARE one, and you know it.'

Me: 'OH I am all for stopping Nazis. You're the one idolising a man who has come to power by appealing to white nationalists, racists and fascists. I would never engage in such sycophancy.'

Magnus: 'So then why don't u help us if you're SERIOUS about stopping the Nazis? U cud be a true force 4 good but instead ure condoning Nazis in the Middle East. It's a plague – ure fanning it with Qatari money. Happy pay day Marc.'

Maybe Magnus was right. I mean, if I was really *SERIOUS* about stopping Nazis maybe I should join the dark side of #MAGA trolls. Maybe I could confront Jessika Aro about stealing all my research. Maybe I could ask him why he was suddenly typing like an angry teenager. Maybe I could finally be happy.

We could talk about all this over Skype, of course.

So when I offered, Magnus became a little cagey, as if he was afraid to Skype me. ... First, he thought our time zones would be a problem. ... Of course, I was very accommodating, but he still resisted, until he suggested that his friend should talk to me instead, because, wait for it … she was 'more fluent'.

> Me: 'I don't mind the time difference, makes no difference as you and I often talk at the same time anyway.'
> Magnus: 'I think it's no good cos she is in the same time zone and can speak English very fluently, thanks. SO I think I also no need 2 tell anyone about it even.'

Wait, what!? Magnus Thesiger Callaghan, a British passport holder with the most British name IN THE UNIVERSE, who loves *Battlestar Galactica* and *Hi de Hi*, admits that he is not fluent in English? For some reason, Magnus had abandoned any pretence that he was a native English speaker?!

Confused, I continued to try and circumvent Magnus's aversion to a Skype conversation. But then he asked:

Will you come to Estonia in the future?

I was perplexed, but played along, informing Magnus that I had actually been to Tartu in Estonia once. He then indicated he was on the Estonian side of the town of Ivanogorod (Ivanogorod is on the border of Russian and Estonia).

> Me: 'Tartu?'
> Magnus: 'Ivanogorod … Narva side of the bridge of course.'
> Me: *google Ivanogorod*… 'Wow, cool-looking fort.'
> Magnus: 'So I need 2 think about how 2 do this. What about Atlantic Council and Ben Nimmo and such personages, will u tell them all this stuff … Cos there's no need 2 tell anyone, thanks.'

After I assured him that I would not tell Ben Nimmo, Magnus said he would block me for OPSEC reasons (operational security), but not before informing me that I would be contacted by someone with the 'code' sveta92.narva. I did not know what this meant, but I presumed she would be my handler.

> Magnus: 'don't forget it, ok. Bye.'

And with that, Magnus blocked me.

Before I had time to grieve, or indeed, be contacted by someone with the code sveta92.narva, millionaire sex offender Jeffrey Epstein killed himself in prison.

Wait, how's that relevant? I hear you ask. Well for some reason this caused Magnus to break his OPSEC-induced vow of silence and message me with the following, two weeks after he had blocked me:

'Seth Rich was killed by the same group. It's terrible.'

I agreed with him; it's terrible, really.

Intrigued by Magnus's return from the dead, I tried to joke with him, to win him back, but he wasn't having any of it. Magnus the Autobot had returned, with his strangely scripted answers that made no sense but simply made it seem more likely that the account was being run by multiple people.

Me: 'Did you miss me?'
Magnus: 'Dunno really cos I don't think so much about stuff really.'

Clearly, I was of no immediate use to him. He then blocked me for a few days (OPSEC of course), only to message me again to ask if I was in Helsinki. Again, he tried to dissuade me from presenting my research:

Magnus: 'Are u in Helsinki, I tried 2 tell u they wud steal all ure stuff in Helsinki.'
Me: 'Who is stealing what?'
Magnus: 'Like I told u 13 days before. SO no need 2 tell nothing about ure research I think cos they will just steal everything. They want research. This is the goal as such'.

For some reason he really cared about me not going to Helsinki as such. For that is the goal. His timeline was also off, as it had been much longer than thirteen days since he had contacted me. Why he felt the need to stipulate the exact number of days was also a little odd.

While I was still waiting to hear from my handler sveta92.narva I would check in periodically on Magnus from another account that had not been blocked by him. Then one day I found that his account had vanished! I was distraught, could he really have just disappeared?

Yet, like the first law of thermodynamics, Magnus can neither be created nor destroyed – he merely changes form. Indeed, Magnus had changed his screen name and user name, but on Twitter, your user ID will stay the same unless you open a new account. Magnus Callaghan had morphed into Jasmine MAGA, a Cuban American teenager who still loved Ariana Grande and President Trump. Gone, though, was the cutting-edge political analysis of Middle East politics. This had been replaced by Spanish-language diatribes against the Marxist Cuban regime! Sure those Cubans exist, but how great is it that Trump has such a diverse support base rather than just white nationalists. This clearly was not propaganda at all!

**

Inspired by my interactions with Jasmine and Magnus, I wrote up the saga in a long Twitter thread. The thread soon went viral, and prompted Twitter to suspend Magnus's account, but not before Magnus sent me a message portraying himself as a victim while also attempting to intimidate me:

> I have reported you to the Met for putting my life at risk. I have also reported you to the British Embassy in the country I am based as you have put me at SEVERE risk of reprisals. I am suing you for loss of earning and emotional stress caused by the extreme danger you have put me in. My solicitor in the UK is absolutely clear there will be closure for me. Contact the MET so that they can arrange a local interview at the embassy with me and verify my identity. They need to hear from you officially to state your side.

Magnus's bluff was a source of bemusement to Twitter users. Some noted the bizarre suggestion that I should contact the Met myself. Others wondered what he meant by loss of earnings – did that mean spreading disinformation via Twitter constituted his main source of income?

A day after I tweeted my story about Magnus Callaghan, I was standing in a hotel lobby in Washington, DC. My phone buzzed.

It was a Facebook call from Magnus Callaghan demanding that we talk. I insisted we communicate in writing. Shortly he stopped trying to phone, and would occasionally troll me on Facebook.

The whole saga left many unanswered questions. Who actually owned the account? Was the real Magnus ever involved? If not, how do they have what looks like a real copy of a British passport? Was it procured by someone with access to his personal documents, perhaps from when he worked in Dammam? How many times has the account changed? Has someone obtained real images from some sort of crude cloud hack and used them to create fake personalities? Has a Twitter account belonging to a real Magnus Callaghan, containing some images such as his passport, been compromised, and have they now been opportunistically used by some hackers or trolls? How many accounts are engaging in this kind of behaviour?

When I examined the biographies of Magnus's followers (over 7,000 of them), I saw that again, the most common theme among them was the MAGA Trump nexus. Around 3,000 of them had MAGA in their bios. That's almost half of his followers. Is it just because MAGAs follow MAGAs? Why did he have so many followers anyway? Is he part of some sort of organised pro-Trump propaganda network? Magnus's account fitted a growing number of suspicious pro-Trump accounts that were emphatic about their opposition to Iran. Although Magnus was almost certainly part of an influence operation, it is not clear how many similar accounts were like his. Was some entity trying to tap into American right-wing populism in order to spread organically an anti-Iranian – and in this case, anti-Qatari – agenda?

Conclusion

Magnus's techniques were somewhat familiar. Like many trolls in the current post-truth climate, he accused anyone who criticised Saudi of being a Qatari agent, or working in connection with a Qatari 'media cell'. What separated Magnus from standard trolls was his attempt to co-opt me into writing about Iranian disinformation. He had also clearly been monitoring my activity and whereabouts to cultivate an intimate relationship that could be used to try to manipulate me more effectively. It never transpired who was truly behind the Callaghan account, although it highlighted what was almost certainly an information operation, designed both to phish for human intelligence and engage in targeted harassment and attempted censorship. Magnus's attempts to convince me of his personal authenticity through the use of cultural competence (or indeed cultural incompetence cues), from *Battlestar Galactica* to Max Boyce, were indicative of the modus operandi of some Internet Research Agency trolls.[2] However, it is not a tactic solely used by them. Indeed, it would behove any vaguely competent troll to attempt to find common cultural ground with whoever they are attempting to target. It also highlights that, without robust verification, social networking websites are ripe for exploitation by foreign intel operatives, deception agents and other malign actors.

CONCLUSION

THE FUTURE OF DECEPTION AND DIGITAL TYRANNY

The Gulf Moment and Theorising MENA Disinformation

This journey of MENA-oriented deception and digital authoritarianism has taken us across the globe; from Algeria to Japan, from Washington, DC to Newcastle upon Tyne. The world of deception has exposed us to a side of reality that is as shocking as it is absurd. We have seen Geordie football fans slut-shaming the grieving fiancée of a slain Saudi journalist. We have seen news outlets as far afield as Hong Kong and Canada duped by fake journalists with AI-generated headshots. We have seen armies of bots producing industrial-level sectarian hate speech and misogyny. We have seen a sockpuppet account of a middle-aged British man promoting Saudi one day and a Spanish-speaking Cuban teenager promoting Donald Trump the next. We have seen an American meteorologist come back from the dead to praise the Saudi state. We have witnessed American congresswomen smeared as Islamist Manchurian Candidates biding their time before unleashing a wave of political Islam across the Middle East for the benefit of Qatar, Turkey and Iran. We have seen ministries flagrantly lie about the results of international arbitration panels. We've witnessed Western companies linked to Cambridge

Analytica promoting conflict in the Gulf by selling deception campaigns. We have seen how the loose regulatory environment and the commercial interests of social media companies have often worked against tackling disinformation. We have seen legions of anonymous accounts with pictures of the Saudi crown prince engage in misogynistic attacks on women journalists. We've seen that, and much more.

Indeed, it would be tempting to say, 'we've seen it all', but this could not be further from the truth. Deception is, by its very nature, secretive. There are countless influence operations occurring across the MENA region, all the time, and while more and more people are devoting their efforts to trying to expose them, it's an uphill struggle. However, we know more now than we did ten years ago. In the post-Arab Spring environment, technologically developed Gulf states have sought to insulate themselves from regime change, and digital authoritarianism has been a large part of this. As countries such as Saudi and the UAE become more tyrannical and sultanistic, increasingly attempting to assert themselves in global and regional politics, they have also become net exporters of deception and disinformation.

This book has attempted to describe the changing face of digital authoritarianism in the Middle East, and the ascendency of the Gulf's post-truth moment – a period of time following the Arab Uprisings characterised by a desire by certain Gulf states, most notably Saudi Arabia and the United Arab Emirates, to dominate the Arabic-speaking social media space through the processes of infiltration, censorship, propaganda, deception and disinformation. The ability to project this influence is the result of the building of digital media power, conceptualised in this book as an actor's ability to use or co-opt digital media technologies in order to assert ideological influence and power over a community (or communities) by regulating or simulating the thought diet of a target demographic, both inside and outside the state.

From employing PR companies to undertake reputation management, to killing journalists and infiltrating Twitter, the gamut of techniques deployed to control the information space points to an almost personalistic authoritarianism in which reputation and ego, and an intolerance of criticism, motivates extreme forms of intervention in the information space. By analysing millions of tweets, and forensically examining dozens of trends, this book has highlighted the extent to which bots, sockpuppets and automation are being used as a form of power to manipulate social media space in order to spread a version of reality desired by the KUBE block. Indeed, as critical voices abandon Twitter through fear, murder and surveillance, and moderate critics are imprisoned, the vacuum left behind is being filled by an a pseudo-civil society of trolls and bots.

The Pseudo-Gulf

Victor Klemperer once noted that truth dies in four modes, the first of which is 'hostility to verifiable reality, which presents the form of presenting interventions and lies as if they were facts'.[1] The post-truth moment has been characterised by a brazen desire to destroy and reinvent reality using social media. The term 'moment' is important, especially when it comes to technology, which changes so rapidly. This post-truth moment has been defined by pseudo-events and pseudo-publics. The Qatar Crisis in particular, and most notably the fake coup documented in Chapter 6, as well as the attendant legions of fake personas, bots and trolls point to the industrialised pseudo-isation of an alternative reality and civil society. The hostility to verifiable reality detailed by Klemperer is evidenced by the scale of the deception: arguing that a coup has occurred, for example, when in fact no such thing took place, or creating dozens of artificial journalists to produce copy in international outlets shows not simply an instrumentalisation of falsehoods for practical ends, but rather an arrogant disdain for, or hostility to, the truth.

Towards Digital Tyranny

The emergence of this post-truth moment is perhaps not surprising. In 2010 Abdulkhaleq Abdulla, a professor of political science at UAE University, wrote about the arrival of the 'Arab Gulf Moment in contemporary Arab history'. According to Abdulla:

The six mostly small but oil-rich states of Kuwait, Bahrain, Saudi Arabia, Qatar, Oman and the United Arab Emirates (the Arab Gulf states or AGS) are taking the lead, influencing events, assuming greater financial responsibilities, projecting socioeconomic confidence, and becoming increasingly conscious of their newly acquired status as a regional power that far transcends the rest of the Arab countries.[2]

Abdulla was right in many ways. However, a corollary of this increased influence is a more dubious superlative – that states such as the UAE and Saudi Arabia are also becoming the region's – and even the world's – most prolific agents of deception, especially after the Gulf Crisis.

The competition for the mantle of deception superpower has resulted from diverging sensibilities within the GCC. Although claims of a Gulf moment within the broader context of Arab history might have been somewhat ambitious, much has changed since Abdulla wrote that paper in 2010. The GCC has splintered, with Saudi Arabia, the UAE and Bahrain on one side, and Qatar on the other. Oman and Kuwait have refused to take sides. Qatar's multilateralism and independence, forged by, among other things, its enormous wealth, has seen it cast aside, despite a more recent easing of tensions.

The Libya conflict is a case in point, with Saudi, Egypt and the UAE backing one side, Qatar and Turkey the other. In many ways, this rift has been the product of the Arab Gulf moment, a testament to an increased desire for certain GCC countries to be the defining force of the trajectory of the future of the region. Saudi and the UAE, in particular, have sought to reimagine the region on their own terms, meeting secretly on a yacht in the Red Sea to form an elite regional alliance designed to contain Iranian and Turkish hegemony.[3] Since then the UAE, and Saudi in particular, resemble what Chris Davidson calls sultanistic regimes. These are highly autocratic but also personalistic, to the extent that the instruments of state become the personal tools of the ruler, and that, when necessary, such rulers 'are able to act arbitrarily beyond any traditional constraints'.[4]

While the term sultanism might be apt, a distinctive aspect of the nature of the deception operations documented over these pages is how they reflect the rise of tyrannical, as opposed to authoritarian, leadership in the region. Tyrannical dictators are characterised by personalism, in which the ruler takes on an almost messianic quality, and whose rhetoric is one of reinventing the nation. In tyrannical regimes, subjects are compelled to compete for degrees of dedication and devotion, to be propagandists as well as proselytisers for the regime. Repetition of slogans and symbols, which is the second mode of the death of truth according to Klemperer, is abundant, and embodied by the constant slogan 'we are all MBS', and there are thousands of fake and real Twitter accounts bearing his image. The billboards in London, his personal role in the killing of Khashoggi, the pettiness of using spyware on private citizens, all point to an egotistical aggrandisement indicative of despotism.

An inevitable outcome of this new vision of the region has been the need to legitimise it through organised persuasive communication, and, more often than not, disinformation, deception and propaganda. To influence is to shape opinions, or rather, to present an interpretation of reality favourable to a particular hegemonic project. Unsurprisingly, this new regional project, and its attendant influence campaigns, mean that much of the disinformation highlighted in this book tends to reflect the foreign policy objectives of the KUBE block, such as containing Iran and attacking political Islam. This also tends to align with the objectives of Israel too. This is not by chance or contrived design; it is backed up empirically by available data, including the fact, for example, that Twitter's database of accounts removed due to state-led manipulation campaigns has been dominated by these countries. Indeed, Saudi, the UAE and Egypt are second only to China in documented evidence of Twitter-led disinformation operations, and certainly ahead of Iran and Russia. This may be a crude barometer of influence operations, but, combined with the other evidence documented in this book, it is probably not an exaggeration to say much of the deception we see in the Arab world emanates from the KUBE countries.

Personality seems to matter too. Just as Trump has shown how personalistic traits impact on the information ecosystem, the same is true of the increasingly autocratic and personalistic policies of MBZ and MBS. The US administration, and its policy in the Middle

East, always impacts on the regional and international politics of Gulf states. Trump's election, for example, immediately prompted a number of human rights abuses in Bahrain.[5] Indeed, within the troika of MBZ, MBS and Trump, the US president enabled and accelerated this tyranny, normalising a cult of personality in which faith displaced reason. In such a world, it is the populist leader, and the tyrant, who positions himself as the voice of the masses, and the sole cure of their ills. The tyrant establishes faith as supplanting understanding.[6]

Indeed, many of the deception campaigns documented here have been a response to specific events that are themselves indicative of a new order in the region. The rise of Mohammed bin Salman, and his totalitarian style of rule, have led to almost unprecedented global scandals. The murder of Jamal Khashoggi is a case in point. The resources poured into attempting to engage in damage control after Khashoggi's killing unleashed a flood of disinformation that still continues today, several years after his murder. Attempts to repackage Khashoggi's legacy as a terrorist will probably continue as long as his murder remains a sticking point in the Saudi–US relationship, which it is certainly likely to be, especially now that Trump has departed the White House. Saudi must now contend with an administration demonstrably less tolerant of its capacity for violence.

While the rise of the likes of MBS and MBZ may play a role in actualising a new vision of the Middle East, they are not necessarily the proximate cause. The Arab Uprisings highlighted the domestic threats to many Gulf regimes. The fear of revolution was particularly acute in the populous and heavily oil-reliant Saudi Arabia. As such, the Arab Uprisings created a reactionary effort from some Gulf states to strengthen the power of the regime, sometimes through brute force, sometimes through top-down reform initiatives, usually both, but always through propaganda. Deception has always been an adjunct necessity of these changes, but digital technology has increased the velocity, reach and breadth of disinformation operations and digital authoritarianism. It has also created new affordances, allowing for the simulation of loyalty via astroturfing and sockpuppets where it might not organically exist. In particular, it allows ambitious regimes to expand efficiently their visions to new, international audiences.

The Discursive and Tactical Qualities of the Gulf Deception Moment

There is no set playbook of deception per se, but certain tropes will usually prompt the interference of bots or trolls. Sockpuppets tend to be almost permanently active, diluting critical Arabic trends with gibberish or spam on matters pertaining to Saudi affairs. They function as a sort of disinformation life support, ticking on in the background. Their tactics develop in order to circumvent Twitter's spam-control filters. Certain events, in particular crises, whether it's the killing of Khashoggi or, say, a Saudi-led killing of civilians in Yemen, will prompt more concerted and complex deception campaigns involving trolls and astroturfing. The creation of pseudo-events, such as the Qatar Crisis, will often involve influencers in addition to bots and trolls. Indeed, while sometimes these accounts focus on driving out negative news, some of the tactics are designed to create pseudo-events that break out into the mainstream media – such as the attacks on Ghada Oueiss, or the Gulf Crisis.

In many ways, this book captures a particular discursive moment in the online public sphere highlighting an interesting theoretical element of disinformation. Abrupt political ruptures that dramatically contradict previous policies result in the need to engage in comprehensive persuasion activities in order to realign expectations of populations. If the on- and offline discursive environment under Obama was one of rapprochement and reconciliation, under Trump it has been one of hostility and belligerence. One cannot underestimate the election of Trump, and his subsequent polices and rhetoric, in filling the sails of the Middle East post-truth moment.

The discursive qualities of the Gulf's post-truth moment emphasise the demonisation and targeting of those who oppose the new vision of the Gulf. Indeed, a defining aspect of much of the Twitter deception is the singling out of those who attack MBS or highlight his role in nefarious activities. The attack on Ghada Oueiss was primarily carried out because she was a woman who drew attention to Khashoggi's murder and was not afraid to criticise Saudi. Even non-criticism can make someone a target. Indeed, another quality of tyrannical rule is that neutrality is almost as treasonous as opposition.[7] Those perceived as remotely critical of the new regional order, or not sufficiently jingoistic, are attacked. As the chapters documenting attacks on Ilhan Omar and Ghada Oueiss have shown, it is also a hostility characterised by misogyny, racism and bigotry. It is also, paradoxically, implicitly Islamophobic. The demonisation of the Muslim Brotherhood and the broader fight against political Islam has, intentionally or not, contributed to the demonisation of Islam in general.

A discursive aspect of many of the accumulated disinformation campaigns documented here positions Saudi Arabia as a victim of some form of a global conspiracy, led in part by the Democrats, Qatar, Turkey, Iran and the Muslim Brotherhood. In this way, disinformation campaigns can be their own form of legitimacy and nationalism building. The politics of victimhood is powerful. As Paul Waldman notes, 'The truth is that victimhood does afford one a certain moral status that can be politically powerful. If we accept that an actual wrong has been done and you are the victim of that wrong, that means you have a legitimate claim not only to redress but also to hold the perpetrator accountable.'[8]

According to this framework of victimhood, Qatar, Turkey, Iran and the Muslim Brotherhood, and a cabal of Democrats, work together with Saudi's internal enemies to undermine Saudi's Vision 2030. In addition to victimhood, promoting anti-Iranian and often sectarian (anti-Shi'a) content has been an enduring aspect of the Gulf post-truth moment. It is on Iran in particular where the goals of the Trump administration, Saudi Arabia and the UAE overlap. The advent of IranDisinfo, a US government agency that attacks its own citizens and journalists for not being militant enough against Iran, is a reflection of how confrontational and bullying politics manifest themselves through institutional behaviour. A key threat, and one of the most alarming takeaways of deception in the Middle East, is the potential ability it has to generate and spawn conflict. Much of the disinformation here, perpetrated by the deception order, has sought to polarise, divide and increase tensions in the Middle East. Further research needs to be done on how successful these campaigns have been in generating actual hatred and violence.

The Gulf Lügenpresse

Just as Trump has railed against what he calls 'the failing *New York Times*' or the 'fake media', the MENA equivalent has been the near-constant attacks on certain media channels. As this book has demonstrated, the tactic of attacking the media has been the modus operandi of many of the deception campaigns in the region. Instead of cries of 'fake news media' (which also do exist), the attacks are more contextual. From the hashtags 'al Jazeera is the channel of pigs', to bots sharing infographics detailing 'Qatar's media snake', social media have been the main platform for the KUBE attacks on what it wishes to brand as the Gulf *Lügenpresse*.[9] The Gulf Crisis is, in many ways, an embodiment of the tension between a dictator's desire to control the media and his inability to do so due to transnational media production. The media wars that have played out in the Gulf Crisis are an extension of a global populism that has sought to re-invoke the notion of the 'lying media'.

For all its faults, Al Jazeera has represented a step change in the media ecosystem of the Arab world. For the likes of MBS and MBZ, Al Jazeera is a victim of its own success and uniqueness in the region, and, as such, must be attacked. This very tension itself is the race to be the official broker of information. The scale of this mobilisation is commensurate with the large influence and reach of Al Jazeera itself, whose journalists and reputation are constantly attacked online by armies of hyper-nationalist accounts and trolls, or targeted with advanced spyware. To be an Al Jazeera journalist in the current Gulf post-truth moment is to be on the frontline of abuse.

In addition to the clear public steers to direct opprobrium against Al Jazeera and its staff, the banning of Al Jazeera in the KUBE bloc has facilitated the creation of an ecosystem of confirmation bias, in which people continually exist in partisan echo chambers that adhere to an existing worldview amenable to a small core of autocratic rulers.

These comforting bubbles provide a heady mix of in-group solidarity, and the comfort born out of never having one's beliefs challenged or contradicted. Another alarming aspect of this problem evidenced in these pages is the co-optation of so-called Western international media brands. Even reputable international outlets such as Sky News Arabia, CNN Arabic and *The Independent* have had their integrity compromised by either being funded by the Saudi government or having an office in the UAE. They have reported, as fact, numerous deception operations without qualification or correction. They have, in some cases, even taken it upon themselves to actively engage in deception.

This new boldness inherent in the Gulf moment has really highlighted the perceived importance of not simply controlling the regional MENA media market, but also what is consumed in key international allies. The capacious Arab Eye network documented in this book, along with its attempts to promote UAE policy to a global audience, is an example of this. It is also telling how the UAE lobbied the US government to get AJ+ registered as a foreign agent in the USA. What amounted to the attempted censorship of AJ+ in the USA was partly the result of a campaign spearheaded by the US law firm Akin Gump, a registered foreign agent of the UAE. What was striking about the AJ+ scandal is that it clearly indicated the overlap and penetration of the Trump administration with the UAE. This was highlighted by the fact that the letter written by the Department of Justice announcing the need for AJ+ to register as a foreign agent included quotes that had been copied and pasted verbatim from a report[10] written by Akin Gump.[11]

Neoliberation Technology and Digital Tyranny

This book has highlighted how assembly lines of disinformation are the product of collaborations with commercial and state actors. At one end of the deception order we have seen, for example, British and American PR companies and consultancies that are seeking to capitalise on conflicts by offering deception services to wealthy clients – be they governments or private actors. As the Boycott Qatar campaign conducted by Project Associates demonstrates, some companies have little regard for the fact that they might be encouraging conflict or destabilising certain regions. On the other end, it is the policy of states pursuing their domestic and foreign policy agendas that prompt them to forge new narratives, be that the demonisation of Iran or saving face by lying about the detrimental findings of a WTO report.

The Gulf's post-truth moment has also laid bare the hypocrisy of tech companies. Although it is one of the most dangerous places in the world for journalists and human rights violations, Twitter continues to operate in Saudi Arabia, a US ally, where MBS the reformer continues to oversee a regime that imprisons activists and cracks down on free speech. This information disorder, and rampant censorship, is so severe that the Lebanese writer Joey Ayoub once described Twitter as a 'direct partner' in the oppression carried out by some Arab regimes.[12] Indeed, with Twitter's now former CEO Jack Dorsey having met MBS twice, and with Saudi moles having infiltrated Twitter, important questions have been raised about the exact nature of the relationship of tech companies with authoritarian regimes. Indeed, many of the proponents of disinformation in this book are repeat offenders based in the UAE and Saudi who have verified Twitter accounts, such as Monther al-Shaykh, Abdul Latif bin Abdullah al-Sheikh or Amjad Taha. Their enormous followings and potential reach are staggering, yet despite their continued and influential role on multiple deception operations, it does not appear that Twitter has even issued warnings for many of these accounts. It took Twitter several years to suspend Saud al-Qahtani, even after he endangered activists and promoted a hashtag designed to initiate an online witch hunt.[13] Even in early 2021 thousands of relatively crude bot accounts still spam hashtags critical of the Saudi regime. It is hard to imagine that Twitter should really have any trouble in tackling this computational propaganda, yet they do.

The high-level and seemingly personal relationships between the likes of Jack Dorsey and MBS point to a new power elite, an unaccountable group of tech gurus and tyrants. The idea of data colonialism has illustrated how big tech firms extract and monetise our data, with limited consent from foreign populations (with the exception of their leaders), in order to profit from advertising revenue. As the saying goes, when something is free, you're probably the product. For social media companies, deregulated markets, free from the stricture of national regulation and political pressure, are a sea of potential human commodities ready to be monetised.

Irrespective of potential political influence, financial incentives still shape much of the disinformation ecosystem. Many of the attempts to remedy disinformation and fake news do ultimately conflict with the profit margins of social media companies. However, increased oversight and moderation requires more manpower, and more manpower requires more cost.

The Gulf's post-truth moment has also challenged the liberation ontology implicit within the exports of Silicon Valley. The Arab Uprisings were initially characterised by an obsession with the liberation potential of technology – the belief that technology would facilitate networked resistance and topple the entrenched dictatorships of the region. This turned out not to be true. If you will permit me an analogy: before cigarettes were considered to be harmful to health, they were described as 'torches of freedom' in a marketing campaign to encourage women to smoke by appealing to women's liberation.[14] Physicians were even used by big tobacco in the 1930s and 1940s to promote cigarettes.[15] Indeed, before the dangers of smoking were widespread knowledge, and before big tobacco was acknowledged as being what was referred to as the nicotine delivery business,[16] engineered to encourage addiction and further consumption, it was seen as an emblem of liberty, patriotism and even good health. Social media companies have, in many ways, fooled the world into thinking that they are torches of freedom – something other than a profit-seeking industry that not only exploits and sells the data of its users, but is benevolently doing so in the name of facilitating such lofty ideals as freedom of speech.

Social media companies are very much part of the disinformation delivery business and the deception order – an outcome of neoliberation technology. Their inaction in effectively tackling disinformation, and their willingness to operate in countries that crush freedom of speech is a reflection of this. Just as conflict and geopolitical tensions are a boon for the arms trade, large-scale deception operations and digital authoritarianism, in general, thrive on conflict. Adversarial content is either a reflection of conflict or an attempt to promote it. Even Facebook employees are increasingly critical about the negative role the company is having in the war on reality. Gregor Hochmuth, a former engineer with Facebook-owned

Instagram, who left in 2014, told the *New York Times*, 'Facebook salaries are among the highest in tech right now, and when you're walking home with a giant paycheck every two weeks, you have to tell yourself that it's for a good cause. ... Otherwise, your job is truly no different from other industries that wreck the planet and pay their employees exorbitantly to help them forget.'[17]

Digital Orientalism

One has to wonder whether companies like Twitter and Facebook view the Middle East in the same manner as arms companies, a place on the periphery of American public opinion where conflict provides opportunities to market their wares without much pushback from US foreign policy objectives. Their perceived apathy in effectively investigating foreign-language moderation has been pointed out numerous times. Journalist Negar Mortazavi highlighted:

> Twitter needs to hire experts who are not only fluent in languages like Persian and Arabic but also understand the social and political nuances of the respective countries. Troll armies are ravaging this platform, making it difficult and dangerous for journalists and activists.[18]

However, with so much Gulf investment in Silicon Valley, and the optics of a Saudi prince being one of Twitter's largest individual investors, it is hard to imagine that the Middle East lingers on the margins of Silicon Valley consciousness. At times it can be unclear whether the Middle East is a regulatory backwater, the Los Alamos for social media companies, where profit can be garnered with minimum concern for accountability, or a space in which authoritarian regimes actually curry favour with social media companies in order to ensure that their products do not harm the balance of power.

Either way reflects a form of digital orientalism – the idea that Silicon Valley can ignore human rights in Gulf markets, exploiting them for profiteering while turning a blind eye to abuses, which are viewed as less significant than domestic affairs. The extent of this perceived complicity of Twitter in abetting digital authoritarianism was demonstrated when Manal al-Sharif, a Saudi activist, deleted her Twitter account onstage at the SuNordic summit; al-Sharif accompanied her very public disavowal of Twitter with the words, 'The very tools we use for our activism are being used to undermine us.'

Indeed, the Tyrant and the Tech bro, when left unattended, produce neo-illiberal affordances.

Despite this transnational element to digital disinformation, states still matter. Big tech companies such as Twitter and Facebook, while private entities, are defined by the regulatory environment afforded by US law. The products and services themselves are a global reality, and as such, what happens in the USA does not stay in the USA. This is why countries such as Germany and Singapore, and also the EU, are increasingly crafting policies that seek to limit the impact of social media disinformation. Their policies must plug the regulatory gaps in the USA that have failed to curtail the platform's use as a weapon. Yet the neoliberation ontology of Silicon Valley documented here has left the door open for tech companies and dictators to break bread together, and benefit mutually from the prospect of large, unregulated markets.

Some will cry foul that attempts to rein in social media companies through regulation will curtail free speech in the Middle East, an area where authoritarianism prevails. However, as I have argued before, 'it is specious, bordering on disingenuous, to argue that censuring deception accounts is an affront to free speech. The real damage to free speech is for social media companies to provide tools for authoritarian regimes to extend their repressive apparatus while denying those platforms to opposition voices.'[19] The argument becomes especially moot if one is defending the free speech of bots and trolls, who do not exist, but are merely programmed or paid to parrot authoritarian polices.

The Coming Pseudo-isation of Reality

Deception campaigns documented in these pages have also highlighted concerns about AI and automation. Scholars of democracy and the internet used to question whether the decline of face-to-face interactions online would be dangerous for civil society, and civility in general. They worried it would decrease empathy and encourage more volatile and aggressive interactions. Similarly, anonymity, while a boon to activists and whistleblowers who need to protect their identity, has been weaponised by malicious actors. Digital technology and automation have facilitated the 'scalability' of deception operations emanating from the Gulf. Hiding behind thousands of fake accounts, adversarial actors promote polarisation and hyper-partisanship.

With AI being able to produce reasonable journalistic copy, and already able to generate images and videos of convincing human beings, the next phase of both journalism and disinformation is alarming in a space where dictators are already maximising their ability to manipulate social media. The Arab Eye network documented here showed how fake journalists can fool newspaper editors for months. That the online public sphere in the Arabic-speaking world is already dominated by trolls and automated software is an indicator of the potential for the online space to be its very own civil society simulacrum. However, while trolls are certainly more convincing and effective as propagandists, advancements in AI could see the return of the bot as a much more affordable and scalable propaganda tool. With rulers who have no qualms about using technology to control the information space, it is hard not to imagine a state of affairs where AI will not be used to undermine the Arab public sphere. In fact, as the numerous examples of bots and automation documented here have shown, that is already evident in the Gulf digital public sphere.

However, while we worry about AI, we also need to worry about how technology changes us. Indeed, we tend to be concerned about robots becoming more human-like, rather than humans becoming more robot-like, but this is what is happening. Accusing someone of being a bot is a recent phenomenon that indicates the success of adversarial politics. There is a tendency to see bots everywhere, even when they are real people. Often when people disagree with others online, and do so in an aggressive manner, they may genuinely believe the other person is a bot. One of the challenges of adversarial politics is that when messages are repeated, and social media platforms provide limited scope beyond soundbites, humans begin to resemble bots. The proliferation of automation has created corollary binary behavioural practices that tend to replicate the adversarial behaviours of computational propaganda. Nuance is crowded out in favour of unwavering commitment to certain talking points, often couched within binary identity politics. This has eroded trust, and often those of different points of view will accuse one another of being a bot, rather than engaging in a bad faith argument.

Deception and the International System

While this book spans disciplines such as communications, media studies and area studies, a book on the transnational nature of digital authoritarianism will naturally invoke questions of what this means for international relations. Christina la Cour asks 'how, when and why states and non-state actors use disinformation, and why disinformation appears to be ever more present in modern-day international politics than ever before'.[20] This book, which has focused on various actors in the MENA region, offers some interesting answers. States might lie when they think the benefits outweigh the costs of telling the truth, especially if the leader(s) in those states wield autocratic power. As the Khashoggi example illustrates, states will often lie until they lose the inability to engage in plausible deniability through competing and superior truth claims. States may also deceive in order to exaggerate the potency or weakness of an enemy, and to legitimise claims of an external foe in order to detract from pressing domestic concerns. Such lies might be part of economic warfare, designed to influence a global public in order to engage in economic warfare with a rival. They might lie to legitimise and justify the costs of certain unpopular actions (such as the Qatar Crisis) among domestic populations. Such lies might be necessary when the incumbent perceives hostility to his specific visions of the region. When a reality that does not exist needs to be justified, a pseudo-public is created to give the illusion of reality. This illusion can also function as a steering, prompting others to 'herd' or nudge in agreement. Tyrants too, or those with autocratic control, might be more inclined to generate disinformation to pursue their own personal goals. Certainly, Saudi Arabia, and the UAE, have shown themselves to be deception superpowers through their manipulation of domestic, regional and global audiences.

Creating a Less Authoritarian Space

While there is no silver bullet able to tackle deception, there are some potential solutions. Better verification could help combat this problem while also preserving anonymity. If it was necessary to confirm that people were real before opening an account, that would at least obviate attempts to create bots or sockpuppets. Here, a trusted third party could verify the user's identity privately, and the user could remain anonymous publicly. At least then if they engaged in criminal behaviour there would be a clear means by which a legitimate organisation could hold them accountable. Of course, this brings its own set of problems. Which entity would be charged with keeping a register of people's personal information? Should national governments be tasked with maintaining such databases, or should it be international organisations such as the UN or EU – the latter having started to legislate around privacy? Even if one believed compulsory verification to be problematic, there could still be an opt-in system. Here people could choose to be verified and, if they wished, only interact with other accounts that were verified. At least people could then engage with others in relatively good faith. After all, what is the point in debating with someone who might be a paid troll, and thus committed to a specific narrative? However, unless individual states make regulatory demands on social media companies, such changes are likely to be ignored, due once again to their potential cost.

The receptiveness of people to disinformation is perhaps, paradoxically, a combination of increasing critical awareness, but also a lack of critical awareness. There is perhaps a growing knowledge of how governments have historically deceived or operated secretive agendas, from the machinations of Sykes–Picot to how Western governments fabricated weapons of mass destruction to legitimise an invasion of Iraq. Such deceptions understandably legitimise distrust in governments, and trust in government has been declining for years, at least in the USA.[21] In the Middle East, the figures are pretty low for most countries.[22] Deception, when recognised, erodes trust, and it is this erosion of trust that allows disinformation actors to exploit increasing disenchantment with established institutions. Trust in institutions is an insulation mechanism against disinformation, but when institutions abuse that trust, our collective immunity weakens. This is why transparency is imperative in rebuilding trust. Similarly, improved digital literacy is imperative for any states wishing to make their populations more resilient to dangerous deception.

Although we are increasingly aware of disinformation and deception, it is not always easy to measure the impact, origins or scale of influence operations. Like any weapon, in the information sphere the contagion, virality and ability of a piece of false information to be absorbed and replicated into the information ecosystem is perhaps a good measure of its success. Deception can be, and often is, insidious. While conventional weaponry can scar, and create enduring traumas, deception can alter perceptions that dictate behaviours and choices for months, decades or even generations. Information seeks to change people's behaviours over time. It is unclear how much extant disinformation will impact upon people's perception of reality over the coming decades. Much of that depends on how much certain administrations value truth. Sadly, little is forgotten on the internet, including the myriad of conspiracy theories, hate speech and propaganda. A generation in the Middle East, and globally, who have been exposed to this 'information disorder' may long be feeling the fallout, even after potential solutions or remedies are implemented. In a region with little trust in government entities, disinformation is, in many ways, a way of life. Further research will be required to document and monitor the long-term effects of particular narratives.

The future role of social media in the Gulf is unclear, although not encouraging. In a 2018 interview with the Atlantic, MBS asserted that Saudi, unlike Iran, did not block social media apps such as Twitter, Facebook or Snapchat. As a consequence, Saudis were relatively free to express themselves. However, as this book has shown, digital technology can be weaponised in so many ways that it becomes a useful adjunct to other mechanisms of repression. However, there is something insidious about digital authoritarianism. It is not as visible as traditional coercion, and operates according to a normative logic that celebrates technological growth as fundamentally liberating. Beyond the authoritarian states of the Middle East, neoliberation technology has resulted in tech monopolies that encourage or facilitate surveillance and disinformation.[23] These elements are perhaps felt more acutely in a region dominated by wealthy autocratic regimes, where digital authoritarianism can thrive with little accountability. With the growing rise and ambitions of powerful autocrats such as MBZ and MBS, the inexorable datafication of global subjects, and the growing global decline of democracy, digital authoritarianism is in its ascendency. Indeed, the Gulf's post-truth moment shows no signs of ending any time soon.

NOTES

PREFACE

1. View all posts by marcowenjones: Marc Owen Jones, Busted! Journalist Liliane Khalil Exposed, 21 March 2020, https://marcowenjones.wordpress.com/2020/03/21/busted-journalist-liliane-khalil-exposed/

2. AJSTREAM, The Stream – The hunt for #lilianekhalil – Marc Owen Jones, 2011 [YouTube Video], https://www.youtube.com/watch?v=TgCp15kVggI&ab_channel=AJSTREAM

3. Elizabeth Flock, 'Liliane Khalil, another possible fake blogger: should we care?', Washington Post, 5 August 2011, https://www.washingtonpost.com/blogs/blogpost/post/liliane-khalil-another-possible-fake-blogger-should-we-care/2011/08/05/gIQAd2XvwI_blog.html

4. Melissa Bell and Elizabeth Flock, '"A gay girl in Damascus" comes clean', Washington Post, 12 June 2011, https://www.washingtonpost.com/lifestyle/style/a-gay-girl-in-damascus-comes-clean/2011/06/12/AGkyH0RH_story.html

5. Christian Fuchs, 'Propaganda 2.0: Herman and Chomsky's propaganda model in the age of the internet, big data and social media', in J. Pedro-Carañana, D. Broudy and J. Klaehn (eds.), The Propaganda Model Today: Filtering Perception and Awareness. London: University of Westminster Press, 2018, DOI: https://doi.org/10.16997/book27

INTRODUCTION

1. https://www.iftf.org/fileadmin/user_upload/images/DigIntel/IFTF_State_sponsored_trolling_report.pdf
2.. A. Polyakova and C. Meserole, 'Exporting digital authoritarianism: the Russian and Chinese models', Brookings, 26 August 2019, https://www.brookings.edu/research/exporting-digital-authoritarianism/
3. S. Feldstein, 'When it comes to digital authoritarianism, China is a challenge – but not the only challenge', 12 February 2020, War on the Rocks, https://warontherocks.com/2020/02/when-it-comes-to-digital-authoritarianism-china-is-a-challenge-but-not-the-only-challenge/
4. Claire Wardle and Hossein Derakhshan, 'Information disorder: toward an interdisciplinary framework for research and policy making (2017)', Council of Europe, https://edoc.coe.int/en/media/7495-information-disorder-toward-an-interdisciplinary-framework-for-research-and-policy-making.html
5. L. Ha, L. Andreu Perez and R. Ray, 'Mapping recent development in scholarship on fake news and misinformation, 2008 to 2017: disciplinary contribution, topics, and impact', *American Behavioral Scientist*, 65, 2 (2021), 290–315, doi:10.1177/0002764219869402
6. http://pubdocs.worldbank.org/en/901061582293682832/Yemen-Economic-Update-January-EN.pdf
7. D. Radcliffe and H. Abuhmaid 'Social media in the Middle East: three big trends to note', European Journalism Observatory, 11 March 2020, https://en.ejo.ch/recent/social-media-in-the-middle-east-three-big-trends-to-note
8. 'Media use in the Middle East', Online and Social Media, Mideastmedia. org, 2018, http://www.mideastmedia.org/survey/2018/chapter/online-and-social-edia/#s226
9. Edelman Trust Barometer, 19 January 2020, https://www.edelman.com/trustbarometer
10. Peter Pomerantsev, *This is not Propaganda: Adventures in the War against Reality*. London: Faber & Faber, 2019.
11. E. D. Richter, D. K. Markus and C. Tait, 'Incitement, genocide, genocidal terror, and the upstream role of indoctrination: can epidemiologic models predict and prevent?', *Public Health Review*, 39, 1 (2018), https://doi.org/10.1186/s40985-018-0106-7
12. Alexandra Stevenson, 'Facebook admits it was used to incite violence in Myanmar', *New York Times*, 6 November 2018, https://www.nytimes.com/2018/11/06/technology/myanmar-facebook.html;

Paul Mozur, 'A genocide incited on Facebook, with posts from Myanmar's military', New York Times, 15 October 2018, https://www.nytimes.com/2018/10/15/technology/myanmar-facebook-genocide.html

13. Dahiya Himanshi, 'Why Rohingya refugees are an easy target for the fake news factory', TheQuint, 20 June 2020, https://www.thequint.com/news/webqoof/rohingya-crisis-how-misinfomation-rests-at-the-heart-of-the-issue

14. A. Coleman, '"Hundreds dead" because of Covid-19 misinformation', BBC News, 12 August 2020, https://www.bbc.com/news/world-53755067

15. Michael A. Peters, 'Education in a post-truth world', *Educational Philosophy and Theory*, 49, 6 (2017), 563–6, DOI: 10.1080/00131857.2016.1264114

16. Jeff Orlowski (dir.), *The Social Dilemma*, Netflix.

17. B. Borel, 'Fact-checking won't save us from fake news', FiveThirtyEight, 4 January 2017, https://fivethirtyeight.com/features/fact-checking-wont-save-us-from-fake-news/

18. Quoted in ibid.

19. Peters, 'Education in a post-truth world'.

20. E. Grieco, 'US newspapers have shed half of their newsroom employees since 2008', Pew Research Center, 20 April 2020, https://www.pewresearch.org/fact-tank/2020/04/20/u-s-newsroom-employment-has-dropped-by-a-quarter-since-2008/#:~:text=The%20long%2Dterm%20decline%20in,about%2071%2C000%20workers%20to%2035%2C000

21. H. Tworek, 'What can prewar Germany teach us about social-media regulation?', The Atlantic, 26 May 2019, https://www.theatlantic.com/international/archive/2019/05/germany-war-radio-social-media/590149/

22. https://www.washingtonpost.com/politics/2020/07/13/president-trump-has-made-more-than-20000-false-or-misleading-claims/

23. Jennifer Kavanagh and Michael D. Rich, *Truth Decay: An Initial Exploration of the Diminishing Role of Facts and Analysis in American Public Life*. Santa Monica, CA: RAND Corporation, 2018, https://www.rand.org/pubs/research_reports/RR2314.html

24. Such vertical organisation of course have their problems in terms of media hegemony and gatekeeping.

25. W. L. Bennett and S. Livingston, 'The disinformation order: disruptive communication and the decline of democratic institutions', *European*

Journal of Communication, 33, 2 (2018), 122–39, https://doi.org/10.1177/0267323118760317

26. 'Facebook's failures to stop misinformation', Amanpour & Co., PBS SoCal, 2020, https://www.pbssocal.org/programs/amanpour-co/facebooks-failures-stop-misinformation-yvxhzl/

27. Julia Carrie Wong, 'How Facebook let fake engagement distort global politics: a whistleblower's account', *The Guardian*, 12 April 2021, https://www.theguardian.com/technology/2021/apr/12/facebook-fake-engagement-whistleblower-sophie-zhang

28. Omar Abu Arqoub, Adeola Abdulateef Elega, Bahire Efe Özad, Hanadi Dwikat and Felix Adedamola Oloyede, 'Mapping the scholarship of fake news research: a systematic review', *Journalism Practice*, 11 August 2020, DOI: 10.1080/17512786.2020.1805791

29. 'Arabic fact-checking site goes online to counter spread of fake news', The New Arab, 28 February 2020, https://english.alaraby.co.uk/english/news/2020/2/28/arabic-fact-checking-site-goes-online-to-counter-fake-news

30. Ibid.

31. A. Leber and A. Abrahams, 'A storm of tweets: social media manipulation during the Gulf Crisis', *Review of Middle East Studies*, 53, 2 (2019), 241–58, DOI: 10.1017/rms.2019.45

32. M. Alimardani and M. Elswah, 'Online temptations: COVID-19 and religious misinformation in the MENA region', *Social Media + Society*, 6, 3 (2020), https://doi.org/10.1177/2056305120948251

33. Giselle Rampersad and Turki Althiyabi, 'Fake news: acceptance by demographics and culture on social media', *Journal of Information Technology & Politics*, 17, 1 (2020), 1–11, DOI: 10.1080/19331681.2019.1686676

34. James Shires, 'Hack-and-leak operations: intrusion and influence in the Gulf', *Journal of Cyber Policy*, 4, 2 (2019), 235–56, DOI: 10.1080/23738871.2019.1636108

35. See, for example, Middle East and North Africa CyberWatch, June 2013, https://citizenlab.ca/2013/07/middle-east-and-north-africa-cyberwatch-june-2013/

36. Ibid.

37. Nick Romeo, 'What can America learn from Europe about regulating big tech?', *New Yorker*, 18 August 2020, https://www.newyorker.com/tech/annals-of-technology/what-can-america-learn-from-europe-about-regulating-big-tech?utm_social-type=owned&utm_medium=social&utm_brand=tny&mbid=social_twitter&utm_source=twitter

38. M. Glasius and M. Michaelsen, 'Authoritarian practices in the digital age| illiberal and authoritarian practices in the digital sphere – prologue', *International Journal of Communication*, 12, 19 (2018), https://ijoc.org/index.php/ijoc/article/view/8899

39. See, for example, E. Bellin, 'Reconsidering the robustness of authoritarianism in the Middle East: lessons from the Arab Spring', *Comparative Politics*, 44, 2 (2012), 127–49, http://www.jstor.org/stable/23211807

40. E. Ferrara, O. Varol, C. Davis, F. Menczer and A. Flammini, 'The rise of social bots', *Communications of the ACM*, 59, 7S (2016), 96–104, https://cacm.acm.org/magazines/2016/7/204021-the-rise-of-social-bots/fulltext

41. S. Heydemann, 'Upgrading authoritarianism in the Arab world', Brookings, 15 October 2007, https://www.brookings.edu/research/upgrading-authoritarianism-in-the-arab-world/

42. Paul C. Sondrol. 'Totalitarian and authoritarian dictators: a comparison of Fidel Castro and Alfredo Stroessner', *Journal of Latin American Studies*, 23, 3 (October 1991), 599–620, DOI: 10.1017/S0022216X00015868

43. Marlies Glasius, 'What authoritarianism is … and is not: a practice perspective', *International Affairs*, 94, 3 (May 2018), 515–33, https://doi.org/10.1093/ia/iiy060

44. S. Khamis, 'The online public sphere in the Gulf: contestation, creativity, and change', *Review of Middle East Studies*, 53, 2 (2019), 190–9, DOI:10.1017/rms.2019.41

45. Ibid., 197.

46. P. Starr, 'How neoliberal policy shaped the internet – and what to do about it now', *The American Prospect*, 2 October 2019, https://prospect.org/power/how-neoliberal-policy-shaped-internet-surveillance-monopoly/

47. D. Harvey, *Spaces of Global Capitalism: Towards a Theory of Uneven Geographical Development*. London and New York: Verso, 2006, 44.

48. S. Zuboff, *The Age of Surveillance Capitalism*. New York: PublicAffairs, 2019.

49. C. Cadwalladr, 'Revealed: Facebook's global lobbying against data privacy laws', *The Guardian*, 2 March 2019, https://www.theguardian.com/technology/2019/mar/02/facebook-global-lobbying-campaign-against-data-privacy-laws-investment

50. L. Diamond, 'Liberation technology', *Journal of Democracy*, 3 (2010), 69–83.

51. Y.-X. Dai and S.-T. Hao, 'Transcending the opposition between

techno-utopianism and techno-dystopianism', *Technology in Society*, 53 (2018), 9–13, DOI:10.1016/j.techsoc.2017.11.001

52. Ibid.

53. Nick Couldry and Ulises Mejias, 'Data colonialism: rethinking big data's relation to the contemporary subject', *Television and New Media*, 20, 4 (2018), 336–49.

54. Randy Bush, 'On techno-colonialism', Psg.com, 2015, https://psg.com/on-technocolonialism.html

55. Starr, 'How neoliberal policy shaped the internet'.

56. Thomas Biebricher, 'Neoliberalism and authoritarianism', *Global Perspectives*, 1, 1 (11 May 2020), 11872, DOI: https://doi.org/10.1525/001c.11872

57. J. Postill and S. Pink, 'Social media ethnography: the digital researcher in a messy web', *Media International Australia*, 145, 1 (2012), 123–34, https://doi.org/10.1177/1329878X1214500114

58. Broadly speaking, the overarching approach to this research, however, has been a digital ethnography within the context of an area studies narrative. A digital ethnography is similar to a traditional ethnography, and 'involves the ethnographer participating, overtly or covertly in people's daily lives for an extended period of time, watching what happens, listening to what is said, asking questions – in fact, collecting whatever data are available to throw light on the issues that are the focus of the research' (M. Hammersley and P. Atkinson, *Ethnography: Principles in Practice*, 2nd edn, London and New York: Routledge, 1995, 1). Inhabiting the social media disinformation space through utilising social media platforms is akin to inhabiting a town or village somewhere an absorbing the behaviours and phenomena in one's immediate environment.

59. This might in some circles be termed 'open source intelligence', or OSINT. My concern with this term lies in the used of the word 'intelligence', which has law-enforcement and security-related connotations which are problematic if the purpose of the research is not for such things.

60. Marc Owen Jones, 'The Gulf information war: propaganda, fake news, and fake trends: the weaponization of Twitter bots in the Gulf Crisis', *International Journal of Communication* [S.l.], 13 (March 2019), 1389–1415, https://ijoc.org/index.php/ijoc/article/view/8994

61. H. Allcott, M. Gentzkow and C. Yu, 'Trends in the diffusion of misinformation on social media', *Research & Politics*, 6, 2 (2019), 1–8, https://doi.org/10.1177/2053168019848554

62. Claire Wardle, '10 questions to ask before covering misinformation', First Draft, 29 September 2017, https://firstdraftnews.org/latest/10-questions-newsrooms/

63. Guidance for Reviewing Protocols that Include Online Sources or Mobile Devices, Uci.edu, 2021, https://research.uci.edu/compliance/human-research-protections/irb-members/reviewing-protocols-online-mobile.html

64. Victoria Clayton, 'The needless complexity of academic writing', The Atlantic, 26 October 2015, https://www.theatlantic.com/education/archive/2015/10/complex-academic-writing/412255/

65. Shannon M. Sliva, Jennifer C. Greenfield, Kimberly Bender and Stacey Freedenthal, 'Introduction to the special section on public impact scholarship in social work: a conceptual review and call to action', Journal of the Society for Social Work and Research, 10, 4 (2019), 529–44.

66. This includes more but shorter chapters and variations in narrative style.

67. K. Warchał, 'Humour in professional academic writing', Theory and Practice of Second Language Acquisition, 5, 1 (2019), 43–54, https://doi.org/10.31261/TAPSLA.2019.05.03

1. DIGITAL AUTHORITARIANISM, DECEPTION AND INFORMATION CONTROLS

1. M. O. Jones, Political Repression in Bahrain. Cambridge: Cambridge University Press, 2020.

2. W. A. Gamson, The Strategy of Social Protest. Homewood, IL: Dorsey, 1990, p. 125.

3. C. la Cour, 'Theorising digital disinformation in international relations', International Politics, 57 (2020), 704–23, https://doi.org/10.1057/s41311-020-00215-x

4. Corneliu Bjola and Krysianna Papadakis, 'Digital propaganda, counterpublics and the disruption of the public sphere: the Finnish approach to building digital resilience', Cambridge Review of International Affairs, 33, 5 (2020), 638–66 at 644, DOI:10.1080/09557571.2019.1704221

5. Claire Wardle, 'The need for smarter definitions and practical, timely empirical research on information disorder', Digital Journalism, 6, 8 (2018), 951–63, DOI: 10.1080/21670811.2018.1502047

6. Josephine Lukito, 'Coordinating a multi-platform disinformation campaign: internet research agency activity on three US social media

platforms, 2015 to 2017', *Political Communication*, 37, 2 (2020), 238–55 at 238, DOI: 10.1080/10584609.2019.1661889

7. Cited in L. John Martin, 'Disinformation: an instrumentality in the propaganda arsenal', *Political Communication*, 2 1 (1982), 47–64, DO: 10.1080/10584609.1982.9962747
8. V. Bakir, E. Herring, D. Miller and P. Robinson, 'Organized persuasive communication: a new conceptual framework for research on public relations, propaganda and promotional culture', *Critical Sociology*, 45, 3 (2019), 311–28 at 312, https://doi.org/10.1177/0896920518764586
9. F. Zollmann, 'Bringing propaganda back into news media studies', *Critical Sociology*, 44, 3 (2019), 329–45.
10. Ibid.
11. Ibid.
12. Ibid.
13. H. D. Lasswell, *Propaganda Technique in World War I*. Cambridge, MA: MIT Press, 1971.
14. Fuchs, 'Propaganda 2.0'.
15. Benjamin D. Horne, Jeppe Nørregaard and Sibel Adali, 'Robust fake news detection over time and attack', *ACM Transactions on Intelligent Systems and Technology*, 11, 1 (2019), https://dl.acm.org/doi/abs/10.1145/3363818#sec-terms
16. B. Decker and C. Fagan, *Adversarial Narratives: A New Model for Disinformation*, Global Disinformation Index, August 2019, https://disinformationindex.org/wp-content/uploads/2019/08/GDI_Adverserial-Narratives_Report_V6.pdf
17. K. Starbird, 'The surprising nuance behind the Russian troll strategy', Medium, 20 October 2018, https://medium.com/s/story/the-trolls-within-how-russian-information-operations-infiltrated-online-communities-691fb969b9e4
18. C. Timberg, 'Cambridge Analytica database identified black voters as ripe for "deterrence", British broadcaster says', *Washington Post*, 28 September 2020, https://www.washingtonpost.com/technology/2020/09/28/trump-2016-cambridge-analytica-suppression/
19. McKay Coppins, 'The 2020 election will be a war of disinformation', The Atlantic, 6 February 2020, https://www.theatlantic.com/magazine/archive/2020/03/the-2020-disinformation-war/605530/
20. D. Vilares, M. Thelwall and M. A. Alonso, 'The megaphone of the people? Spanish SentiStrength for real-time analysis of political

tweets', *Journal of Information Science*, 41, 6 (2015), 799–813, https://doi.org/10.1177/0165551515598926

21. S. Vosoughi, D. Roy and S. Aral, 'The spread of true and false news online', *Science*, 359, 6380 (2018), 1146–51, https://doi.org/10.1126/science.aap9559

22. Kevin Roose, Mike Isaac and Sheera Frenkel, 'Roiled by election, Facebook struggles to balance civility and growth', *New York Times*, 24 November 2020, https://www.nytimes.com/2020/11/24/technology/facebook-election-misinformation.html

23. Bakir et al., 'Organized persuasive communication'.

24. https://public-assets.graphika.com/reports/graphika_report_operation_redcard.pdf

25. 'August 2020 coordinated inauthentic behavior report', Facebook, 2 September 2020, https://about.fb.com/news/2020/09/august-2020-cib-report/

26. Bakir et al., 'Organized persuasive communication'.

27. This word is an alternative to the conventional *fuṣḥa* word for chicken, *al-dajjaj*.

28. Zafar Gilani, Reza Farahbakhsh, Gareth Tyson and Jon Crowcroft, 'A large-scale behavioural analysis of bots and humans on Twitter', ACM Transactions on the Web, 13, 1, Article 7 (February 2019), https://doi.org/10.1145/3298789.

29. K. Munger, 'This researcher programmed bots to fight racism on Twitter: it worked', *Washington Post*, 17 November 2016, https://www.washingtonpost.com/news/monkeycage/wp/2016/11/17/this-researcher-programmed-bots-to-fight-racism-on-twitter-itworked/?utm_term=.9d664101618a

30. 'Weapons of mass deception', BBC, 2018, https://www.bbc.co.uk/programmes/n3ct4f1t

31. S. Shorey and P. Howard, 'Automation, big data and politics: a research review', *International Journal of Communication*, 10 (2016), 5032–55.

32. Gilani et al., 'Do bots impact Twitter activity?'

33. Z. Chu, S. Gianvecchio, H. Wang and S. Jajodia, 'Detecting automation of Twitter accounts: are you a human, bot, or cyborg?', *IEEE Transactions on Dependable and Secure Computing*, 9, 6 (2012), 811–24.

34. Ibid.

35. Ferrara et al., 'The rise of social bots'.

36. Shorey and Howard, 'Automation, big data and politics'.

37. S. Woolley and P. Howard, 'Computational propaganda worldwide: executive summary', Computational Propaganda Research Project, Oxford Internet Institute, https://comprop.oii.ox.ac.

uk/wp-content/uploads/sites/89/2017/06/Casestudies-ExecutiveSummary.pdf

38. Jones, 'The Gulf information war', 1393.
39. L. Nadarevic and A. Aßfalg, 'Unveiling the truth: warnings reduce the repetition-based truth effect', *Psychological Research*, 81 (2017), 814–26, https://doi.org/10.1007/s00426-016-0777-y
40. D. Arnaudo, Computational Propaganda in Brazil: Social Bots during Elections, working paper, Computational Propaganda Research Project, Oxford Internet Institute, DemTech | Computational Propaganda in Brazil: Social Bots During Elections (ox.ac.uk), http://comprop.oii.ox.ac.uk/
41. Philip N. Howard, Samuel Woolley and Ryan Calo, 'Algorithms, bots, and political communication in the US 2016 election: the challenge of automated political communication for election law and administration', *Journal of Information Technology & Politics*, 15, 2 (2018), 81–93, DOI: 10.1080/19331681.2018.1448735
42. Tobias R. Keller and Ulrike Klinger, 'Social bots in election campaigns: theoretical, empirical, and methodological implications', *Political Communication*, 36, 1 (2019), 171–89, DOI: 10.1080/10584609.2018.1526238
43. Marco T. Bastos and Dan Mercea, 'The Brexit botnet and user-generated hyperpartisan news', *Social Science Computer Review*, 37, 1 (February 2019), 38–54, https://doi.org/10.1177/0894439317734157
44. J. Vincent, 'Twitter taught Microsoft's AI chatbot to be a racist asshole in less than a day', The Verge, 24 March 2016, https://www.theverge.com/2016/3/24/11297050/tay-microsoft-chatbot-racist
45. Ibid.
46. Julia Carrie Wong, 'Revealed: the Facebook loophole that lets world leaders deceive and harass their citizens', *The Guardian*, 12 April 2012, https://www.theguardian.com/technology/2021/apr/12/facebook-loophole-state-backed-manipulation
47. S. Gallagher, 'Red astroturf: Chinese government makes millions of fake social media posts', Ars Technica, 13 June 2016, https://arstechnica.com/information-technology/2016/06/red-astroturf-chinese-government-makes-millions-of-fake-social-media-posts/
48. K. Darwish, D. Alexandrov, P. Nakov and Y. Mejova, 'Seminar users in the Arabic Twitter sphere', in G. Ciampaglia, A. Mashhadi and T. Yasseri (eds.), *Proceedings of the Ninth International Conference on Social Informatics*, SocInfo '17, Lecture Notes in Computer Science 10539. Oxford: Springer, 2017, 91 - 108, DOI: 10.1007/978-3-319-67217-5_7

49. N. Maréchal, 'Automation, algorithms, and politics: when bots tweet: toward a normative framework for bots on social networking sites', *International Journal of Communication*, 10 (2016), 5022–31, http://ijoc.org/index.php/ijoc/article/view/6180/1811

50. https://ajph.aphapublications.org/doi/pdf/10.2105/AJPH.2018.3 04567?fbclid=IwAR0EItOl3ftWDEGTLqhpeNzg0PFZwFOLZorU XbjoIiUX8ch4ZASRaQ-jhGg&

51. 'PR company proposed campaign against Sting', Bureau of Investigative Journalism, December 2011, https://v1.thebureauinvestigates. com/2011/12/01/pr-company-proposed-campaign-against-sting/

52. Ibid.

53. https://www.brookings.edu/wp-content/uploads/2020/09/ Nimmo_influence_operations_PDF.pdf

54. J. Shires, 'The simulation of scandal: hack-and-leak operations, the Gulf states, and US politics', *Texas National Security Review*, 13 August 2020, https://tnsr.org/2020/08/the-simulation-of-scandal-hack-and-leak-operations-the-gulf-states-and-u-s-politics/

2. THE DECEPTION ORDER AND PSEUDO-REALITY INDUSTRIES

1. Polyakova and Meserole, 'Exporting digital authoritarianism'.

2. *The Fake News Machine: Inside a Town Gearing up for 2020*, CNN, 2020, https://money.cnn.com/interactive/media/the-macedonia-story/

3. R. Booth, 'PR firms make London world capital of reputation laundering', *The Guardian*, 3 August 2010, https://www.theguardian. com/media/2010/aug/03/london-public-relations-reputation-laundering

4. Ibid.

5. J. Waterson, 'Claims of misogynistic culture at offices of Lynton Crosby firm', *The Guardian*, 1 August 2019, https://www.theguardian.com/ politics/2019/aug/01/claims-of-misogynistic-culture-at-offices-of-lynton-crosby-firm

6. Ibid.

7. J. Waterson, 'Revealed: Johnson ally's firm secretly ran Facebook propaganda network', *The Guardian*, 1 August 2019, https://www. theguardian.com/politics/2019/aug/01/revealed-johnson-allys-firm-secretly-ran-facebook-propaganda-network

8. T. Snyder, *Twenty Lessons from the Twentieth Century*. Crown, 2017, p. 65 (e-book).

9. Waterson, 'Claims of misogynistic culture'.

10. Coppins, 'The 2020 election will be a war of disinformation'.
11. M. Ekström, M. Patrona and J. Thornborrow, 'Right-wing populism and the dynamics of style: a discourse-analytic perspective on mediated political performances', *Palgrave Communications*, 4, 83 (2018), https://doi.org/10.1057/s41599-018-0132-6
12. J. C. Stauber and S. Rampton, *Toxic Sludge is Good for you: Lies, Damn Lies, and the Public Relations Industry*. Monroe, ME: Common Courage Press, 1995.
13. Ibid.
14. Ibid.
15. Ibid.
16. E. Caesar, 'The reputation-laundering firm that ruined its own reputation', *New Yorker*, 18 June 2018, https://www.newyorker.com/magazine/2018/06/25/the-reputation-laundering-firm-that-ruined-its-own-reputation
17. T. John, 'The British PR firm disgraced by a South African racism scandal', *Time*, 5 September 2017, https://time.com/4926830/bell-pottinger-jacob-zuma-guptas-racism-scandal/
18. David Segal, 'How Bell Pottinger, PR firm for despots and rogues, met its end in South Africa', *New York Times*, 4 February 2018, https://www.nytimes.com/2018/02/04/business/bell-pottinger-guptas-zuma-south-africa.html
19. Thor Halvorssen, 'PR mercenaries, their dictator masters, and the human rights stain', HuffPost, 19 May 2011, https://www.huffpost.com/entry/pr-mercenaries-their-dict_b_863716
20. Caesar, 'The reputation-laundering firm that ruined its own reputation'.
21. Ibid.
22. Ibid.
23. Ibid.
24. Crofton Black and Abigail Fielding-Smith, 'Fake news and false flags', Bureau of Investigative Journalism, 2 October 2016, https://www.thebureauinvestigates.com/stories/2016-10-02/fake-news-and-false-flags-how-the-pentagon-paid-a-british-pr-firm-500m-for-top-secret-iraq-propaganda
25. S. Kolhatkar, 'McKinsey's work for Saudi Arabia highlights its history of unsavory entanglements', *New Yorker*, 1 November 2018, https://www.newyorker.com/news/news-desk/mckinseys-work-for-saudi-arabia-highlights-its-history-of-unsavory-entanglements
26. P. Blumberg, 'Twitter denies it failed to warn Saudi dissident of account

hack', Bloomberg, 17 December 2019, https://www.bloomberg.com/news/articles/2019-12-17/twitter-denies-it-failed-to-warn-saudi-dissident-of-account-hack

27. Channel 4 News, *Cambridge Analytica Uncovered: Secret Filming Reveals Election Tricks*, YouTube, 2018, https://www.youtube.com/watch?v=mpbeOCKZFfQ&ab_channel=Channel4News

28. Nanjala Nyabola, 'Politics in the digital age: Cambridge Analytica in Kenya', Al Jazeera, 22 March 2018, https://www.aljazeera.com/opinions/2018/3/22/politics-in-the-digital-age-cambridge-analytica-in-kenya/

29. L. Madowo, 'How Cambridge Analytica poisoned Kenya's democracy', *Washington Post*, 21 March 2018, https://www.washingtonpost.com/news/global-opinions/wp/2018/03/20/how-cambridge-analytica-poisoned-kenyas-democracy/

30. E. Auchard, 'Cambridge Analytica stage-managed Kenyan president's campaigns', Reuters, 20 March 2018, https://uk.reuters.com/article/uk-facebook-cambridge-analytica-kenya-idUKKBN1GV302

31. 'Uni drops Cambridge Analytica executive as fellow', BBC News, 22 March 2018, https://www.bbc.com/news/uk-england-devon-43506270

32. Madowo, 'How Cambridge Analytica poisoned Kenya's democracy'.

33. M. Newman, 'Caught on camera: top lobbyists boasting how they influence the PM', *The Independent*, 6 December 2011, https://www.independent.co.uk/news/uk/politics/caught-on-camera-top-lobbyists-boasting-how-they-influence-the-pm-6272760.html

34. Ibid.

35. Ibid.

36. H. Weber, 'Wikipedia investigates unethical edits by PR firm, Bell Pottinger', The Next Web, 8 December 2011, https://thenextweb.com/insider/2011/12/08/wikipedia-investigates-unethical-edits-by-pr-firm-bell-pottinger/

37. Jones, *Political Repression in Bahrain*, 305–6.

38. Ibid., 304.

39. *The Fake News Machine*.

40. C. Davies, 'Undercover reporter reveals life in a Polish troll farm', *The Guardian*, 31 October 2019, https://www.theguardian.com/world/2019/nov/01/undercover-reporter-reveals-life-in-a-polish-troll-farm

41. Bakir et al., 'Organized persuasive communication'.

42. Glasius and Michaelsen, 'Authoritarian practices in the digital age'.

43. Ibid.
44. A. Marantz, 'Facebook and the "free speech" excuse', *New Yorker*, 31 October 2019, https://www.newyorker.com/news/daily-comment/facebook-and-the-free-speech-excuse
45. https://www.buzzfeednews.com/article/craigsilverman/facebook-ignore-political-manipulation-whistleblower-memo
46. Ibid.
47. L. Mirani, 'Millions of Facebook users have no idea they're using the internet', Quartz, 9 February 2015, https://qz.com/333313/milliions-of-facebook-users-have-no-idea-theyre-using-the-internet/
48. Couldry and Mejias, 'Data colonialism'.
49. 'The "Facebook revolutions" that weren't', The Take | Podcasts, 2021, Al Jazeera, https://www.aljazeera.com/podcasts/the-take-2/
50. Ibid.
51. 'Facebook's failures to stop misinformation'.
52. A. Truong, 'Billionaire Saudi prince Alwaleed is now Twitter's second largest shareholder, with larger stake than Jack Dorsey', Quartz, 7 October 2015, https://qz.com/519388/this-saudi-prince-now-owns-more-of-twitter-than-jack-dorsey-does/
53. Anand Giridharadas, 'Silicon Valley's Saudi Arabia Problem', *New York Times*, 12 October 2018, https://www.nytimes.com/2018/10/12/opinion/silicon-valley-saudi-arabia.html
54. Dania Akkad, 'Revealed: Twitter boss met Mohammed bin Salman months after Saudi spy discovered', Middle East Eye, 9 November 2019, https://www.middleeasteye.net/news/exclusive-twitter-ceo-met-mbs-six-months-after-saudi-spy-discovered
55. A. Kantrowitz, 'How Saudi Arabia infiltrated Twitter', BuzzFeed News, 19 February 2020, https://www.buzzfeednews.com/article/alexkantrowitz/how-saudi-arabia-infiltrated-twitter
56. Akkad, 'Twitter boss met Mohammed bin Salman months after Saudi spy discovered'.
57. 'Jack Dorsey: technology for a better world', SMU Engage, 2015, https://engage.smu.edu.sg/jack-dorsey-technology-better-world
58. M. Zuckerberg, 'Mark Zuckerberg: Big tech needs more regulation', *Financial Times*, 16 February 2020, https://www.ft.com/content/602ec7ec-4f18-11ea-95a0-43d18ec715f5
59. https://www.middleeasteye.net/news/twitter-palestine-israel-accounts-suspended-ministry-report
60. Ibid.
61. 'Twitter suspends accounts of Palestinian Quds News Network',

Al Jazeera, 2 November 2019, https://www.aljazeera.com/news/2019/11/2/twitter-suspends-accounts-of-palestinian-quds-news-network

62. Ibid.
63. D. Filipov, 'The notorious Kremlin-linked "troll farm" and the Russians trying to take it down', *Washington Post*, 7 October 2017, https://www.washingtonpost.com/world/asia_pacific/the-notorious-kremlin-linked-troll-farm-and-the-russians-trying-to-take-it-down/2017/10/06/c8c4b160-a919-11e7-9a98-07140d2eed02_story.html?wpisrc=nl_daily202&wpmm=1; 'My life as a troll – Lyudmila Savchuk's story', DIIS, 2015, https://www.diis.dk/en/my-life-as-a-troll-lyudmila-savchuk-s-story
64. J. Lukito, J. Suk, Y. Zhang, L. Doroshenko, S. J. Kim, M.-H. Su and C. Wells, 'The wolves in sheep's clothing: how Russia's Internet Research Agency tweets appeared in US news as vox populi', *International Journal of Press/Politics*, 25, 2 (2020), 196–216, https://doi.org/10.1177/1940161219895215
65. Ibid.
66. M. Bastos and J. Farkas, '"Donald Trump is my president!": the Internet Research Agency propaganda machine', *Social Media + Society* (2019), https://doi.org/10.1177/2056305119865466
67. A. Breland, 'Shadowy Facebook account led to real-life Trump protests', The Hill, 1 August 2018, https://thehill.com/policy/technology/400010-shadowy-facebook-activities-led-to-real-life-trump-protests; see also M. Kosoff, 'How Russia secretly orchestrated dozens of US protests', *Vanity Fair*, 30 October 2017, https://www.vanityfair.com/news/2017/10/how-russia-secretly-orchestrated-dozens-of-us-protests
68. 'Powerful "Putin's chef" Prigozhin cooks up murky deals', BBC News, 4 November 2019, https://www.bbc.com/news/world-europe-50264747
69. Sheera Frenkel and Julian E. Barnes, 'Russians again targeting Americans with disinformation, Facebook and Twitter say', *New York Times*, 1 September 2020, https://www.nytimes.com/2020/09/01/technology/facebook-russia-disinformation-election.html
70. E. Burke, 'Facebook and Twitter take down Russia-linked accounts targeting US users', Silicon Republic, 2 September 2020, https://www.siliconrepublic.com/enterprise/facebook-twitter-peace-data-internet-research-agency
71. Mona Elswah and Philip N. Howard, '"Anything that causes chaos": the

organizational behavior of Russia Today (RT)', *Journal of Communication*, 70, 5 (October 2020), 623–45, https://doi.org/10.1093/joc/jqaa027

72. Janine di Giovanni, 'Why Assad and Russia target the White Helmets', *New York Review of Books*, 26 June 2020, https://www.nybooks.com/daily/2018/10/16/why-assad-and-russia-target-the-white-helmets/

73. The exact tally is disputed.

74. P. Owen, 'Syria: Russia blames opposition "terrorists" for attack on Aleppo University – as it happened', *The Guardian*, 16 January 2013, https://www.theguardian.com/world/middle-east-live/2013/jan/16/syria-us-denies-assad-regime-has-used-chemical-weapons-live-updates#block-50f6be6495cb5d055131b566

75. K. Starbird and T. Wilson, 'Cross-platform disinformation campaigns: lessons learned and next steps', Harvard Kennedy School Misinformation Review, 14 January 2020, https://doi.org/10.37016/mr-2020-002

76. Ibid.

77. C. York, 'The "useful idiots: how these British academics helped Russia deny war crimes at the UN', HuffPost UK, 29 January 2020, https://www.huffingtonpost.co.uk/entry/the-useful-idiots_uk_5e2b107ac5b67d8874b0dd9d?guccounter=1&guce_referrer=aHR0cHM6Ly93d3cuZ29vZ2xlLmNvbVS8&guce_referrer_sig=AQAAAFh_msKTQE6TyhmEnk7pOs1dyrU_fbc_-JOcOLq6wmx7qjXP6fUMk0koKBhwer3t6y1Jxe6GQiTA9fXc_Uscmh WfGzgUKreLBZfglYshRruG7UjeuxjjQU97jgmRsh7Pyt2wBKdGv1 3OREGUc-Wc2migOhpgOUbxWoVgritU6oue

78. Ibid.

79. Malcolm Brabant, 'Mysterious death of White Helmets co-founder spotlights toxic propaganda', PBS NewsHour, 24 December 2019, https://www.pbs.org/newshour/show/mysterious-death-of-white-helmets-co-founder-spotlights-toxic-propaganda

80. Starbird and Wilson, 'Cross-platform disinformation campaigns'.

81. Christopher Bing and Joel Schectman, 'Project Raven: inside the UAE's secret hacking team of American mercenaries', Reuters Investigates, 30 January 2019, https://www.reuters.com/investigates/special-report/usa-spying-raven/

82. Joel Schectman and Christopher Bing, 'The Karma hack: UAE used cyber super-weapon to spy on iPhones of foes', Reuters Investigates, 30 January 2019, https://www.reuters.com/investigates/special-report/usa-spying-karma/

83. Ibid.
84. https://twitter.com/marcowenjones/status/894132429363060736
85 https://www.youtube.com/watch?v=Wtprg3zann8&ab_
channel=%D8%A8%D8%B1%D8%A7%D9 %85%D8%AC%D8%
AE%D8%A7%D8%B5%D9%87
86. برنامج (6102). خاصه. برامج TwtVoter [YouTube Video]. In YouTube.
https://www.youtube.com/watch?v=c3Q3vr2ijPc&t=350s&ab_
channel=%D8%A8%D8%B1%D8%A7%D9%85%D8%
AC%D8%AE%D8%A7%D8%B5%D9%87
87. برنامج (6102). خاصه. برامج TwtVoter [YouTube Video]. In YouTube.
https://www.youtube.com/watch?v=c3Q3vr2ijPc&t=350s&ab_
channel=%D8%A8%D8%B1%D 8%A7%D9%85%D8%AC%D8%
AE%D8%A7%D8%B5%D9%87
88. برامج FastReply خاصه. (8102). برنامج الرد التلقائي على المشاهير
[YouTube Video]. In YouTube. https://www.youtube.com/
watch?v=xDgCRrVK6LU&t=7s&ab_channel= %D8%A8%D8%
B1%D8%A7%D9%85%D8%AC%D8%AE%D8%A7%D8%B5
%D9%87
89. برنامج (6102). خاصه. برامج Search & Retweet [YouTube Video]. In
YouTube. https://www.youtube.com/watch?v=NgpaPWWN7
eE&ab_channel=%D8%A8%D8%B1%D8%A7%D9%85%D
8%AC%D8%AE%D8%A7%D8%B5%D9%87
90. This software was offered to Faisal Al Manaia, a Saudi citizen
implicated in numerous pro-Saudi influence campaigns.
91. https://www.facebook.com/middleeasteye (2020); Marc Owen
Jones, 'How IS uses hacked accounts to flood Twitter with
propaganda', Middle East Eye, 17 February 2020, https://www.
middleeasteye.net/opinion/how-uses-hacked-accounts-flood-
twitter-propaganda
92. Foreign Lobby Watch, 'FARA spending by country since 2016',
OpenSecrets, https://www.opensecrets.org/fara/countries
93. Glasius, 'What authoritarianism is … and is not'. \

3.   MAKING ARABIA GREAT AGAIN

1. Sondrol, 'Totalitarian and authoritarian dictators'.
2. 'Saudi crown prince's billboard welcome', BBC News, 8 March 2018,
https://www.bbc.com/news/av/world-43325614/saudi-crown-
prince-s-billboard-welcome
3. Dania Akkad, 'MBS, and the million-dollar Saudi charm offensive
you can't ignore', Middle East Eye, 12 March 2018, https://www.

middleeasteye.net/news/mbs-and-million-dollar-saudi-charm-offensive-you-cant-ignore

4.   Ibid.
5.   Ibid.
6.   Author's dataset.
7.   Jones, 'The Gulf information war'.
8.   Marwan M. Kraidy, 'Saudi Arabia, Lebanon and the changing Arab information order', *International Journal of Communication*, 1 (2007), 139–56, quoted in P. Cochrane, 'Saudi Arabia's media influence', Arab Media & Society, 1 October 2007, https://www.arabmediasociety.com/saudi-arabias-media-influence/
9.   Marwan M. Kraidy, 'Saudi Arabia: from national media to global player', in Carola Richter and Claudia Kozman (eds.), *Arab Media Systems*, Open Book Publishers, 2021, Openbookpublishers.com. https://www.openbookpublishers.com/htmlreader/978-1-80064-059-7/ch6.xhtml#_idTextAnchor017
10. Saïd K. Aburish, *The Rise, Corruption and Coming Fall of the House of Saud: With an Updated Preface*. London: Bloomsbury, 2012; eBook, 2020.
11. Cochrane, 'Saudi Arabia's media influence'.
12. Ibid.
13. Mohammad Yaghi, 'Media and sectarianism in the Middle East: Saudi hegemony over pan-Arab media', *International Journal of Media & Cultural Politics*, 13, 1/2 (March 2017), 39–56, DOI: 10.1386/macp.13.1-2.39_1.
14. M. Kraidy, 'The rise of transnational media systems: implications of pan-Arab media for comparative research', in D. C. Hallin and P. Mancini (eds.), *Comparing Media Systems beyond the Western World*. Cambridge and New York: Cambridge University Press, 2012, 177–200.
15. Quoted in Cochrane, 'Saudi Arabia's media influence'.
16. Yaghi, 'Media and sectarianism in the Middle East'.
17. Lebedev was recently made a lord by Boris Johnson, despite being the son of a former KGB agent and being deemed a security risk by Russian experts and a former MI6 officer.
18. 'Saudi Arabia expanding its media dominance beyond the Middle East', Fanack.com, 6 February 2019, https://fanack.com/saudi-arabia/society-media-culture/saudi-media/saudi-arabia-expanding-media-dominance-beyond-middle-east/
19. Khoa Tran and Anh Tuyet Nguyen, 'Twofour54 media free zone: promoting media industry in a censored country', *Journal of Legal, Ethical and Regulatory Issues*, 23, 6 (2020), https://ssrn.com/abstract=3756634

20. https://www.facebook.com/middleeastmonitor; 'UAE-owned Sky News Arabia removes "Palestine" from interview backdrop', Middle East Monitor, 21 September 2020, https://www.middleeastmonitor.com/20200921-uae-owned-sky-news-arabia-removes-palestine-from-interview-backdrop/

21. The small but technologically developed Gulf states feature very highly in such metrics, with Bahrain, Qatar and the UAE having some of the highest social media uptake in the world.

22. Silja Baller, Soumitra Dutta and Bruno Lanvin (eds.), *The Global Information Technology Report 2016*, World Economic Forum, 2016, http://www3.weforum.org/docs/GITR2016/WEF_GITR_Full_Report.pdf

23. Ibid.

24. Jack Goldstone, 'Population and security: how demographic change can lead to violent conflict', *Journal of International Affairs*, 56, 1 (2002), 3–21.

25. Hicham Alaoui, 'Youth, technology, and political change in Saudi Arabia', Hoover Institution, 22 April 2019, https://www.hoover.org/research/youth-technology-and-political-change-saudi-arabia

26. Anuj Chopra, 'Saudi Arabia seeks to tame powerful cyber armies, Techxplore.com, 6 August 2020, https://techxplore.com/news/2020-08-saudi-arabia-powerful-cyber-armies.html

27. Madawi Al-Rasheed, 'The new populist nationalism in Saudi Arabia: imagined utopia by royal decree', Middle East Centre, LSE, 5 May 2020, https://blogs.lse.ac.uk/mec/2020/05/05/the-new-populist-nationalism-in-saudi-arabia-imagined-utopia-by-royal-decree/

28. N. Couldry, 'The hidden injuries of media power', *Journal of Consumer Culture*, 1, 2 (2001), 155–77, https://doi.org/10.1177/146954050100100203

29. Stuart Hall, 'Culture, the media and the "ideological effect"', in J. Curran, M. Gurevitch and J. Wollacott (eds.), *Mass Communication and Society*. London: Edward Arnold, 1977, 315–48.

30. https://www.chinhnghia.com/Media-and-Power.pdf

31. Mattha Busby, 'Schools in England told not to use material from anti-capitalist groups', *The Guardian*, 27 September 2020, https://www.theguardian.com/education/2020/sep/27/uk-schools-told-not-to-use-anti-capitalist-material-in-teaching

32. Marcus Michaelsen, 'The digital transnational repression toolkit, and its silencing effects', Freedom House, 2020, https://freedomhouse.org/report/special-report/2020/digital-transnational-repression-toolkit-and-its-silencing-effects

33. T. O'Connor, 'Saudi crown prince's aide fired over Khashoggi's death also oversaw torture of woman, report says', *Newsweek*, 8 December 2018, https://www.newsweek.com/saudi-prince-aide-fired-khashoggi-torture-woman-1250976

34. file:///C:/Users/marco/Downloads/260cbda4-fb75-4659-9c01-10da2ba31760_.pdf

35. Reuters staff, 'How the man behind Khashoggi murder ran the killing via Skype', Reuters, 22 October 2018, https://www.reuters.com/article/uk-saudi-khashoggi-adviser-insight/how-the-man-behind-khashoggi-murder-ran-the-killing-via-skype-idUKKCN1MW2H4

36. 'Lord of the Flies: an open-source investigation into Saud al-Qahtani', Belling Cat, 26 June 2019, https://www.bellingcat.com/news/mena/2019/06/26/lord-of-the-flies-an-open-source-investigation-into-saud-al-qahtani/

37. Leber and Abrahams, 'A storm of tweets'.

38. 'Twitter bots and fake accounts "blocking news From Yemen"', Telesurenglish.Net, 22 November 2017, https://www.telesurenglish.net/news/Twitter-Bots-and-Fake-Accounts-Blocking-News-From-Yemen-20171122-0041.html

39. Craig's followers were downloaded using a script, and arranged in tableau by account creation date in order to visualise over anomalies. Bot detection was premised on the anomalous mass creation, but also stylistic similarities between accounts (gibberish names, no profile pictures, and little tweet activity).

40. 'Thousands of Twitter bots are attempting to silence reporting on Yemen', Albawaba, 22 November 2017, https://www.albawaba.com/loop/original-saudi-bots-yemen-suffering-1051564

41. Ibid.

42. 'RSF unveils 20/2020 list of press freedom's digital predators', Reporters Without Borders, 10 March 2020, https://rsf.org/en/news/rsf-unveils-202020-list-press-freedoms-digital-predators

43. Ibid.

44. Katie Benner, Mark Mazzetti, Ben Hubbard and Mike Isaac, 'Saudis' image makers: a troll army and a Twitter insider', *New York Times*, 20 October 2018, https://www.nytimes.com/2018/10/20/us/politics/saudi-image-campaign-twitter.html

45. Ibid.

46. Ibid.

47. Ibid.

48. David D. Kirkpatrick, 'Israeli software helped Saudis spy on Khashoggi, lawsuit says', *New York Times*, 2 December 2018, https://www.

nytimes.com/2018/12/02/world/middleeast/saudi-khashoggi-spyware-israel.html

49. D. Pegg, 'Bahraini Arab Spring dissidents sue UK spyware maker', *The Guardian*, 11 October 2018, https://www.theguardian.com/world/2018/oct/11/bahraini-arab-spring-dissidents-sue-uk-spyware-maker

50. United States Department of Justice, 'Two former Twitter employees and a Saudi national charged with acting as illegal agents of Saudi Arabia', Justice.gov, 7 November 2019, https://www.justice.gov/opa/pr/two-former-twitter-employees-and-saudi-national-charged-acting-illegal-agents-saudi-arabia

51. K. Paul, 'Twitter suspends accounts linked to Saudi spying case', Reuters, 20 December 2019, https://www.reuters.com/article/us-twitter-saudi/twitter-suspends-accounts-linked-to-saudi-spying-case-idUSKBN1YO1JT

52. 'About MiSK', MiSK Foundation, 27 January 2019, https://misk.org.sa/en/about-misk/

53. United States District Court, Northern District of California, Criminal Complaint, 5 November 2019, https://www.justice.gov/opa/press-release/file/1215836/download

54. https://cdn.vox-cdn.com/uploads/chorus_asset/file/20712296/file0.482752717836899.pdf

55. Ibid.

56. Bradley Hope and Justin Scheck, *Blood and Oil: Mohammed bin Salman's Ruthless Quest for Global Power*, New York: Hachette, 2020.

57. Ibid.

58. Paul, 'Twitter suspends accounts linked to Saudi spying case'.

59. 'Saudi man arrested as a result of Twitter breach, sister says', MSN, 19 August 2020, https://www.msn.com/en-us/news/politics/saudi-man-arrested-as-a-result-of-twitter-breach-sister-says/vp-BB188bj7

60. https://cdn.vox-cdn.com/uploads/chorus_asset/file/20712296/file0.482752717836899.pdf

61. Massimo Ragnedda and Maria Laura Ruiu, 'Digital capital: a Bordieusian perspective on the digital divide', Emeraldinsight.com, 29 January 2020, https://www.emerald.com/insight/publication/doi/10.1108/9781839095504

62. https://twitter.com/verified

63. Tavish Vaidya, Daniel Votipka, Michelle L. Mazurek and Micah Sherr, 'Does being verified make you more credible? Account verification's effect on tweet credibility', in *CHI '19: Proceedings of the 2019 CHI Conference on Human Factors in Computing Systems*, paper no. 525, May

2019, https://doi.org/10.1145/3290605.3300755

64. This analysis was achieved by downloading all the accounts being followed by Twitter's verified accounts – which follows all those with verification status. The user-reported location of each of these accounts was then used to determine the location of those accounts. Inferred location was not used.

65. Twitter Safety, 'New disclosures to our archive of state-backed information operations', Twitter.com, 20 December 2019, https://blog.twitter.com/en_us/topics/company/2019/new-disclosures-to-our-archive-of-state-backed-information-operations.html

66. The combined synopsis of all Twitter data dumps was taken from their state-backed information operations archive. As Twitter do not tabulate the data, the individual country cases were aggregated to give their totals. Some data was merged, such as Russia and the St Petersburg Internet Research Agency (after all, this is state-backed info ops).

67. R. Choma, 'Donald Trump has a serious Saudi Arabian conflict of interest', Mother Jones, 10 October 2018, https://www.motherjones.com/politics/2018/10/donald-trump-has-a-serious-saudi-arabian-conflict-of-interest/

68. Mark Mazzetti, David D. Kirkpatrick and Maggie Haberman, 'Mueller's focus on adviser to Emirates suggests broader investigation', New York Times, 3 March 2018, https://www.nytimes.com/2018/03/03/us/politics/george-nader-mueller-investigation-united-arab-emirates.html

69. A. England, 'US and Middle East: strongmen contemplate post-Trump era', Financial Times, 20 September 2020, https://www.ft.com/content/132ad76d-0ad4-4cf8-9dc7-acd1797c9e6d

70. J. Swaine, 'Trump inauguration crowd photos were edited after he intervened', The Guardian, 6 September 2018, https://www.theguardian.com/world/2018/sep/06/donald-trump-inauguration-crowd-size-photos-edited

71. This is significant because the potential date range of Twitter account creation goes back to 2006.

72. An account being suspended is not the only way to determine with a substantial degree of action that the account is malicious. Accounts may change their handles (Switching or get deleted). Legitimate users may change their handles.

73. C. Wells, D. Shah, J. Lukito, A. Pelled, J. C. Pevehouse and J. Yang, 'Trump, Twitter, and news media responsiveness: a media systems approach', New Media & Society, 22, 4 (2020), 659–82. https://doi.org/10.1177/1461444819893987

74. https://blog.twitter.com/en_us/topics/company/2020/suspension

75. Damian J. Ruck, Natalie Manaeva Rice, Joshua Borycz and R. Alexander Bentley, 'View of Internet Research Agency Twitter activity predicted 2016 US election polls', First Monday, 27, 7 (1 July 2019), Firstmonday.org, https://firstmonday.org/ojs/index.php/fm/article/view/10107/8049

76. US Embassy in Egypt, Readout of President Donald J. Trump's Call with King Salman of Saudi Arabia, 5 November 2017, https://eg.usembassy.gov/readout-president-donald-j-trumps-call-king-salman-saudi-arabia/

77. Ibid.

78. Editorial Board, 'How Trump enabled the abuses of Saudi Arabia's crown prince', Washington Post, 10 October 2018, https://www.washingtonpost.com/opinions/global-opinions/too-close-of-an-embrace-of-prince-mohammed/2018/10/09/dacd8658-cbe0-11e8-a360-85875bac0b1f_story.html

79. 'Saudi king Salman earns more retweets than Trump, study says', The Peninsula, 2 June 2017, https://www.thepeninsulaqatar.com/article/02/06/2017/Saudi-king-Salman-earns-more-retweets-than-Trump,-study-says

80. Bear in mind that this number is skewed by the inordinately high numbers of new accounts.

81. A further examination indicates that the majority were deleted.

82. Increasingly, many are able to tweet or retweet from iPhone or Android. This is not unusual per se, but it has been said that it has been harder to do this. You can see, for example, in the graph on p. 000, that 127 android accounts were created on 7 November 2017.

83. Lev Muchnik, Sinan Aral and Sean J. Taylor, 'Social influence bias: a randomized experiment', Science, 341, 647 (2013), 647–51, DOI: 10.1126/science.1240466.

84. Alexei Abrahams, 'Regional authoritarians target the Twittersphere', MERIP, 292, 3 (2019), https://merip.org/2019/12/regional-authoritarians-target-the-twittersphere/

4. AUTOMATING DECEIT

1. GPT-3, 'A robot wrote this entire article: are you scared yet, human?', The Guardian, 8 September 2020, https://www.theguardian.com/commentisfree/2020/sep/08/robot-wrote-this-article-gpt-3

2. Ibid.

3. J. Waterson, 'Microsoft's robot editor confuses mixed-race Little Mix singers', *The Guardian*, 9 June 2020, https://www.theguardian.com/technology/2020/jun/09/microsofts-robot-journalist-confused-by-mixed-race-little-mix-singers#:~:text=Microsoft's%20decision%20to%20replace%20human,of%20the%20band%20Little%20Mix

4. Andrew Griffin, 'Saudi Arabia grants citizenship to a robot for the first time ever', *The Independent*, 26 October 2017, https://www.independent.co.uk/life-style/gadgets-and-tech/news/saudi-arabia-robot-sophia-citizenship-android-riyadh-citizen-passport-future-a8021601.html

5. Ibid.

6. R. Bsheer, 'The limits of belonging in Saudi Arabia', *International Journal of Middle East Studies*, 52, 4 (2020), 748–753, DOI: 10.1017/S002074382000104X

7. Ibid.

8. Quoted in J. Vincent, 'Pretending to give a robot citizenship helps no one', The Verge, 30 October 2017, https://www.theverge.com/2017/10/30/16552006/robot-rights-citizenship-saudi-arabia-sophia

9. 'Saudi Arabia: cracking down harder', Reporters Without Borders, 2018, https://rsf.org/en/saudi-arabia

10. Ibid.

11. Omar Abdulaziz, 'Saudi spies hacked my phone and tried to stop my activism. I won't stop fighting', *Washington Post*, 14 November 2019, https://www.washingtonpost.com/opinions/2019/11/14/saudi-spies-hacked-my-phone-tried-stop-my-activism-i-wont-stop-fighting/

12. http://whois.domaintools.com/saudinews50.co

13. K. Paul, 'Update 2: Twitter suspends accounts linked to Saudi spying case', Reuters, 21 December 2019, https://af.reuters.com/article/companyNews/idUSB5N28M002

14. Twitter accounts containing in their biographies any words using specific news-related terminology were downloaded using a Tweeple Search – a Twitter account director tool that allows users to download Twitter accounts based on their biographical data. The keywords were 'news' 'media', and 'newspaper'. Accounts with fewer than 25,000 followers were filtered out on the basis that they were not substantially influential. Locational data from user-reported locations was grouped into the respective country. For example, Cairo would be grouped with Egypt, Doha with Qatar, etc. The accounts were downloaded in September 2019, and so the figures will have now changed. Certain

known extant news sites were excluded at the time of data collection because they were suspended at the time. For example, AjelNews24, a Saudi-based Twitter news account, has 7.4 million followers, but was not included.

15. http://24saudi.tv/

16. شراكه اعلامية بين صحيفة عين تبوك ومجموعة قنوات 24 الفضائية « عين تبوك, Aen-Tabuk.com, 2016, https://www.aen-tabuk.com/241700.html

17. https://web.archive.org/web/20141223003432/http://www.washingtonagencynews.com/

18. https://web.archive.org/web/20140210105824/http://www.swissnewsnetwork.com/

19. https://web.archive.org/web/20130810200044/http://www.belgiumfornews.com/

20. Thanks to Bill Marczak who provided the comprehensive list of domains.

21. https://www.courthousenews.com/wp-content/uploads/2020/12/1-20cv25022-002.pdf

22. Jones, 'The Gulf information war'.

23. Marc Owen Jones, 'Chuto no Tsuitta Kai ni Miru Shuhateki Chusho no Bunpu' (Mapping sectarian slurs in the Middle East Twittersphere), International Politics in Transition, 83-104, DOI: 10.13140/RG.2.2.18449.28000

24. Ibid.

25. Ibid.

26. Ibid.

27. مجزرة_صنعاء and مجزرة_القاعة_الكبرى

28. There are fewer studies on the Middle East on how bots are disseminating seemingly official news content in large quantities. These range from accounts promoting international satellite channels such as Saudi 24 to accounts targeting regional Saudi hashtags. Taken together it can be hypothesised that there has been an organised attempt to target specific geographical hashtags with large volumes of state-approved propaganda. This research seeks to utilise data gathered from regional and national hashtags, and analyse it to determine (a) the extent of automated journalism in the Arabic Twittersphere, (b) the potential impacts of such journalism and (c) the nature of the content. In order to do this, content will be downloaded from Twitter's streaming API.

29. Marc Owen Jones, 'Pro-Saudi spam bots on Twitter try to drown out news of $1.5 billion loan to Egypt', 26 July 2016, https://

marcowenjones.wordpress.com/2016/07/26/pro-saudi-spam-bots-on-twitter-try-to-drown-out-news-of-1-5-billion-loan-to-egypt/

30. See the appendix for more.
31. It is useful to note that maintaining the historical records allows us to conduct such audits. By having archives of the accounts from 2016, it was possible to cross-check the account with the new followers. This was necessary, as Twitter do not release such specifics.
32. Ferrara et al, 'The rise of social bots'.
33. Ibid.
34. Not his real name.
35. Yarno Ritzen, 'How armies of fake accounts "ruined" Twitter in the Middle East', Al Jazeera, 15 July 2019, https://www.aljazeera.com/news/2019/7/15/how-armies-of-fake-accounts-ruined-twitter-in-the-middle-east
36. Ibid.
37. https://twitter.com/marcowenjones/status/120378544433 8667520
38. M. O. Jones, 'Digital de-citizenship: the rise of the digital denizen in Bahrain', *International Journal of Middle East Studies*, 52, 4 (2020), 740–7 at 746, doi:10.1017/S0020743820001038
39. Keller and Klinger, 'Social bots in election campaigns',

5. THE US RIGHT-WING–SAUDI ANTI-IRAN NEXUS

1. T. Cullis, 'The undeniable cruelty of Trump's "maximum pressure" on Iran', Responsible Statecraft, 8 October 2020, https://responsiblestatecraft.org/2020/10/08/the-undeniable-cruelty-of-trumps-maximum-pressure-on-iran/
2. Karen DeYoung, 'Trump administration says it's putting Iran "on notice" following missile test', *Washington Post*, 1 February 2017, https://www.washingtonpost.com/world/national-security/2017/02/01/fc5ce3d2-e8b0-11e6-80c2-30e57c57c05d_story.html
3. Azadeh Moaveni, 'Faking the online debate on Iran', The Listening Post, Al Jazeera English, 2018, https://www.youtube.com/watch?v=JKfSFa5tE_w&lc=UgxhErQz-8YyqfZr0PJ4AaABAg&ab_channel=AlJazeeraEnglish
4. Ben Norton, '"Trump Will Destroy Iran!" Saudis cheer on anti-Muslim president', Alternet, 8 February 2017, https://www.alternet.org/2017/02/trump-destroy-iran-saudi-arabia-twitter/
5. Ibid.

6. Again, using TweetBeaver, the original sample of 7,066 run through the 'bulk account' lookup to determine how many accounts had either been suspended, changed their names, or been deleted.

7. Norton, '"Trump Will Destroy Iran!"'.

8. Ibid.

9. https://twitter.com/EllieGeranmayeh/status/131645078 5895604226

10. 'Iran: confusion and misinformation over social media take-downs fuels online harassment', Article 19, 1 May 2019, https://www. article19.org/resources/iran-confusion-and-mis-information-over-social-media-take-downs-fuels-online-harassment

11. Cited in Derek Davison, 'Is the State Department funding attacks on activists?' LobeLog, 31 May 2019, https://lobelog.com/is-the-state-department-funding-attacks-on-activists/

12. J. Borger, 'US cuts funds for "anti-propaganda" Iran group that trolled activists', The Guardian, 31 May 2019, https://www.theguardian. com/us-news/2019/may/31/us-cuts-funds-for-anti-propaganda-group-that-trolled-activists

13. Ibid.

14. Ibid.

15. Eli Clifton, 'FDD aligned with State Department to attack supporters of Iran diplomacy', LobeLog, 1 June 2019, https://lobelog.com/fdd-aligned-with-state-department-to-attack-supporters-of-iran-diplomacy/

16. E. Clifton, 'FDD emerges as hub for online harassment against critics of Trump's State Department', Responsible Statecraft, 14 October 2020, https://responsiblestatecraft.org/2020/10/14/fdd-emerges-as-hub-for-online-harassment-against-critics-of-trumps-state-department/

17. https://twitter.com/golnarM/status/1316810078763257864

18. https://twitter.com/SanamF24/status/131712945163378 2785?s=20

19. https://twitter.com/NegarMortazavi/status/13172676595710 56641

20. A. Breland, 'Trump's propaganda war on Iran started long before Soleimani's killing', Mother Jones, 9 January 2020, https://www. motherjones.com/politics/2020/01/qassem-soleimani-iran-disinformation-project/

21. Twitter. https://twitter.com/marcowenjones/status/1256322145 900064769

22. Eli Clifton, 'The radical think tank harassing critics of Trump's State Department', The American Conservative, 14 October 2020,

https://www.theamericanconservative.com/articles/business-with-the-devil-the-radical-anti-iran-think-tank-thats-harassing-trump-critics/

23. https://twitter.com/HMATehran/status/1256630063040286727
24. Clifton, E. (2020, October 14). FDD emerges as hub for online harassment against critics of Trump's State Department – Responsible Statecraft. Responsible Statecraft. https://responsiblestatecraft.org/2020/10/14/fdd-emerges-as-hub-for-online-harassment-against-critics-of-trumps-state-department/
25. J. Ofir, 'German censorship campaign targets scholar over BDS and applies "antisemitism" charge', Mondoweiss, 20 April 2020, https://mondoweiss.net/2020/04/german-censorship-campaign-targets-scholar-over-bds-and-applies-antisemitism-charge/
26. D. Sheen, Benjamin 'Weinthal in his own words', 2020, https://www.youtube.com/watch?v=uVHeNpjKYTE&ab_channel=DavidSheen
27. M. Jones, 'How a hawkish DC think tank is trolling critics of the UAE–Israel rapprochement', Responsible Statecraft, 11 September 2020, https://responsiblestatecraft.org/2020/09/11/fdd-trolling-critics-of-the-uae-israel-rapprochement/
28. J. B. Judis, 'Inside the small, pro-Israel think tank leading the attack on Obama's Iran deal', Slate Magazine, 18 August 2015, http://www.slate.com/articles/news_and_politics/foreigners/2015/08/foundation_for_the_defense_of_democracies_inside_the_small_pro_israel_think.html
29. A. Rawnsley, 'New York Post reporter's identity stolen to spread Iran propaganda', Daily Beast, 8 January 2020, https://www.thedailybeast.com/new-york-post-reporters-identity-stolen-to-spread-iran-propaganda
30. https://twitter.com/marcowenjones/status/1252988725233139715
31. https://www.facebook.com/murtaza.hussain.1428; Murtaza Hussain, 'An Iranian activist wrote dozens of articles for right-wing outlets: but is he a real person?', The Intercept, 9 June 2019, https://theintercept.com/2019/06/09/heshmat-alavi-fake-iran-mek/
32. 'Faking the online debate on Iran', The Listening Post, Al Jazeera English, 2018, https://www.youtube.com/watch?v=JKfSFa5tE_w&lc=UgxhErQz-8YyqfZr0PJ4AaABAg&ab_channel=AlJazeeraEnglish
33. C. Newton, 'What is QAnon, the conspiracy theory spreading throughout the US?', Al Jazeera, 8 October 2020, https://www.

aljazeera.com/news/2020/10/8/what-is-qanon-the-conspiracy-theory-spreading-throughout-the-us

34. Ibid.

35. Byron Crawford, 'The Republican embrace of QAnon goes far beyond Trump', *New York Times*, 20 August 2020, https://www.nytimes.com/2020/08/20/us/politics/qanon-trump-republicans.html

36. Sheera Frenkel, 'Facebook amps up its crackdown on QAnon', *NewYork Times*, 6 October 2020, https://www.nytimes.com/2020/10/06/technology/facebook-qanon-crackdown.html

37. Lake, E. (2018, January 3). The Iranian Game-Show Host Urging His Fans to Burn Mosques. Bloomberg.com; Bloomberg. https://www.bloomberg.com/opinion/articles/2018-01-03/the-iranian-game-show-host-urging-his-fans-to-burn-mosques

38. Ibid.

39. Jeremiah Goulka, Lydia Hansell, Elizabeth Wilke and Judith Larson, *The Mujahedin e-Khalq in Iraq: A Policy Conundrum*, Rand Corporation, 2009, https://www.rand.org/content/dam/rand/pubs/monographs/2009/RAND_MG871.pdf

40. https://twitter.com/marcowenjones/status/1369623690636312580

41. https://twitter.com/maasalan/status/1369944977640407043

42. J. Stubbs, 'Special report: how Iran spreads disinformation around the world', Reuters, 30 November 2018, https://www.reuters.com/article/us-cyber-iran-specialreport-idUSKCN1NZ1FT

43. Ibid.

44. Ibid.

45. Donie O'Sullivan, 'Facebook takes down more Iranian pages targeting US and UK', CNN Business, 26 October 2018, https://www.cnn.com/2018/10/26/tech/facebook-iran-removed-pages/index.html

46. 'Facebook finds more fake accounts from Iran', BBC News, 26 October 2018, https://www.bbc.co.uk/news/technology-45995724

47. D. Leprince-Ringuet, 'Iran has its own fake news farms, but they're complete amateurs', WIRED UK, 25 October 2018, https://www.wired.co.uk/article/iran-fake-news

48. Donie O'Sullivan, 'Trump speaks after ordering strike on top Iran general', CNN Business, 3 January 2020, https://edition.cnn.com/2020/01/03/tech/iran-disinformation/index.html

49. Megha Rajagopalan, 'The coronavirus: Iran-linked accounts flooded Twitter with pro California independence tweets', BuzzFeed News, 22 April 2020, https://www.buzzfeednews.com/article/meghara/coronavirus-california-independence-iran-twitter

50. https://twitter.com/marcowenjones/status/1247581464524460 033

51. BBC Trending, '"Russian trolls" promoted California independence', BBC News, 4 November 2017, https://www.bbc.co.uk/news/ blogs-trending-41853131

52. Reuters staff, 'US dismantles global disinformation campaign tied to Iran: Justice Department', 8 October 2020, https://www.reuters. com/article/us-usa-election-iran-disinformation-idUSKBN 26T1MR

53. Ibid.

54. Jones, *Political Repression in Bahrain*.

55. Maanvi Singh, 'Mike Pence pushes 9/11 conspiracy theories to justify Suleimani killing', *The Guardian*, 4 January 2020, https://www. theguardian.com/us-news/2020/jan/03/mike-pence-iran-911- suleimani

56. Bjola and Papadakis, 'Digital propaganda'.

6.   THE GULF CRISIS NEVER HAPPENED

1.   Daniel J. Boorstin, *The Image. A Guide to Pseudo Events in America: From News Gathering to News Making: A Flood of Pseudo-Events* (2021 [1962]), see http://www.columbia.edu/itc/journalism/j6075/edit/boor. html

2.   Kristian Coates Ulrichsen, 'What's going on with Qatar?', *Washington Post*, 1 June 2017, https://www.washingtonpost.com/news/ monkey-cage/wp/2017/06/01/whats-going-on-with-qatar/

3.   BBC Trending, 'The online war between Qatar and Saudi Arabia', BBC News, 2 June 2018, https://www.bbc.com/news/blogs- trending-44294826

4.   N. Browning, 'Qatar investigation finds state news agency hacked: foreign ministry', Reuters, 7 June 2017, https://www.reuters.com/ article/us-gulf-qatar-cybercrime/qatar-investigation-finds-state- news-agency-hacked-foreign-ministry-idUSKBN18Y2X4

5.   'Qatar state news agency's hacking linked to Riyadh', Al Jazeera, 4 June 2018, https://www.aljazeera.com/news/2018/06/qatar- state-news-agency-hacking-linked-riyadh-180604065614055.html

6.   O. Boyd-Barrett, *Media Imperialism*. Los Angeles: Sage Publications, 2016.

7.   Jones, 'The Gulf Information War', 1390.

8.   For a full account of the political dimensions of the Gulf Crisis, see K. Ulrichsen, *Qatar and the Gulf Crisis*. London: Hurst, 2020.

9. https://www.facebook.com/middleeastmonitor; 'Dubai based PR firm hired producer of fake terrorist videos to make anti-Qatar film', Middle East Monitor, 24 April 2018, https://www.middleeastmonitor.com/20180424-dubai-based-pr-firm-hired-producer-of-fake-terrorist-videos-to-make-anti-qatar-film/

10. J. Purkiss and A. Fielding-Smith, 'Executive who oversaw "black ops" in Iraq hired for anti-Qatar attack, Bureau reveals', Bureau of Investigative Journalism, 23 April 2018, https://www.thebureauinvestigates.com/stories/2018-04-23/ex-bell-pottinger-psyops-manager-made-qatar-doc

11. 'FBI "mistakenly reveals Saudi official linked" to 9/11 attackers', Al Jazeera, 13 May 2020, https://www.aljazeera.com/news/2020/5/13/fbi-mistakenly-reveals-saudi-official-linked-to-9-11

12. C. Newton, 'Saudi lobby pays $138,000 for anti-Qatar ads in the US', Al Jazeera, 25 July 2017, https://www.aljazeera.com/news/2017/07/saudi-lobby-pays-138000-anti-qatar-ads-170725041529752.html

13. K. Dozier and Lachlan Markay, 'Hillary's pals made ads for Saudis to influence Trump', Daily Beast, 12 August 2017, https://www.thedailybeast.com/hillarys-pals-made-ads-for-saudis-to-influence-trump

14. M. R. Wilson, 'Lobby firm registers as foreign agent for Saudi group', The Hill, 18 August 2017, https://thehill.com/business-a-lobbying/347122-lobby-firm-registers-as-foreign-agent-for-saudi-group-feuding-with-qatar

15. Ibid.

16. Ibid.

17. The Qatar Insider, 4 December 2017, https://web.archive.org/web/20180912120235/https://theqatarinsider.com/

18. Josh Wood, 'How a diplomatic crisis among Gulf nations led to a fake news campaign in the United States', The World, 24 July 2018, https://www.pri.org/stories/2018-07-24/how-diplomatic-crisis-among-gulf-nations-led-fake-news-campaign-united-states

19. Spinwatch, 'New Spinwatch report! The UAE lobby: subverting British democracy?', Spinwatch.org, 24 July 2018, https://spinwatch.org/index.php/issues/lobbying/item/6003-the-uae-lobby-subverting-british-democracy

20. W. Siegelman, 'From the Seychelles to the White House to Cambridge Analytica, Erik Prince and the UAE are key parts of the Trump story', Medium, 9 April 2018, https://medium.com/@wsiegelman/from-the-seychelles-to-the-white-house-to-cambridge-analytica-erik-prince-and-the-uae-are-key-6d860808da91; FARA

Filing, https://efile.fara.gov/docs/6473-Exhibit-AB-20171006-1.
pdf; FARA Filing, https://efile.fara.gov/docs/6473-Supplemental-
Statement-20180531-1.pdf

21. Matt Naham, 'There's new evidence "defeat Crooked Hillary" PAC
illegally coordinated with 2016 Trump campaign through Cambridge
Analytica: complaint', Lawandcrime.com, 16 October 2020,
https://lawandcrime.com/2020-election/theres-new-evidence-
defeat-crooked-hillary-pac-illegally-coordinated-with-2016-trump-
campaign-through-cambridge-analytica-complaint/

22. FARA Filing, https://efile.fara.gov/docs/6473-Supplemental-
Statement-20180531-1.pdf

23. FARA Filing, https://efile.fara.gov/docs/6473-Informational-
Materials-20171013-1.pdf

24. Ibid.

25. Ibid.

26. Luigi Baresi, 'Charity investigated for terror ties received Qatar
funding', New Europe, 19 September 2017, https://www.
neweurope.eu/article/charity-investigated-terror-ties-received-
qatar-funding/

27. J. Waterson, 'This pro-Saudi Tory MP was paid £15,000 for his work
on a conference criticising Qatar', BuzzFeed, 11 February 2018,
https://www.buzzfeed.com/jimwaterson/this-pro-saudi-tory-mp-
was-paid-ps15000-for-his-work-on-a?utm_term=.dyNz2ODy2#.
hqazQ3e8Q

28. Andy McSmith, 'Daniel Kawczynski: "Honorable member for Saudi
Arabia" up in arms over prison training reversal', The Independent,
14 October 2015, https://www.independent.co.uk/news/uk/
politics/daniel-kawczynski-honorable-member-saudi-arabia-arms-
over-prison-training-reversal-a6694471.html

29. J. Waterson, 'Football and fat fees: questions raised over funding of
sporting conference', The Guardian, 16 July 2018, https://www.
theguardian.com/football/2018/jul/16/football-and-fat-fees-
questions-raised-over-funding-of-sporting-conference

30. Waterson, 'Pro-Saudi Tory MP was paid £15,000'.

31. Jones, 'The Gulf information war'.

32. Ibid.

33. Ibid.

34. Ibid.

35. Foo Yun Chee and Katie Paul, 'Twitter suspends Saudi royal adviser
Qahtani, fake Gulf accounts', Reuters, 20 September 2019, https://
www.reuters.com/article/us-twitter-saudi-idUSKBN1W50O0

36. Leber and Abrahams, 'A storm of tweets'.
37. Leber and Abrahams, 'A storm of tweets'.
38. J. Waterson, 'Questions raised over paid protest timed for Qatari leader's No. 10 visit', *The Guardian*, 23 July 2018, https://www.theguardian.com/world/2018/jul/23/qatar-accuses-gulf-rivals-of-paying-for-political-protest-in-london
39. https://www.facebook.com/middleeasteye; Areeb Ullah, 'London anti-Qatar demo "no show" amid claims PR agency tried to hire protesters', Middle East Eye, 1 August 2018, https://www.middleeasteye.net/news/london-anti-qatar-demo-no-show-amid-claims-pr-agency-tried-hire-protesters
40. Neptune PR Ltd – filing history (free information from Companies House), 2019, Service.gov.uk, https://find-and-update.company-information.service.gov.uk/company/11332435/filing-history
41. https://twitter.com/josephmdurso/status/1021731958915850240 https://twitter.com/tse_tsefly/status/1021321276525293568
42. Helen Chapin Metz (ed.), *Persian Gulf States: A Country Study*. Washington: GPO for the Library of Congress, 1993.
43. Hussain al-Qatari and Jon Gambrell, 'Qatar: exiled sheikh promoted by Saudi Arabia now in Kuwait', Associated Press, 17 January 2018, https://apnews.com/article/d40a183d81b94bb6bd44c2fef807decf
44. Ibid.
45. Tweet translated by Ben_Firnas.
46. https://twitter.com/Ben_Firnas/status/1192740528372305921
47. Jones, 'The Gulf information war'.
48. https://twitter.com/marcowenjones/status/1198949971627692032
49. https://twitter.com/marcowenjones/status/1260675685124841473
50. https://twitter.com/khalifa1996_Q/status/1260693208524341248
51. https://twitter.com/search?q=marcowenjones%20video%202018&src=typed_query&f=live
52. https://twitter.com/marcowenjones/status/1259462949317509120
53. https://www.independentarabia.com/articles-author/%D8%A3%D9%8A%D9%85%D9%86-%D8%A7%D9%84%D8%BA%D8%A8%D9%8A%D9%88%D9%8A. (2020, May 5). هل تشهد قطر محاولة انقلاب ثالثة؟. اندبندنت عربية https://www.independentarabia.com/node/117401/%D8%A7%D9%84%D8%A3%D8%AE%D8%A8%D8%A7%D8%B1/%D

9%87%D9%84-%D8%AA%D8%B4%D9%87%D8%AF-
%D9%82%D8%B7%D8%B1-%D9%85%D8%AD%D8%A7%D9
%88%D9%84%D8%A9-%D8%A7%D9%86%D9%82%D9%84%
D8%A7%D8%A8-%D8%AB%D8%A7%D9%84%D8%AB%D8%
A9%D8%9F

54. Ibid.

55. Stanford Internet Observatory, 'Analysis of Twitter takedowns linked to Cuba, the Internet Research Agency, Saudi Arabia, and Thailand', All Internet Observatory News, 8 October 2020, https://cyber.fsi. stanford.edu/io/news/twitter-takedown-october-2020

56. A. Parasiliti, 'The takeaway: Qatari official sees encouraging signs in diplomacy to end GCC divisions', Al-Monitor, 24 November 2020, https://www.al-monitor.com/pulse/originals/2020/11/takeaway-qatar-official-diplomacy-end-gcc-rift-saudi-uae.html

7. FOREIGN INTERFERENCE IN ELECTIONS, REVOLUTIONS AND PROTESTS

1. Economist Intelligence Unit, Democracy Index 2019, eiu.com, 22 January 2020, https://www.eiu.com/public/topical_report. aspx?campaignid=democracyindex2019

2. Using TweetBeaver it is possible to bulk look up Twitter accounts to see if they have been deleted, renamed or suspended. Of the 836 accounts that had been created between 1 and 4 October 2019, TweetBeaver returned only 609, meaning that around 27% (227) of the accounts on that hashtag have either been deleted, suspended or renamed. That is a seemingly high attrition rate. The overall fall off for the entire sample is around 13%.

3. العراق_تنتفض

4. https://twitter.com/marcowenjones (2019). Thread by @ marcowenjones: [Thread] 1/ This one is on Iraq/Iran/US. An interesting hashtag is trending. 'انا عراقي البرلمان لا يمثلني' - which translates as 'I am Iraq…. Threadreaderapp.com; Thread Reader. https://threadreaderapp.com/thread/1214175182652358656. html

5. https://twitter.com/marcowenjones/status/1198914529880502 273/photo/1

6. https://twitter.com/marcowenjones/status/1198913651727425 537

7. Analysis of April 2020 Twitter takedowns linked to Saudi Arabia, the UAE, Egypt, Honduras, Serbia, and Indonesia, 2020, Stanford.

edu, https://cyber.fsi.stanford.edu/io/news/april-2020-twitter-takedown

8. Fanar Haddad, 'The Iraqi people will pay the price for Iran-US rivalry, again', Al Jazeera, 9 January 2020, https://www.aljazeera.com/opinions/2020/1/9/the-iraqi-people-will-pay-the-price-for-iran-us-rivalry-again/

9. ‎معك يابن الصدر‎ and ‎ادعم مقتدى‎.

10. Reuters staff, 'Clashes in Iraq's Najaf kill 8 after cleric's followers storm protest camp: medics', Reuters, 5 February 2020, https://www.reuters.com/article/us-iraq-protests-idUSKBN1ZZ2RW

11. https://twitter.com/marcowenjones/status/1225740307435859968

12. Joey Ayoub, 'A look at the Lebanon uprising through its chants', Shado Magazine, 9 November 2019, https://shado-mag.com/do/a-look-at-the-lebanon-uprising-through-its-chants/

13. https://twitter.com/marcowenjones/status/1186387185479671808/photo/2

14. Barbie Latza Nadeau, 'Saudi Arabia disinformation accounts jump on Beirut blast', Daily Beast, 6 August 2020, https://www.thedailybeast.com/saudi-arabia-disinformation-accounts-jump-on-beirut-blast?source=articles&via=rss

15. https://twitter.com/Dhahi_Khalfan/status/1290680609925472258

16. Mona Alami, 'Hezbollah was taking Beirut ammonium nitrate to produce weapons: source', Al Arabiya English, 12 August 2020, https://english.alarabiya.net/en/News/middle-east/2020/08/12/Hezbollah-was-taking-Beirut-ammonium-nitrate-to-produce-weapons-Source

17. J. Borger, 'US accuses Hezbollah of stockpiling weapons and ammonium nitrate across Europe', The Guardian, 17 September 2020, https://www.theguardian.com/world/2020/sep/17/us-accuses-hezbollah-weapons-ammonium-nitrate-iran

18. David Daoud, 'Ammonium nitrate didn't belong to Hezbollah, but they knew about its dangers', Atlantic Council, 7 August 2020, https://www.atlanticcouncil.org/blogs/menasource/ammonium-nitrate-didnt-belong-to-hezbollah-but-they-knew-about-its-dangers/

19. N. Beau, 'Le rectificatif de Mondafrique sur Marc Owen Jones – Mondafrique', Mondafrique, 4 October 2019, https://mondafrique.com/rectificatif-la-grossiere-erreur-de-mondafrique-sur-marc-owen-jones/

20. Simon Hooper, 'EU trained Algeria and Morocco police in online disinformation tactics', Middle East Eye, 20 November 2020,

https://www.middleeasteye.net/news/algeria-morocco-european-union-trained-police-data-harvesting

21. https://www.aljazeera.com/news/2021/7/28/tunisia-crisis-prompts-surge-in-foreign-social-media-manipulation

8. YOU ARE BEING LIED TO BY PEOPLE THAT DO NOT EVEN EXIST

1. https://twitter.com/realDonaldTrump/status/12798842130559 26272(2020.

2. Goulet eventually deleted the tweet after speaking to the Daily Beast. (When informed of the Daily Beast's reporting, the lawmaker replied: 'Easy to tell after but thanks, I will be careful.')

3. David Reaboi, 'Khashoggi: Qatari asset in life; Qatari asset in death', Security Studies Group, 23 December 2018, https://securitystudies. org/jamal-khashoggi-and-qatar-in-the-echo-chamber/

4. 'Palestinian politician to continue Irish defamation action against Facebook', Irish Legal News, 10 September 2019, https://www. irishlegal.com/article/palestinian-politician-to-continue-irish-defamation-action-against-facebook

5. This was performed through an analysis of the RiskIQ database.

6. The following names were claimed to be journalists working for Arab Eye: Amira Khan, Michel Haddad, Raphael Badani, Lisa Moore, Joyce Toledano, Sharif Neil, Abdulrahman Al-Hussein, Amin Farhad, Taimur Hall, Joseph Labba, Anass Shalhoub Amani Shahan, Navid Barani, Salma Mohamed, Omer Demir, Adam Brafman, Cindy Xi, Lin Nguyen, Mikael Virtanen, Xavier Palacios, Judy Anderson, Muhammed Serhan, Rasim Derya, Jebediah Kazhdan and Maitha Bitar.

7. A. Rawnsley, 'Right-wing media outlets duped by a Middle East propaganda campaign', Daily Beast, 6 July 2020, https://www. thedailybeast.com/right-wing-media-outlets-duped-by-a-middle-east-propaganda-campaign

8. Ibid.

9. Ibid.

10. Ibid.

11. https://twitter.com/AAboudouh/status/1280580809917968385

12. https://twitter.com/AAboudouh/status/1280580809917968385

13. https://twitter.com/tomgrundy/status/1280536286818779136

14. https://twitter.com/tomgrundy/status/1280532957871013888

15. https://www.facebook.com/middleeasteye (2020); MEE staff, 'Media sites hoodwinked by Middle East propaganda ruse using

fake journalists', Middle East Eye, 7 July 2020, https://www.middleeasteye.net/news/fake-journalists-middle-east-propaganda-media-hoodwinked-ruse

16. https://twitter.com/YahooNews/status/12806168784451174 41?s=20

17. 'Lin Nguyen', *South China Morning Post*, 2019, https://www.scmp.com/author/lin-nguyen

18. J. Toledano, 'A fresh start for Iraq?', Spiked-Online.com, 6 May 2020, https://www.spiked-online.com/2020/05/07/a-fresh-start-for-iraq/

19. 'Qatar is destabilizing the Middle East', Human Events, 3 December 2019, https://humanevents.com/2019/12/03/qatar-is-destabilizing-the-middle-east/

20. https://twitter.com/willchamberlain/status/1280575796835495 940?s=20

21. https://twitter.com/stillgray/status/1280582423802032128

22. Kavanagh and Rich, *Truth Decay*.

23. Daniel Victor, 'How a conservative news site thrived on Facebook and Google, *New York Times*, 22 August 2019, https://www.nytimes.com/2019/08/22/us/western-journal-highlights.html

24. G. Lim, 'Burned after reading: Endless Mayfly's ephemeral disinformation campaign', the Citizen Lab, 14 May 2019, https://citizenlab.ca/2019/05/burned-after-reading-endless-mayflys-ephemeral-disinformation-campaign/

25. Ibid.

26. Ibid.

27. Ibid.

28. Ibid.

29. Brian Whitaker, 'Who is Suzan Hadad?', al-bab.com, 10 August 2011, https://al-bab.com/blog/2011/08/who-suzan-hadad

30. Lim, 'Burned after reading'.

31. Ibid.

32. ibid.

9.   FOOTBALL CRAZY

1. https://www.facebook.com/middleeasteye (2020); Rayhan Uddin, 'Newcastle fans share MBS memes and joke about Saudi rights abuses', Middle East Eye, 22 April 2020, https://www.middleeasteye.net/news/newcastle-united-saudi-arabia-mbs-memes-joke-abuses

2. 'UAE "used spying tool" to target Qatar's emir, other rivals', Al Jazeera, 30 January 2019, https://www.aljazeera.com/news/2019/1/30/uae-used-spying-tool-to-target-qatars-emir-other-rivals

3. 'Qatar must not drop the ball on workers' rights', Amnesty International, 18 November 2020, https://www.amnesty.org/en/latest/news/2020/11/qatar-must-not-drop-the-ball-on-workers-rights/

4. J. Waterson, 'Revealed: Lynton Crosby's £5.5m offer to undermine 2022 Qatar World Cup', *The Guardian*, 10 February 2019, https://www.theguardian.com/politics/2019/feb/10/lynton-crosby-2022-qatar-world-cup-ctf-partners

5. Ibid.

6. Anthony Harwood and Alex Delmar-Morgan, 'Revealed: the multi-million campaign to strip Qatar of World Cup 2022', Inews.co.uk, 16 August 2018, https://inews.co.uk/sport/football/world-cup/qatar-world-cup-2022-england-campaign-khalid-al-hail-fifa-187309

7. Waterson, 'Football and fat fees'.

8. Ben Nimmo, Camille Francois, C. Shawn Eib and L. Tamora, 'Operation Red Card', Graphika, 2 March 2020, https://graphika.com/reports/operation-red-card/

9. Ibid.

10. Ibid.

11. Ibid.

12. Tariq Panja, 'The brazen bootlegging of a multibillion-dollar sports network', *New York Times*, 9 June 2018, https://www.nytimes.com/2018/05/09/sports/bein-sports-qatar-beoutq.html

13. J. M. Dorsey, 'The Gulf wants to buy the English Premier League', Fair Observer, 30 May 2019, https://www.fairobserver.com/region/middle_east_north_africa/newcastle-uae-qatar-manchester-city-psg-premier-league-football-news-99524/

14. Ibid.

15. Joint statement by FIFA, the AFC, UEFA, the Bundesliga, LaLiga, the Premier League and Lega Serie A regarding the activities of beoutQ in Saudi Arabia, BeIN SPORTS, 31 July 2019, https://www.beinsports.com/en/football/news/joint-statement-by-fifa-the-afc-uefa-the-bund/1255337

16. Football Association, Financial Regulation (2020), https://www.thefa.com/football-rules-governance/policies/financial-regulation#:~:text=The%20purpose%20of%20the%20Test,for%20clubs%20in%20their%20leagues

17. 'Khashoggi's fiancé Hatice Cengiz is a deep-cover agent of Turkish spy agency', Blitz, 1 December 2018, https://www.weeklyblitz. net/news/khashoggis-fiance-hatice-cengiz-is-a-deep-cover-agent-of-turkish-spy-agency/

18. https://twitter.com/K3NNY420/status/1260888787338567681

19. See, for example, https://www.chroniclelive.co.uk/sport/ football/football-news/newcastle-takeover-headlines-jamal-khassogis-18284809

20. Tweet deleted.

21. E. Farge, 'WTO says Saudi broke global rules in Qatar broadcast dispute', Reuters, 16 June 2020, https://www.reuters.com/article/ us-trade-wto-saudi-qatar-idUSKBN23N2A1

22. R. Harris, 'World Trade Organization: Saudis facilitated sports piracy', Washington Times, 16 June 2020, https://www.washingtontimes. com/news/2020/jun/16/world-trade-organization-finds-saudi-links-to-spor/

23. 'KSA at WTO: real dispute with Qatar related to Gulf security interests', Saudi Gazette, 15 June 2020, https://saudigazette.com. sa/article/594287/SAUDI-ARABIA/KSA-at-WTO-Real-dispute-with-Qatar-related-to-Gulf-security-interests

24. https://www.independentarabia.com/articles-author/%D8%B2%D9%8A%D8%A7%D8%AF-%D8%A7%D9%84%D9%81%D9%8A%D9%81%D9%8A-0. (2020, June 16). التجارة العالمية" ترفض شكاوى قطر ضد السعودية. اندبندنت عربية." https://www.independentarabia.com/node/127746/%D8%A7%D9%84%D8%A3%D8%AE%D8%A8%D8%A7%D8%B1/%D8%A7%D9%84%D8%AA%D8%AC%D8%A7%D8%B1%D8%A9-%D8%A7%D9%84%D8%B9%D8%A7%D9%84%D9%85%D9%8A%D8%A9-%D8%AA%D8%B1%D9%81%D8%B6-%D8%B4%D9%83%D8%A7%D9%88%D9%89-%D9%82%D8%B7%D8%B1-%D8%B6%D8%AF-%D8%A7%D9%84%D8%B3%D8%B9%D9%88%D8%AF%D9%8A%D8%A9?utm_medium=Social&utm_source=Twitter#Echobox=1592342723

25. 'Saudi enabling of sports piracy "threatens existence of sport as we know it", says UEFA after WTO ruling', The Independent, 16 June 2020, https://www.independent.co.uk/sport/football/world-trade-organization-saudi-arabia-sports-piracy-bein-beoutq-qatar-middle-east-a9569071.html

26. https://twitter.com/marcowenjones/status/1272939140124901376

27. https://twitter.com/KSAMOFA/status/1272942405625528325

28. https://twitter.com/KSAMOFA/status/1272942405625528325
29. https://twitter.com/marcowenjones/status/1272940818224029 696
30. Sign the Petition (2020), Change.org, https://www.change.org/p/boris-johnson-an-independent-investigation-into-the-epl-takeover-process
31. https://www.change.org/p/boris-johnson-an-independent-investigation-into-the-epl-takeover-process?redirect=false&use_react=false
32. Newcastle United: Saudi Arabian-backed takeover completed. (2021). BBC Sport. https://www.bbc.com/sport/football/58826899
33. For a discussion of identity fusion as it pertains to football fans, see Martha Newson in N. McGeehan, '… football just got a little bit dirtier', Medium, 22 July 2019, https://medium.com/@NcGeehan/trollerball-188bfad1e63a

10. COVID19'S DISINFORMATION SUPERSPREADERS

1. 'The COVID-19 infodemic', *The Lancet Infectious Diseases*, 20, 8 (2020), 875, https://doi.org/10.1016/s1473-3099(20)30565-x
2. R. Abcarian, 'Why does Trump downplay real threats and inflate fake ones?', *Los Angeles Times*, 12 September 2020, https://www.latimes.com/opinion/story/2020-09-12/column-trump-woodward-book-lies-covid-pandemic
3. Twitter (2020), https://twitter.com/marcowenjones/status/1237103075002929153/photo/1
4. Geoff Goldberg, 'K-pop army battle royale', Medium, 29 April 2019, https://medium.com/@geoffgolberg/k-pop-army-battle-royale-1774ccda4c55
5. Nabih Bulos, 'Coronavirus is a weapon in Mideast disinformation campaigns', *Los Angeles Times*, 8 April 2020, https://www.latimes.com/world-nation/story/2020-04-08/coronavirus-becomes-new-front-in-middle-east-battle-for-influence
6. https://twitter.com/marcowenjones/status/1234333227772456960/photo/1
7. Nasser Karimi, 'Virus ravaging Iran kills confidant of its supreme leader', AP NEWS, 2 March 2020, https://apnews.com/article/2ab5535d09074fd0e1c70fc78fef2fad
8. 'Saudi Arabia profile', BBC News, 25 February 2019, https://www.bbc.com/news/world-middle-east-14703480
9. https://twitter.com/Norashanar/status/1233042964479447043

10. https://www.facebook.com/middleeasteye (2020); Ragip Soylu, 'In Libya, Turkey and Qatar deepen their footprint amid deadlock in negotiations', Middle East Eye, 20 August 2020, https://www.middleeasteye.net/news/libya-turkey-qatar-military-deal-haftar-gna

11. Naseem Tarawnah, 'MENA region battles the infodemic: from fake news to hashtag-washing in the region's ongoing information wars', Global Freedom of Expression, 15 September 2020, https://globalfreedomofexpression.columbia.edu/publications/mena-region-battles-the-infodemic-from-fake-news-to-hashtag-washing-in-the-regions-ongoing-information-wars/

12. S. Grossman, H. Khadija R. DiResta, T. Kheradpir and C. Miller, 'Blame it on Iran, Qatar, and Turkey: an analysis of a Twitter and Facebook operation linked to Egypt, the UAE, and Saudi Arabia (Takedown)', Freeman Spogli Institute for International Studies, 2019, https://fsi.stanford.edu/publication/twitter-facebook-egypt-uae-saudi

13. 'Analysis of April 2020 Twitter takedowns linked to Saudia Arabia, the UAE, Egypt, Honduras, Serbia, and Indonesia', Stanford Internet Observatory, 2 April 2020, https://cyber.fsi.stanford.edu/io/news/april-2020-twitter-takedown

14. Bulos, 'Coronavirus is a weapon in Mideast disinformation campaigns'.

15. Grossman et al., 'Blame it on Iran, Qatar, and Turkey'.

16. Alimardani and Elswah, 'Online temptations'.

17. K. Aramesh, 'Science and pseudoscience in traditional Iranian medicine', Archives of Iranian Medicine, 21, 7 (2018), 315–23.

18. 'Applying essential oil to anus "cures coronavirus": Iranian cleric', The New Arab, 25 February 2020, https://english.alaraby.co.uk/english/news/2020/2/25/applying-essential-oil-to-anus-cures-coronavirus-iranian-cleric

19. Alimardani and Elswah, 'Online temptations'.

20. Jones, 'Mapping sectarian slurs'.

21. J. A. Mirza, 'Pakistan's Hazara Shia minority blamed for spread of Covid-19', Institute of Development Studies, 17 April 2020, www.ids.ac.uk/opinions/pakistans-hazara-shiaminority-blamed-for-spread-of-covid-19/

22. 'Zionist elements developed a deadlier strain of Coronavirus against Iran: academic', PressTV, 5 March 2020, https://www.presstv.com/Detail/2020/03/05/620217/US-coronavirus-James-Henry-Fetzer

23. A. J. Caschetta, 'Is Iran on the brink of a coronavirus coup?', The Hill, 14 April 2020, https://thehill.com/opinion/international/491952-is-iran-on-the-brink-of-acoronavirus-coup

24. Ben Nimmo, Camille Francois, C. Shawn Eib and Léa Ronzaud, 'Iran's IUVM turns to Coronavirus', Graphika, 2020, https://drive.google.com/file/d/1z9feAsuF5iEKbK8-LELAmkM3YviJR8Ee/view

25. Abuzar Royesh and Shelby Grossman, '#Covid1948: the spread of an anti-Israel hashtag', Stanford Cyber Policy Center, 13 August 2020, https://cyber.fsi.stanford.edu/news/covid1948-hashtag

26. Navid Barani, 'Could Covid-19 herald regime change in Iran', albawaba, 1 April 2020, https://www.albawaba.com/opinion/could-covid-19-herald-regime-change-iran-1348192

27. Caschetta, 'Is Iran on the brink of a coronavirus coup?'.

11. SILENCING JOURNALISTS

1. G. A. Lopez and M. Stohl, 'State terrorism: from the reign of terror to 1984 terrorism', *Chitty's Law Journal*, 32, 5 (1984–7), 25.

2. Y. Cheng, 'How social media is changing crisis communication strategies: evidence from the updated literature', Journal of Contingencies and Crisis Management, 26, 1 (2016), 58–68, https://doi.org/10.1111/1468-5973.12130

3. C. Philp, 'Jamal Khashoggi: Saudis invoke Muslim Brotherhood link', *The Times*, 19 October 2018, https://www.thetimes.co.uk/article/jamal-khashoggi-saudis-invoke-muslim-brotherhood-link-pvws2wlxd

4. I. Tsukerman, 'Amnesty International and Qatari information warfare', Begin-Sadat Center for Strategic Studies, 2 August 2020, https://besacenter.org/perspectives-papers/amnesty-international-qatar/

5. Joby Warrick, 'Records shed light on online harassment of Jamal Khashoggi before his killing', *Washington Post*, 7 September 2020, https://www.washingtonpost.com/national-security/records-shed-light-on-online-harassment-of-jamal-khashoggi-before-his-killing/2020/09/07/1811c100-eed5-11ea-b4bc-3a2098fc73d4_story.html

6. Ibid.

7. Ibid.

8. Snyder, *Twenty Lessons from the Twentieth Century*, 123.

9. There is no reason to assume that Saudi remained more committed to one hashtag mentioning Khashoggi than did other states.

10. '5-year jail, 3 million fine for rumormongers', Saudi Gazette, 13 October 2018, https://saudigazette.com.sa/article/545523

11. A random convenient sample was then taken from multiple JSON files downloaded from Twitter's streaming API. To determine the location of most of the users, location date was extracted from the user input field when possible. Thanks to Alexei Abrahams for this.

12. The top tweets were ranked, and those with fewer than 200 retweets were filtered. The accounts were then coded in Boolean categories based on whether they supported or rejected the official Saudi government narratives that occurred mostly before Saudi's admission of its role.

13. When the data was cleaned to remove null inputs for user location, Saudi accounts amounted to around 33% of the total sample of accounts active on the hashtag.

14. L. Feiner, 'Twitter bans bots that spread pro-Saudi messages about missing journalist', CNBC, 19 October 2018, https://www.cnbc.com/2018/10/19/twitter-bans-bots-spreading-pro-saudi-messages.html

15. This was based on a random sample of 75,000 tweets.

16. Cheng, 'How social media is changing crisis communication strategies'.

17. '#BotSpot: journalist's death followed by fake accounts', Medium, DFRLab, 25 October 2018, https://medium.com/dfrlab/botspot-journalists-death-followed-by-fake-accounts-e8ff7f1d23f1

18. Twitter (2020), https://twitter.com/Ben_Firnas/status/1220258525395505152

19. Twitter also rewards novelty. New hashtags will be more likely to trend than hashtags that have trended before. In theory (although highly unlikely), if Jamal_Khashoggi was the only hashtag trending in Saudi it would probably cease to trend after a number of days.

20. Marc Owen Jones, 'Profit for propaganda: Twitter still complicit in whitewashing the murder of Jamal Khashoggi', DAWN, 8 March 2021, https://dawnmena.org/profit-for-propaganda-twitter-still-complicit-in-whitewashing-the-murder-of-jamal-khashoggi/

21. R. Costa, 'Conservatives mount a whisper campaign smearing Khashoggi in defense of Trump', *Washington Post*, 19 October 2018, https://www.washingtonpost.com/powerpost/conservatives-mount-a-whisper-campaign-smearing-khashoggi-in-defense-of-trump/2018/10/18/feb92bd0-d306-11e8-b2d2-f397227b43f0_story.html

22. W. Sommer, 'Trump Jr. boosts smear tying missing journalist Jamal Khashoggi to Islamic terrorism', Daily Beast, 12 October 2018, https://www.thedailybeast.com/trump-jr-boosts-smear-tying-missing-journalist-jamal-khashoggi-to-islamic-terrorism?ref=wrap

23. Costa, 'Conservatives mount a whisper campaign'.

24. R. Kampeas, 'Why are some pro-Israel voices speaking out against Jamal Khashoggi?', Jewish Telegraphic Agency, 19 October 2018, https://www.jta.org/2018/10/19/politics/pro-israel-voices-joining-whisper-campaign-jamal-khashoggi

25. Reaboi, 'Khashoggi: Qatari asset in life; Qatari asset in death'.

26. Akbar Shahid Ahmed, 'Think tank led by man who warned high schooler's clock was "half a bomb" says it's advising White House on Qatar Crisis', HuffPost, 1 August 2017, https://www.huffpost. com/entry/think-tank-led-by-man-who-warned-high-schoolers-clock-was-half-a-bomb-claims-its-advising-white-house-on-qatar-crisis_n_5980e768e4b02b36343e9920?guccounter=1&guce_ referrer=aHR0cHM6Ly93d3cuZ29vZ2xlLmNvbS8S8&guce_ referrer_sig=AQAAAGzqC7bnLRAJiDP7zPUIot6aOybPQhJMa7 JpaKcvMIf-3yFyrMQQDHZrfR7zM-KhkGpqqtHRJq6UBtkXAP dvEVk77scjiKLBafDljDg8yfr7Q7A8bKjCEoblivKCuKXzO0nzinv LzvOgjImDyicvMc4gTKnFtbfchnUuMt_6mA52

27. Ibid.

28. The overlap among figures in the disinformation order highlights a continuity of stances between some of its members. David Reaboi is also connected to Jason Epstein, the head of Southfive Strategies LLC, a PR firm contracted by the Muslim World League, through SAPRAC, to hold an interfaith conference in New York, the same month Khashoggi was killed. According to FARA filing Jason Epstein texted David Reaboi to promote the event.

29. S. Harris, 'Crown prince sought to lure Khashoggi back to Saudi Arabia and detain him, US intercepts show', Washington Post, 11 October 2018, https://www.washingtonpost.com/world/national-security/crown-prince-sought-to-lure-khashoggi-back-to-saudi-arabia-and-detain-him-us-intercepts-show/2018/10/10/57bd7948-cc9a-11e8-920f-dd52e1ae4570_story.html

30. L. Matsakis, 'Does Jeff Bezos have a legal case against the National Enquirer?', Wired, 8 February 2019, https://www.wired.com/ story/jeff-bezos-legal-case-national-enquirer/

31. J. Peters, 'Read the report that concluded Saudi Arabia hacked Jeff Bezos' phone', The Verge, 23 January 2020, https://www.theverge. com/2020/1/23/21078828/report-saudi-arabia-hack-jeff-bezos-phone-fti-consulting

32. B. Marczak, 'Some directions for further investigation in the Bezos hack case', Medium, 22 January 2020, https://medium.com/@

billmarczak/bezos-hack-mbs-mohammed-bin-salman-whatsapp-218e1b4e1242

33. S. Kirchgaessner, 'Jeff Bezos hack: Amazon boss's phone "hacked by Saudi crown prince"', *The Guardian*, 22 January 2020, https://www.theguardian.com/technology/2020/jan/21/amazon-boss-jeff-bezoss-phone-hacked-by-saudi-crown-prince

34. Shires, 'The simulation of scandal'.

35. https://twitter.com/marcowenjones/status/1220301649706655744

36. https://twitter.com/marcowenjones/status/1220311774421037057

37. جيف بيزوس... .(22 January ,2020) .SultanBinBandar سلطان بن بندر (جدة)
     الهارب من «الخطيئة» بـ«الاتهام». Okaz; okaz. https://www.okaz.com.sa/variety/na/2006704#.XiiRbKRuRbs.twitter

38. S. Ellison, 'As a sale of the National Enquirer collapses, some wonder if the tabloid is too hot to handle', *Washington Post*, 25 August 2020, https://www.washingtonpost.com/lifestyle/media/as-a-sale-of-the-national-enquirer-collapses-some-wonder-if-the-tabloid-is-too-hot-to-handle/2020/08/25/0777e954-e6e3-11ea-97e0-94d2e46e759b_story.html

39. Editorial Board, 'Since the murder of Jamal Khashoggi, the cruelty of Saudi Arabia's ruler has only grown', *Washington Post*, 1 October 2020, https://www.washingtonpost.com/opinions/2020/10/01/since-murder-jamal-khashoggi-cruelty-saudi-arabias-ruler-has-only-grown/?arc404=true

40. Warrick, 'Records shed light on online harassment of Jamal Khashoggi'.

41. Ibid.

42. https://www.facebook.com/middleeasteye (2018); Rayhan Uddin, 'Khashoggi murder film "The Dissident" targeted by suspicious negative reviews, Middle East Eye, 22 January 2021, https://www.middleeasteye.net/the-dissident-jamal-khashoggi-negative-reviews

12. ATTACKING WOMEN

1. Ghada Oueiss, 'I'm a female journalist in the Middle East. I won't be silenced by online attacks', *Washington Post*, 8 July 2020, https://www.washingtonpost.com/opinions/2020/07/08/im-female-journalist-middle-east-i-wont-be-silenced-by-online-attacks/

2. Jones, Marc Owen. "State-aligned misogynistic disinformation on Arabic Twitter: The attempted silencing of an Al Jazeera journalist"

Open Information Science, vol. 5, no. 1, 2021, pp. 278-297. https://doi.org/10.1515/opis-2020-0126

3. Ghada Oueiss, 'I'm a female journalist in the Middle East. I won't be silenced by online attacks', *Washington Post*, 8 July 2020, https://www.washingtonpost.com/opinions/2020/07/08/im-female-journalist-middle-east-i-wont-be-silenced-by-online-attacks/

4. https://twitter.com/AgnesCallamard/status/1270596303198851075

5. https://twitter.com/marcowenjones/status/1270994496130605063

6. S. Castelier, 'Oman weighs costs of bailout from Gulf neighbors', Al-Monitor, 29 June 2020, https://www.al-monitor.com/pulse/originals/2020/06/oman-bailout-public-finances-cost-regional-role-gcc.html

7. B. Marczak, 'The great iPwn: journalists hacked with suspected NSO Group iMessage "zero-click" exploit', Citizen Lab, 20 December 2020, https://citizenlab.ca/2020/12/the-great-ipwn-journalists-hacked-with-suspected-nso-group-imessage-zero-click-exploit/

8. Mehul Srivastava, 'Al Jazeera journalist sues Saudi crown prince and UAE leader over phone hack', *Financial Times*, 10 December 2020, https://www.ft.com/content/63d363e1-63bd-47ec-85d2-689330e9032a

9. N. Suzor, M. Dragiewicz, B. Harris, R. Gillett, J. Burgess and T. Van Geelen, 'Human rights by design: the responsibilities of social media platforms to address gender-based violence online', *Policy & Internet*, 11, 1 (2018), 84–103, https://doi.org/10.1002/poi3.185

10. D. Boyd, 'What world are we building?', Everett C Parker Lecture, 20 October 2015, Washington, DC, http://www.danah.org/papers/talks/2015/Park

11. For the sake of conceptual clarity, cyber-violence is a useful umbrella term to describe cyberbullying, cyber-harassment or cyber-assault.

12. Á .Zsila, R. Urbán, M. D. Griffiths and Z. Demetrovics, 'Gender differences in the association between cyberbullying victimization and perpetration: the role of anger rumination and traditional bullying experiences', *International Journal of Mental Health and Addiction*, 17, 5 (2018), 1252–67, https://doi.org/10.1007/s11469-018-9893-9

13. F. Mishna, K. J. Schwan, A. Birze, M. Van Wert, A. Lacombe-Duncan, L. McInroy and S. Attar-Schwartz, 'Gendered and sexualized bullying and cyber bullying', *Youth & Society*, 52, 3 (2018), 403–26, https://doi.org/10.1177/0044118x18757150

14. Sarah Sobieraj, 'Bitch, slut, skank, cunt: patterned resistance to women's visibility in digital publics', *Information, Communication & Society*, 21, 11 (2018), 1700–14, DOI: 10.1080/1369118X.2017. 1348535

15. *State-Sponsored Trolling: How Governments are Deploying Disinformation as Part of Broader Digital Harassment Campaigns*, Institute for the Future, 2018, https://www.iftf.org/fileadmin/user_upload/images/ DigIntel/ IFTF_State_sponsored_trolling_report.pdf

16. The offensive keywords directed at Ghada Oueiss (to:ghadaoueiss) were input into ScrapeHero, a cloud-based scraping platform that allows one to scrape historical tweets. The results were inserted into tableau and a time series graph generated to determine episodes of increased usage.

17. E. Kavanagh, C. Litchfield and J. Osborne, 'Sporting women and social media: sexualization, misogyny, and gender-based violence in online spaces', *International Journal of Sport Communication*, 12, 4 (2019), 552–72.

18. This data was gathered via ScrapeHero, which allows users to scrape Twitter for any keywords that are visible in publicly available posts. The search terms used here were terms designed to be sexually degrading, suggestive or aggressive, and included: 'شرموطة (whore), انكحك (I will fuck you) , زب (dick) , طيزك (your arse) , الفشخة (slut), 'زبي في بقك' (dick in your mouth) , القحبة (bitch) , ممحونة (horny/ slutty bitch) , ايري (my dick) and (my balls) بيضي'

19. The reason for the uptick in trolling Twitter since 2018 was that Ghada did not really tweet until April 2018, when she was informed of another hashtag attacking her.

20. D. Harman, 'Backstory: the royal couple that put Qatar on the map', Christian Science Monitor, 5 March 2007, https://www.csmonitor. com/2007/0305/p20s01-wome.html

21. https://twitter.com/mime20_/status/1328823692743356417

22. https://twitter.com/irinatsukerman/status/1262162265979211 776

23. H. Al-Khamri, 'Torture, reform and women's rights in Saudi Arabia', Al Jazeera, 30 November 2018, https://www.aljazeera.com/ opinions/2018/11/30/torture-reform-and-womens-rights-in- saudi-arabia

24. Sondrol, 'Totalitarian and authoritarian dictators'.

25. The offensive keywords directed at Negar Mortazavi (to:negarmortazavi) were input into ScrapeHero, a cloud-based scraping platform that allows one to scrape historical tweets. The

results were inserted into tableau and a time series graph generated to determine episodes of increased usage.

26. This data was gathered via ScrapeHero, which allows users to scrape Twitter for any keywords that are visible in publicly available posts. The search terms used here were terms designed to be sexually degrading, suggestive or aggressive, and included: فاحشه (whore), جنده (cunt), bitch, cunt, slut, whore, 'fuck you', شلخته (bitch) cock, dick, or 'blow job'.

27. A. A. Dashti, H. H. Al-Abdullah and H. A. Johar, 'Social media and the spiral of silence: the case of Kuwaiti female students political discourse on Twitter', *Journal of International Women's Studies*, 16, 3 (2015), 42–53, https://vc.bridgew.edu/jiws/vol16/iss3/4/

28. https://twitter.com/marcowenjones/status/1270475823947173 888?s=20

29. Pamela Paul, 'Rejection may hurt more than feelings', *New York Times*, 13 May 2011, https://www.nytimes.com/2011/05/15/fashion/is-rejection-painful-actually-it-is-studied.html?auth=login-google

30. E. A. Jane, 'Online misogyny and feminist digilantism', *Continuum: Journal of Media & Cultural Studies*, 30, 3 (2016), 284–97, https://doi-org.eres.qnl.qa/10.1080/10304312.2016.1166560

31. Oueiss, 'I'm a female journalist in the Middle East'.

32. Jane, 'Online misogyny and feminist digilantism'.

33. https://twitter.com/farnazfassihi/status/1292562677903110147

34. https://twitter.com/monaeltahawy/status/1092870110660849664

35. 'Saudi Arabia's Absher app: controlling women's travel while offering government services', Human Rights Watch, 6 May 2019, https://www.hrw.org/news/2019/05/06/saudi-arabias-absher-app-controlling-womens-travel-while-offering-government

36. 'An official source at Ministry of Interior denounces systematic campaign targeting (Abshar) Application', Saudi Press Agency, 16 February 2019, https://www.spa.gov.sa/viewfullstory.php?lang=en&newsid=1886305#1886305

37. 'Surging Saudi reviews hit apps', DFRLab, Medium, 20 March 2019, https://medium.com/dfrlab/surging-saudi-reviews-hit-apps-d44a8094bcbc

13. STIGMATISING MUSLIMS

1. P. Seargeant, 'What conspiracy theories have in common with fiction – and why it makes them compelling stories', The Conversation, 18 December 2019, https://theconversation.com/what-conspiracy-

theories-have-in-common-with-fiction-and-why-it-makes-them-compelling-stories-128046

2. S. Overly and A. Levine, 'Facebook announces first 20 picks for global oversight board', Politico, 6 May 2020, https://www.politico.com/news/2020/05/06/facebook-global-oversight-board-picks-240150

3. Schectman and Bing, 'The Karma hack'.

4. Joel Schectman and Christopher Bing, 'Exclusive: UAE used cyber super-weapon to spy on iPhones of foes', Reuters, 30 January 2019, https://www.reuters.com/article/us-usa-spying-karma-exclusive-idUSKCN1PO1AN

5. https://twitter.com/marcowenjones/status/1259390376751792128

6. https://twitter.com/marcowenjones/status/1260265641870790658

7. https://twitter.com/marcowenjones/status/1260265641870790658/photo/2

8. https://www.facebook.com/middleeasteye (2020); Yasmina Allouche, 'Tawakkol Karman faces targeted Gulf criticism for new Facebook role, Middle East Eye, 11 May 2020, https://www.middleeasteye.net/news/tawakkol-karman-criticised-facebook-monitoring-position

9. Tawakkol Karman, 'Morsy is the Arab world's Mandela', Foreign Policy, 9 August 2013, https://foreignpolicy.com/2013/08/09/morsy-is-the-arab-worlds-mandela/

10. https://twitter.com/YaqeenMustafa/status/1262006331336261632/photo/1

11. https://twitter.com/marcowenjones/status/1262105789910695939

12. D. Coady, 'Are conspiracy theorists irrational?', Episteme, 4, 2 (2007), 193–204, doi:10.3366/epi.2007.4.2.193

13. A. Fichera, 'Trump's long history with conspiracy theories', FactCheck.org, 20 October 2020, https://www.factcheck.org/2020/10/trumps-long-history-with-conspiracy-theories/

14. Matthew Gray, 'Explaining conspiracy theories in modern Arab Middle Eastern political discourse: some problems and limitations of the literature', Critique: Critical Middle Eastern Studies, 17, 2 (2008), 155–74 at 169, DOI: 10.1080/10669920802172353.

15. Ibid.

16. Ibid.

17. Claire Wardle, Understanding Information Disorder, First Draft, 2019, Introduction, 5, https://firstdraftnews.org/wp-content/uploads/2019/10/Information_Disorder_Digital_AW.pdf?x76701

18. M. Lynch, 'Attempts to designate the Muslim Brotherhood a terrorist organization have failed before. Why is it returning now?', *Washington Post*, 1 May 2019, https://www.washingtonpost.com/politics/2019/05/01/designating-muslim-brotherhood-terrorist-organization-has-failed-before-why-is-it-returning-now/

19. جدلية, J. Mohamad Elmasry, 'Unpacking anti-Muslim Brotherhood discourse', Jadaliyya, 28 June 2013, جدلية. https://www.jadaliyya.com/Details/28855

20. https://www.facebook.com/middleeasteye (2020); Ahmad Rashed Said, 'Saudi propaganda is demonising Islam and the Palestinian cause', Middle East Eye, 29 May 2020, https://www.middleeasteye.net/opinion/saudi-propaganda-regime-shooting-itself-foot

21. Lynch, 'Attempts to designate the Muslim Brotherhood a terrorist organization have failed before'.

22. Hamid Dabashi, 'Why Saudi Arabia hates Muslim women in the US Congress', Al Jazeera, 27 January 2019, https://www.aljazeera.com/opinions/2019/1/27/why-saudi-arabia-hates-muslim-women-in-the-us-congress/

23. O. Salem, 'Saudi Arabia declares war on America's Muslim congresswomen', Foreign Policy, 11 December 2018, https://foreignpolicy.com/2018/12/11/saudi-arabia-declares-war-on-americas-muslim-congresswomen/

24. S. Westrop, 'Disinformation campaign targets Ilhan Omar and Qatar?', Middle East Forum, 27 November 2019, https://www.meforum.org/59981/disinformation-campaign-targets-omar-qatar

25. Ibid.

26. R. Mackey, 'How a fringe Muslim cleric from Australia became a hero to America's far right', The Intercept, 25 June 2019, https://theintercept.com/2019/06/25/mohamad-tawhidi-far-right/

27. M. Elzoheiry, 'Hillary, Al-Jazeera: joint dream to spread chaos in Middle East', Sada El Balad, 11 October 2020, https://see.news/hillary-al-jazeera-a-joint-dream-to-spread-chaos-in-the-middle-east/

28. 'Hillary Clinton emails: thousands of new pages released', BBC News, 1 September 2015, https://www.bbc.com/news/world-us-canada-34111855

29. https://twitter.com/alain_4u/status/1316329150043418627

30. D. Ignatius, 'The Saudi crown prince, Interpol and an alleged assassination plot', *Washington Post*, 6 August 2020, https://www.washingtonpost.com/opinions/the-saudi-crown-prince-interpol-and-an-alleged-assassination-plot/2020/08/06/b172b3a6-d821-11ea-9c3b-dfc394c03988_story.html

31. سكاي نيوز عربية. (11 October 2020). ..بريد هيلاري؛
نافذة على 'مطبخ' الإخوان وآلتهم الدعائية. سكاي نيوز عربية؛
سكاي نيوز عربية. https://www.skynewsarabia.com/
world/1383278-%D8%A8%D8%B1%D9%8A%D8%AF-
%D9%87%D9%8A%D9%84%D8%A7%D8%B1%D9
%8A-%D9%86%D8%A7%D9%81%D8%B0%D8%A9-
%D9%85%D8%B7%D8%A8%D8%AE-%D8%A7%D9%84%D8%
A7%D9%95%D8%AE%D9%88%D8%A7%D9%86-%D9%88%D
8%A7%D9%93%D9%84%D8%AA%D9%87%D9%85-%D8%A7
%D9%84%D8%AF%D8%B9%D8%A7%D9%8A%D9%94%D9%
8A%D8%A9

32. F. Gardner, 'Family of exiled top Saudi officer Saad al-Jabri "targeted"',
BBC News, 25 May 2020, https://www.bbc.com/news/world-
middle-east-52790864

33. New Arab staff, 'Saudi crown prince seeking $15 billion from rival
cousin Mohammed bin Nayef in "shakedown"' The New Arab, 6 July
2020, https://english.alaraby.co.uk/english/news/2020/7/6/
saudi-arabias-mbs-demands-15-billion-from-jailed-prince

34. B. Hope, J. Scheck and W. P. Strobel, 'Saudi Arabia wants its fugitive
spymaster back', *Wall Street Journal*, 17 July 2020, https://www.wsj.
com/articles/a-spymaster-ran-off-after-saudis-say-billions-went-
missing-they-want-him-back-11595004443

35. https://www.facebook.com/middleeasteye (2020); David Hearst,
'The Saudi who could bring down Mohammed bin Salman', Middle
East Eye, 10 August 2020, https://www.middleeasteye.net/opinion/
saad-jabri-saudi-arabia-mbs-not-die

36. Ignatius, 'The Saudi crown prince, Interpol and an alleged assassination
plot'.

37. Reuters staff, 'Saudi social media campaign targets former crown
prince', 20 July 2020, https://www.reuters.com/article/us-saudi-
arrests-idUSKCN24L2AK

38. S. Hsu, 'Former Saudi intelligence officer accuses crown prince of
ordering his assassination in Canada', *Washington Post*, 6 August 2020,
https://www.washingtonpost.com/local/legal-issues/former-
saudi-intelligence-officer-accuses-crown-prince-of-ordering-his-
assassination-in-canada/2020/08/06/04aab9a4-d7e3-11ea-9c3b-
dfc394c03988_story.html

39. https://twitter.com/marcowenjones/status/12916876
61976137728

40. Shires, 'The simulation of scandal'.

41. Ibid.

14. TALKING PRO-MBS ZOMBIES

1. 'Dave Schwartz, 63, dies; was Weather Channel meteorologist', *New York Times*, 1 August 2016, https://www.nytimes.com/2016/08/01/business/media/dave-schwartz-63-dies-was-weather-channel-meteorologist.html

2. Bin Nahit was briefly imprisoned for taking a video of himself criticising the Saudi media's onslaught against Qatar during the outbreak of the Gulf Crisis. It is not clear why that retweet would remain on the account after all others had been deleted – although it would appear that whoever was in control of the dead man's account had been tweeting 'at' the Al Qassim account to praise the region of Al Qassim, and its governor, Prince Faisal bin Mishal Al Saud. This has led to some speculation that the account may have, at some point, belonged to the Saudi prince himself. Upon his release, bin Nahit issued an anti-Qatar poem. It was rumoured that his release was contingent upon him criticising Qatar, and toeing the Saudi government line.

3. Twitter Help Center (17 September 2020), Verified account FAQs, Twitter.com, https://help.twitter.com/en/managing-your-account/twitter-verified-accounts

4. Ibid.

5. marcowenjones, 18 February 2019, Twitter accounts hijacked to tweet anti-Qatar propaganda and challenge the French embassy's demands to issue Raif Badawi an amnesty, https://marcowenjones.wordpress.com/2019/02/18/twitter-accounts-hijacked-to-tweet-anti-qatar-propaganda-and-challenge-french-embassys-demands-to-issue-raif-badawi-an-amnesty/

6. (يا حمار مقاطعه ما هي حصار).

7. marcowenjones, 18 February 2019, Twitter accounts hijacked to tweet anti-Qatar propaganda and challenge the French Embassy's demands to issue Raif Badawi an amnesty, https://marcowenjones.wordpress.com/2019/02/18/twitter-accounts-hijacked-to-tweet-anti-qatar-propaganda-and-challenge-french-embassys-demands-to-issue-raif-badawi-an-amnesty/

8. https://twitter.com/marcowenjones/status/1177614135435169794

9. https://twitter.com/marcowenjones/status/1260825163911831553

10. https://twitter.com/marcowenjones/status/1260825163911831553

11. Vaidya et al., 'Does being verified make you more credible?'.

12. Stephanie Edgerly and Emily K. Vraga, 'The blue check of credibility: does account verification matter when evaluating news on Twitter?', *Cyberpsychology, Behavior, and Social Networking*, 22, 4 (5 April 2019), https://www.liebertpub.com/doi/10.1089/cyber.2018.0475

15. THE RISE AND FALL OF MAGNUS CALLAGHAN

1. This chapter is an adaptation of a Twitter thread I wrote in August 2019 about my experience with Magnus Callaghan, a mysterious Tweep I met in May 2020. All the quotes used are true, as is the chronology. It is written more in a narrative style, to convey the absurdity and humour of the situation.

2. Yiping Xia, Josephine Lukito, Yini Zhang, Chris Wells, Sang Jung Kim and Chau Tong, 'Disinformation, performed: self-presentation of a Russian IRA account on Twitter, Information', *Communication & Society*, 22, 11 (2019), 1646–64, DOI: 10.1080/1369118X.2019. 1621921

CONCLUSION

1. Quoted in Snyder, *Twenty Lessons from the Twentieth Century*.

2. A. Abdulla, 'Contemporary socio-political issues of the Arab Gulf moment', research paper, Kuwait Programme on Development, Governance and Globalisation in the Gulf States, Number 11, 2010, https://core.ac.uk/download/pdf/19578257.pdf

3. https://www.facebook.com/middleeasteye (2020); David Hearst, 'Exclusive: the secret yacht summit that realigned the Middle East', Middle East Eye, 27 December 2018, https://www.middleeasteye. net/news/exclusive-secret-yacht-summit-realigned-middle-east

4. Christopher M. Davidson, *From Sheikhs to Sultanism: Statecraft and Authority in Saudi Arabia and the UAE*. London: Hurst, 2021.

5. Jones, *Political Repression in Bahrain*.

6. Snyder, *Twenty Lessons from the Twentieth Century*.

7. Sondrol, 'Totalitarian and authoritarian dictators'.

8. P. Waldman, 'How Trump and Republicans wield the politics of victimhood', *Washington Post*, 29 October 2018, https://www. washingtonpost.com/blogs/plum-line/wp/2018/10/29/how-trump-and-republicans-wield-the-politics-of-victimhood/

9. Jones, 'The Gulf information war'.

10. The Akin Gump Report was written by written by former House foreign relations chair Ileana Ros-Lehtinen.

11. Marc Owen Jones, 'US ruling on AJ+ projects Emirati power into the heart of American justice', Alaraby, 18 September 2020, https://english.alaraby.co.uk/english/comment/2020/9/18/aj-ruling-projects-emirati-power-into-us-justice-system

12. https://twitter.com/joeyayoub/status/1057677994804891648

13. K. Fahim, 'Twitter suspends account of former top Saudi aide implicated in Khashoggi killing', *Washington Post*, 20 September 2019, https://www.washingtonpost.com/world/twitter-suspends-account-of-former-top-saudi-aide-implicated-in-khashoggi-killing/2019/09/20/9d35d96c db8c-11e9-a1a5-162b8a9c9ca2_story.html

14. J. 8 Lee, 'Big tobacco's spin on women's liberation', *New York Times*, City Room, 10 October 2008, https://cityroom.blogs.nytimes.com/2008/10/10/big-tobaccos-spin-on-womens-liberation/

15. M. N. Gardner and A. M. Brandt, '"The doctors' choice is America's choice": the physician in US cigarette advertisements, 1930–1953', *American Journal of Public Health*, 96, 2 (2006), 222–32, https://doi.org/10.2105/AJPH.2005.066654

16. R. Leung, 'Battling big tobacco', CBS News, 13 January 2005, https://www.cbsnews.com/news/battling-big-tobacco/

17. Kevin Roose, Mike Isaac and Sheera Frenkel, 'Facebook struggles to balance civility and growth', *New York Times*, 24 November 2020, https://www.nytimes.com/2020/11/24/technology/facebook-election-misinformation.html

18. https://twitter.com/NegarMortazavi/status/1312201061327794178

19. Marc Owen Jones, 'How the Saudi regime silences those who discuss the Khashoggi affair online', Jadaliyya - جدلية., 21 November 2018, https://www.jadaliyya.com/Details/38185

20. La Cour, 'Theorising digital disinformation in international relations', 719.

21. 'Public trust in government: 1958–2021', Pew Research Center, 17 May 2021, https://www.pewresearch.org/politics/2019/04/11/public-trust-in-government-1958-2019/

22. Abdul-Wahab Kayyali, 'The Arab world's trust in government and the perils of generalization', Arab Barometer, 23 June 2020, https://www.arabbarometer.org/2020/06/the-arab-worlds-trust-in-government-and-the-perils-of-generalization/

23. Starr, 'How neoliberal policy shaped the internet'.

INDEX

Note: Page numbers followed by "*n*" refer to notes, "*f*" refer to figures

Abdulaziz, Omar, 54–5, 87
Abdulla, Abdulkhaleq, 301–2
Abdurahman, Fahima, 67
Abouammo, Ahmed, 87, 88
Abou Zeinab, Tarek al-Khitab, 108, 264
Abrahams, Alexei, 99, 150
Abrewis, Georgia, 200, 205
Absher (android app), 257–60
Abu Dhabi, 13, 78, 250. *See* United Arab Emirates (UAE)
AC Milan, 117
al-Ahmed, Ali, 194–5
Ahmed al-Jabreen. *See* al-Mutairi, Ahmed
AJArabic. *See* Al Jazeera Arabic
Akin Gump (UAE foreign agent), 308
Akta Group, 148
Al Arabiya, 77, 104, 108, 208
Al Ihsan Charitable Society, 147
Al Jazeera Arabic, 78, 104–5, 106
Al Jazeera English, 78
Al Jazeera Sports, 204
Al Jazeera, 133

and Ali Milan, 118
automated bot accounts
  criticising, 148–9
being out of control of Saudi
  media, 77, 229, 307
compliant on UAE, 251
investigation on pretexts,
  attributed to Qatar, 142
Khashoggi killings coverage
  effects, 229, 232–3, 252
tropes at Iraq protests, 168–9
Al Wesal, 77, 104
Alabama, 92
Alaoui, Hicham, 79
Alavi, Heshmat, 132–5
'Algeria votes/is voting', 174
Algeria, 173–5
  See also Hirak movement
    (Algeria)
Ali Milan (Facebook page), 118
Alimardani, Mahsa, 218–19, 254
al-Jasser, Turki bin Abdul Aziz, 88
Almoteari, Noura, 215–16
al-Qaeda
  Bell Pottinger dissents list, 54

Saudi campaign prompting, 242–3
Alshamrani, Mohammed Saeed, 118–19
al-Shariyyaa, 107
al-Wakra, 155–6
AlYemen Now, 83
Amnesty International, 200–1
Ananny, Mike, 4–5
Andreae & Associates, 144
Andreae, Charles, 144
Anomalies, 75
al-Ansari, Salman, 134, 145
Application Programming Interface (API), 19
Arab Eye, 186–8, 190, 196, 217, 220, 264, 313, 354n6
Arab News, 208
Arab Uprisings (2010)/Arab Spring, 77, 262, 271, 310
led digital authoritarianism, 12, 300, 304, 310
Arab world, 4, 14, 271
democracies in, 165–6
'market share' in, 104
Arabian Enterprise Incubators, 74
ArabSat, 76
Artificial intelligence (AI), 101–2
AI robots, 102–3, 312–14
GAN (deep fake technology), 188
al-Asaker, Bader, 87
Al-Asaker, Naif, 249
Asia Times, 183, 192
Assad, Bashar, 64, 65
Associated Press, 145, 216
Atlantic Council, 258–9
authoritarian regimes, 45, 48, 68
deception media control, 5–7, 15–16, 309
information controls, 29–30

close connection with deception order of state, 62
extractive capitalism character of, 17, 20
hegemony-building projects, for shaping criticism, 80–1
AWDnews (website), 136
'axis of evil', 13–14, 23, 141–2
Ayoub, Joey, 171, 309

Badani, Raphael, 217
Facebook article of, 183–4
profile of, 182–3
BAE (UK defence), 74
al-Baghdadi, Abu Bakr, 263
Bahrain uprising (2011), 56
Bahrain, 3, 40, 64, 143
Bell Pottinger (PR firm) contribution to, 52–3, 54
Bell Pottinger scandal on Wikipedia, 56
Qassim (Isa) issues, 110–11
al-Bandar, Abdallah, 155–6, 209
Baresi, Luigi, 147
Baron of the Flies. See al-Joufi, Sultan
BBC (British Broadcasting Corporation), 67, 128–9
BBC Trending, 150
Beau, Nicolas, 175
beIN SPORTS, 204
Beirut, 172–3
Belarus, 264
Bell Pottinger
contribution to Bahrain government, 52–3, 54
Google search results, manipulating, 55–6
and Gupta Empire, 52–3
and Sarawak (Malaysia government), 53

Bell, Lord, 52
Bender, Alan, 268
beoutQ (be out Qatar), 204–7
Bezos, Jeff, 239–42
    'Jeff Bezos is immoral', 20–1
    'Jeff Bezos liar', 240–1
BGR Gabara, 44
Biden, Joe, 63, 236
bin Abdullah, Yusuf bin Alawi, 67
bin Jassim, Hamad, 157
bin Nahit, Ziyad, 280
Bishara, Azmi, 149
Black Lives Matter movement, 36,
    63
blockading countries
    criticising Qatar, 141, 143–50,
        214, 266–9
    'oppose Qatar visit' hashtag,
        152
    See also KUBE
Bolton, John, 133
bots, 39, 120
    with AI and automation
        technology, 312–14
    and trolls, 40, 101–2
    anti-Shi'a sectarianism bots,
        108–11, 114, 219
    searching 'Botmaster', 116–19
    anti-Qatar bot accounts,
        148–50, 152–3
    See also under individual countries
Bouteflika, Abdelaziz, 174
'boycott Amazon products', 240–2
Brave New World (Huxley), 16
Brexit, 50
Brooke, Graham, 136
Brown, Clare Rewcastle, 53
Bruen, Brett, 127
Bryson, Joanna, 103
Bsheer, Rosie, 102
BTS (Korean boy band), 215

Bush, George, 51
Bush, Randy, 17
BuzzFeed, 8

California, 136–7
Callamard, Agnes, 229–30
Cambridge Analytica, 37, 55, 146
    'data neocolonialism' at Kenya,
        55
Capitol Hill, 94
Cengiz, Hatice, 206, 228, 235, 239
Chamberlain, Will, 192–3
Channel of Saudi Achievements,
    107
China, 43, 47, 184
    'Chinese Virus', 216
CIA (Central Intelligence Agency),
    243, 244, 272
Citizen Lab (University of
    Toronto), 9, 117
    on Operation Endless Mayfly,
        194–6
Clifton, Eli, 127–8
Clinton, Hillary, 261, 269–74
    'Hilary's emails' hashtag, 270
    Muslim Brotherhood related
        conspiracies, 271–2
CNN Arabic (news channel), 78,
    250–1
CNN, 76
Cockburn, Steve, 201
commodification, 15–16, 47
coordinated inauthentic behaviour
    (CIO), 39
'corrupt Saad Al Jabri', 273
'the corruption of Saad Al Jabri',
    273
Counter-Terrorism, 107
'coup in Qatar', 155, 157, 158,
    160
Covid-19 pandemic, 213, 221

and disinformation, 213–4
disinformation in Libya, 217–18
disinformation leads
    sectarianisation, 218–20
and Qatar crisis, 214–17
Craig, Iona, 84, 338n39
'crooked Hillary', 274
CTF Partners, 47–50, 201
Cullis, Tyler, 124, 128
'cyberwars, 15
Cyborgs, 43

Daesh, 4, 8–9, 67
Daily Beast, 146, 183, 190
Daily Telegraph (newspaper), 57
al-Dakhil, Turki, 125
Dar El-Nimer, 78–9
Dark Matter, 66
Darwish, K., 43
'data neocolonialism', 55, 59
deception actors, 44–5
    See also journalists; Saudi Arabia;
        Trump, Donald; United Arab
        Emirates (UAE); United
        States (US)
deception order, 68–9
    cronyism, 69
    Entrepreneur/Mercenary, 66–7
    PR firm from, 47–58, 308–9
    programmers, 67–8
    from social media, 58–62
    within state borders, 62–6
    through rent-a-crowds, 151–3
deception
    authoritarian space, creating
        less, 315–17
    bots and trolls, 40–3
    data deception study, 20–1
    deception playbook (Bell
        Pottinger), 53, 55–6
    deception players, 11–12

and digital authoritarianism,
    14–15, 300, 314
and disinformation, 3–4, 39–40
in neoliberalism, 16–18
nexus of anti-Iran entities,
    134–5, 269
press and media deception, 5–6
rise of pseudo-public, 44, 314
as sportswashing, 204–7
'surveillance capitalism', 15–16
'techno-utopianism' and
    techno-dystopianism
    concept, 16
weaponized deception, 31–2,
    31f
as whitewashing, 55–8
'demonising propaganda', 34–5
dhaba̅b iliktru̅niya (electronic
    flies), 40
Diavolo, 118
digilantism, 256
digital authoritarianism, 2, 9–11,
    69, 244, 255, 317
    authoritarian space, creating
        less, 315–17
    neo-liberation technology,
        14–18
    post-truth moment (Gulf)
        contribution to, 12–14
    US officials contribution, 66–8
    See also deception
digital ethnography, 19, 324n58
digital media, 2, 251
    as disinformation distribution
        tool, 33
    global collaboration effect,
        65–6, 95
    globalisation of, 6, 7
    key projectors of, 12, 141
    press deception, 5–6
    role of, 10

Saudi digital media, evaluation of, 75–82
digital predators, 84–5
digital technology, 2, 3, 13
  to protect authoritarian status, 12
  and automation, 312–14
  provoke cyber-violence campaigns, 251
  under regime control, 81
  using in personalised propaganda, 37
disinformation and propaganda, 14, 32–3
  became weaponized deception, 31–2, 31*f*
  IranDisinfo Project, 126–9
  Pretexts, 142–3
  from Trump's election against Iran, 124–6
  See also Facebook; propaganda; twitter
disinformation campaigns, 32
  adversarial narratives, 35–6
  astroturfing campaigns, 44, 62, 64, 93–4, 151–3, 258–9
  through billboards, 75, 152
  cyber-violence campaigns against women, 251–4
  drive adversarial narratives, 35–6
  drive pseudo-events, 143–9
  influence campaign, 33–4
  London campaign, 74–5, 152
  multiple information collaboration, 65–6
  political actors legitimacy campaigns, 172
disinformation, 31, 98–100
  censorship, 37, 61–2, 75–6, 83–6, 119, 225–6, 308–9

Cold War paradigm, 7–8
cronyism nature, 69
ephemeral disinformation, 196
and fake news, 2–3, 4, 42
information ecosystems, 7
pro-Iran disinformation, 135–7
being leverage, 172–3
Nayirah disinformation, 51–2
relate to moral promiscuity, 240–1
relate to Muslim Brotherhood, 261–75
religious disinformation terms, 109–10
research on, 8–10
as typical warfare, 45
See also deception
Dissident, The (flim), 244
Doha, 155–60
Dorsey, Jack, 60
DotDev, 150
Downing Street, 151
Dubai
  paid Andreae & Associates for investigation of Qatar status, 144
  Project Associates contribution to isolation of Qatar, 146–7

e-baltajiyya (e-thugs), 40
Economist Intelligence Unit's Democracy Index, 165
Egypt, 3, 43, 52, 135, 143, 215, 270
Elaph (newspaper), 216
Elite Media Group, 107–8
El-Menawy, Abdellatif, 147
Elswah, Mona, 218–19
Eltahawy, Mona, 256–7
Emmerson, Jeff, 282
Erdoğ an, Recep Tayyip, 218

Europe
  disinformation research, 10
  European fascism (1930s), 8
  European Union campaign in
    Algeria, 177–8
  as MENA deception base, 68
European Union Agency of
  Law Enforcement Training
  (CEPOL), 177–8
Evgeny Lebedev, 78, 336n17
'Expose Tawakkol', 262
Extra People (UK casting firm),
  151–2
extractive capitalism, 17, 20

'Facebook Caliphate', 263–4
Facebook, 3, 58, 59, 60, 62, 80,
  133, 169, 175
  Badani strange message on, 182
  Cambridge Analytica users, 146
  on Daesh, 4
  fake accounts, 39, 42
  Iran users against US, 136
  'No to Facebook', 262
  oversight committee of,
    189–90, 241, 262
  platform regulation actions
    against disinformation, 61
  on Russian Internet Research
    Agency, 63
  Silverman on, 8
  usage of CIO, 39
  war on reality, 310–11
al-Faisal, Turki, 134
@faisalva, 155
fake blogs, 53, 55–6
'fake news media', 5, 38, 235
fake news
  and disinformation, 2–3, 4
  'government by lying', 5
  'source-hacking', 42

from trolls, 42
  See also malinformation;
    misinformation
Far, Tara Sepehri, 127
FARA. See Foreign Agents
  Registration Act (FARA)
al-Fares, Ola, 248, 249, 250, 256
'Farm of Hamad bin Thamer',
  248–9
Farrah, Raouf, 175
al-Farraj, Ahmad, 267–8
fatbyanno (Jordanian-based), 9
Faulkner, Harris, 238
FBI (Federal Bureau of
  Investigation), 63, 87
Ferrara, E., 117
Fetzer, James, 219–20
Filkins, Dexter, 243
Finspy (spyware), 87
Fitz-Pegado, Lauri, 52
Florida, 118, 119
Flynn, Michael, 124, 125
Forbes (newspaper), 132
Foreign Agents Registration Act
  (FARA), 144–5, 147
  Qataris letter, 145–6
foreign policy, 13, 49
  bad actors impacts, 8–9, 63–6
Foundation for Defense of
  Democracies (FDD), 131
  nexus of anti-Iran entities,
    134–5, 269
  overlap with IranDisinfo, 127–9
  and Weinthal, 130–1
France24 (newchannel), 128
FTI Consulting, 240

Gabrielle, Lea, 127
Gaid Salah, Ahmed, 174
Gambrell, John, 216
Gaza, 62

Geranmayeh, Ellie, 126
Germany, 312
'Ghada insults Oman', 250
'Ghada jacuzzi', 249
Ghasseminejad, Saeed, 128, 129
al-Ghawi, Hussain, 242
Ghebreyesus, Tedros Adhanom,
    214
Giridharadas, Anand, 60
Glasius, Marlies, 57–8
global consultancy firm, 54–5
Global Engagement Center (US
    State Department), 127, 138
Global Inventory of Organized
    Social Media Manipulation, 10
Global North, 8
GNA. *See* Government of National
    Accord (GNA)
Goulet, Nathalie, 184
'government by lying', 5
Government of National Accord
    (GNA), 217
"GPT 3", 102, 103
Graphika, 203
Gray, Matthew, 264
Great Hall (Yemen Massacre), 114
Grundy, Tom, 191
Guardian, The (newspaper), 57, 92,
    202, 258
Gulf Cooperation Council (GCC),
    12, 142, 302
Gulf states, 11, 12
    billboards as whitewashing, 75
    US official facilitating digital
        authoritarianism in, 66, 68
Gulf War, 50, 76, 81
Gupta brothers, 52

Haaretz (newspaper), 130
Hack Forums, 82–3
Hacking Team, 82

al-Haddad, Fanar, 169
Haddow, Robert, 185
Haftar, Khalifa, 217–18
al-Hail, Khalid, 149, 152
    'multi-million-pound marketing
        campaign' arrangement,
        201–2
    as Qatari opposition leader,
        147–8
al-Hamli, Rashed, 156–7
Hanson Robotics (Hong Kong),
    102
Hasbara, 62
al-Hathloul, Loujain, 254
'herd effect', 98
Hernández, Juan Orlando, 42
Heyrani, Hassan, 132–3
Hezbollah, 171–3
'Hezbollah's ammonia burns
    Beirut', 172–3
Hill & Knowlton, 51, 52
Hirak movement (Algeria), 173–8
    activists evaluation, 174–5
    European Union against, 177–8
    misinformation effects, 175–6
    Zeghmati actions against, 176–7
Hong Kong, 102, 183, 299
Hosier, Adam, 74
Hosseini, Seyed Mohammad, 134
Houthis, 83, 84
Hudson Institute, 144
Human Events, 192–3
Human Rights Watch
    on Absher crisis, 257–8
    accused US State Department-
        funded entity, 127
    on LGBTQ, 200–1
Hussein, Saddam, 51, 76, 143

'I am Iraqi' hashtag, 167
Ignatius, David, 271

illiberal dictators, 50
Independent Arabia, 160, 208, 211
Independent (newspaper), 78
  on FDD journalist attack, 128
Independent Voices (El-Menawy), 147
India, 203
influence campaign, 13, 33–4
  originator and target of, 32
  related to Clinton, 270–4
  of Russia, 62–6
  umbrella term usage, 33
  See also Saudi Arabia: influence
    campaign; Trump, Donald;
    United Arab Emirates (UAE)
information space, 37
  gamut technics, 25, 83, 300–1
  See also disinformation and
    propaganda; propaganda
Ingham, Frank, 53
The Intercept, 132
International Covenant on Civil
  and Political Rights (ICCPR),
  35, 126
International Policy Digest, 191
International Union of Virtual
  Media (IUVM), 136, 220
Interpol, 272
iPhones, 66–7, 200, 262, 341n82
Iran, 8, 119, 137–9, 166, 170,
  221, 259, 306
  Covid-19 disinformation
    campaign involvement,
    219–20
  fake articles criticising, 189
  fake network of, 194–6, 197
  Iran Disinformation Project/
    IranDisinfo Project, 126–9,
    255
  pro-Iran disinformation, 135–7,
    138
  MEK contribution, 132–5

Saudi media emphasis as anti-
    Iranian behaviour, 77, 97,
    107
  social media discussions, after
    break JCPOA, 124–6, 135,
    138
  US right-wing digital
    ecosystem, 133–5, 269
  women harassment campaigns
    at, 254–6
Iran's Revolutionary Guard Corps
  (IRGC), 137, 220
'Iraq Revolts', 167
Iraq, 5, 178
  crisis since US invasion, 166
  foreign influencers campaign,
    166–9
  al-Sadr campaign, 169–70
Israel, 13, 68, 125, 139
  FDD and IranDisinfo, 127–9
  inauthentic behaviour online,
    61–2
Israeli Ministry of Strategic Affairs,
  61
Istanbul, 65, 226, 228

al-Jabri, Saad, 242, 272–4
Jamal_Khashoggi (hashtag), 234–6,
    361n11–13, 361n19
Jane, Emma, 256
Jerusalem Post, 192
Jobs, Steve, 60
Johnson, Boris, 50
Joint Comprehensive Plan of
  Action (JCPOA), 138–9
  Trump abandonment from, 123,
    124, 138
Jones, Alex, 65
al-Joufi, Sultan, 107, 114
journalists, 9, 21, 23, 24, 30, 37,
    49

on 'A Grave Danger to Freedom
of Speech', 182–6
control news in regional,
114–16, 115*f*
from Facebook, 39, 42
fake accounts, 38
fake articles of fake journalist,
188–90, 189*f*
fake journalists, 186–8, 264
fake network, 194–6, 197
real journalist editors and fake
journalists, 190–4
and robots, 102–3
Saudi domination, 103–7
from Saudi twitter users, 87,
88, 93, 105, 108–9
with 'source-hacking', 42
'source-hacking', 42
US domination on Iran
journalist, 127, 128
Jubilee Party, 55

KAG (Keep America Great), 133
Kalashnikova, Avtomat, 45
Kalbasi, Bahram, 128
Karma (spyware), 66–7, 262,
341*n*82
Karman, Tawakkol, 189–90, 241,
262–4, 265
@katomilan, 117–18
Kawczynski, Daniel, 148
Kazakhstan, 44
'KELLON YAANI KELLON'
slogan, 171
Kenyatta, Uruhu, 55
Khalfan, Dhahi, 173, 249
Khameini, Ayatollah Ali, 125
Al-Khamri, Hana, 254
Khamsat, 117–18
Khashoggi (Jamal), assassination of,
30, 76, 82, 104, 118

attempts to justice, 229–30
Bezos related disinformation,
239–42
Jamal_Khashoggi (hashtag),
234–6, 361*n*11–13, 361*n*19
Khashoggi as a terrorist, 237–9
murder environment, 228–9
profile of Khashoggi, 226–8
Saudi censorship action, for
reform, 206–7, 225–6
Saudi smear actions to, 231,
233–7, 244–5
searching algorithms creation
false narratives, 231–2
Soufan subject to Saudi
campaign, 242–4
Trendogate results, 232–3,
233*f*
Kleidman, Daniel, 192
Krieg, Andreas, 130
KUBE, 23, 92, 119, 148, 301
delegitimise campaign on Qatar
through World Cup (2022),
201
KUBE block, 303
'Kung Flu', 216
Kuwait, 50–2

Laleh Karahiyya (twitter bot,
Arabic), 40–1
Lapis Communications (Dubai),
144
Le Mesurier, James, 65–6
'Lebanese Revolts', 171
Lebanon, 170–3, 178
Leber, Andrew, 150
Levine, Mark, 238
LGBT (Lesbian, gay, bisexual, and
transgender)
LGBTQ issues as delegitimise
tool, 200–1

Weinthal accusations on LGBTQ, 130–1
Libya, 217–18, 302
London, 48, 68, 69, 75, 202
    PR disinformation campaign against Qatar, 152
#LondonRejectsTaminsVisit, 152
'Lord of the Flies'. *See* al-Qahtani, Saud
Lügenpresse (German term), 5–6, 307–8
'lying media', 5

Macaire, Rob, 129
MacArthur, John, 52
Macedonia, 47, 57
Madowo, Larry, 55
MAGA (Make America Great Again), 133, 134, 146, 269, 292, 297
'Make Arabia Great Again', 73, 99–100
Make Iran Great Again, 134
Malaysia, 53
malinformation, 31, 35, 41, 65, 200, 239–42
    See also women
Mahmud, Abdul Taib, 53
Manangoi, Elijah Motonei, 97
al-Maqdashi, Mohammed Ali, 114
Marantz, Andrew, 58
Marczak, Bill, 117–19, 240
Maréchal. N, 43
Martin, Justin, 130
Massachusetts Institute of Technology (MIT), 98
May, Theresa, 50, 151
Mayfair, 48, 49
MBN. See Mohammed bin Nayef (MBN)

MBS. *See* Mohammed bin Salman (MBS)
MBZ. *See* Mohammed bin Zayed (MBZ)
McGeehan, Nicholas, 202
McKinsey, 54–5
Médecins Sans Frontières (MSF), 83–4
media
    'media power', 80
    Trump attack on, 5–6, 235, 307
MEK. *See* Mujahedin e-Khalq (MEK)
MENA (Middle East and North Africa), 24
    conspiracism, 264–5
    digital technology variation, 3
    information controls, 29–30
    digital orientalism, 311–12
    disinformation research methods, 8–10, 11–12
    gamut techniques, 25, 83
    GCC-deception superpowers, 166
    Russian disinformation campaign, 64–6
    Twitter's neutrality in, 88–9
    UK PR firms, 49–55, 308
Michaelsen, Marcus, 57–8
Microsoft, 42
    robots usage, 102, 103
The Middle East and North Africa CyberWatch, 9
Middle East Eye, 184
Middle East Forum, 268–9
Misbar, 9
misinformation, 31
    Covid-19 misinformation, 213–4
    and disinformation, 2

Hirak misinformation, 175–6
Nguyen on, 184, 191
See also Covid-19 pandemic
MiSK, 87
Moaveni, Azadeh, 124
Mohammed bin Salman (MBS), 13,
59, 60, 104, 266, 274
Abdullah Al Thani videos, 153
CTF Partners 48–9, 50
Dorsey and, 309
'Make Arabia Great Again', 73
and MBN, 272–4
and MBZ tyrannical tactics,
303–4
reform activities after
Khashoggi murder, 226, 227,
239–44
Saudi's digital media,
contribution to, 79–80
women misogyny
encouragement, 253
Mohammed bin Nayef (MBN),
272–4
Mohammed bin Zayed (MBZ), 13,
42, 50, 303–4
Mondafrique, 175
Mortazavi, Negar
on FDD, 128
as target of 'IranDisinfo
project', 255
Motevalli, Golnar, 128
Moza, bint Nasser Shaykha, 253
Mujahedin e-Khalq (MEK)
Iran disinformation project,
contribution to, 132–5
producing virulent
disinformation against Iran,
125
Musk, Elon, 60
Muslim Brotherhood, 13–14, 23,
141–2, 306

attempts to smear Karman as
agent of, 263
blockading countries smear
actions on Omar as, 266–9,
306
Clinton crisis relation to, 271–2
conspiracy of, 265–6, 306
Saudi fake journalist criticising,
189
Saudi fake narratives, 235, 236,
261
Muslim Brothers. See Muslim
Brotherhood
al-Mutairi, Ahmed, 87, 88
Myanmar, 59, 320–1n12

Al Nahyan, Mohamed bin Zayed.
See Mohammed bin Zayed
(MBZ)
Nasrallah, Hassan, 171–3
National Council of Resistance of
Iran (NCRI), 134
National Inquirer (magazine), 240–1
National Interest (Badani's article),
192
neoliberalism, 16–18, 48
Neo-liberation technology, 18, 24,
25
data colonialism, promoting, 59
digital authoritarianism,
contribution to, 14–18
and digital tyranny, 308–11
Neptune PR (UK), 151–3
New Atlantis (Bacon), 16
New Europe (website), 147
'A New Saudi Arabia', 74, 166–7
New York Times (newspaper), 85,
133, 258
New Yorker (magazine), 53, 58
Newcastle United Football Club
(NUFC), 199

Saudi NUFC fans usage for sportswashing, 204–7, 210–11
unlikely football fans, 200
Newsmax (US news outlets), 183, 192
newspaper editors, 181
Newsweek (magazine), 73
Nguyen, Lin
list out fake articles, 188–9
profile of, 183–4
signal out The Middle East Eye misinformation, 184–5
Nile Net Online/Nile Net, 135
9/11 attacks, 138, 144, 242, 243
Nix, Alexander, 146

Obama, Barack, 305
Trump unlike policy of, 92, 123, 124
Office of the Director of National Intelligence (ODNI), 236
Ofir, Jonathan, 131
Okaz, 104
'Ola sauna', 249
Oman, 250
Omar, Ilhan, 266–9
al-Omeisy, Hisham, 84
'on notice', 125
One America News Network (OANN), 5–6
OPC (organised persuasive communication), 33
Open AI, 102
Operation Endless Mayfly (fake network), 194–6, 197
'oppose Qatar visit', 97, 153
#OpposeQatarVisit, 152
Oueiss, Ghada, 365*n*19
on impact of women online attacks, 255–6

malinformation of, 247–51, 305
misogynistic terms around, 252, 365*n*16
Saudi and Emirate propaganda against, 94
Oxford Internet Institute, 10

Pakistan, 219
Palestinian Authority (PA), 61
Panja, Tariq, 204
Peace Data, 63
Pegasus (spyware), 87, 251
Pensacola Naval Air Station (Florida), 118
Pentagon, 54, 119
Persia Now (fake article), 186–8, 196
Peters, Michael, 5
PetersBah (Bahrain Wikipedia user), 56–7
Podesta Group, 145, 146
Podesta, John, 145
Pomerantsev, Peter, 3–4
Pompeo, Michael, 270
populism
results commodification of falsehoods, 50
right-wing populism, 6, 49–50
Post Millennial, 192
post-truth moment (Gulf), 4, 5, 101–2, 221, 305–6
cyberwars, 15
deeply misogynistic among women, 247, 253–5, 259–60
evolution from digital authoritarianism, 12–14
Khashoggi murder impacts, 226, 245
KUBE bloc, 141–2, 197
'surveillance capitalism', 15–16
terrorism narratives, 261

Trump administration impacts, 123, 137

led tyrannical and totalitarian tendencies, 13–14, 92

PR firms/PR companies, 47–50, 68, 211–12, 300

astroturfing behaviour, 151–3

legitimise the foreign policy, 50–2

as political consultancies, 52–5, 308

became right-wing, 49–50

Western PR companies contributing for Qatar isolation, 146–8, 151–3

whitewashing character of, 37, 55–8, 74–5

'PR mercenaries', 53

PR playbook, 53, 55–6

'PremierLeagueisCorrupt', 209

Press TV (news channel), 219–20

press: authoritarian regimes precarious usage, 5–6

Private Eye (magazine), 78

Project Associates, 146–7, 308

Project Raven, 66, 67

propaganda

'computational propaganda', 41

contain truths, 34, 137–8

Daesh propaganda, 68

'demonising propaganda', 34–5

pro-Haftar propaganda, 217–8

MBS propaganda for gaining digital media power, 80

pro-MEK propaganda, 132–5

personalised propaganda, 37

pro-Saudi propaganda, 49

pro-Trump propaganda, 125

twitter's anti-Shiʿa propaganda, 40–1, 109–14, 111–13*f*

pro-Saudi entities/pro-Saudi networks

criticising Qatar, 97

for Trump administration, 93, 96–7, 97*f*, 264

pseudo-events, 141, 300

Pseudo-Publics, 44, 300

as result of 'creation of the enemy', 141–2

al-Qahtani, Saud, 104, 108, 207, 227

criticizing Qatar, 153–4, 155

cyber army trolls, 84–5

playbook of, 82–3

profile of, 82

suspense accounts of, 83–4

Qassim, Isa, 110–11

The Qatar Insider (news site), 145, 146

Qatar News Agency's (QNA), 142

'Qatar the bankroller of terror', 149

Qatar, 3, 40, 68, 105, 119, 184, 301, 302

Absher app crisis, 257–9

Al Jazeera network tropes, 168–9

blockading countries rent-a-crowds and astroturfing campaigns, 151–3

coup rumours, 154–60

cyberattack on, 142–3

federal case on emir of, 268–9

global influence campaigns in sports of, 200–4

KUBE bloc, 141–2

al-Qahtani anti-Qatar behaviour, 153–4

anti-Qatar bot accounts, 148–50, 152–3

Saudi Arabia influence in Qatar
    sports, 204–7
Saudi criticising elite women
    of, 253
think tankers for anti-Qatar
    propaganda, 97, 143–9
Weinthal accused academics of,
    130–1
See also Al Jazeera; think tanks
    (against Qatar)
Qatar: A Dangerous Alliance (flim),
    144
Qatari Media Channel, 158–9
'Qatari pitches kill workers',
    202–3
Quds News Network, 61

Rahman, Mona A., 194–5
Rajavi, Maryam, 132
Rajesh Gupta, 52
Rand Corporation, 134
Rawnsley, Adam, 183, 186–8
Reaboi, David, 184
Real People (fake article), 193
Real Stories (fake article), 193
Reichman University (Israel), 62
Reporters Without Borders (RSF),
    84–5, 104
Responsible Statecraft, 128
Restart (twitter user), 134
Reuters
    on Iran deception campaign, 135
    on al-Sadr, 169
    on WTO report against Saudi,
    208
Riyadh, 2
    Khashoggi crisis, 237–9
    Riyadh Summit, 93
    Saudi fake farm at, 85
    See also Saudi Arabia; Saudi
    Arabia: influence campaign

Rohingya, 4
Russia Today (RT), 63
Russia, 36, 47, 69, 142, 340n66
    anti-White Helmets campaign,
    65–6
    deception order support in
    California secession, 136–7
    Russian-backed Syrian regime
    campaigns, 64–6
    US politics, interference in,
    62–3, 95

SA_EG_AE, 92
Sada Social, 61
al-Sadr, Moqtada, 169–70
Safavid Plan, 107, 109
Salem, Ola, 267
Salman (King of Saudi Arabia),
    148
    and Trump, 95–6
    Abdullah Al Thani meeting, 153
San Francisco, 87
Sanaa Massacre (Yemen), 114
Sarawak Bersat, 53
Sarawak, 53
Sarnes, Emily, 200, 205
Sarsour, Linda, 268, 269
Saudi 24 (news channel), 104,
    343n28
    as 'Botmaster', 116–19
    sectarian hate speech,
    promoting, 109–11, 113–14
    subsidiaries of, 107–8
    swamping behaviour in twitter
    accounts, 114–16, 115f
Saudi 24 Sports, 107
Saudi Al Youm, 107–8
Saudi American Public Relations
    Affairs Committee (SAPRAC),
    134, 144–7
Saudi Arabia, 3, 59, 98–100, 110,

125, 135, 138, 139, 143, 166, 178, 259
'A New Saudi Arabia', 74
affected by software, 67–8
automating social media journalism, 103–7, 107*f*
became digital capital, 89–90, 300
became export of deception, 302
as Biggest Cyberbullies, 90–2, 91*f*
control on youth bulge, 79
CTF try to reform, 48–9
digital media content regulation, 80–2
digital media evaluation, 75–80
digital tyrannical behaviour, 301–4
infiltrating Twitter, 86–9
Lebanon's protest involvement, 171
MBS slogan, 73–4
McKinsey and Abdulaziz, 54–5
on Muslim Brotherhood, 189, 235, 236, 266, 261
producing coup rumours against Qatar, 154–60
anti-Qatar hashtags, 148–50, 155
SAPRAC effects for promoting anti-Qatar propaganda, 144–7
Saudi-led coalition's brutal bombing (Yemen), 114
Saudi regime, 75–6, 86–7
Sophia Saudi (robot), 102–3
troll farm of, 84–6
and Trump, 92–8
pro-Trump propaganda, 125–6
as victim of conspiracy, 306

WTO report on Qatar complaints, 207–11
See also Khashoggi (Jamal), assassination of; al-Qahtani, Saud; Saudi 24 (news channel)
Saudi Arabia: influence campaign, 78, 87, 199, 215, 274–5
Absher (android app) crisis, 257–9
conspiracy theory relate to Clinton, 272–4
influence campaigns to WTO report, 208–11
in Iraq politics, 166–8
as leverage campaign in Beirut Port bombing, 172–3
Public Investment Fund (PIF) action on Qatar sports, 204–7
pro-Saudi influencers to Oueiss (women misogyny), 249–51
twitter accounts hacking for spreading propaganda, 280–4
and UAE Karman related campaigns, 262–4
Saudi Electronic Brigade/troll farm (Saudi Arabia), 84–6
Saudi Gazette, 208
Saudi Research and Marketing Group (SRMG), 78
"SaudiNews50", 105, 106
Al Saud, Bader bin Abdullah bin Mohammed bin Farhan, 78
Al Saud, al-Waleed bin Talal bin Abdulaziz, 60, 79
'save the Iraqi ppl' hashtag, 166–7
Schwartz, David, 279–81, 284–5
SCL Social Limited, 146–7
ScrapeHero, 365*n*16, 365*n*18, 365–6*n*25–6

search engine optimisation (SEO),
55
Security Studies Group (SSG),
184, 238
Shaake, Mariatje, 10
Shabaz, Hassan, 133
Shaner, Nora, 216, 217
Shantyaei, Shanam, 128
al-Shaykh, Abdlatif, 156
al-Shaykh Mubarak, Monther, 156,
209, 309
al-Sheikh, Abdul Latif Abdullah,
249, 250, 309
Al Shibly, Rami, 167
Shires, James, 240
Silicon Valley, 17, 58–62, 310
    Middle East domination on,
    311–12
    as neoliberation dimension,
    68–9
Silverman, Craig, 8
S,ims,ek, Mehmet, 67
    'coup in Qatar' trending,
    155
    federal case on, 268
    malinformation related with
    Oueiss, 248–9
    UK visit, 152
Singapore, 312
Sky News Arabia, 78–9, 271–2
SMAAT
    fake accounts of, 88, 91–2, 105,
    108
    SaudiNews50 project, 105
Smith, Debbie, 281
Smith, Iain Duncan, 148
Sobieraj, Sarah, 251–2
social media, 2, 55, 79
    action against disinformation,
    61, 310
    under authoritarian regimes

control, 15–16, 17, 44–5,
    86–7, 103–7
Bell Pottinger usage for political
    client, 54
as counter-revolutionary
    repression tool, 12, 37–8
as deception order, 58–62
flooding the social media
    emphasis, 150
ownership structures of, 60
political actors usage, for their
    legitimacy, 172
Syrian and Russian groups'
    usage for criticism, 64–5
See also Facebook; Twitter
'sockpuppet' (accounts), 43, 53,
    135, 156, 305
    involving Karman crisis, 263–4
AlSohimi, Musaid, 156
Soleimani (Iranian general), 169
Sondrol. C, 73
Sophia Saudi (robot), 102–3, 119
Soros, George, 65
Soufan Center, 242
Soufan, Ali, 242–4
Source (TV channel), 107
South Africa, 52, 53
South China Morning Post, 192
spamming, 40, 43, 119
Spencer, Richard, 5
Spiked Online, 192
sportswashing, 204–7
St Petersburg (Internet Research
    Agency, Russia), 36, 62–3, 95,
    340n67
Stanford Internet Observatory,
    9–10
Starbird, Kate, 66
Starr, Paul, 15
Stewart, Kate, 206, 207
Strategies Global, 145

Subedar, Anisa, 67
Such jobs, 57
Sudan Now (news channel), 107
Sudanese uprising (2018 and 2019), 40
Suiche, Matt, 182–3
Suleiman, Ibrahim, 249
'Support Moqtada', 169
'surveillance capitalism', 15–16
Syria, 64–6

Taha, Amjad, 171, 209, 309
Tawhidi, Mohammed, 269
Tay (twitter bot, Microsoft), 42
techno-colonialism, 17
techno-dystopianism, 16
'techno-utopianism, 16
    and neoliberal thought, 16–17
Telegram, 85
Al Thani, Shaykh Abdallah, 153
al-Thani, Sheikh Tamim bin Hamad, 67, 142, 150
think tanks (against Qatar), 143–9
    Andreae & Associates contribution, 144
    Dubai-based firm Project Associates, 146–7
    Qatar, Global Security and Stability Conference, 147
    Saudi lobbying firm SAPRAC, 144–7
Tiger Squad, 228, 230, 242, 273
Timoney, John, 56–7
Tirana HQ (of MEK), 133
Tlaib, Rashida, 267, 269
Todd, Chuck, 145
Toledano, Joyce, 187, 188, 191, 192
Trendogate, 232–3, 233f, 264
trolls, 42–3
    The Guardian troll, 57

Magnus Callaghan, 287–98, 371n1 (ch.15)
    troll farm of Saudi Arabia, 84–6
'Trump warns Iranian aggression' hashtag, 125
'Trump Will Destroy Iran' hashtag, 125
Trump, Donald, 138, 142, 153, 183, 241–2, 266
    Covid-19 conspiracies of, 214, 216
    'fake news media' media attack, 5–6, 235, 307
    FDD as 'brains trust', 127–9
    MBS, connection with, 73
    online discursive environment under, 305
    precarious press, 5–6
    QAnon conspiracism, 133, 264–5
    and Saudi Arabia, 92–8
    Saudi propaganda against Iran, 124–6
    twitter suspend twitter accounts of, 94, 125–6, 345n6
    US–Iran relationship, changing, 123–4
Turkey, 306
    'Neo-Ottomanism' coup, 157–9, 218
    Turkish authorities and Khashoggi murder, 228–9
Turnbull, Mark, 55
al-Tuwaijri Khaled, 82
Tweeple Search, 342–3n14
TweetBeaver, 345n6
Tweetdeck, 114
Twitter Web App, 96, 263
Twitter Web Client, 93, 96–7
Twitter, 3, 43, 53, 60, 62, 64, 80, 176–7, 208, 220

anti-Qatar hashtags bot
accounts, 148–50
automation software of, 67–8
blue tick verification badge,
280–1
deception study, 19–20
@faisalva account influence
behaviour, 155
fake followers, 84, 104–5, 116,
344n31
Fassihi on, relate to online
misogyny, 256–7
hacking accounts, 279–84
high-profile accounts, fail to
censor, 217, 237, 259
IranDisinfo's Twitter accounts,
127–9
Iraq campaign tweets, 167, 170
Magnus Callaghan troll
accounts, 287–98, 371n1
(ch.15)
MBS_MBSKSA, 241, 262
Nasrallah praised tweets, 172
new accounts, 105–6, 106f
pro-NUFC takeover accounts,
205–7
pro-Saudi Twitter accounts,
96–8, 97f, 167, 171, 209–10
pro-Trump propaganda related
accounts, 85, 125–6, 133–4
Saudi infiltration activities,
86–9, 99–100, 309
Saudi influencer accounts,
155–61
sectarian hate speech,
promoting, 40–1, 109–14,
111–13f
trending of Saudi calling code
and hashtags, 67
Trendogate archives results of,
232–3, 233f

Twitter bots, 40–1
verification users, 89–90
Weinthal's tweets, 131
Tyrannical dictators, 303

UAE Media Council, 146, 147
UN Security Council, 64, 65
United Arab Emirates (UAE),
12, 68, 138, 139, 143, 166,
178, 190, 194, 197, 204, 215,
274–5, 300
digital media consumption, 3
digital tyrannical behaviour,
301–4
DotDev's anti-Qatar social
media campaign, 150
foreign agent of, 308
foreign officials, engagement
with, 66–8
international news channels of,
78–9
on Muslim Brotherhood, 13–
14, 23, 141–2, 266, 271–2
negative campaign to Qatar,
through World Cup,
202–3
Ola and Oueiss crisis (women
harassment) involvement,
250–1
with part of nexus of anti-Iran
entities, 125, 129, 134–5,
269
pro-UAE briefings, 146
and Saudi as deception export,
302
smear campaigns on Karman,
262–4
United Kingdom (UK), 147
and MBS, 74–5
PR firm MENA region, 49–55,
151–3, 211–12

support Russia deception order, 65, 136
UK-based actors criticising Qatar, 151–2
United Nations (UN), 249–50
United States (US), 8, 36, 57, 59, 146, 173, 259, 266
anti-American sentiment, 169–70
animosity development with Iran, 124–7
Arab speaking world hacking people accounts of, 281–3
conspiracism in, 264, 274
data regulatory environment, 59
Department of Justice on Andreae & Associates, 144
efforts to control pro-Iran disinformation, 137
FDD, 127–31
foreign twitter platforms interference in elections, 62–3, 95
intelligence officials of MENA, 66, 68
and Iran campaigns at Iraq, 167–8
Iran Disinformation Project, 127–9
Pentagon's agreement with Saudi Arabia, 118–19
PR firm for MENA, 49–52, 308
Trump administration changing US policy, 123–4
'whisper campaign', involving, 238–9
See also Trump, Donald
The University of Toronto, 9, 87

Velshi, Ali, 243
Vox (news outlet), 63

Wales, Jimmy, 56
'war against reality', 4, 7, 29, 211–12
Wardle, Claire, 2, 320n4 (intro)
Washington, DC, 2, 68
SAPRAC adverts, 145
Washington Examiner, 192
Washington Post (newspaper), 55, 76, 242, 271
intervention in Khashoggi assassination, 239–42
Oueiss column on, 256–7
repot on 'whisper campaign', 238–9
Washington Times, The, 208
'water armies', 43
'we are all Zegmati', 176
weapons of mass destruction (WMD), 143
websites, 19, 82, 83
new channels websites, 108
of young English speakers (Macedonia), 49
Weinthal, Benjamin, 130–1, 202
The Western Journal, 193
Western PR companies. See PR firms/PR companies
Westrop, Sam, 268–9
Whataboutism, 43
WhatsApp, 4, 85
MBS messages to Bezos, 239–40
Whiliams, Jhon, 135
White Helmets, 64–6
whitewashing, 37, 55–8
UK PR campaigns as, 74–5
Wictor, Thomas, 236
Wikipedia, 56–7
Wilson, David, 56
Wilson, Tom, 66
Wirthlin Consulting Group, 51

women
  Absher crisis, 257–9
  Cyber-violence campaigns
    against, 251–4
  digilantism and feminism,
    256–7
  Iran related campaigns of,
    254–6
  as malinformation, 35,
    247–51
  women activists, 49
Working Group on Syria,
  Propaganda and Media
  (WGSPM), 65, 136
World Cup Football (2022)
  CTF 'Project Ball' documents,
    201–2
  negative campaign, 202–3
  'Operation Red Card'
    campaign, 203
  as opportunity for Qatar,
    200–1
  Saudi influence in Qatar sports,
    204–7
World Trade Organisation (WTO)
  Qatar case files against Saudi,
    205
  report on Saudi deceptive
    action, 207–11
World War I, 52

'WTO rejects Qatar complaints',
  208, 209
WWG1WGA (Where we go one,
  we go all), 133, 134

Xi, Cindy, 185–6, 217

Yaghi, Mohammad, 77–8, 110,
  336n16
Yahoo News, 192
Yates, John, 56–7
Yemen, 3, 118
  campaign against MSF, 83
  Covid-19 disinformation
    campaigns against, 215–18
  Saudi hashtags through hacking
    accounts, 282
  Saudi Twitter account influence
    of, 84, 114
  twitter accounts of, 110
Yoonoo (software), 116
York, Jillian C., 59
YouTube, 45, 64, 65

al-Zabarah, Ali, 87, 88
Zeghmati, Belkacem, 175
Zhang, Sophie, 8, 42, 58
Zollmann, Florian, 33
Zuboff, Shoshana, 15
Zuckerberg, Mark, 61, 262